AF607943

Reading to Learn, Reading the World

Reading to Learn, Reading the World

How genre-based literacy pedagogy is democratizing education

Edited by

Claire Acevedo, David Rose & Rachel Whittaker

SHEFFIELD UK BRISTOL CT

Published by Equinox Publishing Ltd.
UK: Office 415, The Workstation, 15 Paternoster Row, Sheffield, South Yorkshire S1 2BX
USA: ISD, 70 Enterprise Drive, Bristol, CT 06010

www.equinoxpub.com

First published 2023
© Claire Acevedo, David Rose, Rachel Whittaker and contributors 2023
All rights reserved. No part of this publication may be reproduced or transmitted in any form or by any means, electronic or mechanical, including photocopying, recording or any information storage or retrieval system, without prior permission in writing from the publishers.

British Library Cataloguing-in-Publication Data
A catalogue record for this book is available from the British Library.

ISBN-13 978 1 80050 323 6 (hardback)
978 1 80050 324 3 (paperback)
978 1 80050 325 0 (ePDF)
978 1 80050 380 9 (ePub)

Library of Congress Cataloging-in-Publication Data

Names: Acevedo, Claire, editor. | Rose, David, 1955- editor. | Whittaker, Rachel, editor.
Title: Reading to learn, reading the world : how genre-based literacy pedagogy is democratizing education / edited by Claire Acevedo, David Rose and Rachel Whittaker.
Description: Bristol, CT : Equinox Publishing Ltd, 2023. | Includes bibliographical references and index. | Summary: "This volume showcases a range of Reading to Learn (R2L) projects from around the world in a variety of educational settings in many different languages"-- Provided by publisher.
Identifiers: LCCN 2023001609 (print) | LCCN 2023001610 (ebook) | ISBN 9781800503236 (hardback) | ISBN 9781800503243 (paperback) | ISBN 9781800503250 (ePDF) | ISBN 9781800503809 (ePub)
Subjects: LCSH: Reading. | Reading promotion. | Critical pedagogy.
Classification: LCC LB1050 .R4316 2023 (print) | LCC LB1050 (ebook) | DDC 372.4--dc23/eng/20230331
LC record available at https://lccn.loc.gov/2023001609
LC ebook record available at https://lccn.loc.gov/2023001610

Typeset by Sparks Publishing Services Ltd – www.sparkspublishing.com

Contents

Foreword

J R Martin

I have been involved in educational linguistics conference since 1979, when Michael Halliday organised a 'Working Conference on Language in Education' at the University of Sydney. Since then I have attended dozens of seminars, workshops and conferences around the world which focus on the genre-based literacy programs of what has come to be known as the 'Sydney School'. For me, among all these meetings, two moments stand out. One was the 1989 'Working with Genre' conference held at the University of Technology Sydney, which brimmed with the excitement and energy of the educators, linguists, feminists and critical theorists involved and would come to have a considerable impact on language teaching and learning around the world. The second was the 2018 'International Systemic Functional Linguistics Congress' held at Boston College, which overflowed with the same level of excitement and energy as educators and linguists from all over the world gathered to report on their implementation and renovation of the project as they tuned in to the needs of their students – across sectors, across disciplines, across languages and across cultures. I was moved in particular by the day long 'Learning to Write, Reading to Learn' colloquium, which featured presentations of work going on in Australia, South Africa, Hong Kong, Indonesia, Portugal, Argentina, Colombia, Chile, Spain, Sweden and the United States. It was so heartening to see how far our work had progressed from our modest beginnings when working in the Disadvantaged Schools Program in Sydney circa 1986–1993. As I commented in my tribute to Halliday, who had died just two months before the conference, I was confident that he would be more than a little bit proud of all the amazing teaching and learning that had evolved from the working conference he organised in 1979.

This wonderful volume reports on work by many of the key presenters at that colloquium and significant others who could not be there. As the chapters make clear, David Rose has been the inspiration for these initiatives. Although he is a brilliant educator and linguist, David eschewed a career in academe in order to fulfil a pledge he made to himself on behalf of his adopting Indigenous Australian parents – namely to develop pedagogy and curriculum which would ensure that every student can participate equally in schooling, regardless of the background from which they come. To do this he took the foundational work of Joan Rothery and her colleagues in the Disadvantaged School Program and developed the second generation Sydney School reading and writing program known as Reading to Learn. As the name signals, this program foregrounds learning from reading as fundamental if students are to access the uncommon sense knowledge of schooling.

As several chapters in this volume presage, a third generation of Sydney School pedagogy and curriculum is now underway. These developments have been triggered by the implementation of genre-based literacy programs in schools where two or more languages are used for teaching and learning. This raises important questions for curriculum – i.e. what is the ultimate goal as far as accessing knowledge is concerned? Are we aiming for access in one language (perhaps a 'national' or 'international' one), or two or more? And it also raises important questions for pedagogy – i.e. which language (local, national or international) should be used when? And how might this change as students gain control of second, third languages or more in school? However this resolves, I am confident David and his colleagues can be more than a little bit proud of what they will have achieved. I had tears in my eyes in Boston; I have tears in my eyes as I write this now. The commitment and achievements of the educational linguists in this volume are stunning. I commend them to you.

J R Martin, Professor of Linguistics,
University of Sydney, Australia
Sydney, June 2022

Introduction

Claire Acevedo, David Rose & Rachel Whittaker

The methodology that became Reading to Learn (R2L) emerged over two decades from a coalescence of idealism, academic research and teachers' experience in schools and classrooms. One ideal shared by everyone involved in R2L has been to become a more effective teacher, and to help others do so. Underlying this drive to excel is the democratic ideal that education should be equally available, inclusive and effective for every student. Two principles that inform the R2L methodology are that:

- teaching should enable every student to participate and succeed equally,
- learning from reading is essential for confident participation and success.

The democratic ideal informs each of the contributions to this volume in myriad ways. In Chapter 1, David Rose recounts the origins of Reading to Learn in work with Indigenous Australian children in primary and secondary school, informed by genre writing and scaffolded reading pedagogies. A key insight from this research is that Indigenous children's struggles with school literacy are part of a wider problem in schools of inequality of participation and access to knowledge through literacy. The R2L methodology evolved in response to these challenges, guided by the needs of teachers participating in professional learning programs. This chapter describes the development of the methodology in these contexts, and explains its components.

In Chapter 2, Ingrid Freeman and Jane Kelly describe the methodology's impact in an Australian primary school with a high proportion of children with special needs. Over three years, R2L became a whole school pedagogy, leading to the successful integration of special needs students into mainstream classes, and accelerating the whole school's learning results well above national averages. Chapter 3, by Sarah Culican, describes an early R2L project in an Australian secondary school with a high proportion of disadvantaged students, that achieved exceptional results within its first year. Sarah was also a leader, together with Claire Acevedo, of the first major R2L training program, with Melbourne Catholic schools. Chapter 4, by Zena Carusi-Lees, describes a successful whole school secondary program, in which teachers across subject areas have been trained in R2L strategies over several years, and continue to support each other with curriculum and planning.

The success of genre pedagogy in Australian schools attracted South African education activist Mike Hart. In Chapter 5, Mike recounts the efforts of Reading to Learn South Africa to train teachers in urban and rural schools, in a nation with one of the world's widest gaps in educational achievement. Mike also led R2L training in large-scale teacher programs in Kenya, Uganda and Tanzania. R2L was also introduced to academic programs in South African universities, in which Tracey Millin participated. In Chapter 6, Tracey outlines three projects flowing from these academic programs, that achieved considerable success.

A conference in Sweden organized by Ann-Christin Lövstedt brought R2L to Europe, at a time when large scale migration was widening inequalities in schools. Working with Claire Acevedo, Ann-Christin introduced the methodology to Swedish schools. In Chapter 7, Ann-Christin describes an extraordinary project to adapt the methodology for teachers working in Swedish Sign Language (SSL) in a school for deaf and hearing-impaired students. Chapter 8, by Pernilla Andersson Varga, Annette Mitiche, Jaana Sandberg and Susanne Staf, describes the achievements of a long-term project training teachers in disadvantaged schools in Gothenburg, Sweden.

The growing success of R2L in Sweden attracted the interest of Danish educators, so Claire Acevedo and Ann-Christin Lövstedt applied for funding from the European Union for a multi-national training program. They eventually recruited five teams of educators from Sweden, Denmark, Scotland, Spain and Portugal for a three-year project, known as *Teacher Learning for European Literacy Education*, or TeL4ELE. In Chapter 9, Claire Acevedo outlines how the TeL4ELE project unfolded and spread R2L pedagogy into the European education context. In Chapter 10, Rachel Whittaker, Isabel García-Parejo and Aoife Ahern describe how this project has blossomed in Spain into a range of activities, including pre-service teacher education and service-learning. In Chapter 11, Carlos Gouveia, Marta Filipe Alexandre and Fausto Caels outline its outcomes in Portugal, particularly in a project to describe the genres of the school curriculum.

In the Americas, R2L and genre pedagogy have appealed to educators working with Spanish and Portuguese speaking students. In Chapter 12, Andrés Ramírez and María Gabriela Gutiérrez describe their work in a US community education project with Spanish speaking mothers learning English. In Chapter 13, Sergio Álvarez, Norma Barletta, Teresa Benitez and Nayibe Rosado-Mendinueta discuss an academic literacy project in their university in Colombia that has involved educators from multiple disciplines. In Chapter 14, Patricia Meehan, Angélica Gaido, Liliana Anglada and María Belén Oliva describe the literacy outreach program from their university in Argentina for teachers from disadvantaged local schools. In Chapter 15, Samiah Hassan and Cristina Boccia evaluate the R2L methodology in comparison with other literacy methods currently used in Argentina as part of a teacher education program. Chapter 16, by Ingrid Westhoff and Raimundo Olfos in Chile, provides an analysis of the R2L methodology for teaching mathematics.

Finally, Chapter 17, by Harni Kartika-Ningsih, describes a project to teach scientific literacy with Indonesian school students, in both Indonesian and English. While most of the R2L projects discussed in this volume are multilingual, Harni takes this a step further to describe the linguistic basis of bilingual R2L pedagogy.

ABOUT THE AUTHORS

Claire Acevedo is an Australian educator now based in the United Kingdom where she is an affiliated researcher in Language and Literacies at The Centre for Research in Education and Educational Technology (CREET) at the Open University. She concurrently provides educational services to schools and education sectors across Europe and South America where she leads professional development (in English, Spanish and Swedish). She is experienced in using Systemic Functional Linguistics via 'Sydney School' genre pedagogy to improve reading and writing outcomes for underachieving students in all areas of the school curriculum. She has collaborated with Dr David Rose, University of Sydney, over two decades on the latest research into genre-based reading and she specializes in delivering *Reading to Learn* literacy acceleration professional development to teachers and teacher educators. She is the co-founder and deputy chair of *Reading for Life* (http://reading4life.org) a non-profit association that promotes social justice in society and equity in education all over the world.

David Rose is Director of Reading to Learn and an Honorary Associate of the University of Sydney. His research includes literacy teaching practices and teacher professional learning, analysis and design of classroom discourse. His books include *The western desert code: An Australian cryptogrammar*, 2001; and, with J.R. Martin, *Working with discourse, Genre Relations* and *Learning to write, Reading to learn: genre, knowledge and pedagogy in the Sydney School.*

Rachel Whittaker, PhD (English Department, Universidad Autónoma, Madrid), coordinated Spain's team in the project: *Teacher Learning for European Literacy*

Education (tel4ele.eu) which brought *Reading to Learn* to a number of European countries (see http://telcon2013.com/, formule.es) and *Lenguaje y Textos* monograph 2017, co-edited with Isabel García Parejo), and supervised the translation of Rose & Martin's *Learning to Write, Reading to Learn* into Spanish as *Leer para aprender: lectura y escritura en las áreas del currículo* (Pirámide 2018). She is active in teacher education and has published a number of articles on *Reading to Learn* pedagogy and on CLIL in Spain.

1

Learning to teach

David Rose

ABSTRACT

This chapter describes the evolution of the Reading to Learn teaching methodology and teacher education program. It starts with its origins in genre-based writing and scaffolded reading with Indigenous Australian children, followed by expansion of the methodology and teacher training, across the curriculum and grade levels. Descriptions of teaching/learning activities and pedagogic principles are embedded in the story of their development, in collaboration with teachers. The settings for these developments have been schools, universities and teacher education programs across Australia and the rest of the world.

THE PREHISTORY OF READING TO LEARN

In my own experience, the ideal of democratizing the classroom was first shaped by working for the Anangu Pitjantjatjara[1] people in central Australia, who were then in the throes of remaking their communities after decades of government and mission control. In the 1980s, these communities were also coping with a youth substance abuse crisis, and were adamant that they wanted their children to read and write the English they needed for success in school, further education and work (Rose, 2010). My task became to seek out the most effective available methods for providing this literacy.

This quest naturally led to the genre-based writing pedagogy of the 'Sydney School', and the knowledge about language (KAL) that informed it (Martin, 1997, 2000; Martin & Rose, 2012; Rose, 2008). While studying, researching and teaching in Sydney, I was able to apply the pedagogy with adult Aboriginal students[2] at the

University of Technology Sydney (UTS), with promising results. Students whose school education had been very brief were soon able to write coherent, structured arguments, and other genres expected of their academic courses and workplaces. Through teacher-guided collaborative writing, genre pedagogy focused attention on the staging of target genres, and some of the language features that served to organize them. Crucially these adult students were able to read genre models, and texts in their academic curricula, with teacher support to unpack the dense technicality and abstraction that characterizes academic texts.

However, on returning to the desert, I found that genre writing pedagogy was insufficient for Pitjantjatjara speaking students who had little or no experience of reading in English. It was effective for learners with some reading experience to construct successful texts, using language resources accumulated through reading. But for learners without this experience, written language could only be sourced from the teacher or other students during writing activities. In this respect, it is not hard to see why teacher-guided writing activities were more effective than the so-called 'process writing' method, which only allowed teachers to intervene after students had first attempted writing on their own. Anangu children's universal response to this pervasive practice was to write very short texts, throughout their primary schooling, using only words they knew how to spell, that would not be corrected by the teacher.

In the late 1990s, I asked Brian Gray and Wendy Cowey of Canberra University to collaborate on an action research project with teachers in Anangu community primary schools and the *Wiltja* annexe program for Anangu secondary students in Adelaide (Rose et al., 1999). The research methodology combined genre writing pedagogy, and its associated KAL, with a method for scaffolding reading and writing that was being used in Canberra to support primary school children who were struggling with literacy. The basic principle of the method, influenced by Vygotsky's and Bruner's social psychology, was to prepare learners for each learning task, and then hand over control for the task. At a macro scale, its sequence was influenced by the SFL language model, starting with meaning in context of whole texts, followed by close reading of word groups in sentences, then by spelling of its words, and finally rewriting text passages, using this accumulated experience of language in a text. At a micro scale, the close reading activity used cycles of interaction that prepared students for tasks such as identifying word groups in sentences. In Canberra, it had been deployed in one-on-one sessions with children at risk, using popular story books (Axford et al., 2009).

Leading the secondary project in Adelaide was a steep learning experience. Anangu students were enrolled in mainstream secondary classes, with junior primary level reading and writing skills. Despite intensive support, including ESL trained teachers, their skills barely improved from year to year. The challenge was to use the annexe program to embed reading and writing in mainstream curriculum tasks. Essential to this was knowledge about the written genres and language of schooling developed in Sydney School research, particularly the *Write it Right* project, to which I'd contributed (Rose, 1997, 1998; Rose et al., 1992). The Wiltja teachers needed skills to analyze and teach with a variety of curriculum texts, in both reading and writing lessons. Techniques such as *Paragraph-by-Paragraph Reading* and joint *Notemaking* were first developed in this context. In addition, scaffolding interaction cycles had to be redesigned, from one-on-one support to working with whole classes, and teachers had to learn how to use the techniques. In this work, the Wiltja teachers became the community that directed me to help them choose and analyze curriculum texts for lesson planning, to design and demonstrate activities with their classes, and observe and feedback on their teaching.

Working with Anangu students and their teachers in classrooms across the school years prompted several insights that informed the development of Reading to Learn. One was the practice, at all stages of education, of requiring students to practise tasks independently, that are then evaluated. The evaluation is often couched as 'feedback', in which the teacher either corrects, or guides learners to make their own corrections. In some form, this practice is equally a feature of 'teacher-centred' and 'learner-centred' pedagogies. I have called it the 'repair' model of pedagogy, in contrast to *preparing* learners sufficiently to succeed equally with independent tasks. It conflates practice with assessment, so that students who practise successfully experience feedback as affirmation and can learn from it, while students who struggle experience it as criticism and cannot.

Rather than changing pedagogies, the traditional response was to stratify classes and curricula, so that weaker students may succeed with less demanding tasks, while stronger students progress more quickly. In contemporary primary schools, this overt stratification has been recast as 'differentiation' within classes, purportedly to meet students' individual needs, but still assigning different levels of individuated tasks. Behind these practices are age-old assumptions of innate intellectual differences, that are rarely explicitly stated these days, but still serve to divert attention from ineffective pedagogy. When exposed to R2L's redesigned approach, teachers can readily see the advantages of preparing instead of repairing, but some still worry about 'spoonfeeding' learners, or 'transfer' from teacher-led to independent practice. These concerns, like the practices, are compounded by perceived pressures for continual assessment, as well as popular theories in teacher education.

Another insight was the types of literacy development that are expected and assumed in each stage of school, from learning to read independently in the early years, to learning from reading in middle primary, to reading across the curriculum in upper primary, and independently learning from reading in the secondary school. As children are expected to apply these skills in each subsequent school stage, they are evaluated on the skills they have acquired in the preceding stages (Rose, 2004). This evaluation begins in the early years, where children's rate of literacy learning depends on orientations to written texts acquired through parent–child reading in the home. This critical first step in the school's literacy development sequence clearly disadvantaged Anangu children, who had little or no experience of parent–child reading. Their literacy skills consequently developed so slowly that few were reading with comprehension by the end of primary school. In this respect they were not alone. All secondary teachers reported that only a minority of their students could independently learn from reading, and that they consequently avoided extensive reading activities, except for English literature lessons. All primary teachers confirmed that children's positions on the assessment ladder were unlikely to vary from the beginning to the end of their primary years.

A third insight was the inequality of participation in teacher/class interactions, observed in every classroom. One result of children developing literacy skills at different rates is the wide 'ability differences' within each class, which all teachers are forced to manage one way or another. A striking effect is teachers' universal reliance on a handful of top students to provide responses to their questions, that can be built on towards their lesson goals. This was apparent in the Wiltja annexe classes, but was even more marked in the mainstream classes, where Anangu students were largely silent, along with many others. On one hand, the Wiltja project had to make up for the stages of literacy development that the students had missed out on in the primary school. On the other, the teachers needed strategies for engaging every student in the classroom conversation, rather than just a confident few.

Addressing these intertwined problems has shaped founding principles of Reading to Learn – to integrate reading and writing with curriculum teaching, prepare every student in each class to succeed with curriculum tasks at the same level, and clearly separate learning from assessment. What became apparent to me at this time, was that Indigenous children's problems with school education were not a consequence of their own cultural or linguistic differences, but of entrenched pedagogic practices that systematically created inequalities in participation and outcomes in schools. If Indigenous students' outcomes were to improve, then these practices would have to be changed.

NEXT STEPS: DESIGNING TEACHER EDUCATION PROGRAMS

One outcome of the collaboration with the Wiltja teachers was a rapid acceleration in their students' literacy skills. By the end of the project's first year, the Wiltja students were reading books close to their age levels, and writing successful extended texts. These independently verified results (McRae et al., 2000) brought the national education minister to the school with the media in tow. The publicity led to numerous enquiries for teacher education in state and independent school systems around Australia, amongst which were the Catholic Education Office Melbourne (CEOM), and the Anangu Teacher Education Program (AnTEP) of the University of South Australia.

In the AnTEP program, the challenge set by the adult Anangu students, who were teacher assistants and trainees, and whose own literacy was very weak, was to train them in a method for scaffolding reading and writing that qualified teachers often struggled to master. The solution we found was a genre-based multimodal teaching sequence that started with discussing videoed literacy lessons, and concluded with students planning, practising and reflecting on their own lessons. The scaffolding teaching sequence, from reading to spelling to writing, was analyzed as a procedure consisting of a series of steps. The AnTEP students were guided to identify each step in lesson videos, and write them down on a whiteboard, as a joint construction of the procedure in verbal form, including the function of each step. They were then guided to identify wordings in sentences, from books that teachers in the schools were reading with children, together with spelling patterns of key words, and to practise learning activities that they would later guide the children in. Armed with this knowledge and practice, each student would then practise the activities with one or two children. The results were spectacular; in less than an hour, the AnTEP students would have every child independently reading and accurately spelling English sentences for the first time in their two or three years of schooling. Finally, the students jointly constructed a reflective recount of the lesson, using the language of the procedure, with additional explanations and evaluations. Through this sequence of activities, their own literacy learning was embedded in learning to teach literacy to the children. The practice sessions were filmed and edited to create a training video that is accessible at https://readingtolearn.com.au/pages/videos.

What I have described here is a *meta-procedure*, designed for training the AnTEP students to practise a literacy teaching procedure (Rose, 2020). Its ingredients included, on the one hand, knowledge about language at the levels of texts, sentences, words and spelling patterns and, on the other hand, knowledge about pedagogy, at the levels of activity sequencing, preparing and handing over control for each learning task, and observing what learners can do. Designing such meta-procedures for teacher training became a key factor in the development of Reading to Learn, as it expanded to train many more teachers, and the training was taken over by more teacher educators.

THE CEOM PROFESSIONAL LEARNING PROGRAM

A key setting for this expansion was a large-scale teacher professional learning program coordinated by Claire Acevedo and colleagues with the CEOM, including Sarah Culican (Culican, Chapter 3 this volume). The program had been focused on the 'middle years' of upper primary and junior secondary, using the genre writing pedagogy, along with functional grammar training. It was well organized and resourced, including series of face-to-face workshops, followed by in-school guidance from specialist consultants. Claire, Sarah and their team asked me to lead a training program in the reading and writing pedagogy developed at Wiltja, which presented a number of challenges. One was working with a wide variety of school curricula and programming constraints. While teachers in primary schools had dedicated literacy time each day, in secondary schools the pedagogy had to be embedded in their crowded curriculum programs. Another was figuring out how teachers could give all their students the support they needed, in classes with wide ranges of literacy skills and language backgrounds. Yet another was leading workshops with up to 60 teachers, with a multitude of needs and experience (Rose & Acevedo, 2006).

One thing that became clear in these workshops was how much of school teaching was a set of tacit practices, gained more through experience than design. I was often surprised by the number of teachers' questions that seemed to be about basic teaching practice, aside from literacy, such as how to manage their classes, how to deal with 'ability differences', engage their students' interest, fit skills into their programs along with curriculum content, and so on. For teachers to take on the literacy methodology we were offering, answers to all these broad pedagogic questions had to be woven into the training program.

While the topics of curricula were often an explicit focus of their planning, teaching and evaluation, teachers could rarely name or describe the activities through which they taught these topics, nor the kinds of written texts used for learning and assessment. The Sydney School work on genres of schooling provided a consistent metalanguage for these kinds of texts, including varieties of stories, chronicles, explanations, reports, procedures, arguments and text responses (Martin & Rose, 2008). It also provided a name for the activity designed to guide their writing, *Joint Construction*. But a comparable metalanguage was needed for other activities in the pedagogy, so that teachers could explicitly name them with their students, across different grades and curriculum areas, and share them with colleagues. Moreover, the diversity of teaching contexts meant that new activities had to be designed to meet teachers' demands.

Out of this toing and froing between classroom teaching and teacher training, a general model emerged for designing teaching/learning activities. At the centre of each activity was a learning task that learners could only do themselves. Using this principle we could look at any pedagogic activity and ask what the learners' task was. We could then ask how learners were prepared for the task, how it was focused and evaluated, and how it was followed up, or elaborated (Rose, 2020). For example, the task in the first stage of the scaffolding reading pedagogy is to listen as a text was read aloud by the teacher. If the text includes a lot of meanings that are beyond students' knowledge, then this task must be prepared by telling them what to expect as it was read, not just its subject matter but a preview of the sequence in

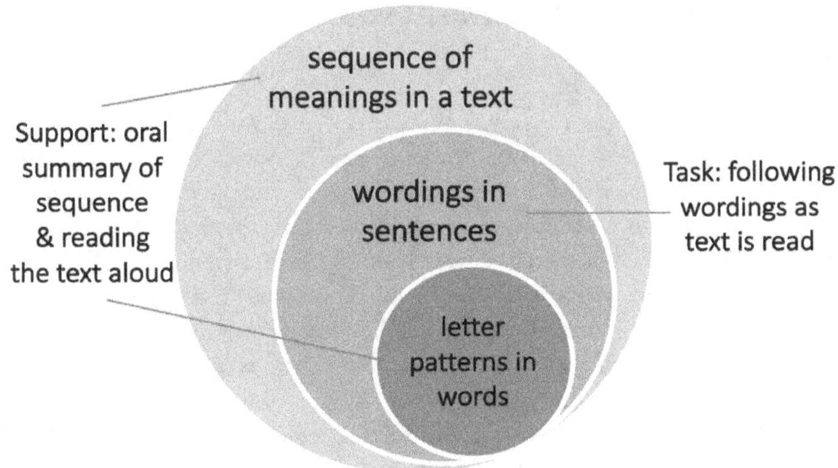

Figure 1.1. How *Preparing for Reading* supports the reading task

which it unfolded in the text. This activity was termed *Preparing for Reading*, including both the preview and the reading. Its lesson plan only required teachers to read the text themselves, and perhaps make notes on how to prepare it. This simple strategy enabled teachers to use texts that were beyond the independent reading skills of some or all of their students, by providing sufficient support for them to follow the text, at two levels. The oral preview supported them to follow its field without struggling to work out what was going on, and reading aloud supported them to follow its wordings without struggling to decode unfamiliar words (Figure 1.1). The reading could then be elaborated with discussion of its meanings, that all students could then participate in.

Preparing for Reading contrasted with some common reading practices that used 'repair' activities. In the primary school these included students reading on their own or in groups, while the teacher circulated and evaluated their reading. As the individual reading was unprepared, it required sets of books at students' independent reading levels. If their reading was assessed as competent, they were allowed to progress to books at the next level. As top students progressed faster than weaker readers, such practices maintained the achievement gap, while providing a profitable market for publishers of levelled reading books. Instead, *Preparing for Reading* enabled teachers to read quality literature with all their students, which they could then practise reading themselves, instead of dull basal readers designed for testing, not teaching. Our advice to teachers was to put these awful books, that every school spent their literacy budgets on, in a cupboard.

READING AND WRITING ACROSS THE CURRICULUM

In secondary schools, teachers reported that reading in class was primarily a feature of English literature lessons. As curriculum texts were beyond many students' independent reading skills, whole short stories or novel chapters might be read aloud, followed by discussion and assessment tasks, which did not advance struggling students' reading skills. The solution we proposed was to use *Preparing for Reading*, and start reading in class, but then gradually hand the task to students. Each story or chapter would be prepared, but students would eventually read the prepared texts themselves. This was also supported by regular *Detailed Reading* sessions with significant passages, daily in primary classes and weekly in secondary subjects, to accelerate students' control of the texts.

In science and humanities classes, reading difficult texts was often avoided, in favour of talking to powerpoints or other media, followed by assessment activities such as written comprehension questions. Such activities enabled teachers to 'cover the content' of their crowded curricula, but again failed to develop students' independent learning skills. As all teachers acknowledged, at the end of each year, those students who could learn from reading would succeed, while those who could not, would probably fail. To enable teachers to cover the curriculum while building their students' reading skills, a procedure for *Paragraph-by-paragraph Reading* was designed. It was first prepared with an oral overview of the text, using images where possible. Each paragraph was then previewed before reading, and then elaborated by identifying and highlighting key information in the paragraph. With practice, long texts could be read and discussed relatively quickly, studying curriculum topics through reading together, while developing reading skills.

Following *Para-by-para Reading,* a procedure for joint *Notemaking* developed as a highly supportive and cooperative activity, that handed control to students. Instead of the typical practice of the teacher controlling the class board, students took turns to scribe notes on the board, while other students dictated information they had highlighted in reading texts. At the same time as reinforcing and extending their comprehension of the field and its terms, this activity built skills in spelling, handwriting, pronunciation and listening, with the teacher's guidance. All students could actively participate and develop both language and content knowledge, no matter what their language or literacy background.

Joint activities like *Para-by-para Reading* and *Notemaking* could then be followed by students continuing to read the text, highlight information, and make notes, on their own or in groups, as the teacher circulated and provided support as needed. Homework could then include further reading of the text, developing students' independent learning skills. This stepwise handover of control addressed the widespread disjunction between teacher-led lessons and individual activities that confused practice with assessment, in all subject areas. Instead, we emphasized a principle of using teacher-led activities to model and jointly practise activities that students would then practise themselves, before assessment tasks.

Where traditional genre-based writing used model texts to imitate their staging with new content, *Notemaking* provided the content for jointly constructing new texts. To prepare for writing, the teacher guided students group the notes into phases of information, that would form paragraphs in the new text, and were then grouped within the stages of the target genre. A metalanguage was developed for labelling these phases, on the board and on students' own notes, that captured the structuring of knowledge in each kind of text and made it explicit. This labelling was based on the terminology developed in Sydney School genre pedagogy, but was finer grained. For example, phases in explanations may be labelled as *steps* or *factors*, or in reports as *types* or *parts*, which sharpened the focus on how the topic was organized, for teachers and students. As with *Notemaking*, students took turns as scribes in *Joint Construction* (Figure 1.2), while the teacher provided guidance in the organization of content and language. This sequence of activities can be seen in action at https://readingtolearn.com.au/pages/videos.

Modelling this teaching sequence with factual texts eventually became the first stage in the teacher training workshops. Using a technical text and diagram, it showed teachers how they could start from students' own knowledge to quickly build a technical field, to prepare for reading. It also demonstrated how to engage and extend every student by focusing on shared experience, affirming responses,

Figure 1.2. ***Joint construction*** **of a factual text**

and elaborating with new knowledge. Using this principle, *Para-by-para Reading* was first demonstrated with teachers in the role of students, by preparing and asking them in turn to identify specific wordings, which were then highlighted and discussed. The activity was then handed over to teachers to consider how they would plan such lessons, by identifying key information in each paragraph of a text, and deciding what needed discussion and how. This practice showed teachers how lesson planning could consider not only the content of a topic, but the texts used to teach it. Practising the cooperative activities of *Notemaking* and *Joint Construction* then showed teachers how to get every student actively involved, while building language knowledge into content teaching, and preparing for assessment tasks.

ANALYSING AND TEACHING TEXTS ACROSS THE CURRICULUM

The focus in these activities, on knowledge structuring in texts, naturally led to text analysis activities in training workshops. Teachers were encouraged to bring copies of texts they were working with in their classes. At first, examples were analyzed and labelled using overhead projectors, and teachers practised with other examples in groups. Eventually, a book of representative texts was created that could be used in workshops and teachers could then use for their own lesson planning. The book included the range of genres described in *Genre Relations* (Martin & Rose, 2008), but its activities guided teachers to identify genres by comparing texts, and then to analyze their stages and phases. Also included was a series of fiction book extracts that modelled a curriculum progression in reading levels, year-by-year through primary and secondary school. Teachers were encouraged to use these as a guide to plan their reading programs, with the goal that all their students would be reading at grade-appropriate levels by the end of each year.

Teachers were introduced to this book following lesson activities with a factual text, story and argument, which grounded the new linguistic knowledge in teaching practice. The first activity in the book was to read a network diagram that grouped genres by their social functions, and the language focus in teaching with them. Stories were classified as *engaging*, since the teaching focus was on resources authors used to engage readers. Factual texts were classified as *informing*, focusing on the information they provided. Arguments and text responses were grouped together as *evaluating*, as the focus was on language resources used to evaluate issues, positions and texts (verbal, visual, musical).

This tripartite division of genres also distinguished types of activities used to teach with them. Stories are prepared with an overview and then read aloud. Passages may then be selected for *Detailed Reading*, and *Rewriting* follows the same patterns of word groups in the passage, but with new settings, characters and events. Joint Construction likewise follows the stages and phases of a model story, and a unique analysis

Table 1.1. Summary of R2L curriculum macro-genres for each genre group: engaging, informing and evaluating

Lang. focus	Genres	Prep & read	Detailed read	Rewrite	New text
engaging	stories	overview	literary	same wordings/ new events	same stages & phases
informing	chronicles, explanations, reports	para-by-para	information	same info/ new wordings	target stages & phases
evaluating	arguments, text responses	target issue or text	evaluative	same wordings/ new issue or text	same stages & phases

of story phase types was developed for this practice (Rose, 2006, 2020, 2021; Martin & Rose, 2008, 2012). Factual texts by contrast, are read using *Para-by-para Reading*, followed by *Notemaking*, and *Joint Construction* using the notes, as described above. *Detailed Reading* and *Rewriting* likewise use notes to rewrite passages of dense text with new wordings, giving students practice in reading and writing technical and abstract language. Working with evaluative texts combines both sets of activities. An issue or text is studied by reading and making notes. Passages from a model of the target argument or text response are then used for *Detailed Reading*, focusing on evaluative language patterns. *Rewriting* follows the same evaluative language patterns, as with story *Rewriting*, but replacing the content with the newly studied issue or text. Finally, the stages and phases of the model are used for jointly constructing the target genre. In terms of genre theory each of these sequences is a *curriculum macro-genre* (Rose, 2020) presented in the summary Table 1.1. They evolved from teachers presenting issues with curriculum teaching, and were presented back to teachers as options for lesson programs. Among the most elaborate macro-genres are experiment reports in science, that include both technical and evaluative sections.

ASSESSING LITERACY GROWTH

To measure the effectiveness of all these activities, a method was needed to track students' growth in writing skills as teachers implemented the pedagogy in their classes. A simple analysis of students' written language resources was developed, that teachers could use with minimal training. It included criteria at the levels of *genre* (stages and phases), *register* (field, tenor, mode), *discourse* (lexis, appraisal, reference, conjunction), *grammar* and *graphic features* (spelling, punctuation, presentation). Each criterion was given a score of 0–3 (absent, weak, good, excellent). Exemplars were then collected of high standard writing in story, factual and evaluative genres

Figure 1.3. Analyzing student writing in workshops

at each stage of school (junior, middle and upper stages in primary and secondary). Teachers were shown how to assess their students' writing against these standard exemplars, practising in the workshops (Figure 1.3). This proved to be a powerful way for teachers to develop knowledge about language, motivated by analysing their own students' texts, using an accessible framework. They were then asked to track improvements in students' writing from top, average and lower cohorts in their classes, to see how effective their teaching was for all their students. These assessments consistently showed lower cohorts improving at an average 4 times expected learning rates, and top cohorts at 1.5 times expected rates (Martin & Rose, 2013; Rose, 2015; Rose & Martin, 2012). As this writing assessment was developed with a small school grant from the Australian government, it was appropriated and adapted (without acknowledgement) as the writing assessment in the National Assessment Program – Literacy and Numeracy (NAPLAN)[3].

ANALYZING AND DESIGNING CLASSROOM INTERACTIONS

A key factor in these literacy growth rates was the activities of *Detailed Reading* and *Joint Rewriting*, that enable all students in a class to read passages of text with detailed comprehension, and use what they have learnt in their writing. A major challenge with these activities was to engage every student while providing sufficient support for all to identify wordings successfully and so benefit from discussion of their meanings.

This challenge led to an analysis of classroom discourse that exposed sources of inequalities in participation, and enabled design of interactions that helped overcome these inequalities (Martin, 2006; Rose, 2004). The ubiquitous 'initiate–response–feedback' cycles of classroom discourse were re-analyzed as micro-learning activities, in which student responses were the learning task. Analyses showed that only a few students in any class responded successfully. Teachers confirmed that only 2–3 or 4–5 consistently responded to their questions, representing around 10–15% of students in any class. Yet the responses of these students were essential for teaching to progress, as teachers continually use their responses to elaborate with new knowledge towards curriculum goals. Analyses also showed initiating moves were typically focus questions that provided insufficient support for many students to respond. From the beginning of school, children learnt that only some students would be affirmed, and simply stopped responding to teachers' questions. This problem was exacerbated by pre-service training that advocated questions requiring 'inferential thinking', that only some children could answer successfully. One result of unequal participation was that teachers could only know if the responding few benefited from their elaborations. Another was that disengaged students could become problems for classroom management. While top students received affirmation for learning, weaker students often received admonishment for behaviour.

In the workshops, teachers were guided to analyze classroom transcripts, and invited to consider their own practice, and where they learnt it. A general model of learning cycles was designed to visualize the analysis (Figure 1.4). For most teachers, this was the first time they had examined their practice this closely, and were highly motivated to continue. A metalanguage was developed for these analyses. Learners' tasks were either to *Propose* a response from their knowledge or to

Figure 1.4. A model of pedagogic activity as teaching/learning cycles

Identify the answer in a text or image. These tasks could be initiated simply with a *Focus* question, or by adding a *Prepare* move that ensured a successful response. Evaluations were either to *Affirm* or *Reject* the response. They could then be *Elaborated* with further knowledge or discussion, and teachers could *Direct* students' actions. It was found that these terms could be applied to any pedagogic practice (Rose, 2014, 2018), and were used to design inclusive practices for *Detailed Reading* and *Joint Rewriting.*

In *Detailed Reading,* the central task in each learning cycle is to identify a wording in a reading passage. This is prepared with the location of the wording in the sentence and the kind of meaning to look for. A focus question is then directed to one student by name, so they can respond successfully and be affirmed. In this way, every student in a class can be engaged in the learning conversation through success and affirmation, while supporting all to read the text. The class is then told precisely which words to highlight in their own copies. As the preparation enables every student to identify the wording, they are all prepared for the elaboration of meanings that follow. This design resolved the typical separation of teaching, management and engagement in pedagogic theories, into a unified practice that managed classes by engaging all students through continual success and affirmation in learning the curriculum.

Such complex interactions around meanings in a text required detailed lesson plans, that teachers could refer to as they taught. Such lesson plans were essential as teachers had to simultaneously focus on patterns of meanings within each sentence, and consider how to prepare and elaborate these meanings with their classes. A procedure was developed to train teachers in designing and using these detailed lesson plans, with a series of steps that supported and gradually handed control to the teachers.

In the first step, *Detailed Reading* was demonstrated with a challenging text passage, with teachers in the role of students. Teachers then copied the passage into a lesson planning proforma, and they highlighted wordings that students would be asked to identify. They considered how to prepare students to identify each wording, and made notes of these meaning cues, then considered which meanings needed elaborating, and wrote notes of these elaborations. Use of this jointly-constructed lesson plan was then demonstrated, again with teachers in the role of students, and teachers then practised using it with each other, taking turns as teacher and students. Some found it a struggle at first to manage the discourse pattern while reading the plan, particularly telling students what to look for instead of habitually asking unprepared questions. But after a few attempts, jointly writing the plan, and practising with each other, most teachers found it flowing more naturally, and were ready to practise with their own students.

A PEDAGOGIC METALANGUAGE FOR PATTERNS IN SENTENCES AND TEXTS

The central aim of *Detailed Reading* is to enable all students to comprehend a text in depth and detail, without necessarily naming types of wordings. But in writing activities, metalanguage is often needed to discuss the kinds of grammatical patterns encountered. Systemic functional grammar was a step towards the metalanguage we needed, but it had two significant shortcomings. Firstly, it is a general linguistic description of grammar systems, whereas *Detailed Reading* and *Rewriting* focus on instances of language patterns in texts rather than features in grammar systems. These instances couple grammar structures with patterns of content and values (or *register*) that vary widely with types of texts and topics. On the other hand, the systems of functional grammars were too much for teachers to learn before applying them in lesson planning and teaching. Many teachers attending R2L training had previously participated in functional grammar training courses. All but a few reported that they remembered little of what they learnt in these courses, and fewer still applied it effectively in their literacy teaching.

Instead of a traditional system-based grammar course, we designed a way in to grammar through patterns of register and pedagogic activities that were already familiar, using the principle of modelling and guided practice. This procedure began with teachers highlighting meanings in a factual and story text, as if planning *Detailed Reading* lessons. They were then guided to label the word groups they had highlighted, simply as *people*, *things*, *process*, *place*, *time* or *quality*. This commonsense perspective from register enabled all teachers to clearly see the structuring of meanings in sentences, firstly as groups of words expressing these types of meanings, then as clauses that combined these word groups. The internal structuring of these word groups was then explored, adapting functional terms such as Describer and Pointer for nominal group functions, together with familiar names for word classes, which in turn provided a platform to unpack grammatical metaphors[4]. Through these steps, a sufficient metalanguage for discussing grammar patterns could be built up in a few hours of workshop practice. Initially teachers used this knowledge to analyze texts for lesson planning, but they could later use the same activities to teach their classes the metalanguage.

As teachers became more familiar with analyzing and teaching language patterns at the level of whole texts and sentences, they were eventually introduced to patterns of discourse semantics in texts. First, patterns of information were explored in the organization of arguments, as the structuring of these genres is a significant concern for many teachers. A principle of information peaks in starting points and end points was applied at the level of whole texts, paragraphs and sentences, building a metalanguage for textual structures at each of these levels. Next, patterns of appraisal were identified and discussed in stories, arguments and text responses, using a simple system of feelings, judgements, appreciation, amplifying and sourcing. The roles of lexical relations in building fields of knowledge were then explored in factual texts, and functions of conjunction and reference were identified in various genres. The approach with each of these discourse systems was to outline a minimal framework, which could be applied to identifying patterns by modelling and guided practice, elaborated with discussion of teaching applications.

EXPANDING TEACHER EDUCATION PROGRAMS

While many of these developments took place in the CEOM program led by Claire and Sarah, the R2L teacher training program was continually expanding across Australia and beyond. The grammar training module, for example, was initiated within a large training program in Brisbane Catholic Education, led by Pauline Chester and Maryanne Fleming, as functional grammar was part of the state and national curricula. In the huge education department of NSW, teacher professional learning was organized in regions, which allowed local managers choices in literacy methodologies, with specialist teachers in the roles of facilitator/trainers. R2L was particularly popular in rural regions with high proportions of Indigenous students. The first training in the region was organized by Lyndall Harrison in the Bathurst/Orange district. This was followed by a major project in the state's far west (Koop & Rose, 2008), which led to a training program for the entire NSW western region, in which teacher facilitators were expected to become the trainers. This in turn led to projects in other NSW regions, including western metropolitan Sydney.

To support such large-scale programs, the R2L materials were organized into a set of resource books provided to teachers. The activities that had been developed in the training program were set out in written form, to be practised with guidance in workshops, as well as studied independently. They included the activities outlined above, along with further activities for teaching foundation skills in reading and writing, beginning literacy in the early years of school, and language in mathematics, all of which were part of the teacher training program.

The maths strategies were developed in the western NSW and Sydney projects. Their major focus was on teachers' common practice of demonstrating maths processes on the board while orally explaining each step, followed by individual practice. This standard method has always been ineffective for many students, who struggle with the individual practice. The R2L solution was not to replace the method, but enhance it with detailed lesson planning and joint practice. Teachers were guided to analyze carefully the steps through which they taught these maths processes, and the language they used, and create detailed lessons plans for themselves.

They would then demonstrate a process using the lesson plan, followed by a series of joint practices of the process, that gradually handed control to students before independent practice (Lövstedt & Rose, 2015; Rose, 2021; Westhoff, Chapter 16 this volume). Along with practising this lesson planning in R2L maths workshops, teachers practised analyzing and teaching written maths genres. The 'word problem' genre, which is supposed to 'contextualize' maths processes, but is simply confusing for many students, was taught by identifying its three elements: data presented, solutions required, and relevant maths processes. Maths definition and explanation genres were taught with *Detailed Reading* and *Rewriting*, to control the highly technical lexicogrammar of maths.

The evolving complexity of the teacher education program, and the range of teaching activities it included, demanded overviews so that teachers could see where each activity was situated. To this end, the activities were summarized as sets of teaching/learning cycles, nested within each other (Figure 1.5). The first cycle dealt with reading and writing whole texts, in *Preparing for Reading* and *Joint Construction*. This level connected directly to the institutional contexts of curriculum, text selection, program planning, and evaluation through writing. The next cycle provided more intensive support, with *Detailed Reading* and *Joint Rewriting* of short passages, and the inner cycle provided most support with the hands-on activities of *Sentence Making*, *Spelling* and *Sentence Writing*. Each cycle included joint reading and writing activities, followed by individual practice with teacher guidance. Crucially,

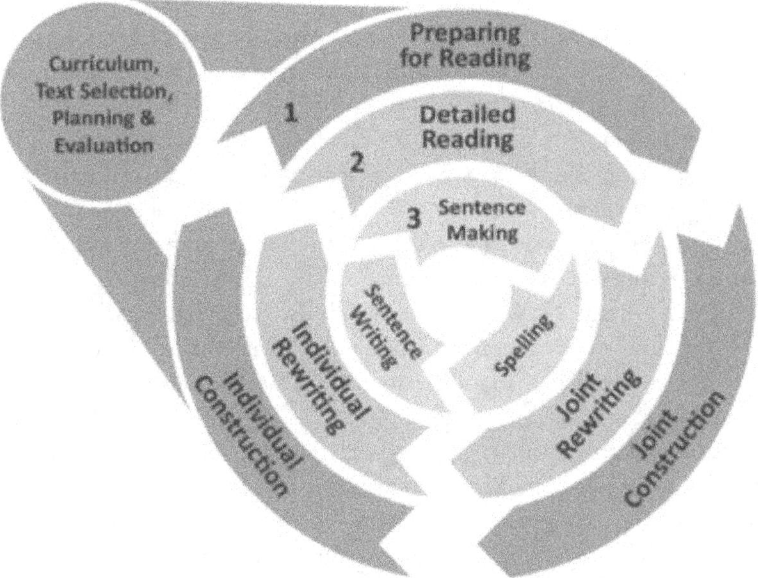

Figure 1.5. Cycles of support in R2L

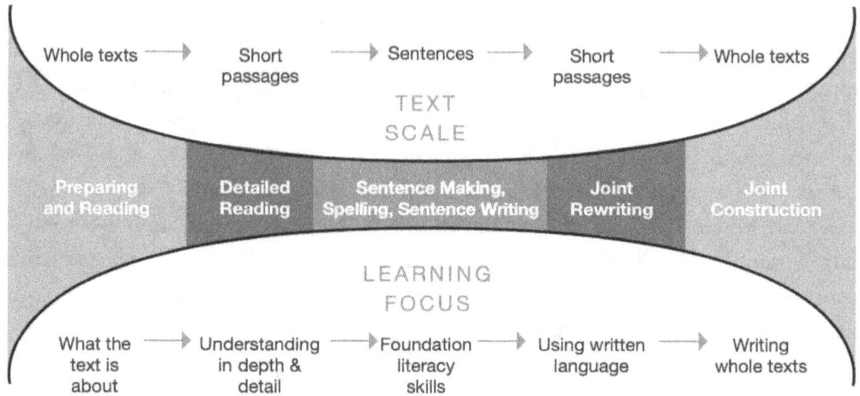

Figure 1.6. R2L programming sequence

it was emphasized that these were all teaching/learning activities, prior to independent tasks for assessment[5].

The various R2L strategies were presented to teachers, not as a fixed program, but as a toolbox to draw on, as their confidence in using them developed. Nevertheless, it was emphasized that the programming sequence always began with reading whole texts, before reading a passage in detail, then optionally the intensive hands-on activities with sentences, and building up writing resources through short passages to constructing texts. This sequence was summarized as the butterfly diagram in Figure 1.6.

Several of the books in the R2L materials were designed to accompany training videos of demonstration lessons, which were filmed in a variety of contexts. The video of reading and writing stories was recorded in a Melbourne Catholic primary school, where most students were children of immigrant families with English as another language. Working with factual texts was filmed in a South African secondary school where all students had English as another language (Rose, 2021). Beginning reading and writing was filmed with AnTEP students teaching Anangu children. Training videos for maths were filmed at a disadvantaged primary school in the town of Orange, NSW, and an ethnically diverse secondary school in western Sydney. The latter video was part of a joint project with the NSW Board of Studies (now NESA), to put demonstration lessons of R2L secondary maths and science lessons on their website (NESA & Rose, 2018a, 2018b). This science lesson was also filmed at the western Sydney high school, and accompanies the activities with factual texts in the R2L books. Strategies for adult ESL lessons, and for teaching academic literacy, were recorded in a project at Charles Darwin University (CDU) in the Northern Territory. Most of these videos are now accessible at https://readingtolearn.com.au/pages/videos.

The ESL video demonstrated how R2L activities explicitly provide sources of new language through talk-around-text in joint reading, notemaking and writing, enabling speakers of other languages to build lexicogrammatical resources while learning new registers and genres. By reversing the traditional ESL bricks-&-mortar approach, from vocabulary items up to grammar structures, it showed how starting with whole texts could rapidly accelerate language learning. Through teacher-guided joint practice, all students could participate actively in practising the target language, at the levels of pronunciation, spelling, lexis, grammar and discourse patterns. These principles for learning other languages have been applied more or less explicitly in many R2L projects. Formal studies of interlanguage learning have been conducted in Hong Kong University, teaching Chinese with speakers of other languages, by Mark Shum and his team (Shum, Tai & Shi, 2016); in Indonesian schools, teaching English with multilingual students, by Harni Kartika (Chapter 17 this volume; Kartika-Ningsih & Rose, 2018); and with Spanish-speaking students in the US, by Andrés Ramirez and colleagues (Chapter 12 this volume). Multilingual learning is also described in the project with the Manilla school for deaf and hearing-impaired students in Sweden, led by Ann-Christin Lövstedt (Chapter 7 this volume), using sign languages to teach reading and writing in Swedish. The work in South African schools by Mike Hart and colleagues (Eminson, 2018; Hart, Chapter 5 this volume), has also focused on teaching multilingual African students to read and write in English. One outcome of the work at CDU was a project to train school teachers in Afghanistan, led by Frances Tolhurst, who had taught on the ESL and academic literacy programs at CDU. The Afghan project was organized by the Aga Khan Foundation (AKF), and proved highly successful for teaching literacy in the local Dari language. As a result, the AKF brought R2L to a very large teacher training program in Kenya, Uganda and Tanzania, for teaching literacy in both English and local languages with multilingual school students. Thousands of teachers have been trained in this project, and 'RtL' is now part of the Ugandan national curriculum (Hart, this volume; Lombardi, 2020).

The academic literacy video was filmed with undergraduate students at CDU. These activities had been gestating since the work with Aboriginal students at UTS in the early 1990s, outlined above, and were further developed with Indigenous adults at the Koori Centre, University of Sydney (Rose et al., 2003), Yooroang Garang Centre for Indigenous Health Studies, University of Sydney (Rose et al., 2008), and with entry programs for international students at the Centre for English Teaching, University of Sydney. The 'scaffolding academic literacy' strategies have been presented at workshops and conferences in South Africa (Rose, 2008) and set out as procedures for teacher education, in a textbook on university teaching (Rose, 2017). South Africa has produced a series of post-graduate theses in scaffolding academic literacy using R2L (Childs, 2008; Makathini, 2015; Millin & Millin, 2014;

Millin, this volume). Academic literacy projects in Spanish are also reported in this volume, by Rachel Whittaker and colleagues in Spain, Nayibe Rosado-Mendinueta and colleagues in Colombia, and Samiah Hassan and Cristina Boccia in Argentina.

In the mid-2000s, Reading to Learn was introduced to Europe, at a Swedish conference organised by Ann-Christin Lövstedt. Ann-Christin recruited Claire Acevedo, who was then in London, for a teacher training program that has gone from strength to strength (Acevedo, 2010), including the *Reading for Life* foundation, the Swedish translation of *Learning to Write, Reading to Learn* (Rose & Martin, 2013), the Gothenburg program (Andersson Varga, Mitiche, Sandberg & Staf, Chapter 8 this volume) and the Manilla school (Lövstedt, Chapter 7 this volume). Of course, another major outcome of Claire and Ann-Christin's partnership was the TeL4EL European teacher training project in Sweden, Denmark, Scotland, Spain and Portugal, in which the EU flew teams of teachers to each other's countries for joint training by Claire and Ann-Christin (Coffin et al., 2013). Outcomes of this project have included the translation of *Learning to Write, Reading to Learn* into Spanish as *Leer para Aprender* (Rose & Martin, 2018), led by Rachel Whittaker, and projects described in this volume by Rachel and her colleagues in Madrid and Carlos Gouveia and colleagues in Lisbon.

Back in Australia, the CEOM program continued under the leadership of Sarah Culican. R2L was introduced to Queensland state schools in a major professional learning program led by Jane Kelly and Ingrid Freeman (Teaching & Learning Unit, Metropolitan Region, Qld State Schooling, 2014). A number of whole-school projects have proved successful in this region, such as Balmoral High (Carusi-Lees, 2017; Chapter 4 this volume). Jane and Ingrid are now based at Kenmore State Primary School, which has a focus on students with special needs, particularly autism spectrum, as well as many students from other language backgrounds. Kenmore has achieved remarkable results in supporting special needs students to participate successfully in their grade classes, and for all their students. This inclusion and success is the focus of Jane and Ingrid's description of the program in Chapter 2 of this volume.

As you can see from this little pocket history of Reading to Learn, its development has been a very human affair, evolving through many conversations between teachers, students and teacher educators, all with the goal of making learning work more effectively for all our students, but particularly for those that come to us with fewer educational advantages. Each of the stories in this volume both illustrate and celebrate how this conversation can play out in all manner of settings. Each provides a model for the reader in how to go, in genre terms, from complication to solution.

NOTES

1 *Pitjantjatjara* is the name of a variety of Western Desert languages (Rose, 2001). *Anangu* is the Pitjantjatjara word for 'people'.

2 These adult students were mainly from First Nations communities in southern and eastern Australian towns and cities. Their schooling had been cut short by historical racist practices and attitudes in Australian schools. Some were training as Community Adult Educators, others were in special entry programs for undergraduate degrees, and others were in general further education courses.

3 Where the R2L writing assessment enables teacher to track students' language growth, the NAPLAN adaptation does not, but is designed to statistically compare students, classes and schools.

4 There are different types of grammatical metaphor but the most common is nominalisation. This is when grammatical forms such as verbs are expressed as nouns. Grammatical metaphor compresses information by reducing the number of clauses in a sentence.

5 The R2L cycles referenced the well-known three stage teaching/learning cycle (TLC) of genre writing pedagogy, centred on *Joint Construction*, with some key differences. The first activity in R2L is not 'deconstruction' of genre models, but preparing and reading source texts. Analysing models is not a separate activity in R2L, but a part of *Joint Construction* and other activities, that varies with text types. The third stage in R2L cycles is not independent writing, but individual practice with guidance, before independent assessment tasks. Finally of course, R2L offers additional layers of support with *Detailed Reading, Rewriting, Sentence Making* and *Sentence Writing*.

REFERENCES

Acevedo, C. (2010). *Will the implementation of Reading to Learn in Stockholm schools accelerate literacy learning for disadvantaged students and close the achievement gap? A Report on School-based Action Research,* Multilingual Research Institute, Stockholm. https://www.researchgate.net/publication/355160739

Axford, B., Harders, P., & Wise, F. (2009). *Scaffolding literacy: An integrated and sequential approach to teaching reading, spelling and writing,* ACER.

Carusi-Lees, Z. (2017). Tackling literacy one classroom at a time: Teaching writing at a whole school level in a Secondary context. *Teachers as Practitioner Research Journal 1* (1) 1–30. https://www.researchgate.net/publication/314230604

Childs, M. (2008). *A reading based theory of teaching appropriate for the South African context* [Doctoral dissertation, Nelson Mandela Metropolitan University, Port Elizabeth, South Africa].

Coffin, C., Acevedo, C., & Lövstedt, A.-C. (2013). *Teacher Learning for European Literacy Education (TeL4ELE) Final Report.* European Union, https://www.researchgate.net/publication/355145686

Eminson, S. (2018). Reading to Learn, South Africa. https://www.cypnow.co.uk/best-practice/article/reading-to-learn-south-africa

Kartika-Ningsih, H., & Rose, D. (2018). Language shift: analysing language use in multilingual classroom interactions. *Functional Linguistics*, 5(1), 9. Springer Open Acess, https://rdcu.be/be2d9

Koop, C., & Rose, D. (2008). Reading to Learn in Murdi Paaki: changing outcomes for Indigenous students. *Literacy Learning: The Middle Years, 16* (1). 41–6. http://www.alea.edu.au/

Lombardi, M. (2020). *Dispatch from the field: From the framework to the field.* Aga Khan Foundation. https://www.akfc.ca/our-work/dispatch-field-framework-field/

Lövstedt, A,-C., & Rose, D. (2015). Reading to Learn maths: A teacher professional development project in Stockholm. *Reading to Learn,* 1–18. https://www.researchgate.net/publication/354521625

Makathini, B. (2015). *Trampoline trajectories: A dialectical analysis of the correlation between the teaching of reading and the learner-academic performance in a South African rural primary school* [Doctoral dissertation, University of KwaZulu-Natal, South Africa].

McRae, D., Ainsworth, G., Cumming, J., Hughes, P., Mackay, T., Price, K., Rowland, M., Warhurst, J., Woods, D. & Zbar, V. (2000). *What has worked, and will again: The IESIP strategic results projects.* Australian Curriculum Studies Association. http://www.acsa.edu.au/pages/images/What%20works_.pdf

Martin, J. R. (1997). Analysing genre: functional parameters, In F. Christie & J.R. Martin (Eds.), *Genre and institutions: Social processes in the workplace and school* (pp. 3–39). Cassell.

Martin, J. R. (2000). Grammar meets genre – Reflections on the 'Sydney School', *Arts: the journal of the Sydney University Arts Association* 22, 47–95.

Martin, J. R. (2006). Metadiscourse: Designing interaction in genre-based literacy programs. In R. Whittaker, M. O'Donnell & A. McCabe (Eds.), *Language and Literacy: Functional approaches* (pp. 95–122). Continuum.

Martin, J. R. & Rose, D. (2008). *Genre relations: Mapping culture*. Equinox.

Martin, J. R. & Rose, D. (2012). Genres and texts: living in the real world. *Indonesian Journal of SFL, 1* (1), 1–21, https://www.researchgate.net/publication/323688001

Martin, J. R. & Rose, D. (2013) Pedagogic discourse: contexts of schooling. N Nørgaard [Ed.] *RASK International journal of language and communication (Special issue in honour of Carl Bache),* 219–264. https://www.sdu.dk/en/om_sdu/institutter_centre/isk/forskning/forskningspublikationer/rask/issues/38, https://www.researchgate.net/publication/355357018

Millin, T. J., & Millin, M. W. (2014). Scaffolding academic literacy using the Reading to Learn intervention: An evaluative study of a tertiary education context in South Africa. *Per Linguam, 30*(3), 26–38.

NESA & D. Rose (2018a). *Learning through reading and writing.* NSW Education & Standards Authority. https://readingtolearn.com.au/pages/reading-to-learn-science

NESA & D. Rose (2018b). *Planning for success in secondary maths*. Sydney: NSW Education & Standards Authority. http://educationstandards.nsw.edu.au/wps/portal/nesa/k-10/learning-areas/mathematics/planning-for-success-in-secondary-mathematics/stage-2-first-guided-practice

Rose, D. (1997). Science, technology and technical literacies. In F. Christie & J.R. Martin (Eds.), *Genre and institutions: Social processes in the workplace and school* (pp. 40–72) Pinter (Open Linguistics Series). https://www.researchgate.net/publication/255649992

Rose, D. (1998). Science discourse and industrial hierarchy. In J.R. Martin & R. Veel (Eds.), *Reading science: Critical and functional perspectives on discourses of science* (pp. 236–265). Routledge. https://www.researchgate.net/publication/255650935

Rose, D. (2004). Sequencing and pacing of the hidden curriculum: How Indigenous children are left out of the chain. In J. Muller, A. Morais & B. Davies (Eds.), *Reading Bernstein, researching Bernstein* (pp. 91–107). Routledge Falmer. http://www.education.uct.ac.za/sites/default/files/image_tool/images/104/readingbernstein04.pdf#page=109

Rose, D. (2006). Reading genre: a new wave of analysis. *Linguistics and the Human Sciences 2*(2), 185–204, https://www.researchgate.net/publication/254011813

Rose, D. (2008). Redesigning foundations: Integrating academic skills with academic learning. Keynote for *Conversations about Foundations Conference*, Cape Peninsula University of Technology, Cape Town, October 2007, https://www.researchgate.net/publication/355357438

Rose, D. (2010). Beating educational inequality with an integrated reading pedagogy. In F. Christie & A. Simpson (Eds.), *Literacy and social responsibility: Multiple perspectives* (pp. 101–115). Equinox. https://www.researchgate.net/publication/323549957

Rose, D. (2014). Analysing pedagogic discourse: An approach from genre and register *Functional Linguistics, 1*:11, http://www.functionallinguistics.com/content/1/1/11

Rose, D. (2015). New developments in genre-based literacy pedagogy. In C A MacArthur, S Graham, J Fitzgerald (eds.) *Handbook of Writing Research, 2nd Edition*. New York: Guildford, 227–242, https://www.researchgate.net/publication/355355349

Rose, D. (2017). Embedding literacy skills in academic teaching. In N. Rolls, E. Chambers & A. Northedge (Eds.) *Teaching at university in times of diversity: Higher education pedagogy and practice* (pp. 202–224). Palgrave Macmillan. https://www.researchgate.net/publication/320447359

Rose, D. (2018). Pedagogic register analysis: Mapping choices in teaching and learning. *Functional Linguistics* 5 (3), 1–33. http://rdcu.be/HD9G

Rose, D. (2020). Building a pedagogic metalanguage I: Curriculum genres and building a pedagogic metalanguage II: knowledge genres II. In J.R. Martin, K. Maton & Y.J. Doran (Eds.), *Accessing academic discourse: Systemic Functional Linguistics and Legitimation Code Theory* (pp. 236–302). Taylor & Francis. https://www.researchgate.net/publication/337114703

Rose, D. (2021). Doing maths: (de)constructing procedures for maths proceses. In K. Maton, J. R. Martin and Y. Doran (Eds.), *Teaching science: Knowledge, language, pedagogy* (pp. 257–286). Routledge.

Rose, D. (in press 2023). Viewing to Learn: intermodal pedagogy in science and mathematics lessons. In *Linguistics and the Human Sciences*, 19pp.

Rose, D., & Acevedo, C. (2006). 'Closing the gap and accelerating learning in the middle years of schooling', *Australian Journal of Language and Literacy, 14*(2), 32–45. www.alea.edu.au/llmy0606.htm

Rose, D., Gray, B., & Cowey, W. (1999). Scaffolding reading and writing for Indigenous children in school. In P. Wignell (Ed.), *Double power: English literacy and Indigenous education* (pp. 23–60). National Language & Literacy Institute of Australia (NLLIA). https://www.researchgate.net/publication/242091988

Rose, D., Lui-Chivizhe, L., McKnight, A., & Smith, A. (2003). Scaffolding Academic Reading and Writing at the Koori Centre. *Australian Journal of Indigenous Education*, [30th Anniversary Edition] *33*, 41–9. https://www.researchgate.net/publication/292306229

Rose, D., & Martin, J. R. (2012). *Learning to write, Reading to learn: Genre, knowledge and pedagogy in the Sydney School*. Equinox.

Rose, D., & Martin, J. R. (2013). *Skriva, läsa, lära (Writing, reading, learning)*. Hallgren & Fallgren.

Rose, D., & Martin, J. R. (2018). *Leer para aprender: Lectura y escritura en las áreas del currículo*. Ediciones Pirámide.

Rose, D., McInnes, D., & Korner, H. (1992). *Scientific literacy (Write it Right Literacy in Industry Research Project – Stage 1)*. Metropolitan East Disadvantaged Schools Program. [reprinted Sydney: NSW AMES 2007].

Rose, D., Rose, M., Farrington, S & Page, S. (2008). Scaffolding literacy for Indigenous health sciences students. *Journal of English for Academic Purposes 7*(3), 166–180. https://www.researchgate.net/publication/223069027

Shum, M. S. K., Tai, C. P., & Shi, D. (2016). Using 'Reading to Learn'(R2L) pedagogy to teach discussion genre to non-Chinese-speaking students in Hong Kong. *International Journal of Bilingual Education and Bilingualism, 21*(2) 237–247. http://www.tandfonline.com/doi/abs/10.1080/13670050.2016.1159653

Teaching & Learning Unit, Metropolitan Region, Qld State Schooling. (2014). *Building depth of practice: Metropolitan Region Reading to Learn Network*. Education Queensland. https://www.readingtolearn.com.au/the-results/

ABOUT THE AUTHOR

David Rose is Director of Reading to Learn and an Honorary Associate of the University of Sydney. His research includes literacy teaching practices and teacher professional learning, analysis and design of classroom discourse. His books include *The western desert code: An Australian cryptogrammar*, 2001; and, with J.R. Martin, *Working with discourse, Genre Relations* and *Learning to write, Reading to learn: genre, knowledge and pedagogy in the Sydney School.*

2

Inclusion and success for all children: A whole-school approach

Ingrid Freeman & Jane Kelly[1]

ABSTRACT

Reading to Learn (R2L) has become the vehicle for a whole-school approach to literacy at Kenmore State School since 2014. During this time many lessons have been learned about the nature of literacy and the conditions under which it can flourish. The purpose of this chapter is to record how our attempts to teach through reading have brought into sharper focus our understandings of contemporary issues for education, both in equity and efficacy. It is also the story of the way R2L's unique approach to differentiation has consolidated a common ethos and success for all our students, including students with disability and students for whom English is an additional language or dialect (EALD). The significance of R2L in supporting inclusion and success for all cannot be overstated. Finally, our aim is to share some of the implementation strategies and on-site professional development processes we have put in place to support depth of practice in R2L and, we would argue, education in general.

CONTEXT – KENMORE STATE SCHOOL

In 2020, Kenmore State School, like most schools, has a diverse community to support (Table 2.1).

Table 2.1. Population data for Kenmore State School

Location	Brisbane Metropolitan Region, Queensland, Australia
Year levels	Prep to Year 6 (Aged 4.5–11)
Enrolment	410
Indigenous enrolment percentage	0.3%
Students with verified disability enrolment percentage	7.8%
Students with English as a Second Language or Dialect enrolment percentage	31%
Index of Community Socio-Educational Advantage[2] (ACARA, 2016)	92%

While our particular circumstances are unique, they are not remarkable. All schools work hard to attend to the broad range and diverse needs of our students. What might be a little different is the degree of confidence we have in our ability to respond effectively and increase our capacity to meet educational challenges. This is in great part due to what we have learned through implementing R2L in our school.

THE SHORT HISTORY OF IMPLEMENTATION

Before 2014, Kenmore State School was a small school where enrolment numbers were falling. Although the school's Special Education Program had a good reputation, this was in some ways working against creating a diverse and inclusive community as many local families with children with no special needs chose schools outside the catchment area. At the same time, the national testing program in literacy and numeracy (NAPLAN) had begun in 2008; and, while our educational systems and institutions were still unsophisticated in interpreting the data, schools were asked to show measurable improvement. Kenmore, like all Queensland schools, was being encouraged to lift the 'tail' of low literacy and accelerate the 'upper two bands' of high achievers. Our search for a way to do both cohesively brought us to R2L.

In 2014, the school hosted an 8-day vacation professional development course for a group of local schools, but, internally, targeted training for our own early years and Special Education Program (SEP) teachers. For the first two years, R2L training provided focus for the professional development within the school. Teachers experimented in their own classrooms, running R2L pedagogy alongside other programs and familiar routines. Even though implementation worked at a fairly personal level at this time, there was enough evidence of early success to extend the training to all year levels and put in some structures to support whole-school implementation.

In 2015, the first school-wide processes for on-site and continuous professional development were instituted to support teachers following their initial training. Regular planning days focussed on English curriculum development through an R2L lens. Assessment knowledge and skill was developed through regular guided marking against R2L criteria and tracking of the data gathered. These practices created a more consistent approach to curriculum and pedagogy in classrooms, as well as developing an assessment culture.

In 2016, a more formalised teacher-feedback process through pedagogical instructional rounds was introduced. While some feedback had been provided earlier through consultants, the leadership team and a local R2L network, the instructional rounds process gave teachers more opportunities to see colleagues at work and reflect on teaching practice at a whole-school level.

For the past three years, these three processes for supporting on-site professional development of curriculum, assessment and pedagogy have provided the rhythm of the work of the school. New classroom teachers and more of our specialist staff continue to be trained by David Rose each year as we host a program also made available to local schools.

On-site, our new teachers are apprenticed into the culture of the school and the R2L methodology through regular planning days, instructional rounds and staff meetings devoted to formative evaluation and analysis.

At the end of 2018, the review of the school by the Education Queensland School Improvement Unit reported:

> Teachers are respected by students and parents as caring professionals who are receptive to communicating regarding student learning and issues affecting that learning. Teachers, teacher aides and school leaders have a strong sense of purpose nurtured in a positive and proactive environment. Parents, students and teachers describe the relationship between members of the school community as caring and respectful. A distinct sense of embracement of multicultural inclusion and diversity exists throughout the school.
>
> Teachers are experts in the Reading to Learn (R2L) approach and confidently apply these strategies within their classrooms. Teacher anecdotes regarding student progress, student bookwork and school data attest to the success of the processes utilised by teachers to differentiate for students.

Curriculum, assessment and pedagogy 'talk' to each other in real and dynamic ways in our school, as Figure 2.1 shows. This is why our school has grown in literacy achievement, student numbers, educational depth, cohesive mission and confidence.

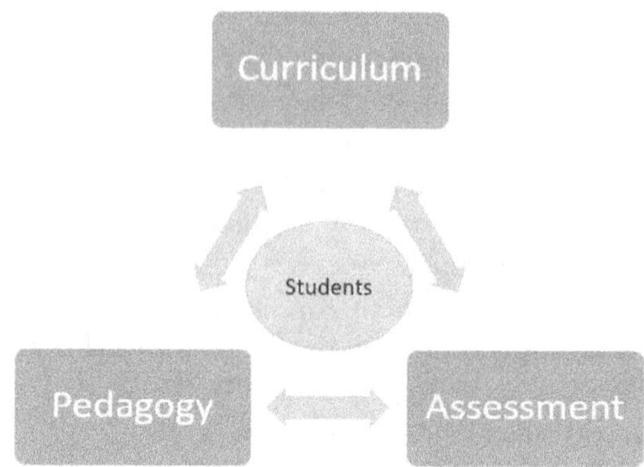

Figure 2.1. Alignment of Curriculum Pedagogy and Assessment

DEVELOPMENT OF THE KENMORE APPROACH TO ON-SITE PROFESSIONAL DEVELOPMENT IN R2L

Six years of work supports the following assertion: if you are proposing whole-school implementation, a long-term, multi-faceted and flexible commitment is necessary because it is a deep systemic and cultural change that is being attempted. Change requires consistent, practical and iterative tending; it needs room to move and generous resourcing; and it demands measurable and generative outcomes to ensure participants value it enough to persist.

In our experience, R2L has provided the tools to pull curriculum, pedagogy and assessment into closer alignment, so that teachers can see more precisely the impact of their pedagogical choices on student achievement, as shown in Figure 2.2. Our challenge was to provide and refine whole-school processes that would encourage a shared depth of knowledge and support precision through alignment.

GROWING UNDERSTANDINGS OF CURRICULUM

As we worked together, over time, out of our experience we distilled these 'big ideas':

- Regular collaborative planning is essential for building shared knowledge.
- Curriculum/assessment alignment is the first and most important task.
- Continuity planning across year levels drives aspiration.
- Genre analysis can de-clutter and deepen curriculum.
- Shared detailed communication around differentiation has potential as an inclusion game-changer.

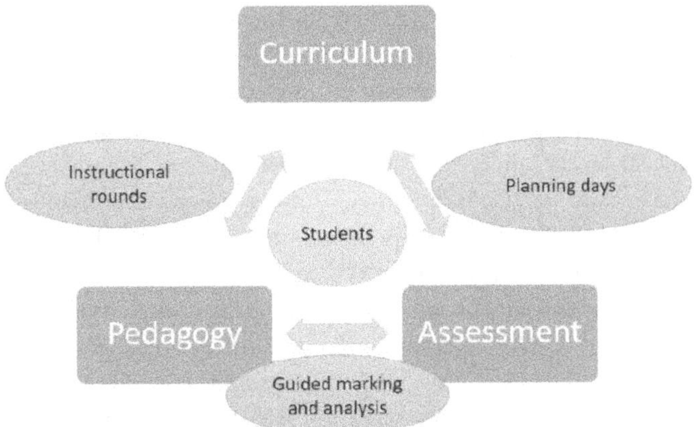

Figure 2.2. Scheduled school-wide processes to co-ordinate and refine the alignment of pedagogy, curriculum and assessment

- Iterative school processes are the best platforms for on-site professional learning and teacher induction.

This is how the big ideas play out in our school. The English curriculum, analysed through the lens of R2L, is currently supported in our school by one day per term of collaborative year-level planning. The aim of these planning days has changed over time. Initially, the focus was to re-structure state-developed units of work to accommodate R2L methodology. This, in the main, involved modifying assessment tasks which had complicated generic structures, and improving alignment to the curriculum texts being read. As teachers' knowledge and confidence in text analysis grew, better text selection and assessment design was possible. Adjustment to the state-developed curriculum/assessment program naturally led to renewed analysis of the national *Australian Curriculum: English*, to refine and balance the choices made in adjusting the state-provided models.

One particularly useful decision was to plan the English program so that all year levels were studying the same genre family at the same time. The *AC: English* calls for students to study imaginative, informative and persuasive texts. By scheduling units for each text type concurrently for Years 1–6, professional development delivered through staff meetings or on student-free days can be genre-specific and timely for all teachers, and can build to a more detailed and relevant continuum of learning for students. This process has extended and deepened teacher knowledge of text and curriculum. There is a growing appreciation that previous assumptions about 'student capability' and 'year level appropriateness of curriculum' arose out of traditional pedagogies that gave students opportunities to practise, but did not fundamentally change, the literacy understanding and skills they brought with them to school.

R2L text analysis gave the school's re-engagement with the national curriculum documents greater purpose and rigour. While the *AC: English* had a functional model of language as one of its informing frames, some historical approaches to implementation have fragmented this. Teachers can see the 30–40 content descriptors for each year level as independent skills to be clustered by mode or topic, and to be planned for and taught in isolation. While not a practice encouraged by the *AC: English*, some of these heritage practices maintain their hold on school routines. This accounts for (or at least allows) the traditional practice of separate activity strands or implementation of commercial programs within the English/Literacy curriculum; reading, writing, spelling, grammar, handwriting, phonics, literature, critical literacy, etc. The integration of all these strands into our current R2L program at Kenmore took time and diplomacy. Teachers were encouraged, at first, to continue with some discrete programs alongside the school-developed R2L units until such time as they were confident that they were achieving better student progress through R2L. Spelling, as a discrete program, held out the longest, but the year the R2L approach to spelling was fully adopted, the school's national testing data in spelling improved.

Our current curriculum work is building shared teacher knowledge of the way the *AC:English* content descriptors cluster meaningfully in specific texts (Table 2.2). Using the R2L criteria frame as a guide, we cluster the content descriptors to see what can be profitably learned through reading and re-writing the studied text. In the example below, where students study and write a new chapter for Roald Dahl's *The Twits*, just over half of the curriculum objectives for Year 4 can be addressed in the one unit.

But this is not an exercise in 'ticking off' objectives. By seeing the content descriptors in this format, teachers can more easily identify how the need to create tension drives the phasing, conjunction and grammar within the text. The specific characterisations in Dahl's text are produced through tenor choices in lexis and appraisal, dialogue and illustration. This clustering produces depth in text analysis that can be conveyed to students; and likewise, by using a consistent metalanguage when comparing with future texts studied, can help students discover and use intellectual tools for literary analysis themselves.

As such, R2L has provided a platform for de-cluttering the curriculum, allowing for both greater depth and the amount of repetition required to promote mastery. In this way, just as teachers are discovering that students can do more than they had expected, teachers also have more to offer.

This is not to say that our curriculum work is over. We understand more fully now that curriculum work must be iterative to allow for the fact that teachers are learners too, and their understandings develop at different rates and in different directions. There is always more to learn. The focus for the work changes in response to capacity and need. Our school has a long-standing commitment to inclusion, so

Table 2.2. Curriculum descriptors clustered by R2L criteria for specific text studied

R2L criteria	*AC:English* – Year 4 Content descriptors
Genre	Make connections between the ways different authors may represent similar storylines, ideas and relationships (ACELT1602) Use metalanguage to describe the effects of ideas, text structures and language features of literary texts (ACELT1604) Discuss literary experiences with others, sharing responses and expressing a point of view (ACELT1603) Identify characteristic features used in imaginative, informative and persuasive texts to meet the purpose of the text (ACELY1690)
Staging	Create literary texts by developing storylines, characters and settings (ACELT1794)
Phasing	Discuss how authors and illustrators make stories exciting, moving and absorbing and hold readers' interest by using various techniques, for example character development and plot tension (ACELT1605)
Field	Use comprehension strategies to build literal and inferred meaning to expand content knowledge, integrating and linking ideas and analysing and evaluating texts (ACELY1692) Understand that the meaning of sentences can be enriched through the use of noun groups/phrases and verb groups/phrases and prepositional phrases (ACELA1493)
Tenor	Investigate how quoted (direct) and reported (indirect) speech work in different types of text (ACELA1494)
Mode	Plan, draft and publish imaginative, informative and persuasive texts containing key information and supporting details for a widening range of audiences, demonstrating increasing control over text structures and language features (ACELY1694)
Lexis	Understand, interpret and experiment with a range of devices and deliberate word play in poetry and other literary texts, for example nonsense words, spoonerisms, neologisms and puns (ACELT1606)
Appraisal	Understand differences between the language of opinion and feeling and the language of factual reporting or recording (ACELA1489)
Conjunction	Understand how texts are made cohesive through the use of linking devices including pronoun reference and text connectives (ACELA1491)
Reference	Understand how texts are made cohesive through the use of linking devices including pronoun reference and text connectives (ACELA1491)
Grammar	Understand how adverb groups/phrases and prepositional phrases work in different ways to provide circumstantial details about an activity (ACELA1495)
Spelling	Understand how to use knowledge of letter patterns including double letters, spelling generalisations, morphemic word families, common prefixes and suffixes and word origins to spell more complex words (ACELA1779) Read and write a large core of high frequency words including homophones and know how to use context to identify correct spelling (ACELA1780)
Punctuation	Recognise how quotation marks are used in texts to signal dialogue, titles and quoted (direct) speech (ACELA1492)
Presentation	Write using clearly-formed joined letters, and develop increased fluency and automaticity (ACELY1696) Use a range of software including word processing programs to construct, edit and publish written text, and select, edit and place visual, print and audio elements (ACELY1697) Explore the effect of choices when framing an image, placement of elements in the image, and salience on composition of still and moving images in a range of types of texts (ACELA1496)

Table 2.3. Consistent text and lesson study routines

Prepare and read – whole text: foreground assessment and goals		
Daily routine	Prepare and Read (part text)	10–20 minutes
	Detailed Reading	10–20 minutes
	Sentence Making	10 minutes
	Spelling	5–10 minutes
	Sentence Writing	5–10 minutes
	Joint and *Individual Rewriting*	20 minutes
Prepare and write – whole text: *Joint* and *Individual Construction*		

currently the building of shared curriculum knowledge is focussed on strategic experimentation with EALD, high achievement and special education programs. This experimentation is in its infancy, but there are some signs that deeper shared curriculum knowledge is leading to better shared classroom practice between teachers, support teachers, students and aides, leading to enhanced inclusion.

Our school is also growing, so another focus is apprenticing new staff into a significantly different approach to curriculum, pedagogy and assessment. Collaboratively developed and shared curriculum resources at program, unit, lesson and detailed reading/re-writing levels are a start. The approach to R2L implementation taken at Kenmore means that there is a consistent pattern to the study of a text and a consistent R2L routine in the delivery of most lessons, working from *Preparing for Reading* through to *Independent Rewriting* (Table 2.3).

This routine, and the curriculum resources developed to scaffold delivery, are the stepping-off point for new teachers. However, to truly understand planning you need to take part in it yourself, so we envisage that the collaborative planning days provided each term will continue to refine and refresh curriculum indefinitely.

GROWING UNDERSTANDINGS OF PEDAGOGY

At the same time, our experience has revealed to us these 'big ideas' about pedagogy:

- Pedagogical change requires on-going strategic commitment.
- Teachers need space and support to learn something new.
- Routines provide benefits for staff and students in work quality and well-being.
- Using a text-based pedagogy has advantages in making curriculum and standards more explicit.
- Explicit curriculum and standards allow for more collaboration and innovation within the teams of people supporting inclusion.

- Routined student work producing visible learning allows teachers to make more precise responses to formative evaluations.

The on-site professional development of R2L pedagogy has likewise changed focus over time, but it is a consistent part of the school's processes. After new staff complete initial training, Kenmore now uses an *Instructional Rounds* process to provide feedback and maintain collegial discussion about the purpose and effectiveness of the pedagogical moves within R2L. Figure 2.3 shows the structure of our process for implementing the *Instructional Rounds*[3] professional learning process.

Each term, a focus for feedback is chosen to frame observations of teaching practice, either by the leadership team or by teaching peers. In the early years of implementation, the feedback process was to refine understandings and application of the steps learned through training. Some teachers find the pedagogical moves they have been taught easier to adopt than others. All interpret them through the prism of their own experience and values.

Conventional wisdom says we all teach how we ourselves have been taught, and when push comes to shove, we revert to earliest habits. So one of the guiding principles at Kenmore has been to manage the stress and workload of teachers, while increasing the opportunities for teachers to learn from and support each other in using R2L.

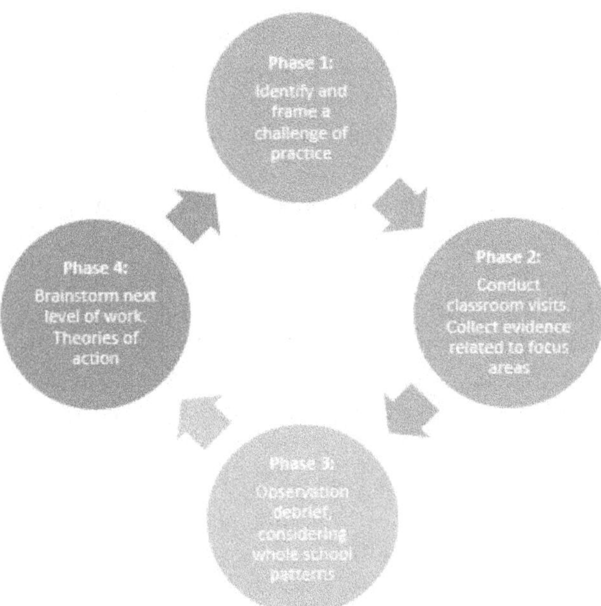

Figure 2.3. Process adapted from: *Instructional Rounds in Education* (City et al., 2009)

One initiative to support teacher learning has been an increase in specialisation within the school. Most primary schools in Australia plan for and deliver eight curriculum areas to their students. Most schools access specialist teachers for Physical Education, Languages and Music. Over time, the infrastructure of Kenmore has been adjusted to add specialist teaching of The Arts and STEM (Science, Technology, Engineering and Maths). What this has meant, in effect, is that the classroom teachers have had increased time and opportunity to become more specialised in the teaching of English. The time gained by the classroom teachers is used for planning and delivering small-group and individual intervention and enhancement activities, supported by greater analysis of a range of formative assessment data sources – of which the R2L monitoring of writing is the most significant. These interventions can be delivered in class, or supplement the whole-class instruction.

The most obvious impact of R2L as you move around the school, however, is the consistency of pedagogical routines used in classrooms. Early experiments in R2L across other local schools had pointed out an effectiveness gain achieved by moving through most of the stages of the pedagogy in quick succession within the one lesson, rather than implementing across a series of lessons over time. Consequently, the resources developed at Kenmore support teachers to deliver a daily lesson for English that is highly predictable in design and, therefore, quite unusual in the Australian context. While primary school teachers have been used to routines in classrooms around aspects of their program (guided reading, spelling or phonics drills), the routines have largely been self or school-selected and lesson design itself has always been very individualised. For some teachers, this variety has been a key element in their perception of what motivates or engages students, and even a key strategy for behaviour management, so it took a while for us to register the benefits of this 'routined' pedagogy, first for students and then for teachers.

The reason we chose R2L as the platform for pedagogical change and improved literacy was the promise that all students could engage and be supported in whole-class learning. But it would be fair to say that we did not really understand the impact the routines would have on student learning and wellbeing. Initially, many teachers had fears that the high level of repetition would be monotonous for students and that behaviour problems would result. However, quite the opposite was true, and a calm contentment began to characterise classroom atmosphere. It appeared that knowing what to do and being sure of success was more important to student wellbeing and engagement than perceived variety of activity.

Indeed, once children had been trained in the processes and were sure of expectations, their ability to concentrate and work productively for extended periods of time improved. Even very young children developed a pride and work-focus in rather endearing ways. It perhaps should not have surprised us to see how this worked. A considerable amount of research and subsequent professional development has highlighted the importance of students understanding what it is they are learning, why they are learning it and how their work will be judged. The R2L pedagogy of supported reading and re-writing of texts achieves this in simple as well as subtle ways. In a very concrete form, students know that the purpose of every lesson is to learn how to read and write the text studied and understand its content. They, as well as their teacher, can easily see how well they are doing by comparing their re-written text with the original exemplar. As they are scaffolded at every stage, there is no fear of failure, just opportunities to improve and become more consistent.

We believe this is one reason for our success with EALD students. We have been amazed and delighted by the progress of students without an English-speaking background. It is clear that the highly-visible, explicit pedagogy and literacy/language expectations have promoted student self-determination. In one class where the teacher had been supplying translations of key terms for EALD students, she was thrilled when a new student looked up, thanked her, but said they were not needed any more. This ability to monitor progress against a tangible goal is useful for all students, but particularly so for our EALD learners.

Likewise, this has aided inclusion and academic progress for students with disability. Our ongoing efforts to make inclusion both a viable and vibrant component of school life have changed over time but have been greatly enhanced by consistent R2L practices in classrooms. The period of time students with disability are learning with their age-level peers has increased and, clearly, will continue to increase. The interaction is mutually beneficial on a human level and educationally. We are discovering new and better ways to support students where they require extra help and, more importantly, when to step back or enlist the support of their peers. Academically, the clear focus of the curriculum and the consistency of the pedagogy makes room for the level of repetition and practice that allows for mastery of skills. In this way, we have seen literacy growth well beyond what had previously been achieved for our students with disability. At the present time we are balancing engagement with the class text and peers and using R2L intensive strategies to make focussed and intensive teaching decisions aligned to the students' Individualised Curriculum Plans. Our aim is not to limit expectations about what can be achieved, while providing appropriate time with text to develop literacy skill. The team of people involved in this enterprise need deep and shared knowledge to be effective. R2L and our school processes for integrating curriculum, pedagogy and assessment have effectively created an action-learning approach to education for us as a staff.

During the recent COVID19 learning@home period, we developed lesson booklets that mimicked as closely as possible our classroom practices for students. The plan was to make use of students' independent management of learning skills and maintain, for them, the comfort of familiar routines. It was observed that a number of our students with learning support needs and disability had flourished while using the booklets. A number of staff are now investigating how and why that worked; whether it was about the increased individualised attention or if the extra visual scaffolding made concentration and completion easier for students who, for various reasons, have interruptions to their focus at school. If it proves successful, we will add it to our repertoire of ways to implement R2L.

Clearly, this patterned routine to pedagogy has not just been a benefit to students. While adopting R2L pedagogy can be challenging for teachers, once learned, it provides a freedom that can be exploited in other ways. Where teachers do not have a consistent, patterned pedagogy, they spend a considerable amount of their time designing, creating, sourcing, balancing resources and activities for individual lessons which may never be used again. More particularly and significantly, the work produced by students from these lessons may never be analysed in enough depth for their teachers to accurately evaluate the quality of the learning taking place and then design better, more effective lessons in response. Because the activities and resources in a R2L lesson are so well known, the focus of the teacher's time can be on the curriculum objectives of the lesson/text, and how students are responding to the instruction and the content. Each step in the R2L pedagogy prepares the student for the next, and, in turn, the way students complete each activity gives the teacher immediate feedback on the effectiveness of the teaching. As students have daily patterned practice in reading, talking, spelling, handwriting, using grammar and text construction skills, teachers have incremental evidence of growth in student literacy and therefore, better information about where and how to intervene.

But it is what teachers do with this extra time, information and clarity that is important. Some of our teachers have used it to deepen knowledge and skill in curriculum and text analysis. Others have used it to enhance classroom management and inclusion practices. What individual teachers learn is of great benefit to their students, but also contributes to our shared understanding and ethos.

GROWING UNDERSTANDINGS OF ASSESSMENT

And, finally, here are the 'big ideas' which have been generated in the area of assessment:

- A rigorous and consistent platform for formative evaluation is necessary to drive improvement in pedagogy and student results.
- Teachers need to be able to see how a change in their pedagogy improves student performance – the direct link between R2L's 14 criteria and the steps of the pedagogy makes this possible on a daily basis.
- Shifting teacher focus from curriculum inputs to assessment outputs changes teacher understanding of pedagogy fundamentally.

- Increased awareness of the impact of pedagogy on student achievement, and the unintended impact of some traditional methodologies, inspires in most teachers a greater passion for equity and inclusion.

Staff meetings are used each term to host the assessment and moderation practices of our school and support purposeful connections between curriculum, pedagogy and assessment. R2L has been crucial to the refinement of this work. It has provided Kenmore with a more stable platform for a more rigorous approach to formative evaluation than was previously possible.

Each term, teachers are supported to mark student writing using the 14 criteria and the modelled standards in the R2L materials (Rose, 2020, *Booklet 3, Assessing writing*) and then analyse the class data to refine curriculum, pedagogy and assessment design. At first, it is typical for teachers to see the data purely in terms of student strengths and weaknesses. This perception is useful enough, because, uniquely, there is a clear and workable link between the pattern of information drawn against the 14 criteria used and the steps in the R2L pedagogy that can be used to address the issue. It is not an exaggeration to say that very little data at the disposal of teachers has such a direct relationship to a set of pedagogies needed to effect change in the results. Certainly, none can be accessed in such a timely manner that it will allow teachers to track the impact of their efforts from term to term and even lesson to lesson. At our school, it has meant that teachers' assessment knowledge and skill has increased, and this has resulted in more precise and effective differentiation and feedback. Sometimes you only know how far you have come by looking back at distance travelled. Today, our earlier understandings of differentiation seem very unsophisticated. Now we understand that differentiation without a reliable means of measuring the impact of the intervention is just wishful thinking.

Seeing student work improve towards tangible standards is very motivating for teachers. In Australia, while there is an acceptance of a standards-based approach, our national curriculum documents have achievement standards and demonstration portfolios of work that are broadly described. Our national collection of data for Years 3 and 5 literacy and numeracy (NAPLAN) uses mainly standardised-testing protocols with the exception of the Writing Test, which is marked by trained panels against standards and marking guides. The text-based exemplars and consistently described literacy standards provided within R2L give us an extra layer of precision which helps to drive measurable improvement.

This is not to say that the national collection of data has not been useful to us. On the contrary, the data drawn from the NAPLAN measures help triangulate against our internal R2L marking. This process has demonstrated that the achievement growth mapped by teachers (essentially self-reporting against R2L scales) has validity on a wider scale, as our NAPLAN results in literacy have also indicated a significant upward trend over the same period. It is, however, the formative and generative R2L data that drives the co-ordination and refinement of English curriculum and pedagogy at our school.

Over time, our teachers usually come to see that the quality of student work directly reflects the quality of the curriculum and pedagogy offered. This is a game changer for most teachers. All of us have learned, in deeper ways than first imagined, that all students can learn, and learn well, given the right conditions. Clearly, then, the traditional attitudes and structures of education have worked against many children in the past.

What this realisation often means for teachers is a re-doubling of efforts to manage their practice to factor out impediments to learning. But the realisation does not mean that teacher practice changes overnight or forever more. Understanding grows slowly, often hampered by expectations, habits and values that we do not even know we have. But if you accept that context is everything in student learning, you have to accept the same for teachers, too. For the leadership team, this means continued efforts to lead the thoughtful and useful analysis of data, and support the enhanced implementation of curriculum through R2L.

As part of our professional development program, and in line with systemic expectations, we participate in cross-school moderation of student work in English. At these meetings, teachers from a number of local schools present examples of student work and discuss grading. This reaffirmed our belief that our 'alternative' approach is promoting student achievement. Additionally, the growth in confidence of our teachers at these meetings, articulating understandings of the deep relationships between curriculum, pedagogy and assessment, has been confirmation that the school's implementation of R2L and on-site professional development approach is heading in the right direction.

FINAL THOUGHTS: R2L AS AN APPROACH TO DIFFERENTIATION THAT FOSTERS INCLUSION

The learnings at Kenmore over the past six years have all confirmed that a deeper and more detailed alignment of curriculum, pedagogy and assessment is necessary to make differentiation and inclusion effective. Reading to Learn has been our platform for achieving what we have to date and will be our framework for digging deeper in the future.

We have demonstrated to ourselves that it is the speed at which we ask students to move through the curriculum that is the greatest impediment to developing learning and literacy skills. Curriculum needs to be of a size to allow mastery, but not limit the potential of the broadest range of students. R2L's approach of teaching through texts helps to do this. It takes knowledge, skill and an amount of discipline to choose texts that not only instantiate the curriculum fully but are small enough to be examined in detail through the steps of the R2L pedagogy. We are getting better at programming vertically across year levels, as the benefits are obvious. Crucially, it means all students in a class are being scaffolded towards the same curriculum, not provided with a plethora of different programs pitched at different levels. Learning support and curriculum extension are, likewise, available to all students through the staging of the pedagogy. We do not need to make assumptions about student 'ability' that ultimately serve to limit their curriculum options. Equally important is the impact of having a visible, overt curriculum in the form of texts. The impact of this on student learning and ability to monitor progress was mentioned earlier, but the value for teachers is equally impressive. The challenge is not in providing a range of curriculum offerings, but in bringing all students to deeper understandings of the one curriculum, exemplified through the text studied. This is a unique approach to differentiation which has benefits for teacher knowledge, equitable student access to curriculum and the development of an inclusive ethos in the classroom.

The R2L pedagogy is the means through which students are supported to deeper understandings and greater levels of proficiency than they would manage independently. The underpinning R2L cycle of Prepare–Task–Elaborate[4] means that differentiation is attended to, meeting the needs of all students, within the flow of activities provided to all. Importantly, the activities are such that all students can participate in them, and find challenge in them, at the same time. One of the joys of visiting a classroom at Kenmore during an English lesson is to see the whole class working in concert and with focus. You have to look very closely to identify who has a disability, who is in the early days of learning English and who is the most adept and creative writer. This creates a sense of calm and purposeful community which is very supportive of inclusion. While these differences are invisible to the casual observer, the teacher is able to see the different needs of students with great clarity and make small but significant adjustments to activities, lessons and units of work to provide students with the time and repetition to build mastery. Teachers must learn and deploy a raft of skills in formative evaluation and pedagogical response to make this work unobtrusive. In doing so, our teachers have been in the process of shifting the focus from inputs to outputs. This is necessary for any genuine student-centred approach which places the emphasis on learning, but R2L does it in a way that increases teachers' knowledge and skill without exhausting them. The repetition and approach to mastery in R2L pedagogy is as useful to the teachers as it is to the students. In teaching this way you learn more about the students and your own craft. This approach to differentiation responds to difference (in teachers and students) without exacerbating it, and this fosters inclusion and excellence in teaching and learning.

Most approaches to differentiation seem to place an emphasis on varying inputs and not on the means by which teachers diagnose the need for the variation nor the measure of the success of the intervention. We certainly have more resources at our disposal to design disparate curriculum, activities and resources than we have to accurately measure progress over time. In Queensland, the major process for determining the quality of student work has been social moderation: peer discussion matching student work to criteria. This process has the advantage of being flexible enough to respond to social expectation and growth in teacher knowledge, but it requires significant investment in time and expertise to build shared expectations within schools, and across schools. Nationally, the NAPLAN standardised testing assesses individuals more against cohort performance than clearly defined standards in literacy. It is our contention that detailed performance standards-based assessment continua should be more widely used in Australia, as we have seen what it has achieved for us through the R2L program. For us, the knowledge contained in the R2L progressions helps us to build a more detailed picture of progress that co-ordinates teacher work to the benefit of students. We have been working to give 'flesh' to these statements through examples of student work and the choice of texts for study.

Ultimately, these texts provide students with an aspirational standard to work towards and teachers with a stable measure against which to measure student progress. The measurement of student work against a clearly defined standard, even while describing marked differences in student performance, is not anti-inclusion. It delivers the information to make differentiation effective. It celebrates the achievement of all students, but particularly the acceleration in learning for groups of children often perceived at an educational disadvantage. It provides the focus and impetus for genuine collaboration between teachers and students. The goal becomes progress and excellence for all students, and it is a goal that can be pursued collaboratively and over time.

Differentiation and inclusion are not contradictory aims, but they have potential to work against each other in their implementation and, subsequently, place great pressure on schools and teachers. At Kenmore State School, Reading to Learn has provided us with the knowledge and skills to make both viable, valued and embedded in the way we work. As such, there isn't an end point in our learning or implementation, just the promise of good things to come.

NOTES

1 Permission to publish granted by the Queensland Department of Education, Australia, October 2021, https://education.qld.gov.au/

2 The Index of Community Socio-Educational Advantage (ICSEA) was created by the Australian Curriculum, Assessment and Reporting Authority (ACARA) to provide an indication of the socio-educational backgrounds of students. It is used to enable fair comparisons between schools with similar student populations on the National Assessment Program – Literacy and Numeracy (NAPLAN) test achievement in schools across Australia.
3 *Instructional Rounds* (City et al., 2009) is a professional learning process with a set of protocols for teachers to observe classrooms with the aim of improving a school wide problem of practice.
4 See Rose, Chapter 1, this volume for an explanation of the R2L interaction cycle.

REFERENCES

The Australian Curriculum, Assessment and Reporting Authority (ACARA). (2016). *What does the ISCEA value mean?* https://docs.acara.edu.au/resources/About_icsea_2014.pdf
Australian Curriculum, Assessment and Reporting Authority (ACARA) (n.d.). *F-10 Curriculum, English*. https://www.australiancurriculum.edu.au/f-10-curriculum/english/
City, E. A., Elmore, R. F., Fiarman, S. E., & Teitel, L. (2009). *Instructional rounds in education – A network approach to improving teaching and learning.* Harvard Education Press. https://www.hepg.org/hep-home/books/instructional-rounds-in-education
Rose, D. (2020). *Reading to Learn: Accelerating learning and closing the gap (2020 Edition).* Reading to Learn. http://www.readingtolearn.com.au
Rose, D., & Martin, J. R. (2012). *Learning to write, reading to learn: Genre, knowledge and pedagogy in the Sydney school.* Equinox Publishing. https://www.equinoxpub.com/home/learning-writereading-learn/

ABOUT THE AUTHORS

Ingrid Freeman is the Principal at Kenmore State School, a primary school in Brisbane, Australia (https://kenmoress.eq.edu.au). She has undertaken a number of teaching, professional development and leadership roles within a range of contexts across the Brisbane Metropolitan Region. Ingrid has guided and supported teachers in whole-school implementation of Reading to Learn methodology.

Jane Kelly is the Curriculum and Literacy Coach at Kenmore State School. Previously, Jane co-ordinated the development of the Metropolitan Region R2L Network through school support, resource and professional development and teacher conferences. Her major interest is in site-based professional learning in literacy, language, assessment and curriculum.

3

Scaffolding pedagogic change at school and system level: Reading to Learn in Victoria, Australia

Sarah Jane Culican

ABSTRACT

This chapter outlines the author's own 'journey of discovery' of Reading to Learn, described in two projects which document the first trials with teachers and students in Victoria. These projects took place simultaneously in two different education settings – one in the Government sector and one in Catholic education. The chapter discusses the background and context for these projects – in particular, the prevalence of deficit views of literacy underachievement, and the shortcomings of many traditional approaches to literacy intervention. It also discusses both the challenges and the importance of scaffolding teachers in achieving pedagogic change.

INTRODUCTION

In Melbourne, Victoria, *Reading to Learn* (R2L) had its genesis in two parallel initiatives, both of which felt like 'pioneering' work, given the language and literacy education landscape in Victoria at the time. The first initiative resulted from an Australian Government-funded literacy research project, while the second was in the Catholic education sector. My chief involvement in this second research initiative was through my role as Literacy Education Officer in the Catholic Education Office Melbourne (CEOM) where I was part of a large team responsible for providing literacy leadership, advice and support to schools, and for delivering literacy professional learning to teachers.

The next section sets out the general background and context for R2L in Victoria and outlines the two initiatives mentioned above, along with their contribution to anchoring R2L as a significant teacher professional learning program in both the Victorian Government and Catholic education sectors.

BACKGROUND AND CONTEXT: LITERACY INTERVENTION IS 'CONTRACTED THUS'

Throughout the 1990s and into the early 2000s, the so-called 'literacy crisis' and the ensuing federal and state education 'reform agenda' dominated national political and educational discourses in Australia. Successive national policy documents and ministerial declarations identified goals and targets for lifting literacy performance, particularly for target groups of learners identified as underperforming (e.g., *Literacy for all: The challenge for Australian schools,* DEETYA, 1998).

During this time, the research lens was also on student performance and levels of engagement in the middle years of schooling (Years 5–8), which encompassed students in late childhood and early adolescence. Major research reports published during this time in western developed countries – including Australia, North America, the United Kingdom and Canada – argued that the middle years represent a crucial stage of schooling where the spectrum of student achievement widens, and progress for some students slows significantly (Cairney et al., 1998; Hill & Russell, 1999). Of particular concern were vulnerable cohorts such as disadvantaged students, students considered to be 'at risk' and those for whom English is an additional language (EAL students).

Key concerns underpinning the focus on the middle years of schooling were: the need to improve learning outcomes; to build greater cohesion and continuity in the transition from primary to secondary schooling; and to enhance student engagement and wellbeing.

However, as we know, language and literacy education – and the best ways to teach it – are hotly contested topics in education, inextricably linked with often polarised political and educational ideologies. Literacy education in the middle years was no less complex, characterised as it was by a number of practical and ideological 'divides': the divide between the structure and curriculum orientations of primary and secondary schooling; the divide between sociocultural and cognitive skills-based models of literacy development; and the divide between mainstream and 'intervention' literacy pedagogies and practices.

Studies of underachieving students abounded during this time (e.g., Freebody et al., 1995; Rose, 2004, 2005) and while there was never any doubt that significant numbers were disengaged in, and potentially struggling with, school learning, there was at the same time a backlash in terms of questioning the deficit views that seemed to dominate discourses around the perceived 'literacy crisis', and pathologise literacy underachievement. Where were the critiques of what constituted 'institutionalised schooling' and why and how it failed to engage particular cohorts of learners? Where were the closer analyses of 'at-risk' students who were struggling in school learning but whose out-of-school literacies might reveal remarkable competencies, not rated among the traditional subjects and structure of the school curriculum? If EAL learners, along with Aboriginal and Torres Strait Islander students, are among the cohorts described as disadvantaged or 'at risk', what does that tell us about marginality, about the nature of their experiences at school, about the lack of inclusiveness and about their unmet needs? (Freebody et al., 1995).

In Victoria, in 1998, the three education sectors (Government, Catholic and Independent) collaborated in a joint submission for federal funding from the *Successful Interventions* literacy research project (DET, 2001). The aim of this state-wide, cross-sectoral study was to analyse more closely students' experiences of school and classroom learning, with a particular focus on those underachieving in literacy in the upper primary and secondary years.

The first phase of the *Successful Interventions* research was an 'environmental scan' designed to investigate a selection of the literacy programs and practices that schools were implementing for vulnerable student cohorts. The second phase focused on literacy intervention programs for young adolescent learners in the junior secondary years (Years 7–8), while the third phase focused on the middle years of schooling (Years 5–8). The aim of this third phase was to bring together models of effective practice from both mainstream and literacy intervention settings, and to make recommendations for future policy and provision.

Not surprisingly, the first two phases of *Successful Interventions* found varied and inconclusive results. While there were clearly some examples of effectiveness – even excellence – among the 44 research schools, some of these successes may have been influenced as much by affective factors stemming from positive teacher–student relationships, a highly supportive school culture and strong parent/carer involvement, many of which were features of the literacy initiatives being trialled.

For educators and practitioners who, like myself, had spent decades in the field of language and literacy education, the shortcomings of many 'withdrawal' literacy intervention programs were to be expected. The tireless efforts of dedicated teachers notwithstanding, many programs failed to articulate to mainstream curriculum and assessment texts or tasks, or to scaffold students adequately in meeting the literacy demands of an increasingly complex, abstract and specialised curriculum (Christie, 1990; Unsworth, 2001). Further, they often represented a limited learning repertoire that served only to compound the distance between some students' capabilities and the demands of the mainstream school curriculum.

Added to this was the frustrating reality, not unique to Victoria, that teaching is an increasingly demanding and stressful occupation, where teachers are time-poor and schools struggle to allocate adequate resources – whether human, material or financial – to curriculum programs. Schools can also find themselves marketed to by commercial companies offering 'packaged' programs and materials that rely less on the knowledge and expertise of the teacher, and more on the appeal of incremental learning activities that can be worked through at the students' 'own pace', often requiring minimal input from the teacher. Further, many such programs are designed for younger students and therefore lack the capacity in both content and structure to engage older readers and writers.

For struggling middle years students, who typically lack the confidence or capacity to be self-directed 'independent learners', the challenge of working at their own pace can be daunting and ultimately ineffective. However, such programs or approaches often become the default literacy curriculum for disadvantaged or 'at risk' learners, potentially leading to fragmentation of provision for EAL students, Indigenous students, low literacy students, and students with disabilities or special needs (Luke et al., 2003).

Such programs are often selected by schools not because they represent best practice but according to how well they can be accommodated within the existing structures and programs of the school. This is not to suggest that schools and teachers do not do their very best to support students but rather that the narrow options that can be slotted seamlessly into an already crowded school curriculum, or that can operate smoothly within the context of the institutionalised learning environment of the school, come with some, not inconsequential, limitations.

Literacy intervention programs come and go, often leaving the mainstream curriculum largely undisturbed. Literacy intervention teachers may struggle to teach the key literacy knowledge students require in order to meet literacy demands and learning expectations of the mainstream curriculum while, on the other hand, mainstream teachers may remain uninformed as to the learning taking place in the intervention setting, leaving them ill-equipped in activating, reinforcing and building on prior learning.

Several of the shortcomings outlined in previous paragraphs were aptly summarised in the major national report *Beyond the middle*, which found that

> ... many schools have instituted various forms of withdrawal programs as interventions aimed at students at risk of poor literacy achievement in the middle years. Many of these remain focused on deficit or

> remedial approaches, drawing heavily from dated special education materials with an emphasis on individual worksheets, levelled texts and baseline decoding of printed text... Characteristic of these pull-out programs was a mismatch with the practices and pedagogies of the mainstream classroom. (Luke et al., 2003, p. 1160)

From my own observation and experience, reinforced by many research reports, it seemed that, to have maximum impact, an approach to literacy pedagogy designed for learners in the middle years of schooling would require several non-negotiable features. Namely, it must:

- recognise and encompass the broad repertoire of knowledge, skills and capabilities that constitute literacy for adolescent learners
- articulate to the literacy demands and learning expectations of mainstream curriculum texts and tasks
- provide support in all language modes, e.g., listening, speaking, reading, writing and visual/digital literacies
- be adaptable for whole class, small group or even one-to-one settings
- support students to develop the 'transferable' knowledge, skills and understandings for them to progress towards being independent learners, able to apply new knowledge across subject disciplines
- resist 'deficit' approaches to literacy underachievement and 'back to basics' approaches (a common mantra in education at the time)
- include not only traditional written texts but also more complex multimodal texts
- advocate for a common literacy pedagogy that promotes continuity in literacy provision and builds partnerships between middle years teachers in primary and secondary schools.

But where to find a classroom pedagogy that could meet these (apparently) elusive and exacting standards? Those of us who had spent our professional lives advising on, investigating and critiquing the limitations of programs or approaches labelled as 'intervention', 'remediation' or 'back to the basics' questioned where we could find a classroom pedagogy that both avoided the shortcomings described earlier and met the organising principles and features outlined above.

SCAFFOLDING LITERACY, 1998

In 1998, I was invited to join a trip to Canberra by fellow researcher, Sally Milburn, and members of the Victorian Department of Education. The purpose was to investigate the *Scaffolding Literacy* approach that was developed in the Schools and Community Centre at the University of Canberra to support primary students struggling with literacy (Axford et al., 2009). Its attributes were immediately obvious: its focus on a staged teaching cycle to scaffold reading and writing using quality, age-appropriate texts; on explicit teaching of language patterns and structures; and on patterns of teacher–student interaction around written texts. I made reference to the approach in the final report on the third phase of *Successful Interventions* (Culican, et al., 2001). Further, Sally and I were keen to launch a Melbourne-based trial of the pedagogy with teachers and students.

In a parallel development, the Literacy Team at the CEOM, led by Claire Acevedo, were engaged in early discussions and planning for a teacher professional development program aimed mainly at teachers of students in Years 5–8, and focused on struggling readers. At this time, the *Scaffolding Literacy* approach was also being further developed in South Australian schools in the research project *Scaffolding reading and writing for Indigenous children in school*, led by researchers from the Schools and Community Centre, David Rose, Brian Gray and Wendy Cowey (Rose, et al., 1999). The nationally recognised success of this project (McRae et al., 2000) led the CEOM Literacy Team to invite David Rose, from 2002 onwards, to lead workshops in the teacher professional development program, initially under the title *Supporting Struggling Readers in the Middle Years (5–9)*. I was part of the team organising and delivering this program, and Sally also attended the CEOM workshops as a participant.

A SCHOOL CLUSTER APPROACH TO R2L: THE EPPING CASE STUDY

Begun in 2002, the Epping case study was the first documented trial of R2L with primary and secondary school students in Victoria. This was a school cluster initiative that involved a group of government schools – Epping Secondary College and three associate ('feeder') primary schools – located in a culturally diverse, low socio-economic area in Melbourne's outer northern suburbs.

In the mostly working-class area of Epping, where between 50% and 70% of students were struggling with the demands of the school curriculum, a one-to-one remedial approach seemed, in the words of one teacher, as futile as 'trying to save the Titanic with a bucket'. Past years had seen staff in these schools 'burned out' by the pressure to 'fix' each and every student whose low literacy levels prevented active participation in learning. School filing cabinets overflowed with individual students' educational assessments, the Victorian Certificate of Education (VCE)[1] results were distressingly low, and discipline problems dominated the school policy agenda.

The opportunity to trial R2L with the Epping Cluster came with a Victorian state-government initiative called *Restart*, which was designed to improve literacy outcomes for Year 7 students in Victoria's 100 lowest-performing secondary schools. The Epping case study involved 15 teachers from the four participating schools in the cluster, comprising 10 secondary teachers from various learning areas and 5 teachers from the three primary schools. The schools in the cluster had a positive history of working collaboratively on projects to improve primary to secondary school transition. The teachers trialled the pedagogy in their mainstream classes, and Sally taught a class of 13 of the lowest-achieving Year 7 students in the secondary college, which began each school day with a 45-minute lesson, with myself as fellow researcher and 'critical friend'.

This cluster of schools was determined to challenge 'deficit' views of literacy underachievement by embracing a new and different approach. Unlike many traditional approaches to intervention for low-literacy students, which typically offered a differentiated 'diet' based on simplified materials or 'basal readers', this new approach was characterised by high expectations of learners, providing a staged teaching cycle designed to 'scaffold' them to be able to engage with the high-level, age-appropriate texts required by mainstream curriculum and assessment. The mantra for us in this pilot project fast became '*scaffolding up, not dumbing down*'.

A staged approach to professional learning was adopted, and David Rose was asked to present workshops to the group from the four participating schools at strategic intervals throughout the project. Teacher participants were also offered support through mentoring, in-class demonstrations and team teaching.

Even in the earliest days of the project, the teachers seemed to be aware that R2L differed in significant ways from any other approach they had come across. Soon enough, we had basic R2L teacher resource booklets, and have since had the satisfaction of seeing these resources grow and develop over the years. Importantly, back then and in the many subsequent iterations of the R2L resources, David has consistently acknowledged the valuable contribution of the many teachers and collaborators with whom he has worked.

The secondary college was the main source of 'hard' data on student achievement. However, each cluster school collected and recorded their own formative and summative student data – in particular, pre and post data to enable tracking of student progress and achievement, which was important in providing a basis for comparison over time. Throughout the year, students and teachers were regularly asked for feedback on how they felt the project was going based on a number of factors: their observations of student participation, engagement and performance; their key learnings from the professional development sessions; and their questions or 'wonderings' about the approach.

At the end of *Restart* in 2002, the results, feedback and evaluation of the Epping case study exceeded expectations and provided a strong impetus to maintain the

Table 3.1. A comparison of estimated growth in Reading between March 2002 and November 2002

Student	Assessed year level, March 2002	Estimate of growth, November 2002
1	Below Year 1	At least 4 years
2	Early Year 3	More than 2 years
3	Early Year 3	3 years
4	Early Year 3	Small progress
5	Possibly Year 2	2 years
6	Early Year 3	2–3 years
7	Early Year 3	1 year
8	Possibly Year 2	3–4 years
9	Early Year 3	1 year
10	Early Year 3	2–3 years
11	Possibly Year 2	More than 1 year
12	Late Year 3	Barely 1 year
13	Late Year 3	1 year

program in subsequent years within the Epping Cluster (Milburn & Culican, 2003). Table 3.1 gives an overview of the reading development of the 13 (mostly male) *Restart* students at the secondary college. The estimates in the table were based on a pre and post assessment carried out in March and November 2002 using the Australian Council for Educational Research tool, the *Developmental Assessment Resource for Teachers* (Forster et al., 1994), hereafter referred to as 'DART'.

The first column shows the year level standard each student was assessed as being equivalent to in March 2002; the second shows the estimate of growth based on an average of the pre and post DART reading scores in November 2002. Only two students showed less than one year of improvement and, in both those cases, multiple absences from school had impacted their participation in the project.

Clearly, there were a range of factors that may have enhanced the growth in student achievement in the Epping case study. Not least of these was the relative stability for vulnerable students of beginning every school day with a 45-minute session led by the same teacher in a highly supportive small-group setting – a marked departure from the usual structure of the secondary school timetable. However, other factors notwithstanding, when first assessed on the DART in early 2002, the students had just begun their first year of secondary school, whereupon they were assessed as to the age and stage of schooling their assessment performance indicated. By the end of the school year, as shown in Table 3.1, the majority had gained considerable ground, with some accelerating their reading capacity by three years or more.

Among the many evaluations Sally and I carried out in this project, the following three quotations from our first report on the project still stand out in my mind – all the more because of the immense challenge of engaging this group of low-performing students in school learning:

> **Assistant Principal:** If you'd have told me I was going to watch a Year 7 class talking about two paragraphs for a whole period, I'd have said, 'Get out of here'.
>
> **Teacher:** This approach provides tools, instead of rules.
>
> **Student:** Whatever you're doing, it sure is working! (laughs) (Milburn & Culican, 2003)

On the basis of these successful findings, the Epping case study was granted federal funding in 2003 for a further two years via the Australian Government Quality Teacher Program (AGQTP). In a bid to engage interested readers in our 'journey of discovery' of R2L, and also to be more lively and playful than the constraints of academic writing typically allow, Sally and I documented the project as a 'playscript' that included visuals in the form of cartoon drawings. This was presented at the International Federation of Teachers of English (IFTE) Conference in Melbourne in July, 2003. In 2006, the final report, *Scaffolding literacy in the middle years* (Culican, et al., 2006), was submitted to the Department of Education, Science & Training (DEST) in Canberra.

Nevertheless, there were challenges. Teacher feedback in the Epping case study highlighted the considerable difficulty teachers experienced in enacting the dialogue or discourse pattern for talking through print texts in R2L. This emphasised the need for a more strategic approach to scaffolding teacher learning in this important element of R2L pedagogy, a topic to which I shall return later in this chapter.

A SYSTEM-BASED APPROACH TO R2L: CATHOLIC EDUCATION OFFICE MELBOURNE

Around the same time as the Epping Case Study, the CEOM R2L project was initiated in response to two key educational priorities upon which education authorities were compelled to act: the national imperative to improve literacy outcomes for groups of students identified as underperforming, and the middle years reform agenda. This project was a large-scale literacy professional learning program offered to primary and secondary teachers in the Catholic Archdiocese of Melbourne. Key components in its design were as follows:

1. Teacher professional development workshops (4 two-day workshops over a school year)
2. School visits and support by CEOM literacy consultants between workshops
3. Organisation of the most appropriate 'mode of delivery' within the respective school setting: whole class, small group or one-to one
4. Collection of school and student pre and post assessment data
5. Teacher reflective journals
6. Dedicated 'Continuing Teacher' days for previously R2L-trained teachers
7. Accreditation as an R2L practitioner

Workshops were led primarily by David Rose as key presenter, with members of the CEOM Literacy Team as facilitators. This project was the beginning of the *Reading to Learn* professional learning program. It was so successful that it continued to be offered by CEOM until 2018 under the leadership of Claire and myself, in conjunction with David Rose. We worked assiduously to ensure that R2L continued to be firmly anchored within the raft of teacher education programs offered by CEOM (Acevedo & Rose, 2007; Rose & Acevedo, 2006). Between 2003 and 2018, close on 2,000 primary and secondary teachers participated in the CEOM R2L program. A proportion of these were 'Continuing Teachers', who returned for 'refresher' courses designed to build their capacity to mentor new and/or graduate teachers in the R2L pedagogy. As a key strategy in building the R2L 'community of practice' and fostering a culture of continuous improvement in schools, an 'R2L Mentoring' program was initiated in later years where experienced R2L teachers could work across schools to support those new to the pedagogy.

In 2003, a two-year research project was established to 'measure the effectiveness and outcomes of R2L'. Carried out across 2003–2004, *The CEOM Middle Years Literacy Intervention Research Project* continued to deliver the R2L program. However, now framed as a research project, a major focus was on collecting and analysing data to measure the progress and achievement of students, whose teachers were participating in the professional learning program.

Over two years, the project gathered qualitative and quantitative data from approximately 60 middle years teachers who implemented R2L with approximately 400 students across 24 primary and secondary schools in the Melbourne Archdiocese. Teachers in the project were required to trial R2L as part of their mainstream classroom practice. From their classes they also selected a group of underachieving 'target' students and used a range of assessment tools and strategies to track their progress and achievement. In addition, teachers were asked to nominate a 'comparison group' of students who did not receive R2L. Importantly, since most schools could only manage to release one or two teachers to attend the R2L training, students in the 'comparison' group were not seen as 'missing out', but rather as simply continuing as part of the school's 'business as usual'.

This research project culminated in the report, *Learning to read: Reading to Learn: Final report on the middle years literacy intervention research project 2003–4* (Culican, 2005), hereafter referred to as the 'CEOM R2L Report'. The CEOM R2L Report demonstrated that R2L not only closed the gap in achievement for students identified as underachieving or 'at risk' but, importantly, had the potential to accelerate the learning of all students (Culican, 2005) – a finding that is reinforced in papers written by David and Claire (e.g., Acevedo & Rose, 2007; Rose & Acevedo, 2006) and in other studies (e.g., Acevedo, Chapter 9, this volume). These findings were sufficient to set R2L apart from 'deficit' approaches to literacy underachievement in the middle years, and to rewrite teaching practices around texts in the classroom.

The key findings are discussed in greater detail in the CEOM R2L Report; however, in summary, they demonstrated that R2L was successful in improving the literacy performance of over 92% of the target students underachieving in literacy, extending the learning of more able students, and increasing the engagement and participation of all students. In 2003, as measured by the *Victorian Curriculum and Standards Framework* (CSF), over 45% of students made gains of one or more curriculum levels over six months, or approximately double the expected rate of literacy development. In 2004, over half of students made gains of one or more CSF levels over approximately nine months. These gains were approximately 20% greater than those made by the comparison group.

Other significant findings were as follows:

- Teachers reported improved confidence, increased engagement, active participation and better-quality reading and writing of texts across the curriculum learning areas.
- Target students made gains in excess of those of the year level comparison groups in all models of delivery.
- R2L was found to be equally valuable for male and female students, and gains for both male and female students were greater than those of the comparison groups at each year level.
- Gains for students with learning difficulties or disabilities exceeded expectations, and teachers reported higher than usual levels of engagement and participation from these students.
- Gains were greatest where R2L sessions were organised on a regular and consistent basis, and where they were frequent enough to impact positively on students' literacy performance.
- The whole-class model of delivery produced better outcomes than the small-group withdrawal model.

- Greater gains were achieved where teachers worked collaboratively and where there was a school culture of support for pedagogic change and curriculum reform.
- The project provided a model for monitoring the progress of students and for systematic, longitudinal tracking of underachieving students, particularly in the transition from primary to secondary school.
- Where a combination of approaches was used, the most successful combination occurred where the *Detailed Reading* or *Paragraph-by-Paragraph Reading* strategies were used with a whole class, then followed up in small-group work using the Intensive Strategies for those students (such as EAL, at risk and low-literacy students) requiring additional scaffolding and a higher level of support.
- The project showed that R2L was successful in equipping teachers with knowledge about language (KAL) and the teaching skills or pedagogical 'know how' that apply to all aspects of their practice

Finally, the CEOM R2L Report concluded that R2L had an important part to play in middle years literacy provision at system and school levels. Further, the research answered the call for a 'new wave of research' (Luke et al., 2003) into sustainable improvements through mainstream pedagogic reform. The building of teacher knowledge about language, in particular, was a significant driver in improving student literacy outcomes. Equipping teachers with textual and linguistic knowledge that could be imparted in a staged, scaffolded pedagogical teaching cycle was clearly revolutionary for many. As stated by one teacher, these things were 'the missing pieces of the jigsaw', the pieces that he had never received, either in his own schooling, in his pre-service teacher training or in his postgraduate studies.

The word 'intervention' was eventually dropped from the title of the R2L professional learning program in CEOM. This was for several reasons: partly because, in a sense, *all* formalised education can be seen as intervention; partly to avoid the negative connotations sometimes associated with the term 'intervention'; and partly because results had clearly shown that the R2L pedagogy was most effective when enacted in the mainstream classroom context (Culican, 2005).

In 2016, a corporate restructure led the CEOM to reduce the number of professional learning programs offered to schools. Having been one of the longest-running literacy professional learning programs in the history of the CEOM Literacy Team, the R2L program formally ceased at the end of that year but continued under a different contractual arrangement until 2018.

OTHER R2L PROFESSIONAL LEARNING PROJECTS IN VICTORIA AND WIDER AUSTRALIA

In the years between 2005 and 2019, I also worked collaboratively with David in a number of other R2L professional development programs in metropolitan and rural settings, some of which extended over several years. These included programs presented in the Victorian Department of Education, Independent Schools Victoria, the Catholic rural Diocese of Sandhurst in Victoria and the Brisbane Catholic Education Office in Queensland. In these projects, David would lead some workshops, while I led others, and supported teachers in their schools.

THE R2L DISCOURSE PATTERN

When I first encountered the scaffolding approach at the heart of R2L, most startling for me was the realisation that, in all my previous experience and research into approaches to language and literacy education, I had variously focused my attention on the limitations of the teaching, the limitations of the texts, the limitations of the tasks, or the limitations of the setting. Here, 'hiding in plain sight', was the traditional dialogue or discourse pattern governing the majority of teacher–student interactions around print texts, and the significant barrier this pattern could pose for some students in school learning.

R2L pays particular attention to the interactions that take place around written texts in classrooms and proposes a new pattern of classroom talk. However, my early work in R2L (Milburn & Culican, 2003) had demonstrated that changing classroom patterns of interaction is challenging and requires an effort of will as much as an understanding of why and how comprehension-style questioning – or the traditional Q&A teaching pattern – fails to provide sufficient support for many learners. The first step was to bring the traditional pattern of teacher–student talk around texts (best known as the IRE pattern) consciously into view. This was necessary in order that the limitations and unintended outcomes of the pattern for its 'receivers' (particularly EAL, disadvantaged and low literacy students) be fully understood and analysed.

However, it was also easier said than done. In the two R2L projects outlined earlier in this chapter, I recognised how powerful and pervasive was the intuitive and habituated Q&A pattern in teacher talk. Even where teachers understood the consequences of the traditional pattern, they struggled to move away from it in order to take up a more equitable and 'democratised' pattern that made meanings in a text – literal, inferential and interpretive – accessible to *all* the students in a class, which in turn supported student learning and writing on the topic (Rose & Martin, 2012).

This led me to focus attention on what I called 'scaffolding the scaffolding' – the development of a number of workshop activities and resources designed to support teachers in practising and mastering the R2L discourse pattern.

The R2L discourse pattern was a major focus in my doctoral studies in the early 2000s, where I videotaped R2L lessons and then analysed the written transcripts. The resulting doctoral thesis, *Scaffolding pedagogic change in middle years literacy*, completed at Deakin University in 2008, highlighted not only the challenges experienced by the four research participants but also the successes. Further, it drew attention to the value of transcript analysis as a means of raising conscious awareness of the often dramatically different results that can be achieved in student (and teacher) learning as a result of the R2L discourse pattern (Culican, 2007).

In conclusion, to this day – having completed four levels of educational qualification, having spent over 40 years in education and having worked with R2L over the last two decades – R2L remains the single-most significant and 'game-changing' classroom pedagogy I have ever encountered, and one from which, happily, I still continue to learn.

NOTE

1 The Victorian Certificate of Education (VCE) is a key credential available to secondary school students who successfully complete year 11 and 12 in the Australian state of Victoria

REFERENCES

Acevedo, C., & Rose, D. (2007). Reading (and writing) to learn in the middle years of schooling. *PEN, 157*, 1–8. NSW, Primary English Teaching Association. https://www.researchgate.net/publication/355182893

Axford, B., Harders, P., & Wise, F. (2009). *Scaffolding literacy: An integrated and sequential approach to teaching reading, spelling and writing*. Australian Council for Educational Research.

Cairney, T., Buchanan, J., Sproats, E., & Lowe, K. (1998). Literacy in the transition years. *The Australian Journal of Language and Literacy, 21*(2), 98–117. https://search.informit.org/doi/10.3316/aeipt.89909

Christie, F. (1990). The changing face of literacy. In F. Christie (ed.), *Literacy for a changing world*, pp.1–25. Australian Council for Educational Research (ACER).

Culican, S. J. (2005). *Learning to read: reading to learn: A middle year's literacy intervention research project, Final report 2003–4*. Catholic Education Office, Melbourne. DOI:10.13140/RG.2.2.13690.41921

Culican, S. J. (2007). Troubling teacher talk: The challenge of changing classroom discourse patterns. *Australian Educational Researcher, 34*(2), 7–27. https://files.eric.ed.gov/fulltext/EJ776211.pdf

Culican, S., Emmitt, M., & Oakley, C. (2001). *Literacy and learning in the middle years: Major report of the Middle Years Literacy Research Project*. Deakin University, Melbourne. https://digitised-collections.unimelb.edu.au/bitstream/handle/11343/115665/scpp-00181-nat-2001.pdf

Culican, S. J., Milburn, S., & Oakley, C. (2006). *Scaffolding literacy in the middle years: literacy and numeracy innovative projects initiative*. Department of Education, Science and Training. Commonwealth of Australia 2006. https://webarchive.nla.gov.au/awa/20070829204159/http://dest.gov.au/literacynumeracy/innovativeprojects/pdf/oakley_scaffolding.pdf

DEETYA. (1998). *Literacy for all: the challenge for Australian schools*. Canberra, Department of Employment, Education, Training and Youth Affairs.

DET. (2001). *Successful interventions literacy research project*. Department of Education and Training, Victoria. https://rest.neptune-prod.its.unimelb.edu.au/server/api/core/bitstreams/e3119bc0-a918-5044-93d0-e74978d6acae/content

Forster, M., Mendelovits, J., & Masters, G. (1994). *Developmental assessment resource for teachers, DART English*. Australian Council for Educational Research.

Freebody, P., Ludwig, C., & Gunn, S. (1995). *Everyday literacy practices in and out of schools in low socio-economic urban communities* (Vols 1–2). Department of Employment, Education and Training (DEET).

Hill, P., & Russell, J. (1999, March). Systemic, whole-school reform of the middle years of schooling, [Conference presentation]. Centre for Applied Educational Research, University of Melbourne.

Luke, A., Elkins, J., Weir, R. L., Carrington, V., Dole, S., Pendergast, D., Kapitzke, C., van Kraayenoord, C., Moni, K., McIntosh, A., Mayer, D., Bahr, M., Hunter, L., Chadbourne, R., Bean, T., Alvermann, D., & Stevens, L. (2003). *Beyond the middle: A report about literacy and numeracy development of target group students in the middle years of schooling* (Vol 1). Commonwealth Department of Education Science & Training.

McRae, D., Ainsworth, G., Cumming, J., Hughes, P., Mackay, T., Price, K., Rowland, M., Warhurst, J., Woods, D., & Zbar, V. (2000). *What has worked, and will again: the IESIP Strategic Results Projects*. Australian Curriculum Studies Association. www.acsa.edu.au/publications/worked, 24–26

Milburn, S., & Culican, S. J. (2003). *Scaffolding literacy in the middle years*, [a case study funded through the Australian Government Quality Teacher Programme, Canberra: Department of Education, Science & Training (DEST)]. Commonwealth of Australia 2003. https://trove.nla.gov.au/search/category/websites?keyword=Scaffolding%20Literacy%20in%20the%20Middle%20Years

Rose, D. (2004). Sequencing and pacing of the hidden curriculum: How Indigenous children are left out of the chain. In J. Muller, A. Morais & B. Davies (Eds.) *Reading Bernstein, Researching Bernstein* (pp. 91–107). Routledge Falmer.

Rose, D. (2005). Democratising the classroom: A literacy pedagogy for the new generation. *Journal of Education, 37*, 131–167.

Rose, D., & Acevedo, C. (2006). Closing the gap and accelerating learning in the middle years of schooling, *Literacy Learning: The Middle Years*. Australian Literacy Educators' Association, *14*(2), 32–45.

Rose, D., Gray, B., & Cowey, W. (1999). Scaffolding reading and writing for Indigenous children in school. In P. Wignell (Ed.) *Double power: English literacy and Indigenous education* (pp. 23–60). Australian National Languages and Literacy Institute, Deakin.

Rose, D., & Martin, J. (2012). *Learning to write, reading to learn: Genre, knowledge and pedagogy of the Sydney school.* Equinox Publishing.

Unsworth, L. (2001). *Teaching multiliteracies across the curriculum*. Open University Press.

ABOUT THE AUTHOR

Sarah Jane Culican is an experienced consultant and teacher educator from Melbourne, Australia. She specialises in language and literacy education and has been involved in Reading to Learn teacher education for 20 years. Her doctoral research focused on teacher up-take of the Reading to Learn pedagogy. She has worked for education authorities and universities around Australia and currently holds a position at the Department of Education in Victoria.

4

Whole-school implementation of Reading to Learn in a secondary context

Zena Carusi-Lees

ABSTRACT

Balmoral State High School is part of a network of schools in Brisbane that have adopted Reading to Learn (R2L) as a whole-school approach. Beginning in 2014, Balmoral began investing in R2L professional development for teachers across secondary subject areas. Students' literacy growth has been carefully tracked (Carusi-Lees, 2017), showing outstanding results for students in top, middle and lower cohorts. This chapter outlines the path Balmoral took to adopt Reading to Learn, the organization of support for teachers, and the results they achieved.

SCHOOL CONTEXT

Established in 1958, Balmoral State High School is a metropolitan Year 7 to 12 co-educational secondary school located six kilometres from the centre of Brisbane. Since 2014, the school has experienced strong growth with enrolment numbers increasing from approximately 400 to over 850 students in 2022. The school draws from a diverse socio-economic population, and on the Index of Community Socio-Educational Advantage (ICSEA) it has a rating of 1032, slightly above the national average of 1000[1] (ACARA, 2016). Approximately twenty percent of the school's students come from families who speak a language other than English at home.

THE SHIFT TOWARDS EVIDENCE-INFORMED PRACTICE

From the mid 2000s, successive executive leadership teams at Balmoral State High had identified student literacy as a key target area for development. In an attempt to address this concern, the executive had directed substantial funding into a variety of school-based and external literacy initiatives, including the appointment of a Support Teacher for Literacy and Numeracy (STLaN), engaging professional development presenters to work with school staff, budgeting for staff to attend external literacy professional learning opportunities, and the purchase of professional resources. Despite targeted investment, by the start of 2013 the executive had determined that this response to whole-school literacy teaching had not had significant impact on student outcomes.

In that same year, the Queensland Department of Education's 2013–17 Strategic Plan identified literacy (reading and writing) as a *core learning priority* for all schools (Queensland Department of Education, Training and Employment, 2013, p. 2). In addition to recognizing literacy achievement as a performance indicator in the 2013–17 Strategic Plan, this document indicated that schools were to 'strengthen evidence informed decision making using performance data, research, review and evaluation' with 'evidence informed practice and collaboration driving innovation and improvement' (Queensland Department of Education, Training and Employment, 2013, pp. 1–2).

The introduction of this directive calling on schools to assess evidence-based practices as a part of the evaluation and selection process, was a significant shift from the selection practices of the past, which had often favoured: those pre-existing programs within the school context, positive anecdotal feedback and recommendations between teachers or between schools, or promotion of publishing house programs within schools or across regions, among other reasons. In borrowing practices long associated with the scientific and medical communities, schools were being directed to review the effectiveness of a program or a research study based on available external evaluation and replication capacity as determined through rigorous and repeated demonstration of results (Australian Institute for Teaching and School Leadership , 2021).

LOOKING BACK TO MOVE FORWARD

Shortly after the release of the 2013–17 Strategic Plan, Balmoral's executive began scanning and assessing the then current literacy data against past literacy initiatives. It was at this point in the literacy review that my involvement as STLaN began.

These important conversations on literacy were to shape the recommendation procedures for future initiatives, including literacy.

One of the executive team's initial observations was that past selection processes for literacy programs or professional development had not identified an established evidence base as a requirement. This is not to suggest the initiatives failed to provide teachers with useful professional learnings or strategies. However, the finding does indicate a lack of demonstrable evidence that any of the implied student outcomes could be replicated at Balmoral State High, and that the absence of external review meant that suggested program findings were unable to be validated.

Next, the team identified two important and interrelated issues which were affecting teacher performance in the area of literacy. Firstly, many teachers (especially those from non-humanities' subjects) had limited understandings of literacy teaching, compounded with little expertise in how to identify evidence-informed strategies to address literacy teaching in the secondary context. This restricted understanding of literacy and the processes surrounding evaluation of potential programs and strategies is a problem faced by experienced teachers and newly trained, alike. The 2014 Report of the Teacher Education Ministerial Advisory Group (TEMAG) recommended that secondary pre-service teachers require a thorough understanding of the fundamentals of teaching literacy, coupled with the capacity to use a range of evidence-based strategies, in particular citing literacy (The Department of Education, Skills and Employment, 2015, pp. xi–xix). Secondly, some teachers at Balmoral State High, perhaps as a result of limited understanding of literacy theory, struggled to accept that their role included teaching literacy. Informed by the issues identified in their review, the team determined that future literacy initiatives be underpinned by an evidence-base that would develop both teacher understanding and capability, while at the same time building capacity to implement literacy learning across the whole school.

READING TO LEARN EXPLORED

With the review stage completed, and clear guidelines for future selection established, research and evaluation began. In Term 2, 2013, I reached out to two highly experienced primary principals, Debra Cox from Nundah State School and Lisa Morrison of Manly West State School, both of whom were already implementing *Reading to Learn* in their schools, and were strong advocates for the evidence-based methodology. Following these discussions, I gathered research from the Reading to Learn (R2L) website (http://www.readingtolearn.com.au), a number of external research papers and large scale trials by the New South Wales Department of Education (Dione-Rodgers et al., 2012) and The Catholic Education Office of Melbourne

(Acevedo & Rose, 2007; Culican, 2005). This body of research became the focus of ongoing discussions within the executive team.

Three fortuitous opportunities presented in the months following these discussions. The first involved Dr David Rose presenting as keynote speaker at the Metro Reading to Learn Network's weekend *Reading to Learn Mini Conference* in Brisbane, towards the end of Term 3. The principal, deputy principal and I attended the conference, participating in a variety of workshops. During the day we gathered resources, and spoke with other school leaders and teachers, some of whom were in the implementation stage, while others, like ourselves, were scanning and assessing for potential literacy programs. We were encouraged to join the Metro Reading to Learn Network and invited to the AGM later in the year. Over the next few years, the role of the Metro Reading to Learn Network and its member schools would become increasingly important to the success of this literacy initiative at Balmoral State High.

Following attendance at the Mini Conference, I continued to meet regularly with the executive team to evaluate *Reading to Learn*'s published evidence base and its eight-day professional learning model, with particular focus on the program's suitability in a secondary context. Increasingly, the team recognized that implementation of the program was a long-term commitment, necessitating both strategic planning and a carefully costed implementation plan. With commitments around ongoing support, funding and teacher release for whole-school professional development (PD), and flexibility around the selection process for initial teacher participation established with the principal, the focus shifted to organization.

The next opportunity was securing a place in the eight-day Reading to Learn PD program hosted by Manly West State School, commencing late 2013 and finishing early in 2014. Undertaking PD ahead of others enabled me to develop a practical understanding of the program that would assist teachers as they progressed in their literacy learning journeys. The professional development was a deeply engaging experience that invited teachers to recognize the selection and use of texts as fundamental to the teaching and learning process. Instead of a passing parade of articles, textbooks and videos, the focus shifted to the text quality: the capacity of a text to act as the vehicle for learning content through language. Reading to Learn provided the strategies to support teachers to sharpen their focus on the student experience of learning, as well as the tools to evidence student growth. Speaking to and collaborating with other teachers and leaders, it became clear that the program would not only fulfil the requirement for an evidence-base, it would support teachers in developing a deep understanding and capacity for literacy teaching.

The arrival of the third opportunity was a gamechanger. In 2014, the then Queensland Government approved the Department of Education to distribute AU$794.4 million in federal funding under a state-based initiative ('Great Results

Guarantee') now known as 'Investing for Success'. This initiative was designed to address potential literacy and numeracy disadvantage in Queensland schools by giving school leaders and teachers the independence to make decisions and develop programs to best meet the needs of their students (QAO, 2018, p. 2).

WHOLE-SCHOOL PROFESSIONAL DEVELOPMENT

The introduction of Great Results Guarantee secured the school-based funding to implement R2L professional learning across Balmoral State High. The first PD program during 2014–2015, saw twenty-three staff members, or 70% of the total teaching staff participate. One of the first groups to participate in the PD included four heads of department. The decision to target middle leaders across core faculties, Science, English, Special Needs and Maths, was seen as vital to building a cross-curriculum, whole-school literacy approach. The selection process for other teaching staff and teacher aides targeted 'early adopters', a mixture of experienced and beginning career teachers, and the first of two deputies. By 2020, successive principals and deputies had all completed the PD. From 2016 onwards until mid-2021, Balmoral State High committed to and maintained an ongoing rate of 80% of all teaching staff participating in the PD.

The model of R2L professional development over the eight-year period at Balmoral State High has adapted to support the school's changing needs and priorities. From the very first program in 2014, invitations for PD had been extended across the Region and beyond, to schools implementing Reading to Learn, or investigating the program for their own school. The growing Metro Reading to Learn Network was often a central point of reference for these enquiries.

From 2014 to 2017, the majority of the teachers from Balmoral State High attended programs of eight days' duration organized by our school, or in some instances, hosted by Nundah State School. One of our neighbouring secondary schools, Brisbane Bayside State College, trialled a four-day course in 2017, with secondary teachers participating in two groups: Humanities, Arts, English, Health and Physical Education (HPE) teachers in one group, and Maths, Science and Technologies teachers in the other. From 2018 onwards, Balmoral State High made the decision to move to a six-day PD model to contain the increasing costs of the program (teacher release now accounting for almost half of the total budget). This model was in use until the start of 2022. The delayed start to that school year, along with pandemic restrictions, prompted an ongoing review of future PD models.

In the initial years of R2L, the training model Balmoral State High implemented saw David Rose presenting for all of the eight days. When the format was refined from eight to six days, to ensure ongoing affordability of the program for the school,

I presented the first two and last two days, with David hosting the middle two. With over a decade as Head of English, some years working in literacy education across various universities, experience in using Reading to Learn in my classroom, and the incredibly good fortune to observe David Rose in action over a number of program deliveries, I accepted the challenge and have presented at the last four PD programs.

SUPPORTING TEACHERS

Working to build a high performing literacy teaching team across the whole school represented significant cultural change. As Balmoral State High undertook successive waves of PD, it was clear that classroom implementation 'post' training proved to be a substantial challenge. In the initial period of R2L PD, the goodwill and passion of 'early-adopter' teaching staff was pivotal to the success of the program, and to the school's capacity to transition towards a literacy-centred curriculum and pedagogy.

The energy of the teaching staff in this initial phase focused on forming a creative, collegial space, as they consulted educational articles, connected with their professional networks and colleagues at other schools. This effort produced a multitude of strategies identified as successful in building teams, developing and deepening collective understanding, and promoting collaborative learning. Reading to Learn conversation shaped staff forums at every level, from executive team meetings to collegial staffroom discussions. Ideas to promote and build the program's profile across the school were exchanged, discussed and enacted. From before-school book circles and discussion groups, observation visits at other Reading to Learn schools, reciprocal classroom peer observations, coaching training, attendance and participation at Metro Reading to Learn Network meetings, and presenting at Regional conferences, teachers and the leadership team worked tirelessly.

From the many initiatives implemented at the school, the following four strategies have been identified as having the greatest impact in supporting teaching staff:

1 *Peer observation* provided a formative process to 'open classroom doors' and support teachers in sharing their practice. Despite past attempts by the executive team to encourage peer observation, the school's 1950s closed space architecture offered limited opportunities for collaboration. Reading to Learn was instrumental in prising these doors open. Teachers invited colleagues into their classes to observe their work with one or more strategies. Rarely did the observation extend over the whole lesson, making the classroom cover required as short as fifteen to thirty minutes. The teacher conversation and collaboration that ensued from these observations drove a culture

of excellence and creativity, evidenced by peer observations as an established part of the school's annual planning processes.

2 *Quality Standards* for each of the Reading to Learn strategies (*Preparing for Reading, Paragraph-by-paragraph Reading, Notemaking* and so on) were shared with our school courtesy of Nundah State School. These single-sided A4 templates support teachers new to Reading to Learn in their discussion before, during and after a peer observation. They provide a guide for conversations around aspects of the strategy that were working effectively and those that would benefit from attention – effectively shifting the focus from the individual teacher to the strategy. The strength of developing and applying quality standards to the strategy-in-use lies in their function as a guideline to ensure consistency of practice. Feedback from newly trained teachers and observers who apply quality standards in peer observations remains highly positive.

3 The *Metro Reading to Learn Network* provided tangible support for Balmoral State High in numerous ways. Attending the Metro Reading to Learn Network AGM in December of 2013 deepened the school's connection with a number of other schools, many were further advanced in their professional learning, and all were extraordinarily collaborative. At that time, the Network included ten primary schools and two secondary schools, one of which was Balmoral State High. The Network allowed for practical sharing of resources, school observation visits and importantly, provided the capacity to organize and advertize training programs. As the number of schools working with Reading to Learn grew, Metro Region's Teaching and Learning Unit, seconded Jane Kelly, Ingrid Freeman (see Chapter 2, this volume) and Cindy Keong, to support the development of Reading to Learn across the Metropolitan Region. Their roles included assisting program implementation in the Manly West State School and Nundah State School clusters, as well as the continuation of the R2L network. Balmoral State High teachers presented aspects of our work and journey at the 2014 and 2015 Reading to Learn Mini Conferences, developing not only our confidence as practitioners, but our sense of team collaboration.

4 *Assessment workshops* served a number of important purposes in the school. Firstly, these workshops supported teachers who had recently completed Reading to Learn PD, by consolidating and deepening their knowledge of literacy theory, and sharpening their understanding of *when* and *which* strategies to apply to support student literacy development. These scheduled workshops followed the method outlined in the Reading to Learn program where teachers analyzed the most recent student texts for the six students they had identified to track for the year. The workshops involved all R2L

teachers (except those on a full Maths load) and were timetabled over two days mid-term to enable cost effective teacher release.

Another feature of the assessment workshops were the collegial conversations around student scripts and outcomes. Marking of the student texts not only gave teachers a clear view of where their students were making progress – importantly, it also highlighted those areas that needed further development in future units of work. As a means of formative feedback for teachers, the process was invaluable, with teachers leaving workshop sessions formulating a plan of action to implement. One teacher commented: 'It's the first time I have really shared with people outside the Master teacher and close colleagues – but the marking data is starting to kind of... make meaning of it and how it informs my teaching practice... like seeing that I could do more grammar and spelling... see where the data is indicating where you need to do that' (Matt Hodges, teacher 2016).

At these workshops, I supported teachers as they marked their student texts using the fourteen criteria from the Reading to Learn model (Rose & Martin, 2012, pp. 323–324). After the session, I moderated each assessed text to gauge teacher understanding of the criteria, offering feedback and encouragement when assessed texts were returned. Another rational for moderation of the teacher assessment was to provide a level of calibration for whole-school data collection of results. When finalized, these results were entered into spreadsheets to form an annual quantitative school-based data set. Trends from the assessment workshop data, as well as observational and anecdotal data have continued to demonstrate a strong causal relationship between a teacher's capacity to implement R2L strategies with rigour and commitment, and improved outcomes in student writing.

OUTCOMES IN THE INITIAL R2L IMPLEMENTATION PHASE

The assessment workshops provided valuable data to evaluate the program's impact on student literacy outcomes at the classroom level. Reviewing data in the assessment workshops indicated significant improvement in writing, which was observable across many classes, even with teachers implementing Reading to Learn in their first years. This was evaluated as follows by a school leader: 'The data from other places is the reason we decided to go down this path. This was exciting to begin with and now we are producing our own (data) and it is mirroring what we have seen in other places... that makes you want to learn even more – teachers want good results... they want kids to be in a classroom where they are learning.' (Deputy Principal, Gerowyn Lacaze, 2016).

Teachers selected students on the basis of their literacy levels, with two students for each of the low, mid and high ranges. These selections were made at the start of

2015 R2L Target Students Writing Score - Balmoral SHS																														
STUDENT	A					B					C					D					E					F				
	Baseline	Term 1	Term 2	Term 3	Term 4	Baseline	Term 1	Term 2	Term 3	Term 4	Baseline	Term 1	Term 2	Term 3	Term 4	Baseline	Term 1	Term 2	Term 3	Term 4	Baseline	Term 1	Term 2	Term 3	Term 4	Baseline	Term 1	Term 2	Term 3	Term 4
Purpose	1	1	1	2	2	0	1	2	2	NA	1	2	3	2	3	1	2	2	2	2	1	2	3	2	3	2	2	3	2	3
Staging	0	0	1	2	2	0	2	1	2	NA	1	2	3	2	3	1	2	2	2	2	1	2	3	2	3	1	2	3	2	3
Phases	0	0	1	2	1	0	1	1	2	NA	1	2	3	2	2	1	1	2	2	2	1	2	2	2	2	1	2	2	2	3
Field	1	1	1	1	1	1	1	1	1	NA	1	1	2	2	2	1	1	1	2	2	2	2	2	2	2	2	2	2	1	2
Tenor	0	1	1	2	2	0	1	1	2	NA	1	2	2	2	2	1	1	1	2	3	2	2	2	3	2	2	2	2	2	3
Mode	0	1	1	1	2	0	1	1	1	NA	1	2	2	2	2	1	1	2	2	3	2	2	2	2	3	2	2	2	2	3
Lexis	1	1	2	2	2	1	1	2	2	NA	1	2	2	2	3	2	1	2	2	3	2	2	3	3	3	3	2	2	1	3
Appraisal	1	1	1	2	2	0	2	1	2	NA	1	2	3	2	2	2	1	2	2	2	2	3	2	2	2	2	2	2	2	2
Conjunction	1	1	1	2	2	0	0	1	1	NA	1	2	2	2	3	1	2	2	2	3	2	3	2	2	2	2	2	2	1	3
Reference	1	1	2	1	2	0	1	1	1	NA	2	2	3	2	2	2	2	2	2	3	2	3	2	2	2	2	3	2	2	2
Grammar	0	1	1	1	1	0	1	1	1	NA	2	2	2	2	2	2	2	2	2	2	1	2	2	2	2	2	2	2	1	2
Spelling	1	1	1	1	1	2	2	2	2	NA	2	2	2	1	3	2	2	2	2	3	2	2	2	2	3	3	2	3	2	3
Punctuation	0	1	1	2	2	1	1	1	1	NA	1	2	1	1	2	2	2	2	2	2	2	2	2	2	2	2	2	2	1	2
Presentation	2	1	2	2	2	1	1	1	2	NA	2	2	2	3	3	2	2	2	3	2	2	3	2	3	2	2	2	1	2	3
TOTAL	9	12	17	23	24	6	16	17	22	0	18	27	32	27	34	21	22	26	29	34	24	32	31	31	33	28	29	30	23	37
	low										mid										high									

Figure 4.1. Literacy improvement data 2015

the school year based on the writing samples students produced without teacher support. Of particular interest in tracking student outcomes is their improvement across individual criteria, as well as the growth indicated across the 'total' columns. Reading to Learn uses a simple 4-point marking scale for each criterion, relative to the stage of learning in the national curriculum (no evidence of criterion = 0, weak evidence = 1, stronger evidence but not at the top standard for the stage = 2, highest level expected = 3, with the maximum possible total score of 42).

In Figure 4.1, student 'A' has a score of 9 indicating achievement is below the expected standard for the year. In the first writing sample the student demonstrates six criteria with no evidence, or 0. However, by the end of the school year the student no longer receives 0 for any criteria, and only four criteria indicate performance below the standard for the stage of learning. The student's total has moved to 24 points; a shift from *below expected year level standard* to *at year standard*. The other end of the continuum provides information about student 'F' who began the year at 28, or one full calendar year above student 'A'. Student 'Z' builds capacity across a number of criteria including Purpose, Staging and Phases to end the year at 37, which indicates a further full year of literacy progress.

The data in Figure 4.2 demonstrates students' growing competence with literacy and the Reading to Learn approach. The teacher of this class had taught these students in the same subject the previous year and had excellent knowledge of the students. The results show the strong understanding of the Purpose criterion demonstrated by all students. Similarly, students reveal growth across the Stages and Phases criteria, an indication of high levels of understanding of text features and structure. By tracking teachers and their students over these years, it was observed that these first three criteria improved relatively quickly when teachers began to use Reading to Learn consistently in their classrooms; whereas the criteria of Grammar and the graphic features of Spelling, Punctuation and Presentation [paragraphing] improved more slowly.

However, in Figure 4.3, further data from another class shows that despite similar growth trends for most students in 2018, at least two students' progression demonstrates inconsistent results. A number of important factors can be identified as potentially impacting the data.

The lower result for all students in Term 2 raises questions about the task itself. Was the genre unfamiliar to the students, or was it not explicitly taught using quality exemplars to deconstruct its Stages and Phases? Did the assessment task take place under exam conditions? How confident was the teacher with the Reading to Learn pedagogy, and how effectively were the strategies implemented? Each question highlights the importance of teachers having the necessary knowledge about language to deconstruct the features of the texts required for assessment and

2018 R2L Target Students Writing Score - Balmoral SHS																														
STUDENT	G					H					I					J					K					L				
	Baseline	Term 1	Term 2	Term 3	Term 4	Baseline	Term 1	Term 2	Term 3	Term 4	Baseline	Term 1	Term 2	Term 3	Term 4	Baseline	Term 1	Term 2	Term 3	Term 4	Baseline	Term 1	Term 2	Term 3	Term 4	Baseline	Term 1	Term 2	Term 3	Term 4
Purpose	3	3	3	NA	3	3	3	NA	3	NA	3	3	3	3	3	3	3	3	3	3	3	3	3	3	3	3	3	3	3	3
Staging	2	2	3	NA	3	2	1	NA	1	NA	2	2	3	2	3	3	2	3	3	3	2	2	3	3	3	3	2	3	3	3
Phases	2	3	2	NA	2	1	1	NA	1	NA	2	3	3	3	2	2	2	3	2	3	2	3	2	3	3	2	3	3	3	3
Field	1	2	2	NA	2	2	1	NA	1	NA	2	2	2	2	2	2	2	2	2	2	2	3	2	3	3	2	2	3	3	3
Tenor	1	3	2	NA	3	1	3	NA	2	NA	1	3	3	3	2	2	3	2	2	2	2	3	3	3	3	3	3	3	3	3
Mode	1	2	2	NA	2	1	2	NA	2	NA	1	2	2	2	2	2	2	2	3	2	2	3	3	3	2	3	2	3	3	3
Lexis	1	2	2	NA	3	2	2	NA	2	NA	2	3	2	3	2	2	2	3	2	3	2	2	3	3	3	3	3	3	3	3
Appraisal	1	1	3	NA	3	2	1	NA	1	NA	2	1	3	2	3	1	1	2	3	3	2	3	3	2	2	3	3	3	3	2
Conjunction	2	2	2	NA	2	2	1	NA	2	NA	2	2	1	2	2	3	2	2	2	3	2	3	2	2	3	2	3	3	3	2
Reference	2	2	1	NA	2	1	1	NA	2	NA	2	2	2	2	2	2	2	2	2	2	2	3	2	3	3	3	3	2	2	3
Grammar	1	1	2	NA	2	1	2	NA	2	NA	2	1	2	2	3	2	2	2	2	2	2	2	3	3	3	2	3	2	3	2
Spelling	1	2	2	NA	2	2	2	NA	1	NA	2	2	2	2	3	2	2	3	2	2	2	2	2	3	3	2	3	3	2	3
Punctuation	1	1	2	NA	3	1	2	NA	2	NA	2	1	2	2	2	2	1	3	3	2	2	3	3	2	3	3	3	3	3	3
Presentation	3	3	2	NA	3	2	2	NA	1	NA	3	3	3	2	3	3	3	3	3	3	3	3	3	3	3	3	2	3	2	3
TOTAL	22	29	30	0	35	23	24	0	23	0	28	30	33	32	34	31	29	35	34	35	30	38	37	39	40	37	38	40	39	39
	low										mid										high									

Figure 4.2. Literacy improvement data (1) 2018

2018 (2) R2L Target Students Writing Score - Balmoral SHS																														
STUDENT	M					N					O					P					Q					R				
	Baseline	Term 1	Term 2	Term 3	Term 4	Baseline	Term 1	Term 2	Term 3	Term 4	Baseline	Term 1	Term 2	Term 3	Term 4	Baseline	Term 1	Term 2	Term 3	Term 4	Baseline	Term 1	Term 2	Term 3	Term 4	Baseline	Term 1	Term 2	Term 3	Term 4
Purpose	1	2	2	3	2	2	2	2	3	2	2	2	2	2	2	2	3	1	3	2	2	3	2	3	3	1	3	2	3	3
Staging	2	2	2	2	2	1	2	2	2	2	1	1	2	2	2	1	2	2	2	2	2	2	2	2	2	2	2	2	2	2
Phases	1	2	1	2	2	1	2	1	2	2	2	1	1	2	1	2	2	1	2	1	1	3	2	3	2	1	2	2	2	2
Field	1	1	1	2	2	1	2	1	2	1	2	1	1	2	1	2	2	1	2	2	2	2	2	3	3	2	2	1	2	2
Tenor	1	2	2	2	2	1	1	1	2	1	2	2	1	2	1	2	2	1	2	1	1	2	2	2	2	1	2	2	2	2
Mode	1	1	1	2	1	1	1	1	2	1	1	1	1	2	1	2	2	1	1	1	1	2	2	3	2	1	1	2	2	1
Lexis	1	2	2	2	1	1	2	1	2	2	2	1	2	2	1	2	2	1	2	1	2	2	3	3	3	2	2	2	2	2
Appraisal	2	2	2	2	2	2	1	2	2	2	2	2	2	2	2	2	2	2	2	2	1	2	2	2	2	1	2	2	2	2
Conjunction	2	1	1	2	2	1	1	2	1	1	2	2	1	2	1	2	2	1	1	1	1	3	2	3	2	1	2	2	3	2
Reference	2	2	2	2	2	1	2	2	2	2	2	2	1	2	1	2	2	2	2	2	2	3	2	2	2	2	2	2	3	2
Grammar	1	2	2	1	1	1	1	1	2	2	2	1	1	2	1	2	2	1	2	1	2	2	2	2	2	1	2	2	2	2
Spelling	1	2	2	2	2	1	2	1	2	2	2	2	2	2	1	2	2	2	2	1	2	2	3	3	3	1	2	2	3	2
Punctuation	1	1	1	1	2	1	1	1	2	1	2	1	1	2	2	2	2	1	2	2	1	2	2	2	2	1	2	1	2	2
Presentation	1	2	1	2	2	1	2	1	1	1	1	1	1	2	1	1	2	1	2	1	1	2	1	1	2	1	2	1	2	1
TOTAL	18	24	22	27	25	16	22	19	27	22	25	20	19	28	18	26	29	18	27	20	21	32	29	34	32	18	28	25	32	27
	low										mid										high									

Figure 4.3. Literacy improvement data (2) 2018

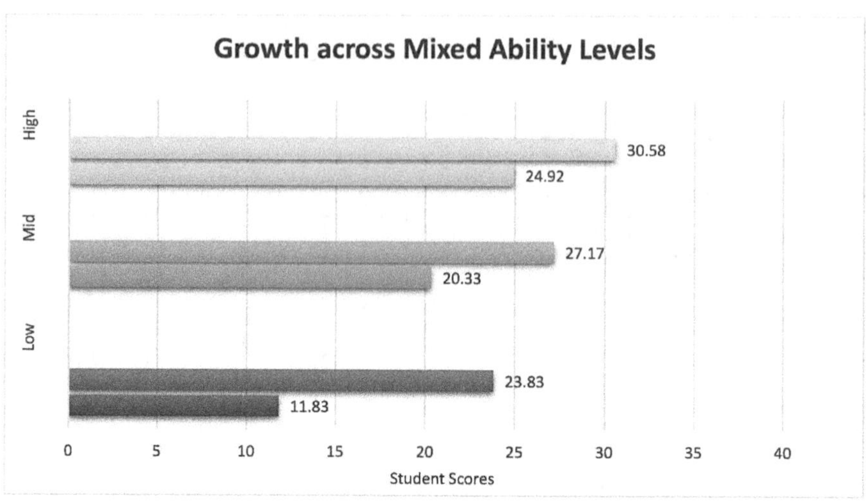

Figure 4.4. Student literacy improvement according to low, mid and high groupings

well-developed skills to successfully scaffold and gradually release responsibility to support student learning. These attributes enable teachers to prepare their students to apply this literacy understanding to the assessment tasks.

One outcome of tracking student performance across these three literacy achievement groupings was the capacity to observe relative gain in each level. Figure 4.4 shows that while each grouping improved their performance in literacy, it was the low range that produced the greatest increase, from an average of 11.83 points to 23.83 points in the course of one year. These findings reflect the stated premise of Reading to Learn methodology – closing the literacy gap between low and high achieving students in schools. Prior to implementation the difference between the low and high groups was 13.09 points. By the end of the year this had been reduced to 6.75 points, almost halving the gulf.

Those early-adopter teaching staff, whose work was critical to the success of Reading to Learn, must be credited with the levels of student literacy growth indicated in the graph. In attempting to build a whole-school expert teaching team, many factors affect the quality of outcomes. However, as the program grew to become one of the school's signature practices, to maintain whole-school capability, increasing numbers of new teaching staff needed to be 'inducted' into the methodology, rather than through self-nomination as in earlier years. This transition, though a normal part of induction procedures across large schools, presented both opportunities and challenges.

BUILDING TOWARDS A SUSTAINABLE FUTURE

Reading to Learn remains the whole-school approach for literacy teaching at Balmoral State High School. With the arrival of new principal Linda Galloway in mid-2016, there was a renewed focus on quality outcomes across the whole of the school, 'rather than pockets of excellence'.

From 2017, student enrolment numbers began to accelerate and, proportionally, staffing levels grew. Numbers of teaching staff have more than doubled over the period from 2014 to 2022, from approximately 33 to 78, making it more difficult to maintain the previous target of 80% of all staff trained in R2L. If we add to these numbers, those R2L teachers who were transferred to other schools, and 'untrained' teaching staff who replaced them, the issues facing sustainability become clear.

Over the period 2017 to 2020, several whole-school learning projects were initiated to address the shortfall between the numbers of incoming teachers without R2L training and the capacity of the school to provide more PD programs. Most substantial of these was the whole-school annual explicit implementation agenda for 2018, narrowed to focus on student literacy under the banner 'Write like a Reader'. To support teaching staff who were not yet trained, key Reading to Learn strategies were unpacked as mini-workshops in staff meetings throughout the year. Teachers were encouraged to share artefacts that represented evidence of this renewed focus on student writing. For one year, school newsletters contained more examples of student writing than ever before.

The two years of pandemic interruptions have impacted heavily on the school's PD program, and on teacher capacity to implement Reading to Learn strategies face-to-face in their classrooms with any continuity. In late 2021, a Literacy Reference Group was instituted to explore issues around Reading to Learn delivery at the school and provide recommendations to the executive team. This group allowed a voice for staff in the strategic direction of literacy in the school. The two areas explored included:

- To create processes to reinvigorate the signature practices, specifically Reading to Learn in the classroom.
- To investigate opportunities for internal PD and observations for interested teachers.

Reinvigoration of anything which has been part of the fabric of a school's culture presents a conundrum of sorts. Can the old be made new? Certainly, teachers who now teach through the clarity of a Reading to Learn literacy lens react with blank stares at the suggestion of retiring the approach.

In Term 2, 2022, the Literacy Reference Group surveyed those teaching staff trained in either the eight-day or six-day models. Feedback collated from thirty-one responses provided potential processes for the revitalization of the program in the school's current context. All of the ideas involved refreshing strategies using the existing meeting schedule. The survey responses provided multiple suggestions (percentages are indicative, not an aggregate): 38% endorsed the idea of including Reading to Learn segments within whole school staff meetings, 39% indicated the same approach for Faculty meetings, with an emphasis on subject-specific application, and finally, 19% recommended further training opportunities, either as refreshers for specific strategies, or to build on current levels of understanding.

With teacher absence levels showing little sign of abating and relief teachers a contested resource, the solution to how and when to organize PD remains unclear. From Term 3 of 2022, there is a possibility of implementing a PD program very different from the eight and six-day models. Half-days appear to offer more flexibility, hence are achievable. 2023 may present different possibilities. For now, and looking forward, Reading to Learn at Balmoral State High is committed to a reconfiguration that, while holding fast to the core of the program, suits this post-pandemic time.

NOTE

1 The Index of Community Socio-Educational Advantage (ICSEA) was created by the Australian Curriculum, Assessment and Reporting Authority (ACARA) to provide an indication of the socio-educational backgrounds of students. It is used to enable fair comparisons between schools with similar student populations on the National Assessment Program – Literacy and Numeracy (NAPLAN) test achievement in schools across Australia.

REFERENCES

Acevedo, C., & Rose, D. (2007). Learning to read, reading to learn – A middle years literacy intervention project. *The International Journal of Learning Annual Review, 12*(11), 73–84. https://www.researchgate.net/publication/307770538_Learning_to_Read_Reading_to_Learn_–_A_Middle_Years_Literacy_Intervention_Project

Australian Curriculum, Assessment and Reporting Authority (ACARA). (2016). *What does the ISCEA value mean?* https://docs.acara.edu.au/resources/About_icsea_2014.pdf

Australian Institute for Teaching and School Leadership. (2021). *Informing teaching: Navigating and translating education best practice.*
https://www.aitsl.edu.au/research/spotlight/informing-teaching-navigating-and-translating-education-best-practice

Carusi-Lees, Z. (2017). Tackling literacy one classroom at a time: Teaching writing at a whole school level in a secondary context. *Teachers as Practitioner Research Journal, 1*(1), 1–30. https://www.researchgate.net/publication/314230604

Culican, S. J. (2005). *Learning to read: Reading to learn: A middle year's literacy intervention research project, Final report 2003–4.* Catholic Education Office, Melbourne. DOI:10.13140/RG.2.2.13690.41921

Department of Education, Skills and Employment. (2015). *Action now: Classroom ready teachers report.* https://www.dese.gov.au/teaching-and-school-leadership/resources/action-now-classroom-ready-teachers-report-0

Dione-Rodgers, M., Harriman, S., Laing, B., & Snitch, W. (2012, March). Report of the Program Evaluation of Reading to Learn. Retrieved from State of New South Wales, Department of Education: https://education.nsw.gov.au/content/dam/main-education/about-us/educational-data/cese/evaluation-evidence-bank/2012-np-literacy-and-numeracy-program-evaluation-of-reading-to-learn.pdf

Queensland Audit Office (QAO). (2018). *Investing for Success Report 12: 2017–18.* https://documents.parliament.qld.gov.au/tp/2018/5618T370.pdf

Queensland Department of Education, Training and Employment. (2013). *Strategic plan 2013–17: Engaging minds, empowering futures.* https://silo.tips/download/strategic-plan-2

Rose, D., & Martin, J. R. (2012). *Learning to write, reading to learn: Genre, knowledge and pedagogy in the Sydney school.* Equinox Publishing.

ABOUT THE AUTHOR

Zena Carusi-Lees is Head of Pedagogy and Performance at Balmoral State High School in Queensland, Australia, where she facilitates whole-school R2L teacher professional development in conjunction with Dr David Rose. She has over a decade of experience as Head of English and some years working in literacy education across various universities. She has experience in using Reading to Learn in her classroom and her current role includes leading professional learning teams, coaching peers and tracking student literacy improvement.

5

The story of Reading to Learn South Africa (RtLSA)

Mike Hart

ABSTRACT

This chapter tells the story of the author's introduction to Reading to Learn, and his work in educating South African teachers in the pedagogy over the last thirty years. It gives a vivid picture of the post-apartheid situation of educational change, with its well-intentioned but unsuccessful adoption of constructivism in the early years. The text documents the varied Reading to Learn initiatives the author has undertaken with a range of groups at different stages of schooling. It includes descriptions of the activities, the actors involved, their successes and challenges and how they faced them.

BACKGROUND

> Language is a political institution: those that are wise in its ways, capable of using it to shape and serve important personal and social goals, will be ones who are 'empowered'... not merely to participate effectively in the world, but able also *to act upon it*... able and willing to take an effective role in democratic processes of all kinds (Halliday & Hasan, 1985, p. x).

The history of Reading to Learn in South Africa began in a second-hand bookshop in Cape Town in 1990, when I came across Jim Martin's 1985 book on genre-based writing pedagogy, *Factual writing: Exploring and challenging social reality.*

At the time I was teaching at the University of Kwa-Zulu Natal, and South Africa was on the cusp of major changes after a decade of increasing resistance and contestation in schools and universities brutally crushed by the Apartheid regime (Gultig & Hart, 1990). In the midst of this turmoil and debate around pedagogy, access to power and literacy, Jim's book brought the promise of a visible, explicit and highly scaffolded text-based literacy methodology linked to the drive for social justice and empowerment.

After exploring the genre-based writing approach in my teaching and development of academic literacy courses in other contexts, I used it for my Master's thesis on the teaching of writing in a South African school in 2000. At the 1999 International Systemic Functional Conference in Singapore, I met Jim Martin and others working with genre pedagogy and, in 2002, I undertook a sabbatical tour of Australia, from Adelaide to Sydney, with the help of John Polias. At the University of Technology in Sydney, I gave a seminar on a program I had developed in a school involving learners writing a range of different genres for real purposes to real audiences. At the end, David Rose stood up and told me that I was doing things the wrong way round, I was trying to teach writing without teaching reading. 'Nobody can write what they can't read'. This started the Reading to Learn journey in South Africa.

POST-APARTHEID CURRICULUM CHANGES

This journey unfolded in the 1990s and beyond during a period of fundamental post-apartheid curriculum changes to drive the radical transformation of everything the crippling Apartheid education system represented. The National Department of Education (DOE) launched *The President's Education Initiative Project* to get an understanding of the state of basic education in 1997/98. It painted a depressingly chaotic picture: 'In many cases schools seemed reconciled to gross inefficiency, maladministration and endemic chaos' (Morrow, 2007, p. 57). Many teachers in their survey had little conceptual grasp of the subjects they were teaching. Classroom teaching was characterised by low expectations of learners; minimal focus on higher order thinking; books and reading were scarce; and learners had little experience of writing beyond single words or short phrases.

The imperative to solve this situation resulted in the importation of Outcomes-Based Education (OBE) and the launching of Curriculum 2005 (C2005) in 1998. C2005 official documents announced that South Africa had embarked on 'transformational OBE', what Taylor (2001, p. 4) described as 'the most radical constructivist curriculum ever attempted in the world'. It was proclaimed as the educational foundation of the social equity drive of the democratic government. In contrast to

Apartheid education, C2005 was touted as transparent, learner-centred with explicit competences outlined in the outcomes. Formal subject knowledge was not specified, and teachers and learners were expected to determine the content and develop the programmes to achieve the specified outcomes.

Critics warned that the likely outcome of a radical constructivist C2005 would be widening inequality across school contexts, the very antithesis of its declared aims (Graven, 2002; Harley & Wedekind, 2004). As evidence of this emerged (Harley & Parker, 1999; Taylor, 2001), a Ministerial Review Committee was tasked in 2005 with evaluating its implementation and impact. It basically called for the scrapping of C2005 as it created unequal access to foundational skills for effective learning. It called for a shift from teacher control over content and learning programmes to 'the conceptual coherence of school knowledge through the systematic development of knowledge' (Taylor, 2001, p. 8). However, the OBE framework was retained in the new National Curriculum Statement in 2007, with some specification of school knowledge to be learned, but teachers were still expected to decide on content, methodology and assessments. In 2012, a third curriculum reform, the Curriculum and Assessment Policy Statement (CAPS), replaced the radical competence-based direction of C2005 and NCS, with prescriptive specifications about predetermined subject content to be taught, how it was to be taught and the pace at which it was to be taught.

Through all these iterations of curriculum reform, the quality of post-apartheid education fell far short of the declared aims of C2005 of erasing the skewed inequality inherited from apartheid education. This was graphically illustrated by the 2016 PIRLS report that just over 78% of South African Grade 4 children could not read for meaning in any of the 11 official languages (Howie et al., 2017).

A series of studies have shown the persistence of unequal access to the literacy levels that count. In 2000, 65% of Grade 6 learners were below the minimum level of reading mastery and unlikely to succeed in the following year of schooling. By 2007, only 22% were reading at appropriate levels of comprehension (Moloi & Chetty, 2011). In 2013, 22% of eleven-year-olds were assessed as illiterate (Taylor, 2014). Spaull (2019) estimated that the actual throughput rate of the school system in 2017 was around 55%. Furthermore, for those students who attained university-entrance qualifications, the Council on Higher Education report of 2012 estimated that 55% of the intake would never graduate and less than 5% of African and coloured youth were succeeding in any form of higher education. It determined that academic skills and literacies were at the heart of the systemic obstacles to student success.

The stubborn persistence of low levels of literacy through all the curriculum changes brings to the fore teachers' capacities and the training and support they received to manage the curriculum changes. Taylor (2019) outlined the different types of knowledge that teachers need to have and put into practice in their classrooms: disciplinary knowledge; pedagogical content knowledge; curriculum knowledge; and pedagogical competence. Taylor and Taylor (2013) found a distinct lack of all four aspects of teaching knowledge and competence in English reading comprehension in both practising teachers and those emerging from teacher training institutions. Studies by Ensor et al. (2009) and Hoadley (2012) found poor disciplinary knowledge amongst teachers; inadequate command of English; teaching practices with little focus on higher order thinking skills; dominance of oral teacher talk; and little focus on reading and writing coupled with a lack of explicit guidance and feedback.

Poor teacher training and support through the curricular changes is acknowledged as the central cause for minimal shifts in teachers' practice and content knowledge. The crucial in-service training and support for teachers to implement new curricula were of short duration and did not provide the means nor the support to enable teachers to internalise and acquire methodologies that disrupted what they were schooled in, and promoted in their teacher training. As one teacher complained 'all you do is microwave us!'. Muller and Hoadley (2019, pp. 118–121) commented that:

> Given the schooling system from which most teachers had emerged, the possibility of teachers and learners co-constructing a curriculum with no guidance was extremely ambitious... there was literally no model of a different repertoire on offer to show the teachers what a different pedagogy would look like. All they had had to fall back on was the old dysfunctional pedagogy of their own schooling and their teacher training.

THE DEVELOPMENT OF READING TO LEARN SOUTH AFRICA (RTLSA)

Reading to Learn South Africa (RtLSA) came into being in the midst of the unfolding developments in education sketched above. After my visit to Australia, as a senior lecturer in the University of KwaZulu-Natal (UKZN) Education Faculty, I started exploring the application of RtL in degree programmes, developing academic literacy skills, as well as applications in schools (Moore & Hart, 2007; Thomson & Hart, 2006). These schools are situated in rural villages, in townships, which are historically segregated urban areas in South Africa, and in suburbs of cities like Pietermaritzburg, Cape Town and Johannesburg.

What follows is a brief history of our RtL teacher training projects in these schools.

In 2004 and 2007, David Rose came to South Africa for a series of workshops on Reading to Learn, with a wide range of educators through the schooling system and tertiary education. During his 2004 visit he gave a series of demonstration lessons at Sobantu secondary school in Pietermaritzburg, with students whose first language was primarily isiZulu. The lessons were professionally filmed and edited and have since been widely used in teacher training and conferences (https://readingtolearn.com.au/pages/videos).

Following David's 2004 visit, I started training small groups of individual teachers. It was often a struggle to get institutional support for this work. An example was a 2007 project with five primary schools in the Richmond area, a small rural town 45 kilometres from Pietermaritzburg. This project was funded for six months by the Media in Education Trust but, despite getting support and buy-in from the teachers, funding for a continuation was not forthcoming.

Over this period four pioneers of RtL emerged: Nana Mthalane and Bonny Todd teaching Grades 2 and 3 respectively in a township primary school; Adrienne Watson teaching in a girls' high school; and Debbie Avery in a private school at secondary level. They all demonstrated the possibilities of RtL, as their learners were coping with and going beyond syllabus requirements. Debbie Avery had taught at all levels of the education system from remedial school to secondary school. She seized upon the RtL methodology, declaring that it gave her 'permission to teach again' in the time of OBE, and that her last year of teaching, using RtL, was the best year she had experienced. She has played a hugely significant role in the development of RtL. In 2010, we registered Reading to Learn South Africa (RtLSA) as a Public Benefit Organisation (PBO), with a management committee of African teachers (https://www.readingtolearnsouthafrica.com/).

Two significant developments emerged from the formation of RtLSA. The first was our participation in the East African Quality in Early Learning (EAQEL) project in primary schools in Kenya, Uganda and Tanzania (APHRC, 2012). This project was organised by the Aga Khan Foundation (AKF) as a large-scale teacher training program. David had first introduced RtL to a pilot EAQEL project in 2008, with a series of workshops with AKF teacher trainers. The success of this pilot led to the large-scale program from 2011, in which Debbie and I trained cohorts of teacher trainers, who then took RtL to the teachers. The project began with a week of intensive training in Mombasa, Kenya, in which David presented the RtL teaching methods, together with the principles of the RtL teacher training program. In the following years, Debbie and I trained and supported Trainers of Teachers (ToTs) and then returned to observe the dedicated and creative teachers they had trained using RtL in their classrooms in diverse and deeply challenging circumstances. RtL was rolled out in thousands of schools across those countries. We learned a great deal and basked in the experience of being ably supported by a powerful and generous organisation like the AKF. Importantly this also provided a much-needed source of initial income for RtLSA.

The second development was the decision in 2011 to focus on whole-school training in keeping with the cross curricular nature of RtL methodology. A committee member, Sybil Maree, introduced us to the wonderfully supportive Mr. Msomi, Principal of Slangspruit Primary School in a local township. We started training the whole staff in 2012, meeting twice a month after school and later twice a term. When Nana Mthalane did a demonstration lesson for Foundation Phase teachers, this brought Bongi Ntombela (Gr I) on board as well as Sthe Qoma (Gr 6) and Gertrude Nkabane (Gr 7), outstanding teachers teaching across the curriculum. They were soon brought onto our committee and became fully fledged and hugely capable trainers. Their impact in training is palpable, as they are practising teachers working in the same contexts as the teachers they are training. Bongi, Nana, Sthe, Gertrude, and Sandra Pretorius were filmed teaching in their classrooms, by Roger O'Neill, a very skilled filmmaker of classroom practice, and we produced training videos from these lessons.

In 2013 we were contacted by Bheka Makhathini, a Director of Curriculum in KwaZulu-Natal's education department, to do his doctoral research on the application of RtL in Mqolombeni Primary School, a remote rural school 65 km from Pietermaritzburg. Debbie and I had trained teachers across the school and curriculum from Foundation Phase through to Grade 7. We experienced first-hand the learners' problems in the transition for Grade 4 learners to English as the medium of instruction. They could not understand basic instructions in English like 'write'. This was representative of the deep literacy issues faced in the majority of schools in South Africa mentioned earlier.

Our response was to develop a bilingual approach to RtL. Debbie worked with two Grade 2 and 3 teachers, using isiZulu texts to develop learners' understanding of the prompts and questions of the RtL cycle. They then covered the isiZulu words of the text with English and taught the story in English. It was heartening to see the development of the learners in both languages and their enthusiasm at being released from the tyranny of texts they could not understand. We worked at the school at regular intervals for 18 months. There was strong take up from the two Foundation Phase teachers and, by 2015, we could see the impact on learner's English comprehension when they graduated into Grade 4.

Also, in 2013 we organised our first Reading to Learn conference at St Nicholas school in Pietermaritzburg. It was a mammoth effort by our small committee in a short space of time. Large numbers of teachers attended from the Pietermaritzburg district and rural schools further afield. Claire Acevedo was our keynote speaker and made a big impression at the conference, both with her keynote address and the workshop she presented. Bheka Makhathini presented a joint paper on his PhD research with his supervisor, Emmanuel Mgqwashu of Rhodes University. Four people involved in our work in East Africa gave a presentation that made a big impact, given the challenging circumstance they were working in. Crucially, we had RtL teachers doing workshops and papers of their work in classrooms that mirrored the contexts that delegate teachers were experiencing, from Foundation Phase to secondary school in isiZulu, English and Afrikaans, from narrative texts to factual texts across the curriculum.

A significant outcome of the conference for RtLSA was being approached by Mr Lucky Lushaba and the principal of Nkelabantwana Full Service Primary School, a rural school 90 km from Pietermaritzburg, to provide training for their staff. Full-service schools are required to accept learners with certain levels of learning difficulties, and they were facing huge problems with literacy levels. Lucky has since played a significant role in RtLSA as a committee member and trainer, and is now completing his Master's degree.

In 2015 we started a joint programme with the Ethekwini North District Branch of the South African Democratic Teachers Union (SADTU). We were tasked with training their branch representatives in that district covering 33 urban and rural schools. The training took place in Tongaat, a small town north of Durban and 120 km from Pietermaritzburg. Debbie and I were joined by the formidable team of Bongi, Nana, GT, Sthe and Vanessa from Mqolombeni school who changed teachers' perceptions on the possibilities of RtL. Despite problems such as travel from remote areas, up to 115 km away, we completed the first phase of the project by observing teachers in their classrooms twice and sometimes three times. We started with 44 teachers but finally certificated 21 as RtL practitioners. Unfortunately, changes in SADTU management meant that Phase 2 was abandoned. This was a big disappointment as it could have provided a model for future development and an avenue for research.

In 2016, we were asked to train teachers from three primary schools in the Edendale township area of Pietermaritzburg, as part of the project *Strengthening Schools to Address Barriers to Learning*, funded by the NGO MIET Africa. Two of the schools went through the whole process of training and observation. Their results were evaluated by Dr Sandra Land, of Durban University of Technology. Literacy growth rates are summarised in Figures 5.1 and 5.2, in which classes are identified by teachers' initials. Growth rates vary between teachers, which is expected as their mastery of RtL takes time to be developed, but the overall improvements were very heartening. In 4 out of 5 classes at Edendale Primary (Figure 5.1), average class marks almost doubled, from less than 50% to around 80%. At Nichols Primary (Figure 5.2), growth rates were around 20–30% for each class.

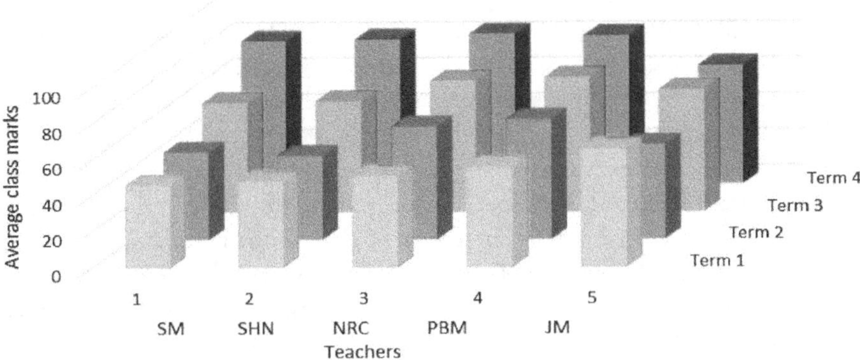

Figure 5.1. Literacy growth by class at Edendale Primary School

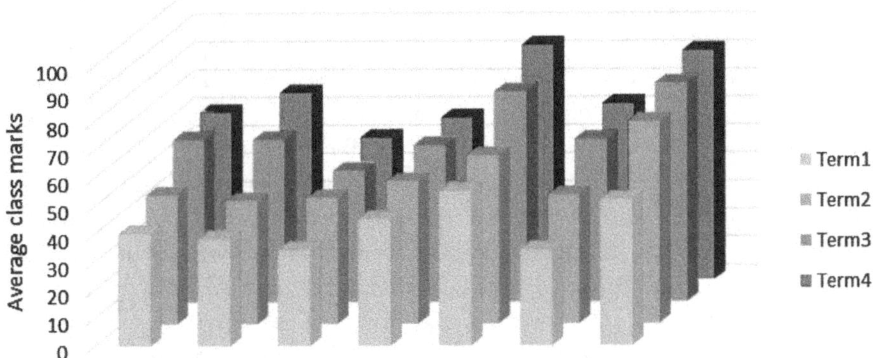

Figure 5.2. Literacy growth by class at Nichols Primary School

Dr Land reported that:

> Teachers report that it takes 6–7 weeks to get used to the process, and once learners are used to the process it speeds up. They say that 'learners with barriers' are responding very well to this methodology, participating more and showing more understanding, because it is clear to them what is expected, and things are done in small achievable steps... Teachers suggest that this enables weak learners to build self-esteem.

The second RtLSA conference was held in 2017 at Pietermaritzburg Girls High School. Keynote speakers were David Rose, Dr Emmanuel Mgqwashu and Dr Carol

Macdonald, one of the doyens of literacy education in South Africa. There was a big turn-out of local teachers, other educationists and NGOs. There was a range of papers and workshops by RtL teachers and others. A highlight for many teachers was the awarding, by David, of RtL practitioner certificates to teachers who had successfully come through our training over the year.

Following the conference, we were asked to train primary school teachers by the Senior Education Specialist for special needs education in full-service schools in the Ugu district, centred in Port Shepstone 120 km south of Durban. We trained 3 teachers from each of 9 chosen Primary schools, one each from Foundation, Intermediate and Senior Phases. We did a week's training at the end of June and then completed one round of observations of teachers in 2018 and another at the beginning of 2019. We were joined in the training and observation by a new committee member, Leonard Hlongwa, a high school teacher in a nearby area. Unfortunately, the Department of Education then introduced a very prescriptive 'Reading Improvement Programme' where each lesson is prepared in advance by planners and teachers. This made many of the teachers fearful of using RtL, given the surveillance required by officials to ensure strict adherence to the step-by-step program. However, our well-trained and confident teachers use RtL as they are able to fulfil, and go beyond, the requirements of these programmes.

In 2019 we had a one-day RtL conference in Pietermaritzburg with David. Importantly, the conference paved the way for a developing relationship with the Western Cape Education Department. Following the conference Urshula Saindon organised for us to train Foundation Phase teachers at Mondeor Eco School in Somerset West near Cape Town. Urshula then went on to train all the teachers in the school, and she has become a driving force for RtL in the Western Cape. This culminated in our third RtL conference held at Mondeor school in conjunction with the Western Cape Education Department. It was a vibrant and joyful conference, opening up RtL to a new area and audience. Claire, Emmanuel Mgqwashu and Carol Macdonald were leading speakers. Our committee members again impressed teachers new to RtL with their presentations of their classroom practice. In a very significant development, Urshula and the WCED are now exploring the possibility of rolling out RtL in the senior phase of Primary school and in the special needs department. She has also been working with the University of the Western Cape (UWC) to train pre-service language teachers.

Two secondary school projects started in 2018–19, but were cut short by COVID. The first project began with seven secondary schools, in Soshanguve near Pretoria and Port Elizabeth in the Eastern Cape. This project was organised by Telkom Foundation, whose aims are to develop youth resilience through innovation and digital transformation to bridge the digital divide in South African schools. However, this program was very sporadic through 2018, with big gaps between training sessions and a lack of continuity. We visited schools at the beginning of 2019 to negotiate further support for teachers, but COVID intervened. The second project was at St Stithians, a private school in Johannesburg, on the invitation of Adrienne Watson. Two other projects emerged from this. One was training teachers in the school's outreach program, Thandulwazi, for 1200 learners from less privileged schools who come to St Stithians for extra tuition. The second was to train all the teachers in Jabula Primary School, a rural school 60 km from Pietermaritzburg, funded by the University of Hull. Unfortunately, COVID put everything on hold until the following year.

Over the years we have trained tutors and academics involved in first year academic literacy development programmes which were linked to faculties but not integrated into mainstream programmes such as Commerce, Law, Medicine, Education and Humanities. Significant people involved in this were Dr Kellie Steinke (2019), Dr Tracey Millin (2011, 2015), Dr Billy Meyer and Jean Moore. Interest was sparked by Dr Nayibe Rosado's presentation at the 2018 ISFC in Boston on the training of mainstream academics in RtL methodology and its integration across academic degree programmes at the Universidad Del Norte in Colombia. At that time Professor Carol Bertram in the UKZN Education Faculty brought up the problem of Masters' students struggling with academic texts. As a result, I ran a course on the application of RtL at tertiary level with academics from Biochemistry, Media, Education, Theology and Biology. This experience gave impetus to the idea of applying to the National Research Fund (NRF) to bring Claire and Nayibe out to do a symposium and workshop on their work in Colombia in November this year. The idea was to invite interested academics from South African universities and to invite contributions on the theme of integrating academic literacy into degree programmes. Again, COVID intervened but we are reviving it online.

REFLECTIONS AND WAY FORWARD

The introduction of a radical constructivist curriculum and subsequent iterations in the post-apartheid South African education system have not really shifted the systemic inequalities exposed in the 1998 President's Education Initiative (Taylor & Vinjevold, 1999). While access to schooling has been provided, it is clear that equal access to the skills and knowledge that schooling is tasked to provide has been denied to the majority of learners. The problem has been exacerbated by the inadequate training and support through the curriculum changes. According to the South African educational leader, Wally Morrow (2007, p. 205), 'One contribution that teachers at all levels of the system, and in all areas of the curriculum, can make to overcoming inequality is to focus strongly and persistently on developing learners' capacity to read and to learn from reading'.

RtL's training responds to these issues by linking training in RtL classroom teaching methodology to teacher professional learning and scaffolding teacher learning about language, literacy and pedagogy. Acevedo (2020) points to the key elements of effective teacher development coaching exemplified in the RtL process: procedural (technical) support; affective (emotional) support; and reflective support (after Swafford, et al., 1997). It is these elements, and crucially affective support, that enable teachers to change practice and to internalise and acquire methodologies that disrupt their already established practices and beliefs. The cycle of expert-led training with authentic modelling of RtL classroom practice, followed by ongoing support, observation and reflection, provides teachers with the explicit knowledge of text and language patterns to integrate the teaching of the content of texts across the curriculum with how to read and write them. It also builds the capacity of experienced RtL teachers to become on-site lead teachers for colleagues and other teachers. This has certainly been the experience of the RtLSA committee members who, after training and regular classroom implementation, began to participate in our training workshops and are now independently training teachers across the curriculum and phases of schooling.

An example of on-site mentoring was when primary schools opened after lockdown for Grade 7 initially. In Slangspruit Primary mentioned earlier, the Grade 7 class was divided into 10 smaller groups. Gertrude Nkabane, one of our trainers, was put in charge of English and allocated two teachers from Grade 3 and 4 to assist her even though they had never taught Grade 7 or been trained in RtL. Gertrude had four classes and the other teachers three each. In an ongoing cycle Gertrude would jointly prepare a lesson which she would demonstrate and model with one of her classes. The teachers would then deliver the lesson to their classes, reflect on their experiences after school and prepare for the next cycle. This went on for less than a month before schools were closed again but, by then, the two teachers were independently managing their classes and motivated by the quality of writing of four genres they were seeing in their classes. The Grade 3 teacher sent a voicemail detailing her initial anxiety and doubts but felt she was now a Grade 7 teacher due to the ongoing support and practice.

Furthermore, in questionnaires and discussions with RtL trainers, they have all referred to their increased knowledge of how texts work and the language patterns that enable different genres to achieve their purposes. They thus feel that they can unpack and teach a wide range of texts beyond their learning area and level of schooling. Bongi Ntombela, a highly skilled Foundation Phase teacher, had to write an entrance test to get admitted to the Master's program in the Faculty of Education at the University of KwaZulu-Natal (UKZN) because she did not have the required Honours level marks. She passed the test, got her Master's cum laude, and is now doing her Doctorate. Lucky Lushaba is completing his Master's degree with a view to starting a Doctorate next year. Both of them get constant affirmation from their supervisors for the coherence of their writing and their lack of plagiarism. They both put this down to the text knowledge built up by the RtL training, their repeated classroom practice and the teacher training they do.

Over the years, funding has been a problem which has impacted on training and long-term support of trained teachers. We are a small organisation, with nine trainers who are also practising teachers. Without state support, it is difficult to sustain a model of regular training sessions with support in the classroom during and after training. Linked to the funding issue is the need to develop our research profile. There is doctoral and masters research (Childs, 2008; Makathini, 2015; Mataka, 2018; Millin, 2011, 2015; Steinke, 2019) and published journal articles, and regular conference presentations, but we need to up our research profile showing evidence of learner development in RtL classrooms. To this end, all our trainers will focus on doing action research in their classrooms and will map the progress of their learners. Their findings can be shared with fellow teachers and state officials in a one-day mini conference and at the annual Literacy Association of South Africa conference. We need evidence-based research to attract funders and to engage with the state. In addition, Carol Macdonald is heading a programme to train teachers in four Catholic Primary schools over a three-year period, mapping learners' progress through Grade 3 into Grades 4 and 5. We will train the trainers and have some regular oversight, but the program will be carried out by Carol.

As COVID has shown us all, we also need to look at alternative ways of doing training and support. We are working on a blended approach mixing face-to-face training with online individual work and using WhatsApp groups working with mentors as a means of support. This would include short clips of classroom practice taken on cell phones with the aim of developing communities of RtL classroom practice.

It has been a long struggle in a difficult educational, social and political context but, as we always say to the teachers we train, 'Reading to Learn gives you and your learners wings!'

REFERENCES

Acevedo, M. C. (2020). *Bringing language to consciousness: Teacher professional learning in genre-based reading pedagogy*. [Doctoral dissertation, Open University, United Kingdom]. http://oro.open.ac.uk/70422/

African Population and Health Research Center (APHRC). (2012). *East African quality in early learning (EAQEL): Impact evaluation report*. https://microdataportal.aphrc.org

Childs, M. (2008). *A reading based theory of teaching appropriate for the South African context* [Doctoral dissertation, Nelson Mandela Metropolitan University, Port Elizabeth, South Africa].

Ensor, P., Hoadley, U., Jacklin, H., Kuhne, C., Schmitt, E., Lombard, A., & Van den Heuvel-Panhuizen, M. (2009). Specialising pedagogic text and time in Foundation Phase numeracy classrooms. *Journal of Education, 47*, 5–30.

Graven, M. (2002). The effect of the South African curriculum change process on mathematics teacher roles. In P. Valero & O. Skovsmose (Eds.), *Proceedings of the 3rd international MES conference Copenhagen* (pp. 1–10). Centre for Research in Learning Mathematics.

Gultig, J., & Hart, M. (1990). The world is full of blood: Youth, schooling and conflict in Pietermaritzburg, 1987 to 1989. *Perspectives in Education, 11*(2), 1–19.

Halliday, M. A. K., & Hasan, Ruqaiya (1985). *Language, Context, and Text: A Social-semiotic Perspective.* Deakin University Press [Republished by Oxford University Press. 1989].

Harley, K., & Parker, B. (1999). Integrating differences: Implications of an outcomes-based national qualifications framework for the roles and competencies of teachers. In J. D. Jansen, & P. Christie, (Eds.), *Changing Curriculum: Studies on Outcomes-based Education in South Africa* (pp. 181–200). Juta and Company.

Harley, K., & Wedekind, V. (2004). Political change, curriculum change and social formation, 1990 to 2002. In L. Chisholm, (Ed.), *Changing Class: Education and Social Change in Post-apartheid South Africa* (pp. 195–220). HSRC Press.

Hoadley, U. (2012). What do we know about teaching and learning in South African primary schools? *Education as Change, 16*(2), 187–202.

Howie, S., Combrinck, C., Roux, K., Mokoena, M., & McLeod Palane, N. (2017). *PIRLS literacy 2016: South African highlights report*. University of Pretoria.

Makathini, B. (2015). *Trampoline trajectories: A dialectical analysis of the correlation between the teaching of reading and the learner-academic performance in a South African rural primary school* [Doctoral dissertation, University of KwaZulu-Natal, South Africa].

Martin, J. R. (1985). *Factual Writing: Exploring and Challenging Social Reality*. Deakin University Press [republished by Oxford University Press, 1989].

Mataka, W. (2018). *Reading to Learn for secondary schooling: An interventionist action research study within a South African under-privileged setting* [Doctoral dissertation, Rhodes University].

Millin, T. (2011). *Scaffolding academic literacy with undergraduate social science students at the University of KwaZulu-Natal using the Reading to Learn intervention strategy: An evaluative study* [Master's Thesis, The University of Edinburgh, Moray House School of Education].

Millin, T. (2015). *Scaffolding academic literacy using the Reading to Learn methodology: An evaluative study* [Doctoral dissertation, University of Stellenbosch, South Africa].

Moloi, M. Q., & Chetty, M. (2011). Trends in achievement levels of grade 6 pupils in South Africa. *Policy brief 1*. The Southern and Eastern Africa Consortium for Monitoring Educational Quality, http://www.sacmeq.org/sites/default/files/sacmeq/publications/achievement_south_africa.pdf

Moore, J. M., & Hart, M. (2007). Access to literacy: Scaffolded reading strategies in the South African context. *Journal for Language Teaching, 41*(1), 15–30. https://hdl.handle.net/10520/EJC59914

Morrow, W. (2007). *Learning to Teach in South Africa*. HSRC Press.

Muller, J., & Hoadley, U. (2019). Curriculum reform and learner performance: An obstinate paradox in the quest for equality. In N. Spaull, & J. D. Jansen, (Eds.), *South African Schooling: The Enigma of Inequality* (pp. 109–125). Springer Nature.

Spaull, N. (2019). Equity: A Price Too High to Pay? In N. Spaull, & D. Jansen, (Eds.), *South African Schooling: The Enigma of inequality: A study of the present situation and future possibilities*. Springer, 1–24.

Steinke, K. (2019). *The pedagogical content knowledge of teachers and its effect on enliterating grade three and four learners* [Doctoral dissertation, North West University, South Africa].

Swafford, J., Maltsberger, A., Button, K., & Furgerson, P. (1997). Peer coaching for facilitating effective literacy instruction. In C. K. Kinzer, K. A. Hinchman, & D. J. Leu, (Eds.), *Inquiries in Literacy Theory and Practice* (pp. 416–426). Chicago, National Reading Conference.

Taylor, N. (2001). 'Anything but knowledge': The case of the undisciplined curriculum. In *Curriculum dialogue seminar: What counts as worthwhile knowledge for the 21st century South African citizen?* https://files.eric.ed.gov/fulltext/ED463253.pdf

Taylor, N. (2014). *NEEDU national report 2013: Teaching and learning in rural primary schools*. National Evaluation and Development Unit, https://www.researchgate.net/publication/330220311

Taylor, N. (2019). Inequalities in teacher knowledge in South Africa. In N. Spaull, & J. D. Jansen, (Eds.), *South African Schooling: The Enigma of Inequality* (pp. 263–282). Springer Nature.

Taylor, N., & Taylor, S. (2013). Teacher knowledge and professional habitus. In N. Taylor, S. van der Berg, & T. Mabogoane (Eds.), *Creating Effective Schools: Report of South Africa's National Schools' Effectiveness Study*. Pearson.

Taylor, N., & Vinjevold, P. (Eds.). (1999). *Getting learning right: report of the President's Education Initiative Research Project*. Joint Education Trust.

Thomson, C., & Hart, M. (2006). Implementing the genre approach in a South African school. In R. Whittaker, M. O'Donnell, & A. McCabe (Eds.), *Language and Literacy: Functional Approaches* (pp. 189–204). Continuum.

ABOUT THE AUTHOR

Mike Hart worked for many years as a literacy teacher and teacher educator at the University of Kwa-Zulu Natal and played a significant role in the struggle for social justice in South Africa. He started working with the genre approach in the early 1990s in both academic literacy development and teacher training and from 2002 with the Reading to Learn methodology. He is currently the director of Reading to Learn in South Africa (RtLSA) and leads a team of teacher trainers who provide professional development in the pedagogy in many locations in South and East Africa.

6

Equity-based models of teaching literacy: Supporting EAL students' English academic writing development with Reading to Learn pedagogy

Tracey Millin

ABSTRACT

Globally, concerns about academic literacy point to the need for educators to embrace alternative approaches to English literacy instruction in different stages of education. With an increase in English Additional Language learners in classrooms that adopt English as the medium of instruction, comes the need for classroom teachers, and tertiary instructors to embrace explicit, specialised literacy instruction to scaffold more advanced forms of English academic reading and writing skills to ensure equitable learning outcomes for all students. This is more pressing for low socioeconomic status students, who tend to be also linguistically marginalised, and so face poor graduation prospects. In response, this chapter offers an overview of two studies that sought to test the efficacy of an English academic literacy intervention. Two small-scale, longitudinal studies were run in three separate educational contexts in South Africa – a low socioeconomic senior secondary school, a high socioeconomic senior secondary school, and a tertiary institution. Results from all three contexts showed the Reading to Learn (RtL) intervention to be successful at raising the level of English academic writing skills of the participants. Furthermore, as in other RtL studies, the weaker-performing students made the greatest gains in their English academic writing skills, showing evidence of a convergence effect when RtL pedagogy is incorporated into literacy programmes. In the one study where literacy instruction deviated significantly from RtL pedagogy in the second half of the programme, student performance stopped improving, thus strengthening the claim of the efficacy of RtL pedagogy.

INTRODUCTION

Globally, large inequalities in literacy skills between and within different countries have been found (Roser & Ortiz-Ospina, 2016). There are groups of students who struggle with basic literacy in primary schools, and in the secondary and tertiary education sectors there are students who have difficulty demonstrating their learning due to a lack of mastery of advanced forms of English academic writing skills. In the multilingual environment in the Republic of South Africa (RSA), English may be a student's third or fourth language, and the school environment may be the only opportunity for English language input. Furthermore, in many schools with an intake of pupils from low socioeconomic backgrounds (SES), the language of teaching and learning may not be English, as prescribed, but an African language can be chosen as the medium of instruction due to students' low level of English proficiency. In such a situation, if teachers are not trained to support students who have English as an Additional Language (EAL) the difficulties students already face in demonstrating their learning in English become greater. It is no surprise, then, that many secondary school teachers in RSA report their frustration at what they see as their inability to adequately support the linguistic needs of their EAL students.

Given this situation, many tertiary providers in RSA find it necessary to invest heavily in school-to-university transition programmes to ensure that the development of English academic literacy skills provides all students with an equal opportunity to succeed in completing their studies in a country with a historically high undergraduate attrition rate. From my experience as a trained secondary English teacher, and academic writing specialist, I have anecdotal evidence to suggest that students enter secondary school with an understanding of what an academic essay is, but fewer students are able to bridge the gap between understanding and actually composing an effective academic argument. In other words, students appear to be equipped with multiple different acronyms to support their essay writing (PEEL, hamburger, PETAL, TEAL, OREO) but still struggle to write effective academic essays. To make things worse, these acronyms used to help students write tend to change from teacher to teacher, year after year, often creating confusion in students. Limited opportunities for students to engage in extended writing is another problem, since it leaves little chance for students to develop mastery of the genres they need. Sadly, this description reminds me of my experience with my own English academic writing development at secondary school.

As a secondary school student, I never excelled at academic writing. I struggled to articulate my points in an argument, and when I asked the teacher how I could express ideas more succinctly, they themselves struggled to demonstrate, or model, what good strong arguments looked like. My teachers were adept at telling me what a good essay should include at a superficial level, but this failed to help me become a better writer. During my first year of undergraduate studies, I enrolled in an academic writing course. Mike Hart was the lecturer, and introduced Reading to Learn (RtL) during the classes (see Hart, Chapter 5 in this volume). Mike used key principles of RtL pedagogy, which included the teaching of academic writing through genre pedagogy and systemic functional grammar. Model texts were used to *show* us how to use specific language features to meet genre conventions (and thus improve our writing), and multiple writing drafts were given detailed, differentiated feedback to scaffold us in the development of discipline-specific academic writing. Multiple learning 'light-bulbs' went on for my peers and me as Mike and his team were able to *show* students what good academic writing was instead of merely *telling* us. This approach has driven my development as a teacher of academic writing, with positive results, as this chapter highlights.

The chapter offers an overview of RtL research carried out by Millin and Millin in RSA between 2010–2015. This includes, firstly, work with a tertiary group of EAL students where RtL pedagogy was incorporated into a specifically-designed academic writing course. The course was split into two halves temporally, with the first half explicitly incorporating RtL pedagogy, and the second half, following 'conventional' writing instruction. The introduction of RtL had a marked impact on student writing development, as commented on in the discussion section. The second study on academic writing interventions took place in two separate secondary schools in RSA, in order to test the efficacy of RtL pedagogy in diverse socioeconomic school contexts. The democratising impact of RtL pedagogy on students' writing performance is highlighted in these two school contexts. The purpose of the chapter is to raise awareness for classroom teachers, literacy instructors, and ESOL teachers of the possibilities and the benefits of incorporating RtL pedagogy into literacy programmes in contexts where inequitable learning outcomes persist.

READING TO LEARN – AN OVERVIEW

RtL was designed to address the literacy performance of Indigenous Australian students where academic reading and writing skills appeared to be key determinants of these students' poorer educational outcomes. The theoretical frameworks underpinning RtL encompass the work of (but are not limited to) Vygotsky (1978) (learning as a social process), Halliday (1989) (language as a text within a social context) and Bernstein (1990) (education as a pedagogic discourse). A number of studies incorporating RtL pedagogy in different countries have indicated the effectiveness of RtL at fast-tracking the development of students' academic literacy skills (see, for example, Acevedo, 2010; McRae et al., 2000; Rose & Acevedo, 2006). Research evidences that, through purposeful scaffolding, the lower the base of students' literacy skills, the greater the gains, effectively democratising the classroom (Rose, 2005; Rose & Acevedo, 2006; Rose et al., 2008).

Reading to Learn is explicit teaching, as David Rose has shown in his work in classrooms around the world and in his many publications (see Rose & Martin, 2012). The R2L pedagogy choices are summarised in Figure 6.1. (below). The concentric circles show the three levels of support available for developing students' reading and writing skills, that can be integrated at various points in any teaching program. R2L teaching begins with preparing students for reading and comprehending curriculum texts, then these readings are used as models for guided and independent writing activities. This contrasts with approaches that use decontextualised, inauthentic reading and grammar exercises to teach reading and writing. In R2L, students learn by interacting with the teacher during joint reading and writing of authentic texts, which enables language and content to be taught at the same time. The second level of support uses *Detailed Reading* strategies to jointly read texts and deepen students' understanding of written texts, and to use the information and language patterns from reading in different genres as models for their own writing. This enables an acceleration of student reading and writing development, as teachers equip students with the necessary skills through modelling and joint writing practice before requiring them to complete tasks independently. A third level of support for sentence and word level teaching and learning is also available as necessary. This teacher scaffolding is gradually reduced to enable learner autonomy over time.

The theoretical basis of RtL (as it is known in RSA) is what gives power to the literacy interventions reported in this chapter. They include: scaffolding of writing; mediated learning; working within each student's zone of proximal development; text modelling through explicit teaching strategies; differentiated teaching and assessment practices; incorporating a process-approach to writing, and drawing on systemic functional grammar and genre pedagogy to support writing development. The RtL cycle acts as a blueprint to help enable teachers to follow a more systematic and structured approach to the teaching of writing skills. In practice, across the three research projects presented in this chapter, not all cohorts of students required the same amount of time to be devoted to each cycle. Rather, time spent within each stage of the cycle in Figure 6.1 is dependent upon student needs.

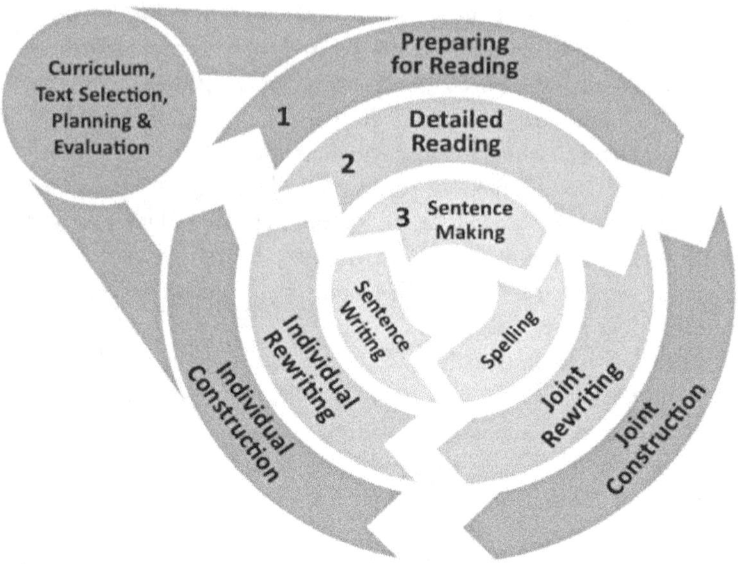

Figure 6.1. Pedagogic cycle of Reading to Learn (Rose & Martin, 2012, p. 147)

Thus, the key element here is differentiated teaching and learning. Diagnostic/baseline testing guides classroom teaching.

RESEARCH CONTEXT

The three RtL research projects all made use of a small-scale, longitudinal research design, generally over a minimum period of one semester. All of the studies adopted a purposive sampling procedure where either specific schools were approached, given their student demographics and SES context (and thus linguistic policy); or, in the case of the tertiary study, students voluntarily enrolled in an academic writing course. Given that the projects made use of a non-random sampling procedure, the results of these studies are not necessarily generalizable to other wider classroom contexts. However, in all three studies, the student samples do comprise interesting heterogeneous characteristics that could be applicable to other similar classroom settings. This includes circumstances related to school environment, linguistic background of students, differences in SES of students, and linguistic needs when transitioning into tertiary studies. All three studies made use of a mixed methods approach to data collection and analysis. Writing samples (qualitative data) were assessed (quantitative data) and both descriptive and inferential statistics were used to analyse RtL's efficacy.

1. South African tertiary study cohort

With the RSA tertiary study, the population of students comprised undergraduate Social Science students at a prominent university that services in general a lower SES community. These were all EAL students.

A diagnostic writing task was set at the onset of the semester course to gauge students' baseline levels of essay writing skills. This diagnostic task served to inform the level of teaching required to enable students to develop the academic writing skills needed to succeed in their studies. Further, by engaging in diagnostic assessment, pedagogic intervention was also more student-centred and allowed for more differentiated literacy instruction to follow. To assess students' ongoing writing development, two separate writing tasks were created. Task 1 and Task 2 had different essay topics, and the level of difficulty increased considerably from Task 1 to Task 2. One of the differences was in the genres used to model academic writing between Task 1 and Task 2. Task 1 utilised a specially written academic argument essay to model genre conventions of an argument, and associated language patterns, thus following RtL principles. However, Task 2 incorporated a recount text extracted from a local gossip magazine. Students were directed to convert the recount text into an academic argument. No model text was used. This was a significant step up in complexity of Task 2 and a marked deviation from the principles of RtL pedagogy. Therefore, when interpreting the results of these students' literacy progress for the research project, this needs to be taken into account (see Figure 6.2), given that Task 2 was not aligned with RtL pedagogy. With both Task 1 and Task 2, students submitted two writing drafts for formative tutor feedback (Task 1.1, 1.2 and Task 2.1, 2.2). Students were expected to engage with tutor feedback to help them in the writing of a final essay with no tutor support at all (which would represent the summative assessment) – the third submission (Task 1.3 and Task 2.3) served as post-intervention test.

2. South African secondary school study cohorts

For the secondary school study, three Grade 11 English classes from two separate schools took part. The choice of schools was based on the Department of Basic Education quantile ranking system, which ranks schools according to SES circumstances. Schools in quintiles 1–3 generally service a lower SES community; whereas, those in quintiles 4–5 service more affluent communities and have more resources at their disposal. Educational outcomes tend to be higher for higher quintile schools. One of the classes in the study – comprised of EAL students enrolled in a quintile 1 school – was representative of a school plagued with crime, drugs and generally non-existent community support. Furthermore, many of these students were migrant students from other African nations, and thus their English proficiency skills were very low. The other two Year 11 classes came from a prestigious quintile 5 school, which is very well resourced. One of these two classes was an English home language class (EHL) whereas the other Year 11 class was also comprised of EAL students. Within the RSA educational system, the language of teaching, learning and assessment is English, but students can be separated into different classes based on home language. This has an effect on the curriculum the class follows, since it varies depending on the language group the class belongs to. Because two of the classes followed an EAL curriculum, it was easier to compare the within-class rate of change of these students' individual writing skills.

This particular RtL study was aimed at addressing poor writing skills of EAL learners at largely lower SES schools given the prevalence of underachievement at these schools. However, many higher SES schools in RSA offer scholarships to lower SES families and are thus experiencing growing literacy inequality inside the classroom too. For this reason, it was decided to extend the RtL study to an English Additional Language class at a quintile 5 school in addition to a quintile 1 school. A higher achieving English Home Language class was also included to test whether RtL pedagogy could still engage learners already performing at a higher academic writing level. The rationale behind this was to show classroom teachers the diverse pedagogic reach RtL could have in secondary school classrooms.

In this particular study, the data comprised of ten pieces of extended writing. All the classes were set a diagnostic/baseline writing task for narrative and argumentative genres. For both genres, each writing draft tackled a different stage of that genre. For example, students were explicitly taught (through text modelling) how to write an essay introduction for the first argument genre task and were then asked to construct their own example (A1). Feedback was given on this (A1) whilst classroom instruction continued to explicitly teach how to construct the body paragraphs (A2). Students then had to submit a redraft of their introduction addressing the feedback and expanding their writing drafts to include the body paragraphs (A2). Feedback was given on the amended introduction and new body paragraphs whilst classroom instruction explicitly modelled to students how to construct a conclusion (A3). Feedback was then given on all three stages of the argumentative essay (A3). A similar pedagogic approach was used for the narrative. To assess whether students were making progress in their ability to internalise the genres and language being taught, a final post-intervention assignment was set (N4 & A4). The topics for N4 and A4 were different, and no teacher support was given to students (see Figure 6.3 below).

OVERVIEW OF HOW RTL PEDAGOGY WAS INTEGRATED INTO CLASSROOM TEACHING AND LEARNING

RtL pedagogy equips classroom teachers and academic writing specialists at a tertiary level with the tools to explicitly scaffold reading and writing skills development across the curriculum, and at various levels within the education sector with the nine sets of strategies, across three pedagogic cycles (see Figure 6.1). This section will offer a brief general overview of how some of these strategies were employed in both the secondary school context and tertiary context. Due to word limitations, this is not an exhaustive discussion of how RtL was used in these research projects, but indications are given of problems or deviations from the strategies and explained.

PREPARING FOR READING

In an effort to support the development of more advanced writing skills, the first effort must be to support students' reading development. Clearly, students need to read with comprehension if they are to develop an understanding of curriculum content, which is then assessed via writing tasks. Thus, the first strategy employed was to thoroughly prepare students for the reading of the model texts that would be used to scaffold their writing skills. With both the narrative and academic argumentative essay, in both the secondary school context, and tertiary context, model texts were specifically designed to exemplify the required genre conventions. Before we unpacked the stages and phases of each text, and the accompanying language features used to create meaning, students were provided with more background information about the texts in general prior to reading them, following the *Preparing for Reading* strategy. The purpose of this activity was to orient students to the field (subject matter) of the text. This included an introductory discussion of the background information of the text, what each text was about at a macro level (global meaning), and a brief overview of the purpose of the genre of the text. This also included an overview of how each text would unfold in stages and phases. For example, the narrative genre lesson included an orientation to the storyline, and the characters that the students would meet. Students were briefed on how the story would unfold (without giving away the resolution). The academic argument introductory lessons included an overview of the main argument (thesis), how the argument unfolded (topic for each supporting paragraph), and looked at some of the key evidence used to persuade the reader to take on the author's viewpoint. We also discussed additional language points that could have been used to enhance the text's argument (building students' repertoire of evidence to draw on for their own writing).

In the secondary school project, the students from the lower SES school were given a much more detailed preview of the texts than the students from the higher SES school. This was largely due to differing baseline literacy skills, and a different amount of classroom time that had already been spent on building students content knowledge prior to the start of the research project[1]. Once all students had been given an overview of the texts, we read the texts aloud making sure students were following. During the reading aloud session, we purposefully engaged with students by using consciousness-raising techniques (questions used to direct students attention to certain aspects of the text). It's important to note that this process was not followed in full for the second half of the tertiary project for various reasons, one being a time issue. In other words, we moved away from RtL pedagogy. Results (see Figure 6.2), show that this affected the upward trend in students' literacy development. The secondary school project, which followed on from the tertiary project, had this pedagogic shortcoming rectified, giving rise to much more positive results with the secondary school project (see Figure 6.3).

DETAILED READING

During the *Detailed Reading* cycle, we moved from unpacking the texts at a macro level first (stages of the genre), then focused explicitly on the paragraph level (phases of the stages), and finally selected sentence level language features, e.g., sign-posting wordings like conjunctives, theme and rheme etc. While we worked exclusively on the argument genre for the tertiary project, within the second half of the teaching time, we used a narrative text and asked students to convert it into an academic argument. We did not engage in detailed reading for this second task and, again, this seems to be one of the reasons student progress stagnated (see Figure 6.2). For the secondary school projects, we broke the detailed reading down into the stages of each genre and directly after unpacking a stage of the narrative or argumentative essay, students engaged in the rewriting of that stage, focussing on replicating the stage and associated phases based on what we had unpacked with the *Detailed Reading*. For the secondary project, this was largely because we only got to see students once in a 5–10 day cycle. Through *Detailed Reading* and unpacking of the texts with the use of the model texts, students became more familiar with the way to structure their own writing more effectively.

An important aspect of our detailed reading cycle entailed the use of constant guiding questions to ask students to focus on key words such as sign post words to show transitions to new phases within specific stages of the genre. Students had to highlight these to ensure they used them in their own writing. We also focused on content words with detailed elaboration to ensure students were building their understanding of the content as well. During this cycle, we allowed translanguaging amongst students to build a deeper comprehension of English vocabulary items. Over and above a focus on structure and language usage, we also brainstormed new ideas that students could use in their own writing. This was done in a whole-class setting, with students volunteering to write up these ideas on the board. We made sure we affirmed all student responses to help students build their confidence. If a response was not really moving a student forward, we gently redirected the student back to the text and elaborated further by drawing on the modelled texts. In this way we made use of RtL's 'prepare–focus–identify–affirm–elaborate' strategy.

JOINT AND *INDIVIDUAL WRITING*

Before embarking on *Individual Writing* of their drafts, students worked in groups to write a joint draft of each stage of the narrative or academic argument using the writing prompts already brainstormed, and documented on the board. This really helped weaker students understand the thought processes needed to delve into the writing process. Throughout this stage, we monitored group responses and provided extensive feedback and support where needed. After completion of the *Joint Construction* of the narrative or argument, students wrote their own individual draft. At this stage, they had now been scaffolded via the *Preparing for Reading*, *Detailed Reading* and *Joint Construction* cycle with extensive teacher and tutor feedback throughout. As students embarked on their individual drafts, we moved around the class to support students who needed additional help. Students then handed in their individual draft of each stage for detailed teacher feedback. This allowed support to be highly differentiated with weaker students being given the greatest amount of written feedback. Given the age of all the students in the secondary school study (Year 12) and the tertiary study, we did not move down to the RtL sentence level activities or spelling. This was not an issue with our cohort of students, but might be an activity for junior secondary school students.

FINDINGS AND DISCUSSION

The following section offers a brief overview of the findings of each RtL project.

1. South African tertiary findings

Figure 6.2 represents data patterns exhibited throughout the RSA tertiary RtL project.

Figure 6.2 shows some interesting patterns when RtL pedagogy was incorporated into this specific academic writing skills development course versus a more traditional approach to literacy development in the second part of the course. Task 1 and its associated subtasks (1.1; 1.2 & 1.3) used RtL pedagogy whereas, due to various constraints, Task 2 and its associated subtasks (2.1; 2.2 & 2.3) reverted to traditional literacy pedagogy. Where students were guided through the reading and writing process with RtL pedagogy (Task 1), a positive upward trend was evidenced with a noticeable improvement in the final draft of Task 1.3. This is important because as students submitted a new draft, the writing demands, and the literacy skills students needed to demonstrate in their writing, increased. Therefore, despite assessment criteria becoming more complex from Task 1.1 through to Task 1.3, students still improved considerably in their writing skills. This is testament to RtL pedagogy. Task 2 presented interesting results too. On the one hand, although students' literacy skills development stagnated throughout Task 2, they still demonstrated a more advanced level of writing than their initial baseline scores, showing the continued effect of RtL pedagogy. In other words, RtL pedagogy for Task 1 provided a solid foundation for developing academic writing skills that was transferred to Task 2. It is important to point out that the complexity of Task 2 was significantly higher than Task 1. However, because a more traditional approach to literacy development was used, students struggled to continue with the same level of upward progress as

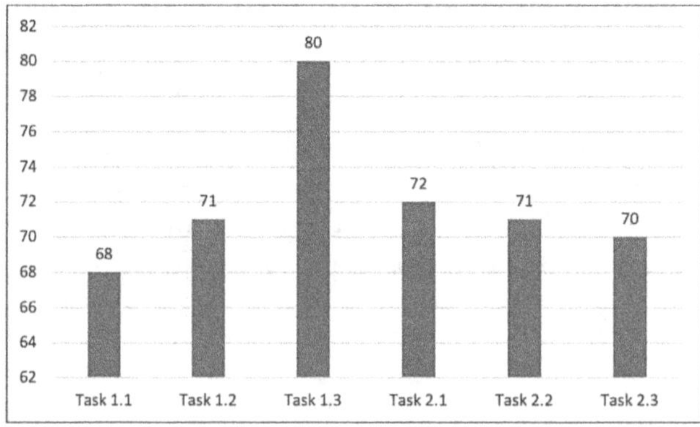

Figure 6.2. Whole class performance for the South African tertiary RtL intervention. (Millin & Millin, 2014)

opposed to when RtL pedagogy was used. What cannot be seen in the data in Figure 6.2 is that, with Task 1, the weaker students (identified through a baseline/diagnostic task) ended up performing on par with academically stronger students (see Millin & Millin, 2014, for a more detailed discussion). As teachers, reflecting on the above data made it clear that the use of RtL pedagogy (Task 1) offers students more scaffolding than traditional pedagogy (Task 2) and this reflection informed the design of the secondary school project.

2. South African secondary school findings

Figure 6.3 offers a graphic representation of student progress with the use of RtL pedagogy within a secondary school context in RSA.

In the RSA secondary school RtL project, all students, regardless of their academic literacy skills base, determined by the pre-intervention baseline assessment, demonstrated improvement in their academic writing. The greatest improvement was in the schematic structuring of both the narrative and the argumentative essay. As a result, students were able to write more cohesive and coherent pieces of extended writing. With the argumentative essay, this also meant a clearer articulation of thoughts, ideas and argument relevant to the essay questions. From a marking perspective, this made it easier to read students extended pieces of writing without having to read, re-read, and back track to earlier sections of the essay to follow a student's line of argument. Thus, access to the 'discourse' of both narrative writing, and argumentative writing was improved through intensive scaffolding, achieved through explicit, purposeful modelling of genre-specific texts, in addition to highly differentiated writing feedback. Importantly, Grade 11B (left bar) – students from the low SES school (see Figure 6.3) started the intervention with the lowest academic writing skills base. Therefore, the most exciting finding of this particular

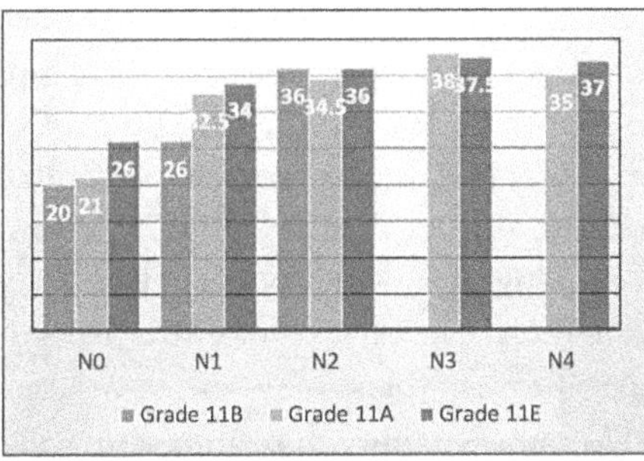

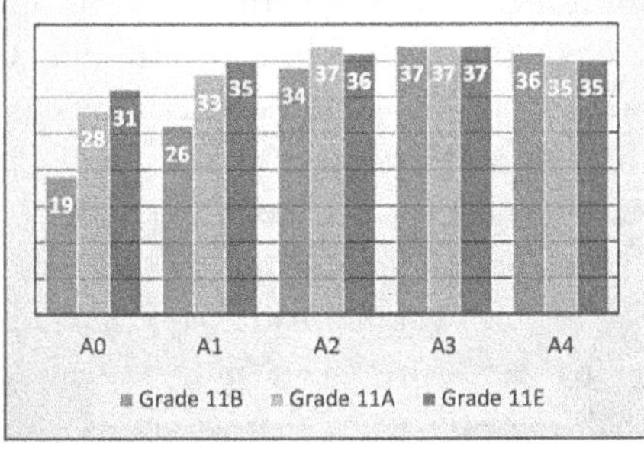

Grade 11B = English First Additional Language, **low SES school** (left bar)
Grade 11A = English First Additional Language, **high SES school** (middle bar)
Grade 11E = English Home Language, **high SES school** (right bar)

Figure 6.3. Across and within class performance for the narrative essay (left) and the argumentative essay (right) (Millin & Millin, 2018)

project was the convergence (or catch-up) effect between students from the lower SES school towards students from the higher SES school (comparisons were made between the two EFAL classes – Grade 11B & Grade 11A). This was especially marked in the argumentative essay, with the lower SES students outperforming students from the higher SES school (A0–A4). This convergence phenomenon demonstrates that when RtL pedagogy is adopted within academic writing interventions, students initially deemed weaker in writing skill may be given an equal opportunity of performing on par with academically stronger students. With the narrative genre, similar patterns emerged, but due to the low SES EFAL students' teacher's illness, access to this class was abruptly halted. This explains why data after N2 is absent for this cohort. Nevertheless, the data we do have suggests this cohort of students were on track for similar convergence effects to the academic writing genre. On a side note, students from the low SES school had been asked if they were going to university at the beginning of the project. None of the students said they would, and explained that they lacked the academic literacy skills to attend university. At the completion of this project, the question was repeated and this time, 80% of the students said that they now felt confident to try. This is further testament to the empowering nature of incorporating RtL pedagogy into classroom instruction.

CONCLUSION

The two projects described here show the importance of explicit teaching of more advanced forms of academic writing, especially in contexts such as ours in RSA. Students need to be supported via purposefully designed literacy interventions that move away from talking about how to write, to showing students how academic texts make meanings in different genres via a focus on reading and supporting their writing using effective models. This needs to be coupled with multiple opportunities for students to practise their writing until a higher level of automaticity is reached. This chapter offered insights into two RtL literacy interventions within three separate educational contexts that sought to support students in the development of more advanced academic writing skills. Data evidences the democratising effect RtL has on student performance, especially in the secondary context, allowing all students an equal opportunity of success and opening the possibility of tertiary study to those for whom it had not been an option. If teachers can embrace RtL pedagogy in their classroom teaching, students can improve in their ability to demonstrate their learning, given that we access formal knowledge through reading and assess that learning through writing. This also gives weaker-performing students access to the same type of writing preparation as stronger students. Although labour intensive, given the amount of time needed to prepare the RtL strategies and to provide writing feedback, the impact on student performance, confidence levels, and ongoing educational opportunities to succeed, are certainly worth it.

NOTE

1 The lower SES school students encountered many barriers to learning. There was community disruption to teaching and learning, students were often late to class, the absence of senior leadership meant other students easily disrupted whole classes, and lower English literacy skills meant the sequencing and pacing of the curriculum was slower. To remediate, more time was spent preparing students for the texts they were going to read, which would also serve as model texts for the writing process.

REFERENCES

Acevedo, C. (2010). *Will the implementation of Reading to Learn in Stockholm schools accelerate literacy learning for disadvantaged students and close the achievement gap? A report on school-based action research*, Stockholm, Multilingual Research Institute. DOI: 10.13140/RG.2.2.12012.69762

Bernstein, B. (1990). *The structuring of pedagogic discourse*. Routledge.

Halliday, M. A. K. (1989). *Spoken and written language*. Oxford University Press.

McRae, D., Ainsworth, G., Cumming, J., Hughes, P., Mackay, T., Price, K., Rowland, M., Warhurst, J., Woods, D. & Zbar, V. (2000). *What works? Explorations in improving outcomes for Indigenous students*. A report prepared for the Commonwealth Department of Education, Training and Youth Affairs by the Indigenous Education Strategic Initiatives Programme (Strategic Results Projects) National Coordination and Evaluation Team. Canberra, ACT: Australian Curriculum Studies Association and National Curriculum Services.

Millin, T., & Millin, M. (2014). Scaffolding academic literacy using the reading to learn intervention: An evaluative study of a tertiary education context in South Africa. *Per Linguam, 30*(3), 26-38.

Millin, T., & Millin, M. (2018). English academic writing convergence for academically weaker senior secondary school students: Possibility or pipe-dream? *Journal of English for Academic Purposes. 31*. 1 – 17.

Rose, D. (2005). Democratising the classroom: A literacy pedagogy for the new generation. *Journal of Education, 37*, 131-167.

Rose, D., & Acevedo, C. (2006). Closing the gap and accelerating learning in the middle years of schooling. *Literacy learning: The Middle Years, 14*(2), 32–45.

Rose, D., & Martin, J. (2012). *Learning to write, reading to learn: Genre, knowledge and pedagogy in the Sydney School.* Equinox Publishing.

Rose, D., Rose, M., Farrington, S., & Page, S. (2008). Scaffolding academic literacy with indigenous health sciences students: An evaluative study. *Journal of English for Academic Purposes*, *7*(3), 165-179.

Roser, M., & Ortiz-Ospina, E. (2016). *Literacy; Our world in data.* https://ourworldindata.org/literacy

Vygotsky, L. (1978). *Mind in society: The development of higher psychological processes* [Edited by M. Cole, V. John-Steiner, S. Scribner, & E. Souberman]. Harvard University Press.

ABOUT THE AUTHOR

Tracey Millin is an Educational Linguist and secondary school English teacher with over 15 years of experience working in the secondary and tertiary sectors, and researching multiple aspects of additional language development. She specialises in the teaching and learning of English as an additional language, with a focus on the development of reading and writing skills for non-native speakers of English in classrooms where English is the medium of instruction. Tracey has taught languages at secondary schools in South Africa and New Zealand, and has been involved in teacher training for the past 9 years – preparing future English as an additional language teachers in South Africa and New Zealand. Tracey is currently the Programme Co-ordinator for the MTESOL, and PGCertTESOL, and subject endorser for the MEd (Teaching and Learning Languages) at the University of Canterbury, New Zealand.

7

Bridging the gap between sign language and written texts for students who are deaf or have a hearing loss

Ann-Christin Lövstedt

ABSTRACT

This chapter tells the story of introducing Reading to Learn pedagogy (R2L) at Manilla School in Stockholm, Sweden, an internationally renowned special school for students who are deaf or have a significant hearing loss. Manilla is a bilingual school where teachers and students communicate in both Swedish and Svenskt teckenspråk (STS), the Swedish deaf community's sign language[1]*. The school initiated an R2L professional development project to improve literacy and learning outcomes for all their students across subject areas in 2015. While R2L has been applied in diverse settings, it had not previously been implemented with this group of students, using sign language as the medium of instruction. The chapter describes the challenges of this innovative undertaking and the reciprocal learning of participating teachers and their educators. The R2L teacher educators, Claire Acevedo and myself, had no prior experience of Svenskt teckenspråk or of working with these students and teachers. As we collaborated with the teachers, via STS interpreters, to develop teacher knowledge about the language of written texts and literacy pedagogy, we came to understand more about signed communication and its relationships with spoken and written language, and with learner identities. The success of this learning journey is demonstrated by the eventual adoption of R2L as a whole-school approach to teaching and learning at Manilla School.*

FIRST STEPS: LEARNING ABOUT THE SCHOOL

In the spring of 2015, Claire Acevedo and I were invited to Manilla School by the principal, Ann-Sofie Montelius, to conduct an information session for the staff about Reading to Learn. R2L is quite well known in the education community in Sweden, as we have been providing teacher professional learning programs since 2009 (see Andersson Varga, et al., Chapter 8 this volume), and our projects' outcomes have been disseminated via lectures (https://urskola.se/Produkter/182462-UR-Samtiden-Flersprakighet-i-fokus-Metodiken-Reading-to-learn-for-alla), conference presentations and publications (Acevedo, 2010, 2014; Acevedo, & Lövstedt, 2014; Acevedo et al., 2016; Coffin et al., 2013). Moreover, the R2L reference book, *Learning to write, Reading to learn* (Rose & Martin, 2012), has been translated into Swedish, as *Skriva läsa lära* (Rose & Martin, 2013), and is included on the reading lists for language education students at a number of Swedish higher education institutions. So the staff at Manilla were keen to learn more about R2L with a view to improving the literacy learning of their students.

The school had ongoing concerns over the underachievement of its students compared to their hearing peers, despite efforts to improve teaching strategies. Only some 40% of the Manilla students reached the curriculum goals in basic compulsory education, compared with about 77% for their hearing peers. These disheartening statistics are commensurate with international data on literacy achievement for these learners (Hendar, 2008; Skolverket, 2014).

The principal, Ann-Sofie, recognized that the integral relationship between oral language and literacy development that typically underpins the teaching of hearing students was not a viable resource for teaching reading to deaf students, nor was it proving effective for teaching students with a hearing loss. Her hope was that by focusing more on the relationship between the students' first language (L1), Svenskt teckenspråk (STS), and literacy development in Swedish (L2) it would be possible to build an effective pedagogical bridge to improved literacy learning for the Manilla students. Likewise, the teachers wanted access to pedagogical tools that would enable their students to comprehend the texts in their coursebooks and write well-developed texts in their subjects across the curriculum.

However, as we planned for the information session, we began to realize that we were entering previously uncharted waters, and they were quite deep! While we recognized deafness as a cultural and linguistic difference, we began to wonder if the R2L pedagogy would provide the Manilla teachers with the pedagogical tools necessary to teach their students via STS. Moreover, we began to question our own ability to lead the learning of these teachers, given our lack of experience in a context where oral language played little or no part at all. And, most importantly, we wondered if the initiative would result in improved reading and writing outcomes for the students.

So, to be as well prepared as possible, we began to investigate the background of Manilla School and its students. We already knew that it was Sweden's first school for students who are deaf or have a hearing loss, opening in 1809. It has played an important role in the development of a world-class education for deaf students via teaching through STS. These efforts have attracted international attention and the school is regularly visited by key figures in the field of deaf education from around the world.

At the time of the project, the school had about 110 students in grades 1–10[2], with a staff of about 40 teachers and teaching assistants. While many students are profoundly deaf, the proportion of students with some hearing had recently increased due to the development of cochlea implants. A number of students also had physical or learning disabilities that the school also catered for. Furthermore, due to the large influx of refugees to Sweden since 2015, some students were newly arrived immigrants. These students sometimes had no school background at all, and some could not communicate in the sign language of their home countries. In such cases, prior to attending Manilla School, their only mode of communication had been via a repertoire of gestures developed within their immediate family circles (known as 'Homesign'). Amongst the teaching staff, about half of the teachers could not hear at all while the rest were able to hear to varying degrees.

While the school's dominant language of communication is Svenskt teckenspråk, spoken Swedish is also used where possible. The school has a policy of bilingualism, which means that each individual has the right and the opportunity to express themselves in STS or in spoken Swedish. If an interpreter is needed, the school will hire one. All students are also given the opportunity to develop both languages if possible. While this opportunity is not available to the profoundly deaf students, it is a requirement for all students to learn and master written Swedish, regardless of their ability to hear.

With this background knowledge, we felt well prepared for our presentation. However, this first presentation made us realize that we had much to learn about communicating via STS interpreters, and that their role would be extremely important throughout the project. We had to become far more conscious about our communication context. For example, we were unable to move freely in front of the audience while giving presentations, we had to remain in fixed positions so that everyone could see the interpreters all the time. In addition, as it was impossible for the teachers to simultaneously look at our presentation slides and at the interpreters, we had to deliver our presentation in just one mode at a time. Dealing with the different languages, Swedish, English and STS as well as the different modalities in the presentation – signs, written language, pictures and diagrams etc. – was more complicated than we had anticipated. We felt that it was visually very demanding for the audience and, above all, it took more time than usual.

Nonetheless, in spite of our unfamiliarity with working through interpreters, we could see by the questions asked and the comments made that our presentation was well received. The teachers were incredibly patient and committed to the notion of learning more about R2L in the hope of improving the literacy learning of their students.

ORGANIZING FOR TEACHER LEARNING

Within a few weeks, a professional learning program was planned over three semesters, between August 2015 and December 2016. Of course, not only would teachers be learning about the pedagogy from us, we would need to learn more about teaching via the visual–spatial mode in the STS classroom from the teachers. Our hope was that by working collaboratively with the teachers, we could all learn how the R2L strategies could work best in this context.

During preparatory meetings with the principal, we learnt more about the background to the school's decision to undertake the R2L project. It was only in the 1980s that Svenskt teckenspråk was recognized as a 'real' language in Sweden, and thus became the school's natural language of instruction[3]. At that time, there were high hopes that the shift to teaching in STS would result in an improvement in student results. However, over time, the school realized that just changing the language of instruction to STS had not been enough to enable the students to achieve the curriculum goals at similar levels to those of their hearing peers and progress to upper secondary school (gymnasium). In order to offer Manilla students the same opportunities as their hearing peers, Ann-Sofie was keen to work with the staff to trial and develop new pedagogical processes that would support students' development in both STS and written Swedish, as well as spoken Swedish where appropriate.

OBSERVING LESSONS

To understand more about teaching in Svenskt teckenspråk, a key part of our preparation was to observe lessons, accompanied by interpreters. We witnessed many examples of remarkable teaching, particularly as some students faced challenges besides hearing loss. Cognitive and physical disabilities compounded the obstacles to learning for numbers of students. The situation often required two teachers for a small group of only 5–12 students. In addition, some students required a dedicated assistant who was responsible for various medical treatments that needed to be carried out throughout the school day. We were amazed that the teachers, despite all the different demands that the disabilities entailed, could still be so relaxed and focused and thereby create a safe learning environment for their students.

Despite this caring practice, a student in a grade seven class revising for a history test brought up an issue that epitomized a key concern for the students in the school. He told his teacher that he had no problem understanding everything that was communicated in STS during the lessons, but when he was required to revise independently by reading the textbook, he could not understand the written language at all. Other students agreed and added that they did not know how to formulate written answers to test questions. They could sign the answers without any problems but writing in Swedish was overwhelming for them.

The class discussion clarified for us that that the current classroom pedagogy was not enabling students to make the connection between the information given by the teacher in STS and the written Swedish in the textbook. We also observed that the textbooks were seldom used as a resource in the classroom, as is the case in many classrooms with hearing students. However, there was an expectation for students to be able to use the textbooks for individual revision of the lessons that had been given in STS. We could see parallels with hearing classrooms where teachers predominantly teach in the oral mode, but set reading for homework without addressing students' varying capacities to learn from reading. As R2L strategies are specifically designed to address this problem, we decided to proceed with our usual professional development program in the hope that the R2L strategies would

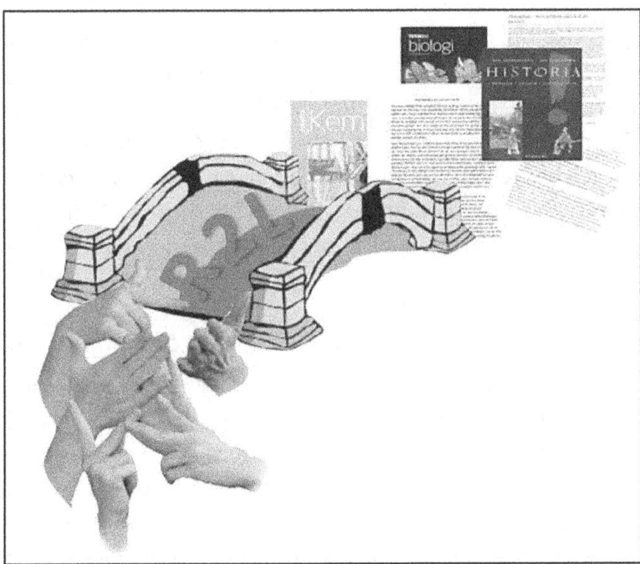

Figure 7.1. Bridging the gap between Svenskt teckenspråk and written texts with R2L

bridge the gap between STS and knowledge in written texts. We hoped that as the teachers became fluent in the R2L strategies, the students would develop subject-specific language in STS and learn to comprehend written texts and express their knowledge in written Swedish. This working model is symbolized in Figure 7.1.

IMPLEMENTING THE R2L PROFESSIONAL DEVELOPMENT PROGRAM

We negotiated with the school leaders for the professional learning program to be carried out over a longer period of time than we allow for in mainstream schools, to enable communication through interpreters. The workshops and school visits were organized over three semesters with six 2-day workshops, rather than the typical four workshops over two semesters. The 40 teachers on the staff were divided into two workshop groups to allow for 'horseshoe' style seating arrangements that enabled visual contact for communication with the interpreters and between the teachers. In addition, teachers received guidance individually or in small groups between workshops. This supported the teachers and enabled us to tailor the workshops to meet the needs of the teachers at each stage of the program (see Table 7.1).

RECIPROCAL LEARNING: R2L AND TRANSLANGUAGING

In the first two-day workshops we jointly analyzed texts from different subjects according to purpose, i.e., genre, stages and phases, and then modelled and practised how to use the knowledge about language from the analysis for *Preparing for Reading*, *Paragraph-by-Paragraph Reading* and *Joint Construction.* Focusing on the context, text and paragraph levels when reading with their students, before moving on to sentence and word levels, was a new experience for the teachers. Previously they had almost entirely focused on the meanings being made by sentences, words and letter patterns. This contrast in approaches is illustrated in Figure 7.2 which shows the different levels of language depicted by the Functional Model of Language.

Analyzing texts, pictures and diagrams using R2L's functional model of language was also new to the teachers. They were, like most teachers in Sweden, used to explaining the meaning of texts without specifically focusing attention on where and how the meaning was made linguistically in the text. As the students' first language was Svenskt teckenspråk (L1) rather than Swedish (L2), the teachers were of course accustomed to explaining words and concepts in written texts, but they were unaccustomed to clarifying the purpose of a text and the overall structure and

Table 7.1. Workshop schedule 2015–2016

Term	Activity	Content
Autumn term 2015	Workshop 1 (2 days)	Knowledge about language: Analysis of texts used in school: purpose = genre, stages and phases Knowledge about pedagogy: R2L strategies: Preparing for reading + Paragraph-by-paragraph reading + Joint construction
	Workshop 2 (2 days)	Knowledge about language: Analysis of texts used in school: purpose = genre, stages and phases Knowledge about pedagogy: Introduction to the Detailed reading strategy (factual texts)
	Tutorials (individual/pairs/small groups)	Support and feedback on teachers' individual R2L work in their classrooms
Spring term 2016	Workshop 3 (2 days)	Knowledge about language: Patterns in sentences Knowledge about pedagogy: modelling and planning Detailed reading for stories
	Tutorials (individual/pairs/small groups)	Support and feedback on teachers' individual R2L work in their classrooms
	Workshop 4 (2 days)	Knowledge about language: Patterns in texts + Abstract language Knowledge about pedagogy: Intensive strategies (Sentence making, Spelling, Rewriting sentences) + Joint rewriting
Autumn term 2016	Workshop 5 (2 days)	Knowledge about language: Deepening understandings and revision of genres, stages, phases, the 5 categories of meanings Knowledge about pedagogy: Practice in implementing strategies
	2 mini-workshops	Training: lesson planning + implementation of plans (in small groups)
	Workshop 6 (2 days)	Knowledge about language: Assessing students' texts according to the R2L assessment criteria Knowledge about pedagogy: the role of formative assessment in teaching connected to the R2L strategies
	Tutorials (individual/pairs/small groups)	Support and feedback on teachers' individual R2L work in their classrooms
	Evaluation (questionnaire)	Discussion of future actions

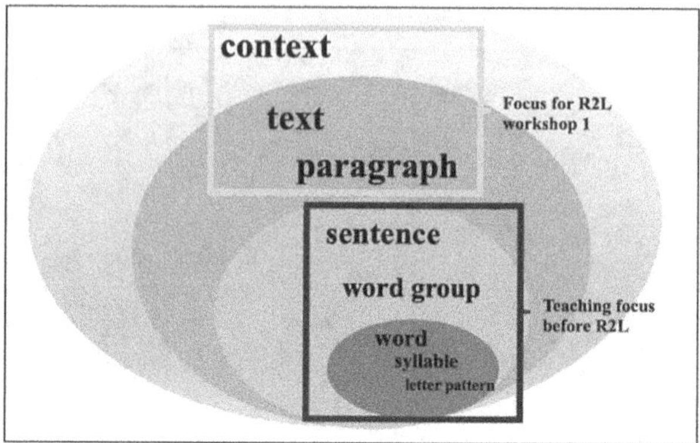

Figure 7.2. The Functional Model of Language showing the difference in reading focus before and after R2L

how the meaning unfolds in stages and phases in written Swedish. They were used to explaining only what a text was *about*, but not what a text was *doing*.

While it is self-evident that students who are deaf or have hearing loss are less able to learn language via the vocal–auditory mode, our classroom observations after the first workshop showed us that they responded very well to R2L activities that draw on the visual–spatial mode to facilitate meaning making from written texts. By making a written text the focal point of a lesson, the teachers were able to use STS to visually guide students to identify and understand meanings as they unfolded in each stage and phase of a text. They could then guide them to identify and understand meanings at the level of grammar and vocabulary in written Swedish, that are different to STS.

Although we had not foreseen this advantage, we soon realized that the R2L activities of *Paragraph-by-paragraph Reading* and *Detailed Reading* were excellent opportunities for so-called *translanguaging*. García (2009, p. 140) describes this as 'the act performed by bilinguals of accessing different linguistic features or various modes of what are described as autonomous languages, in order to maximize communicative potential'. The R2L activities enabled teachers to consciously use students' bilingualism as a resource to teach meaning, so that all the available linguistic resources contributed to enhanced learning outcomes.

Initially we thought that the teachers were working by translating between STS and equivalent meanings in written Swedish, as is common practice when teaching a new language. However, as we began having more technical learning conversations with the teachers, their questions revealed an embarrassing gap in our understanding of the complex nature of signed communication. They began to ask whether they should use STS or sign the Swedish words as they appeared on the page during certain stages of the R2L pedagogy. While we understood that STS is not just Swedish in signed format, we had not initially grasped the nature and extent of the difference between the two languages that meant teachers often needed to use a mediating, multimodal practice that they referred to as 'signing the Swedish as it appeared on the page'[4] even though it did not necessarily convey meaning to the students.

As STS is independent from Swedish, it has its own system of vocabulary and grammar, or *lexicogrammar*.[5] As the teachers explained to us, STS makes meaning with 'polysyntactic' signs, in which lots of things are happening at the same time within one sign. For example, it is not always possible to determine if a hand sign corresponds to a noun or a verb, but the clarifying grammatical information is shown simultaneously via facial expressions, mouthing words, and/or performing the sign in a certain position in relation to the body. This illustrates how STS makes meaning with lexicogrammatical patterns that are very different from what might be described as the consecutive, linear, patterns of written Swedish.

While the teachers could use STS to convey the meaning of whole texts, paragraphs or sentences, it was not as effective in focusing on written Swedish grammar and word choices. So, 'signing the words as they appeared on the page' was an additional language strategy used to teach the students to understand Swedish lexicogrammar, while simultaneously preparing them to use written language patterns from reading texts as a resource for their own writing. This new understanding led us to revise our initial thinking about what the process of reading really entailed for learners who had STS as their first language. For the Manilla students to gain a similar level of comprehension as hearing students during reading aloud with a teacher, an additional step was often involved. STS was used for general comprehension of a text, followed by 'readings' incorporating the signing of strings of words from the texts using signs from STS, even though they could have little relation to the grammar of the language and therefore would not make meaning.

Over the course of the training, we returned to the discussion about the role of 'signing words as they appeared on the page' in written Swedish in the R2L pedagogy on several occasions. This enabled us to identify some similar tendencies amongst the teachers for making choices about using STS or signing strings of words at different stages of the R2L pedagogy. In order for all students to follow a reading passage in class, most teachers projected a text onto a whiteboard or smartboard and pointed to the specific section of the text to be read. The most common approach to preparing for reading a whole text, a paragraph or a sentence was to use STS to preview the meaning. The text, paragraph or sentence was then 'read aloud' by signing the written Swedish, or the students would read silently to themselves. Teachers would then use STS for cues guiding students to identify wordings in the paragraph or sentence that had been read. The students would respond by signing the words, sometimes using finger spelling[6], and the teacher would direct the students to highlight the wordings. Finally the teacher would then elaborate their meanings in STS, or a combination of signing individual words and using STS to elaborate about language features. This intermodal, multilingual practice is illustrated in Figure 7.3.

R2L writing activities also offered further opportunities for translanguaging. In the *Notemaking* activity, information that was highlighted during reading was scribed as notes on the board. Teachers used STS in this activity to guide students to come to the board and write the key information in Swedish wordings. These notes were then used for *Joint Rewriting* of sentences and *Joint Construction* of new texts in Swedish. As with hearing students, these activities provided excellent opportunities to make different grammar and spelling patterns visible. They enabled teachers to focus attention on the patterns of written Swedish, particularly those that cause the most difficulty for students with STS as their first language. Teachers guided students and provided elaborations predominantly in STS, but also signed words and groups of words particularly for grammatical clarifications. These translanguaging activities are illustrated in Figure 7.4.

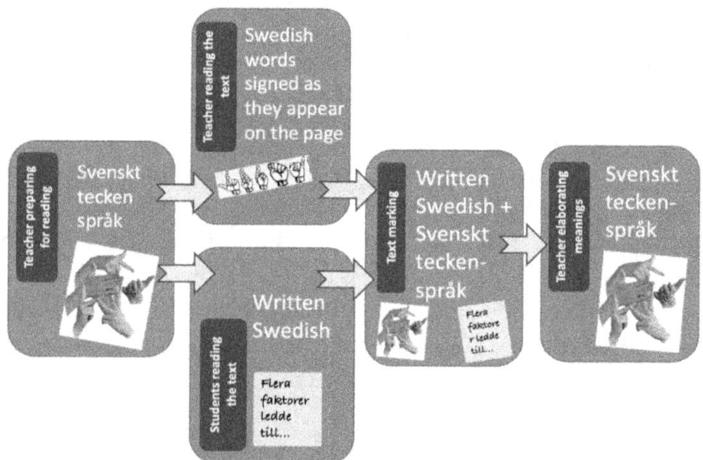

Figure 7.3. R2L strategies using intermodal, multilingual practices

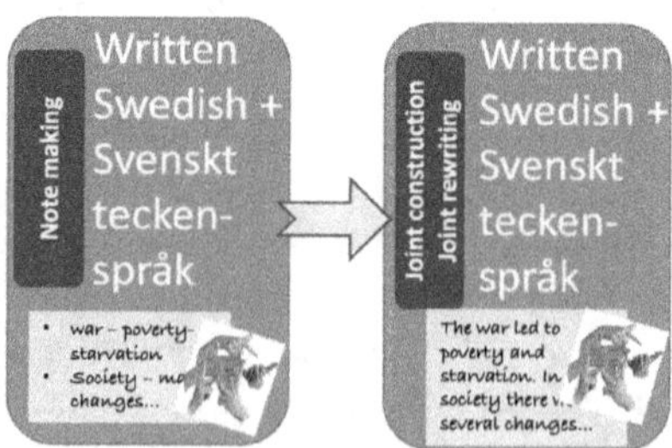

Figure 7.4. Translanguaging in notemaking and writing activities

MENTORING TUTORIALS

As the pedagogy was implemented, we conducted mentoring tutorials with individuals and small groups of teachers. The goals were to provide encouragement and support by answering questions, clarifying and revising elements of the pedagogy, and assisting with practical issues such as text analysis and lesson planning. Some teachers had also filmed themselves in the classroom so we could provide feedback on their teaching.

Teachers' comments were insightful but not unlike comments in other R2L projects (See Acevedo, 2010; Hart, Chapter 5 and Andersson Varga, et al., Chapter 8 this volume). As in other projects, some teachers had questions about how to simultaneously support struggling students while still providing challenges for high-achievers. Like most teachers, they experienced their students' levels of knowledge and/or language as extremely diverse. Our advice was to be very specific with their STS preparations to keep low-achieving students engaged in reading. We drew on models of successful practice in other contexts, to illustrate how to formulate specific cues that guide students to identify the precise wordings in the text. We also provided examples of how to engage the high-achieving students within the same interaction cycle by planning elaborations that were challenging and inferential, using open ended 'thinking' questions.

Some teachers had adopted the R2L *prepare–task–elaborate* interaction pattern without any hesitation. They enthusiastically reported that preparing students to identify wordings and continually affirming them engaged students who usually did not take an active part in the classroom. They were delighted with the increased engagement of their 'hard to reach' students! On the other hand, teachers who had found the use of the R2L interaction pattern challenging also realized how naturalized the practice of asking comprehension questions was, and how closely linked it was to teacher identity. They had struggled to let go of this pattern as, seemingly, asking students just to identify wordings seemed too easy and not like 'good' teaching at first which has also been reported as a response from teachers in other projects (e.g. Meehan et al., Chapter 14 this volume).

LANGUAGE AND IDENTITY

During our discussions with teachers a concern arose that the R2L activities may have too strong an emphasis on the Swedish language at the expense of students' STS development. As language is intrinsic to the expression of culture, perhaps we should not have been surprised that our work could be viewed as a type of cultural incursion that had the potential to impinge on deaf students' identity as competent and proud users of STS as a first language.

We learnt that this was a longstanding concern for the teachers, following the traumatic treatment that generations of deaf learners had to endure from the mainstream school system. It was only in 1981 that the Swedish government recognized Svenskt teckenspråk as the mother tongue of deaf people. For 100 years prior to this, schools were banned from using STS as the language of instruction. Instead, deaf students were supposed to learn the Swedish language through the so-called 'oralism' method, using speech and lip-reading rather than sign language. They were routinely forbidden to sign and were punished if they did. One consequence of this repression of STS was low achievement levels for the students at Manilla school, and a series of government reports that disparaged the ability of deaf students to learn and develop. Furthermore, when the hearing aid was invented in the 1950s, the authorities hoped that it would sweep away the 'obstacle' that deafness posed to learning the Swedish language.

For some of the teachers, this history of shameful treatment was part of their own lived learning experience, which gave us a powerful insight into their concern. We were astounded to learn that they had been deprived of rights that are protected by the UN Convention on the Rights of the Child and the UN Convention on Human Rights, such as the right to education and the right to have their voice and opinion heard. The knowledge of these injustices made us realize that the context of this project was far more complex than we could have imagined. In spite of the burgeoning success of the pedagogy at Manilla, we had to entertain the possibility of pausing the project to enable these issues to be explored more fully.

Unaware of these past injustices, we had entered an environment where we encountered open, inventive and keen teacher-learners. As teachers became confident with the R2L activities, we learnt that they had spontaneously begun using the strategies to also teach STS, and were finding them very supportive of students' development in their first language. In particular, they reported that their newfound knowledge of genres and the stages and phases of texts had direct relevance to effective visual–spatial communication in STS. Already in the primary school years, teachers were able to introduce R2L meta-language. For example, the names of stages and phases of stories could be introduced when they were telling stories in STS. This then enabled them to talk about how both STS and Swedish texts are structured for the purpose of the communication. In the higher grades, teachers across the curriculum discovered that students benefitted by their modelling of the structure of presentations, which are a requirement for their national tests on performance in STS.

EVALUATING R2L WITH THE TEACHERS

In the final workshop of the 2015–16 professional development program, the teachers were asked to anonymously answer a questionnaire about their teaching experiences during the implementation of R2L. The teacher responses allayed our initial doubts about introducing R2L in this unfamiliar context. The new R2L pedagogy had clearly provided them with more effective tools than previously to support their students' literacy development. Every single respondent reported that R2L had given them more teaching strategies to use to support students' reading development. About half stated that they had already observed beneficial or highly beneficial effects of the pedagogy on student learning which they attributed to the changed teaching practices.

At the commencement of the professional development, the teachers at Manilla School, like many other teachers in Sweden, had not been able to articulate what their approaches to teaching literacy actually were. In the final questionnaire, however, they had become far more conscious of their pedagogy and reported retrospectively on their previous teaching approaches. They were able to describe the typical approach to reading by first explaining words and concepts they thought would be difficult for students. They would then 'read' the text by translating into STS, and this 'reading' would be followed by students answering comprehension questions. For young learners, a typical approach had been to look at pictures and try to predict what the text would be about, followed by 'reading' of picture books by translating into STS. These of course are typical activities in mainstream schools, with the difference of signing the text in STS instead of reading aloud. It was not difficult to see why these translating activities were ineffective for learning to read in Swedish. When it came to the writing lessons, the most common activities had previously been decontextualized exercises focusing on the lower levels of language – spelling, grammar and word comprehension. Some teachers had also taught rules of text structure, while others used 'mind maps' and 'process writing' that did not address text structure. Every single teacher reported that R2L writing activities had been helpful in teaching writing.

With respect to students' engagement, many teachers felt that their struggling students benefited most from the R2L strategies, which had effectively engaged students who were usually not so motivated or committed to participating in learning. Half of the teachers said there was increased commitment among the students while about 80% found that the students' self-confidence had increased as they started using R2L. They also said that their students also became more persistent and focused on school assignments compared to before. On the other hand, 45% said that some of the high-achieving students had sometimes felt impatient because it took too long to work through the R2L teaching sequence. Nonetheless, the teachers also recognized that the pace of lessons was slow because they themselves were not yet fluent in the new teaching practices.

In response to a question of whether the students' deafness or hearing loss had created difficulties in implementing the R2L strategies, several teachers pointed to the need for students to constantly shift focus from the teacher signing to the written text:

- Not being able to talk [sign] while I write on the board. It takes longer and more energy than when writing with hearing students.
- Joint reading of the text can be problematic sometimes, I think. Should I use STS or 'sign the Swedish as it is on the page'? Sometimes it is difficult to ask questions about the text, as the students have to move their eyes between me and the text. Students can then lose focus and get lost or find it difficult.
- The students need to see the text at the same time as I 'talk' about it in sign language.

The general issue of translanguaging was also raised by some:

- A challenge to teach English through STS, written Swedish and 'signing Swedish as it is on the page'. Then when we add spoken English and written English and also Swedish combined with STS... puhhh! Sometimes my head spins when I do all this at the same time.

Nevertheless, the teachers proved to be very resourceful and inventive in resolving these issues. Some responses focused on teaching sequences:

- With extra-long preparation before reading, R2L has showed me how to prepare the students well before reading.
- I have talked about the general content in STS, I have elaborated the knowledge by talking about the paragraphs – in STS. Then we read together, and I asked typical R2L questions so that everyone could participate.

Others focused on using the smartboard to guide students:

- When we highlight words, students have the opportunity to look at the text they have in front of them and also on the smartboard. It's so easy to get lost otherwise.
- I had the text on the smartboard, and I sign and point where in the text I am. This is so that students can see the text both in STS and in Swedish.

The final question in the survey asked 'To what extent do you think the R2L strategies help deaf students and students with hearing impairment to meet the knowledge requirements in the curriculum?' As Figure 7.5 shows, 100% thought that R2L was helpful and 92% thought R2L strategies could help to a high degree.

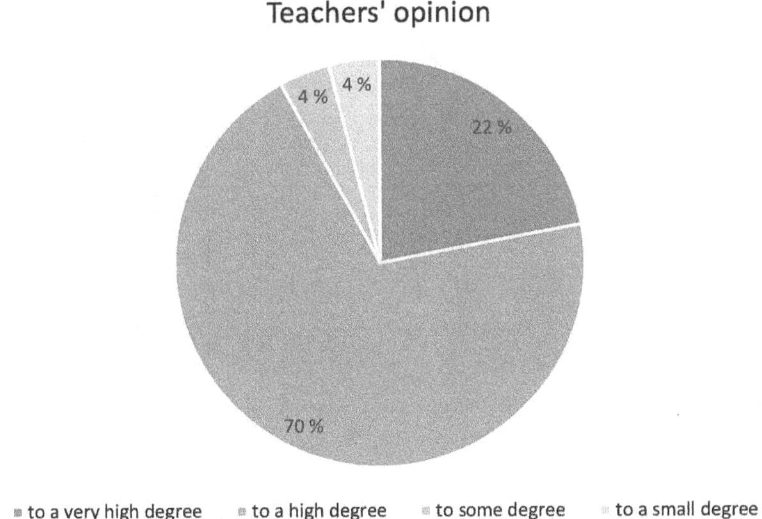

Figure 7.5. R2L strategies could help meet the knowledge requirements in the curriculum

One teacher put it this way:

> R2L is an explicit way to guide students into the initially insipid and abstract text. R2L teaching helps them to see structures that make texts easier to recognize and thus understand. Which in turn makes it easier for them to write different types of texts themselves.

INDEPENDENT PRACTICE OF R2L TEACHING

Following this first project, it was time for the Manilla School to test its wings by planning and implementing R2L teaching on its own. In order for the teachers to continue to be supported, a senior teacher, Åsa Helmerson, was given the task of leading the ongoing R2L development at the school, with my support. Åsa organized regular workshops and planning meetings with her fellow teachers and also invited them to her classroom to observe her R2L teaching. She and I met at regular intervals to jointly develop an action plan for a whole-school approach to R2L. On occasion, Claire and I provided workshops for teachers who were new to the school as well as further workshops for teachers already trained in R2L to revise the pedagogy and deepen their understandings in order to support their cross-curricular planning and whole-school implementation.

Figure 7.6. R2L demonstration lessons in Svenskt teckenspråk with Åsa Helmerson

The school was subsequently contacted by the National Agency for Education, seeking a contribution from a special school about strategies for improving reading. When they learnt about the school's work with R2L, a series of demonstration lessons were filmed with Åsa teaching and explaining the activities, as shown in Figure 7.6. This was an affirmation of the R2L work done by all the Manilla teachers and provided evidence of the innovative contribution they could make to the special education community. The edited demonstration lessons can be seen on the Agency's learning portal:

https://larportalen.skolverket.se/#/modul/5-las-skriv/Specialskola/037_tvasprakig-undervisning-teckensprak/del_07/

MANILA SCHOOL = AN R2L SCHOOL

The adoption of R2L throughout the school gave rise to the notion of Manilla School becoming an 'R2L school', for which they sought official certification from Reading to Learn. This certification would see the whole school come together to review and align their guiding policy documents with the philosophy of R2L that was underpinning their current classroom practices. The teachers provided comprehensive documentation of their R2L teaching, including lessons plans with objectives aligned to national curriculum goals, with prepared texts for reading and writing, using appropriate R2L activities. Some teachers also included photos or short films and reflections on the outcomes of their lessons. For the certification process, I revised the lesson plans and provided feedback.

In February 2020, almost five years after the start of the project, the school became certified as an R2L school. The occasion was celebrated with a ceremony in

Figure 7.7. Manilla teachers with R2L certificates

which the school and the teachers who had completed their documentation were presented with certificates, shown in Figure 7.7. Invitations were extended to interested parties from the special education sector and from Stockholm University. There was a congratulatory video message from David Rose, and a recognition from the Principal and Claire and myself of the outstanding work and professionalism shown by the staff in working together to gain this achievement. Several teachers also showed videos of their classroom work with the students. Other key participants were of course our esteemed interpreters, some of whom had become very well known to us, and without whom our participation would not have been possible.

We are in awe of the good will, tenacity and inventiveness that characterized the outstanding achievements of the staff at Manilla School and we wish them all the best in their ongoing efforts to continue to improve the learning of their students.

NOTES

1 Svenskt teckenspråk (STS) is the official name for Swedish Sign Language. The designation of 'Swedish' in the name (STS) is designed to emphasize that sign language is not universal as each country has its own sign language. In the case of English, even though the spoken language is common to many countries there are a number of different sign languages that are not mutually intelligible e.g., British Sign Language (BSL), American Sign Language (ASL), Auslan in Australia, NZSL in New Zealand and SASL in South Africa.

2 The Special School System in Sweden, that Manilla School belongs to, allows students to receive an extra year to complete compulsory education compared to the nine years that hearing students without any special needs receive.

3 Prior to 1981 when Svenskt teckenspråk was recognized as an official language in Sweden, deaf and hearing impaired students were taught via other methods such as Oralism (using speech and lip-reading) and Signed Swedish, *Tecknad Svenska* (see Note 4 below).

4 The teaching practice of 'signing the words as they appear on the page' is a bridging strategy particularly relevant when teaching the linear word order and grammatical elements in written Swedish which may have little or no correspondence with the polysyntactic signs of STS. It is not to be confused with the now obsolete manually coded form of Swedish that used signs of STS for lexical words, supplemented by additional signs for grammatical words and inflectional endings known as Signed Swedish, *Tecknad svenska.* It was developed in the 1970s in the hope of making Swedish more accessible to the deaf, but was later abandoned for being slow and inefficient. It was never a natural form of communication among deaf people. See, Linus Glansholm (1993) *Teckenspråket och de dövas situation, förr och nu*, http://studierummet.blogspot.com/2016/03/specialpedagogik-att-undervisa-dova-och.html

5 Johnston and Schembri (2007) describe such a contrast between the Australian sign language Auslan and English.

6 Fingerspelling is a typical feature of sign languages where hand signs for letters of the alphabet are used to spell out names of people and places for which there is not a sign. Students may use fingerspelling to spell words that they do not yet know the sign for.

REFERENCES

Acevedo, C. (2010). *Will the Implementation of Reading to Learn in Stockholm schools accelerate literacy learning for disadvantaged students and close the achievement gap? A report on school-based action research*, Multilingual Research Institute, Stockholm. https://www.researchgate.net/publication/355160739_Will_the_implementation_of_Reading_to_Learn_in_Stockholm_schools_accelerate_literacy_learning_for_disadvantaged_students_and_close_the_achievement_gap

Acevedo, C. (2014). Reading to Learn: Scaffolding democracy in literacy classrooms in Stockholm. In H. Emery, & N. Moore (Eds.), *Teaching, learning and researching reading in EFL* (pp. 298–320). TESOL Arabia Publication.

Acevedo, C., Coffin, C., Gouveia, C., Lövstedt, A.-C., & Whittaker, R. (2016). Teacher Learning for European Literacy Education (TeL4ELE) 2011- 2013. In H. de Silva Joyce & S. Feez (Eds.), *Theory, research and practice of literacies* (pp. 327–333). Palgrave Macmillan.

Acevedo, C., & Lövstedt, A.-C. (2014). *Teacher Learning for European Literacy Education: Project outputs from Sweden*. Stockholm Education Administration, European Union. https://www.researchgate.net/publication/355160985

Coffin, C., Acevedo, C., & Lövstedt, A.-C. (2013). *Teacher Learning for European Literacy Education (TeL4ELE) final report.* European Union. https://www.researchgate.net/publication/355145686

García, O. (2009). Education, multilingualism and translanguaging in the 21st century. In T. Skutnabb-Kangas, R. Phillipson, A. K. Mohanty & M. Panda (Eds.), *Social justice through multilingual education* (pp. 140–158). Multilingual Matters.

Hendar, O. (2008). *Måluppfyllelse för döva och hörselskadade I skolan: Redovisning av uppdrag enligt regleringsbrev: Slutrapport.* https://www.yumpu.com/sv/document/read/19810548/maluppfyllelse-for-dova-och-horselskadade-i-skolan-barnplantorna

Johnston, T., & Schembri, A. (2007). *Australian Sign Language (Auslan): An introduction to sign language linguistics.* Cambridge University Press.

Rose, D., & Martin, J. R. (2012). *Learning to write, Reading to Learn: genre, knowledge and pedagogy in the 'Sydney School'*, Equinox.

Rose, D., & Martin, J. R. (2013). *Skriva, läsa, lära (Writing, reading, learning).* Hallgren & Fallgren.

Skolverket. (2014). *Grundskolan: Slutbetyg årskurs 9, våren 2014.* https://www.skolverket.se/download/18.6bfaca41169863e6a65b2ac/1553965806561/pdf3316.pdf

ABOUT THE AUTHOR

Ann-Christin Lövstedt is a freelance teacher educator and consultant based in Sweden. She is an experienced secondary school leader and language teacher with a specialization in multicultural education and teaching Swedish as a Second Language. She has worked throughout Europe in primary, secondary and tertiary education in project management and education research roles. She specializes in whole school development and leading teacher professional learning for literacy education using the genre-based pedagogy *Reading to Learn* in schools in Sweden. She is the Chair of Reading for Life, Sweden, and was the project leader for the European Union funded project *Teacher Learning for European Literacy Education (TeL-4ELE)* 2011–2013.

8

Scaffolding a long-term professional development project in a disadvantaged Swedish context

Pernilla Andersson Varga, Annette Mitiche, Jaana Sandberg & Susanne Staf

ABSTRACT

Since 2013 Reading to Learn has been organized as a professional development program by the Centre for School Development (CfSD) in Gothenburg, the second largest city in Sweden. CfSD is a municipal department supporting preschools, primary, secondary and upper secondary schools in the municipality. The chapter describes the adoption of Reading to Learn pedagogy in this large, long-term project in different school settings, the responses of the teachers participating, how their learning challenges were addressed, and the improved results for the students. It puts special emphasis on the continuing support for the R2L teachers provided by the CfSD, as key to this long-term literacy project in the Swedish context.

BACKGROUND

The Gothenburg Reading to Learn Professional Development Program (R2L PD) started in 2013 when the municipality decided to fund a project to improve teaching in eleven comprehensive schools where the academic results were well below expected levels. The National Agency for Education had noted that 20% of the year 9 students in Gothenburg did not manage to qualify for upper secondary school and highlighted the huge disparity in performance between schools from different areas of the city.

In the past three decades, Sweden has gone from having been one of the most homogeneous nations in the world, to having one of the most ethnically diverse populations in Europe. Sweden is now a multilingual society where 28% of the students in compulsory school have a mother tongue other than Swedish (Skolverket, 2019). This change has had a great impact on society as a whole including the education system, which was substantially transformed during the 1990s, when reforms such as a student voucher system and private schools were introduced. The outcome is that students with a low socioeconomic and migrant backgrounds tend to go to municipal schools in disadvantaged suburban areas, whereas more privileged students gather in municipal schools in affluent areas or in private schools. As a result, school segregation has gradually increased (OECD, 2015). During this period, Sweden also lost its former high-ranking position in international surveys like PIRLS and PISA, and now achieves an average rating. The decline in reading literacy is most notable for students with migrant backgrounds, where boys perform at a particularly low level.

Consequently, pedagogic segregation (Hansson & Gustafsson, 2016) has become evident in schools situated in disadvantaged areas where retaining or even attracting highly qualified and experienced teachers has also become a struggle. Hence, the students from disadvantaged backgrounds, who are most dependent on skilled teachers lose out and underachieve. Again, boys seem to be more vulnerable than girls.

The effects of migration, school reforms and pedagogic segregation were increasingly evident in many Gothenburg schools. The results of a 2012 survey of principals and teachers in schools in the city's disadvantaged areas, attributed low achievement to factors linked to the changes in the student population. Firstly, that the majority of the students lacked proficiency in Swedish and, secondly, that this issue was not being adequately addressed by teachers who lacked the teaching strategies necessary to meet the needs of their students.

In these circumstances, the Centre for School Development (CfSD) was given the task of sourcing a powerful teacher professional development program to enhance teachers' ability to teach literacy, particularly to L2 students. We chose Reading to Learn because the pedagogy had been developed with the intention of supporting students from underprivileged backgrounds; and, in contrast to many other types of professional development, it offered a solid theoretical foundation. In the Swedish context, the concept "teaching to improve language and learning" is often used to refer to a kind of smorgasbord of theories and teaching methods such as highlighting subject-specific vocabulary, prioritizing oral student interaction and writing in more or less specific genres etc. What is missing is a systematic approach to embedding literacy in both pre- and in-service education.

The R2L professional development project was also well in tune with current school development principles (Timperley et al., 2007), including formative teaching, data collection and assessment principles that are applicable in most subjects. Thus, we had reasons to believe that the PD would provide teachers with tools for scaffolding their students' learning regardless of the stage of schooling or subject they taught. Importantly, the classroom implementation of the R2L pedagogy would be supported by mentoring from the expert R2L PD providers, Ann-Christin Lövstedt and Claire Acevedo and our team of local literacy specialists at the CfSD.

The R2L project has been carried out under the auspices of the operations manager of the CfSD, Jan Mellgren, who was inspired by the outcomes of the European R2L project TeL4ELE (see Acevedo, Chapter 9 this volume). The R2L project leadership team at the CfSD brought together a group of four experienced educators with a range of skills. Jaana Sandberg, who has a background in cultural and arts education, functioned as the administrative hub of the project. The other three project leaders all have roles as local R2L facilitators. Pernilla Andersson Varga and Susanne Staf are experienced secondary teachers with an ongoing association with the University of Gothenburg where they have completed their doctoral studies. Annette Mitichie also complemented the team with her background in mathematics and science education.

As literacy is essential in all subjects, we decided to start offering the R2L PD to teachers of late primary and secondary level in several subjects, as well as teachers of Swedish and Swedish as a second language. Following an introductory meeting in April 2013, the first R2L PD began in August 2013 with some hundred teachers from eleven schools. Ten of these schools were situated in disadvantaged areas where more than 90% of the students had a migrant background and only a low percentage qualified for upper secondary education. These schools were also characterized by a large proportion of teachers lacking adequate training, and high staff turnover.

THE GOTHENBURG R2L PROFESSIONAL DEVELOPMENT DESIGN

The Gothenburg R2L PD started with a year-long foundation course in 2013–2014. While the main target group was teachers from disadvantaged schools, participants from other schools were welcome, subject to availability of places, and this has continued to be the recruitment principle. So far, CfSD has organized the R2L

PD for nine consecutive years, making it the long-term project it was intended to be. Although the number of teachers has varied between years, some 400 participants have so far completed the course. The majority come from 24 comprehensive schools where teachers representing different subjects have been trained in the pedagogy. An additional 63 teachers from nine upper secondary schools with academic as well as vocational programs have also completed the course. Moreover, the municipal Language Centre (LC), which employs mother tongue teachers who work in more than 70 languages, has sent some 30 teachers to the R2L PD. Since they teach second language learners in many schools in Gothenburg, their participation has been vital for spreading the word about the R2L pedagogy.

The foundation course (see Table 8.1) consists of four two-day workshops led by Ann-Christin and Claire, our external experts who have been with us from the start. Teachers attend during school hours and the workshops are designed to be delivered bilingually in English and Swedish. The participants are introduced to the theoretical background, the pattern of classroom interaction and the genres of schooling, before being guided through the nine strategies in the R2L Pedagogy Cycle (see Rose, Chapter 1 this volume). The teachers work in groups to practice the strategies in readiness for classroom implementation. Besides practical exercises, all workshops include discussions where the participants reflect on the pedagogy.

Table 8.1. Key components of the Gothenburg R2L PD

Period	Year 1 – Foundation course (8 days)	Additional support	Year 2 – Continuation course (4 days)
August – October	Workshop 1 (2 days) Implementation of strategies for whole texts Collection of pre-data	In-school meeting for teachers and principals Workshop on lesson planning	Workshop 1 (1 day) Revision and extension of Year 1 pedagogy
October – December	Workshop 2 (2 days) Implementation of detailed reading and filming	In-school tutoring Principal meetings Assessment workshop Classroom visits on request	Workshop 2 (1 day) Revision and extension of language & pedagogy according to group needs
January – March	Workshop 3 (2 days) Implementation and recording	In-school tutoring Assessment workshop Classroom visits on request	Workshop 3 (1 day) In-depth exploration of specific issues according to teacher needs
April – June	Workshop 4, (2 days) Implementation Collection of post data Evaluation and course report	Local workshops on text assessment Classroom visits on request	Workshop 4 (1 day) Discussion, planning for whole faculty/school implementation

The workshops are based on the R2L teacher learning materials (Rose, 2016), supported by the reference book *Learning to write, reading to learn* (Rose & Martin, 2012) and its Swedish translation *Skriva Läsa Lära* (Rose & Martin, 2013). Extra material such as handouts or digital presentations from the workshops is located on a digital platform together with additional films, links and communication assets that are presented in the first workshop and updated over the course.

Between workshops the participants are expected to try the R2L teaching strategies in at least one class or subject, as their personal teaching experience is used as a starting point for the following workshop. The fact that all course groups include teachers from different schools, subjects and stages has proven to be a good basis for discussions and provided us as facilitators with lots of examples of how R2L can be implemented in different contexts and teaching situations.

In 2014, we also began offering a four-day follow-on course to support teachers in their second year of classroom implementation. The course, which is optional, was introduced in response to teacher requests for further support in delivering the R2L strategies and a deeper understanding of the linguistic aspects of the pedagogy, such as the appraisal system. Apart from a welcome revision of the pedagogy, the supplementary workshops enable the educators to introduce strategies for whole-school implementation of R2L, something which is still rare in the Swedish context.

SCHOOL-BASED MENTORING

In addition to workshops, both the foundation and the continuation course include two mentoring weeks where the local facilitators team up with the educators to provide support on the implementation of the pedagogy. These in-school sessions are held individually or in small groups to ensure that all participants receive scaffolding and feedback on matters such as choosing relevant teaching material, using a specific curriculum genre or even suggestions for classroom management. During the pandemic, the mentoring sessions were conducted online and they proved so successful that this part of the program has continued to be offered online.

The first mentoring visit often focuses on emotional scaffolding to convince the participants of their capability to try new ways of teaching that allow for teaching in the zone of proximal development to scaffold the reading and writing of texts that are well above what their pupils could accomplish on their own. Equally important is to encourage the teachers to resist giving in to the temptation of returning to well-known routines when they experience the challenges that come with applying a new pedagogy. When the participants become familiar with the pedagogy, the mentoring visits include reflective scaffolding where the focus shifts from verbalizing to reflecting on individual strengths and weaknesses in applying the classroom strategies (Hipkiss & Varga, 2018). These reflections serve as a starting point for immediate or long-term changes and become more frequent when the teachers feel comfortable with using the pedagogy.

DATA COLLECTION

To inform and strengthen the R2L PD, the course includes a research element that requires all participants to collect data of the literacy progression of six students over the course of the year: two high achievers, two average achievers and two low achievers. The data includes texts representing two different genres at the beginning and end of the PD, and results from two reading tests representing the same interval. Apart from student data, the participants fill in an online survey about their use of texts and teaching strategies at the beginning and end of the PD, as well as their plans for using the pedagogy after the course. The data is analyzed and presented in an annual report where the educators include suggestions for strengthening the R2L PD further. A summary report covering the years 2013–2020 is also published on the CfSD website (Lövstedt & Acevedo, 2020).

Collecting and assessing data has proved a challenge from the start. To increase the number of participants who submit a complete set of data we organize assessment workshops where teachers practice applying the R2L assessment criteria, which are quite different from criteria normally applied in Swedish schools. It has proven fruitful in encouraging teachers to discuss the assessment criteria (Rose & Martin, 2012, pp. 323–324) with colleagues. The "top down" approach of R2L assessment, starting with the genre instead of focusing on grammar and spelling, often challenges previous assessment routines.

CONTINUOUSLY STRENGTHENING THE R2L PD

Since most of the schools participating in the R2L PD were characterized as "struggling", we anticipated that the PD would be challenging, since low-performing schools tend to get snowed under with initiatives from different sources. Another prediction was that R2L would challenge the prevailing classroom culture where teachers tend to function like facilitators encouraging students to work with assignments at their own level and pace, rather than instructing the whole group.

We knew from research and personal experience that L2 students risk being met by low expectations for academic achievement. Therefore, we have continuously tried to improve the PD to meet the needs of the participants. So, in addition to the workshops and mentoring visits, the CfSD facilitators – Pernilla, Susanne and Annette – each take responsibility for providing 3–5 schools with a range of additional support to strengthen the impact of the project.

Between the first and second workshop we meet with the principals and teachers at our designated schools. We also offer to come for classroom visits and reflection and to participate in lesson planning to scaffold teachers to incorporate the R2L pedagogy into their teaching.

After the second workshop, the principals are invited to a meeting to engage them as our partners in the professional learning of their teachers. The meeting gives us an opportunity to explain and elaborate on the essence of R2L and the importance of regarding the PD as a long-term commitment as well as discussing any questions that the principals may have. Since the principals are expected to monitor the PD continuously, the meeting also includes advice on how to support the teachers.

To support the use of R2L in mathematics, where the technical language requires a deep understanding, regular workshops have been conducted on applying R2L to problem solving. In one mini-project, a secondary teacher and a mother tongue teacher in Pashto collaborated in a six-month project, using *Preparing for Reading, Detailed Reading*, and *Joint Construction* on mathematical problems. At the end of the project the students reported that R2L had provided them with the necessary scaffolding for learning the process of mathematical problem solving.

We have also taken action to recontextualize the R2L PD to the Swedish context, by organizing the CfSD film team to produce instructional films in Swedish. In the films, two experienced R2L teachers display their reasoning when choosing texts, planning detailed reading and implementing the curriculum genres: *Preparing for Reading, Detailed Reading, Notemaking* and *Joint Rewriting* in the classroom (see Rose, Chapter 1 this volume).

THREE EXAMPLES OF PARTICIPATING SCHOOLS

To illustrate the success and challenges of our R2L project over the years, we present three different learning contexts. These include a municipal comprehensive school, an upper secondary municipal school that provides vocational programs, and the Language Centre for L2 students.

The Language Centre

Since Sweden has a strong governmental mandate for multilingualism (SFS 2010, p. 800), all L2 students in compulsory school have the right to mother tongue education, including study support. In Gothenburg this teaching is provided by the municipal Language Centre (LC) where some 300 teachers of more than 70 languages such as Somali, Arabic, Turkish, Italian, Pashto and German teach students their mother tongue as a subject or provide study support. Over the years the principal at the LC has continuously sent teachers to the R2L PD with the purpose of developing the teaching of mother tongue languages. Their participation has also contributed to a stronger teacher identity.

The comprehensive: Spruce School

The Spruce School could be described as a typical, struggling comprehensive school situated in a disadvantaged area in Gothenburg, where a vast majority of the students have migrant backgrounds. Due to school reforms like the school voucher system[1] the school has continuously experienced decreasing numbers of students.

Spruce School has been sending teachers to the R2L PD every year since its initiation in 2013, and teachers from most subject areas have participated. During the period 2016–2018 the local facilitators gave extra support to teachers who had participated in the PD in previous years in various group constellations. For example, the 7–9 STEM teachers meet once a month to collegially plan how to make disciplinary literacy more visible and tangible for the students.

One challenge was to let go of previous teaching habits such as mainly presenting subject content through PowerPoints and films. Another challenge was to use R2L to teach from texts in science course books that teachers had been reluctant to use because of perceived simplifications and factual errors. For STEM teachers this is often an excuse for not using textbooks at all to teach scientific reading and writing. In the planning meetings, they were supported to carefully examine and modify texts to teach appropriate information. Planned and executed classroom activities were then evaluated by the group.

Another example was a weekly cross-curricular lesson, in which a Swedish teacher and a science teacher worked collaboratively to plan and teach science using R2L pedagogy. This project was recorded in a film produced by CfSD and displayed on our website (https://lartorget.goteborg.se/kategori/tema/sprakutveckling/reading-to-learn/). The teachers quickly noticed the effects of the pedagogy, particularly when it came to the students' writing competence along with their ability to reason. Their reading comprehension also improved as well as their ability to cooperate. The students also appreciated the R2L pedagogy, one explaining that "Everybody shows

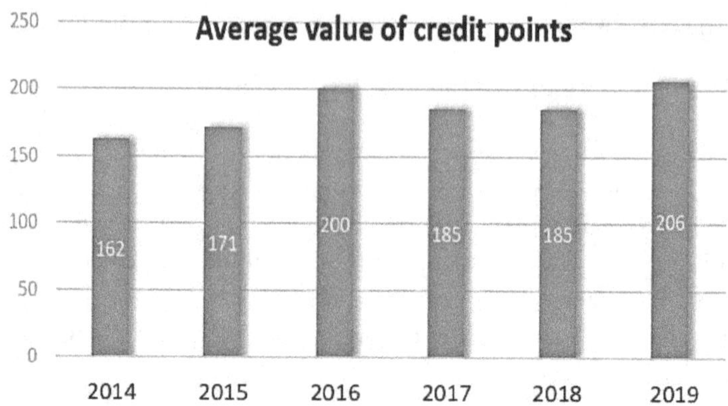

Figure 8.1. Improvement in student achievement at Spruce School in credit points since R2L PD 2014–2019

that they try and that they learn. First, we write a text once all together in class, and then it is easier to write on your own."

The R2L PD appears to have had an overall positive effect on student achievement. This is represented in the graph in Figure 8.1 by the steady increase in the average credit points on leaving school in year 9 from 162 in 2014, to 206 in 2019. When leaving secondary school after Year 9, the maximum is 320 credit points. Thus, in five years, the student average rose from a bare pass to a very creditable one.

Despite the relative success of the R2L PD at the Spruce School, some challenges remain. One is to ensure that all teachers regularly implement the R2L pedagogy. Adopting the R2L interaction pattern in the classroom, involving all students by using preparations to pose well-prepared questions has been an ongoing challenge for some teachers.

The upper secondary: Birch School

While the R2L PD has had no trouble in recruiting teachers from schools that focus on the compulsory years of schooling, far fewer upper secondary schools have shown interest, and teachers can often feel that literacy is not a priority at this stage of schooling. So, when we received a general request for a reading project from the Birch School, we knew we would need to design a bespoke learning pathway for the teachers if they were to benefit from the project. This initial request eventually turned into a three-year-long period of developing the teaching of literacy (Figure 8.2).

The Birch School is a municipal upper secondary school with 400 students from different parts of the city, many of whom are second language learners. A majority of the students attend a three-year program to qualify for vocations such as

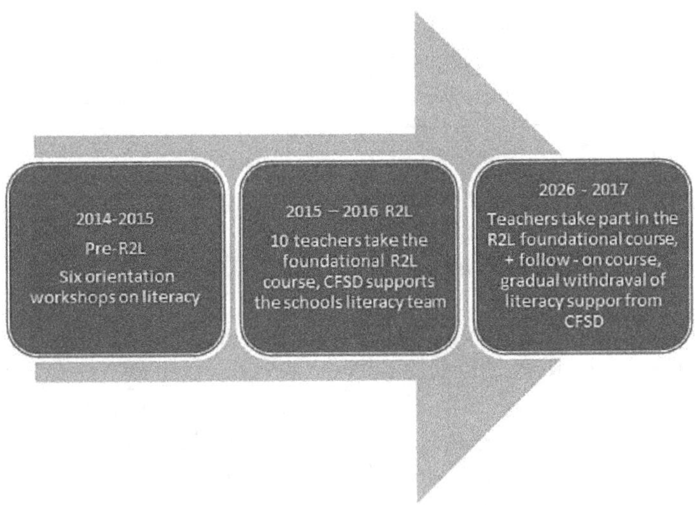

Figure 8.2. Birch School R2L journey

hairdressing, hospitality or childcare, but all vocational programs include academic subjects such as history, civics and natural science. The school also offers programs for students who need to complete their compulsory school diploma and programs for students with diagnoses such as Asperger's syndrome. Thus, many students need qualified teachers who can scaffold their learning by explicitly teaching reading and writing.

We began designing their project in conjunction with the principal and the three lead teachers in 2014, following their request for PD. We decided that the goal for the first year would be to build shared understandings about literacy through a series of workshops on the teaching of texts in all subjects. In the second year, the project continued when ten of the teachers, representing both vocational and academic subjects, attended the R2L foundation course provided by Ann-Christin and Claire. An important factor that led to the success of this project was that the school set aside 2.5 hours per month for teacher team meetings to support the classroom implementation of R2L. The meetings were facilitated by the lead teachers and coordinated with support from the CfSD literacy team. In the third year, the teachers from the Birch School took part in the R2L continuation course while a new group of teachers attended the foundation course. At the school the monthly meetings in peer groups continued, but the meetings between the lead teachers and CfSD team were less frequent during the third year.

In sum, the three-year-long project resulted in positive outcomes in terms of peer learning and cooperation. The fact that the project grew step by step allowed the Birch School to build a solid structure for peer learning which greatly enhanced the quality of their participation in the R2L PD. The principal and lead teachers made the project possible by keeping momentum in close cooperation with the team at CfSD. According to the principal, the participation in the R2L PD resulted in a much stronger focus on the content and quality of teaching, which continues to be present in classrooms and professional conversations.

DISSEMINATING THE SUCCESS OF THE R2L PD

During the nine years that CfSD has been conducting R2L PD, news about it has generated external interest. The R2L PD has been promoted with articles, films and blog posts on our website and local mini-conferences have been organized, where teachers applying the R2L pedagogy have met and shared experiences. Teachers have also participated in national and international conferences giving presentations on how they apply the R2L pedagogy.

One of the private International English schools in Gothenburg has started to send teachers to the R2L PD. Their ambition is that all teachers in Swedish, Swedish as a second language, English, social sciences and natural sciences will take the R2L PD and they have already started to build a R2L infrastructure in their school where mentors support colleagues in applying the pedagogy.

The R2L PD has also attracted the attention of some of our Nordic colleagues. Teacher training students and teachers from Copenhagen, Denmark, have paid visits to CfSD, wanting to learn more about how the R2L PD has been organized. After visiting CfSD in Gothenburg, representatives from the department for adult education in Stavanger, Norway have now undertaken a similar R2L PDP.

In addition to our roles as local R2L facilitators at CfSD, we are now providing lectures and workshops on R2L at the University of Gothenburg, where the teacher training program for the subject of Swedish in secondary and upper secondary school has incorporated R2L in one of their courses. R2L has also been introduced in the Bridge Building teacher training program at Gothenburg university – a fast track program for people with academic qualifications in STEM subjects who want to swap careers and go into teaching.

RESEARCHING THE R2L PD

In 2015 we started to research the R2L PD in cooperation with Anna Maria Hipkiss at Gothenburg University. Various kinds of data have been collected and analyzed, using Legitimation Code Theory (LCT). Research on the in-school tutoring sessions was reported by Hipkiss and Varga (2018). The analyses reveal that the experts play an important role in supporting teachers in both year 1 and year 2 of the R2L PD. The year 1 teachers are much more dependent upon the R2L artifacts such as the illustration of the R2L Pedagogy Cycle and the Map of Genres if they are to discuss the pedagogy. During year 2, the teachers seem more confident, and the expert role becomes more of a supportive and confirming one. Year 2 teachers use a growing number of concepts from the R2L metalanguage but also include more of a general literacy metalanguage, suggesting that both types of metalanguage influence one another, making the teachers more aware and competent in explicitly teaching disciplinary literacy.

An ongoing study by Anna Maria, Pernilla and Susanne focuses on R2L pedagogy in chemistry classes in a middle school classroom, particularly how the teacher elaborates on certain words and concepts in *Detailed Reading*. Analyses of textbook extracts that are used as model texts and students' independently written texts are also included in the study.

AFTER NINE YEARS OF THE GOTHENBURG R2L PD – WHAT HAVE WE LEARNT?

We are happy and proud to state that R2L has become the long-term PD it was intended to be, and some 400 teachers have now completed the course. In accordance with our original intentions, most of the participants represent comprehensive schools where teachers from many different subjects now apply the pedagogy. Since Sweden received large numbers of teenage migrants during 2015–16, an additional 60 upper secondary teachers have also completed the R2L PD, enabling them to improve their teaching of literacy for students who have limited time for completing their studies. In addition, the participation of the mother tongue teachers at the Language Centre has made them familiar with the R2L pedagogy and consequently making them better prepared to support the L2 students they teach.

The teacher data that has been collected for eight years reflects that the degree of support provided by the R2L Pedagogy Cycle which allows the use of more advanced texts where the content is richer and the language more subject specific. Most participants also report on being much more selective in their choice of texts, a result worth noticing since teachers who lack efficient literacy teaching strategies tend to retreat to texts where both content and language is much simplified. As Sweden is often criticized in both national and international surveys about classroom management, it interesting that an important positive side effect of R2L is that it helps teachers to improve classroom organization by keeping students focused, attentive and on task.

Most importantly, the R2L pedagogy has a positive effect on student learning, particularly for low achievers, who can take a more active part in learning activities. This contributes to a more inclusive classroom climate where students learn to trust each other and cooperate, rather than compete for the teacher's attention, which in turn changes the classroom dynamics in a positive direction.

The student text data confirms that the R2L pedagogy decreases the gap between high and low achieving students, which, if not addressed, keeps widening as the students move into higher year levels. As more lesson time is spent on shared reading and writing, fewer texts are just being addressed as homework without further preparation. The introduction and development of a shared metalanguage makes both teachers and students more aware of language and text structure.

The improvement in literacy is visible in students' writing before and after being exposed to the pedagogy. The following example illustrates how a middle school student improved her writing of argumentative texts during two terms of R2L. In the pretext, produced before the student had been exposed to the R2L pedagogy, she argues about the issue of pocket money:

> I WANT more weekly pocket money!
>
> I am a girl aged 11 years and my name is Rose and I WANT monthly pocket money! I want monthly pocket money because then I can buy things and earn money to be able to go on a trip with my mates and I also would like to give money to those who are por [misspelt in Swedish] and learn to take care of money and NOT waste it instantly/directly. And giv [misspelt in Swedish] me monthly pocket money then I give to the poor a lot of money.

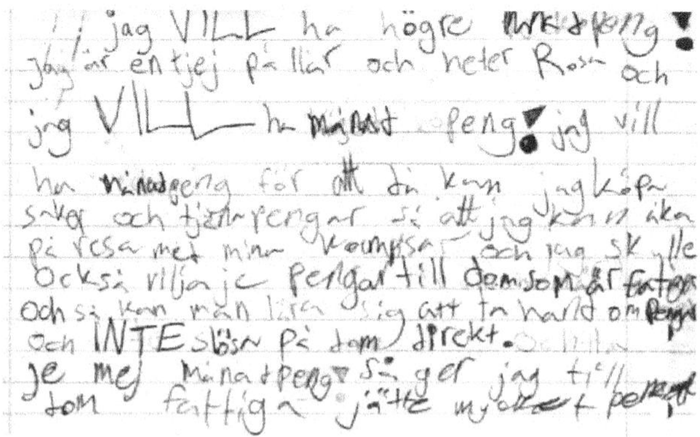

jag VILL ha högre [illegible]peng!
jag är en tjej på 11år och heter Rose och
jag VILL ha [illegible] peng! jag vill
ha [illegible]peng för att då kan jag köpa
saker och tjäna pengar så att jag kan åka
på resa med mina kompisar och jag skulle
också vilja ge pengar till dem som är [illegible]
och så kan man lära sig att ta vård om [illegible]
och INTE slösa på dom direkt.
ge mej månadpeng så ger jag till
dom fattiga jätte mycket [illegible]

Figure 8.3. Argumentative writing before R2L

In the post text, which was written after eight months of the pedagogy, the same student argues about coal energy:

Stop the use of coal fired power

Coal fired power is not good for the environment as it emits carbon dioxide and therefore I think we should not use as much coal for energy.

The biggest problem is the carbon dioxide (CO_2) which is formed during the combustion of the coal. Research is being done to reduce the emission of carbon dioxide worldwide, but the methods are very expensive. Another problem with coal fired power is that coalmining has a big impact on farming and the nature. The coal is also something that will run out.

To sum up I think that although coal is one of the cheapest energy sources it is a big environmental culprit. Firstly, the smoke emitted is polluted with hazardous substances such as sulfur dioxide. Secondly it affects the greenhouse effect since large quantities of carbon dioxide is released into the atmosphere.

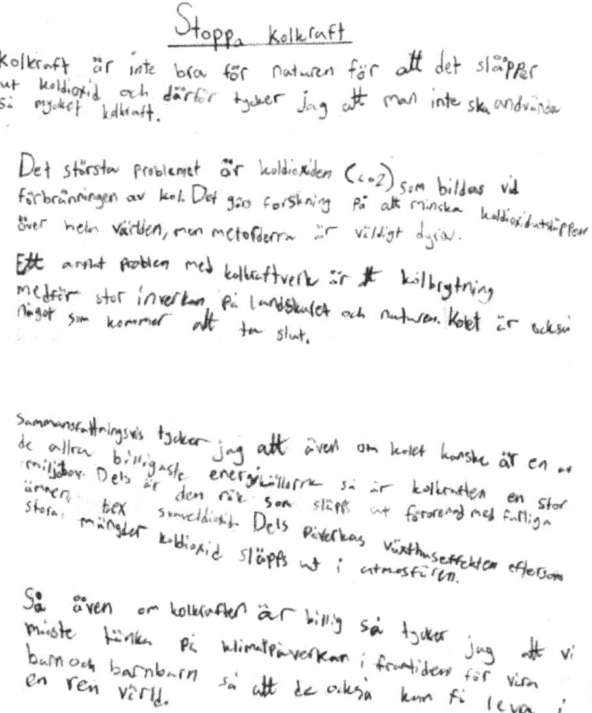

Figure 8.4. Argumentative writing after two terms of R2L

> So even if coal fired power is cheap I think we must think about the climate impact in the future so that our children and grandchildren also can have the right to live in a clean world.

The two texts illustrate the student's writing development in several respects. Both texts are clearly argumentative but where the pretext concerns personal matters (pocket money) and the arguments are based on personal feelings, the post text draws on typical school knowledge that requires subject-specific vocabulary. The post text also shows a better overall knowledge of the genre. For example, the pretext introduces the topic in the heading, in comparison with the post text where the thesis is repeated in the first paragraph and followed by a scientific argument. Another improvement can be seen in the argumentation. In the pretext the student gives several reasons for why she needs more pocket money, but the arguments are not elaborated and the link between monthly payments and learning to care for money remains implicit. In contrast, the post text has a clear structure with separate paragraphs where the arguments are presented and elaborated, and a number of subject specific concepts are used, even though there still is room for improvement. Finally, the writing in the post text is much more accurate than in the pretext, where the punctuation and spelling as well as the use of capital letters in words like WILL and NOT, markers of orality, indicate that the student lacks knowledge about more powerful writing strategies.

As facilitators of the R2L PD it has become evident to us that it can be very challenging for teachers to adopt a pedagogy that requires changing their previous teaching strategies, and adopting the new pattern of classroom interaction seems to be particularly hard. Some teachers also find planning and implementing the R2L pedagogy time-consuming, even though its benefits include less time spent on repairing mistakes and commenting on poorly written texts. Secondary teachers often claim they have difficulties finding time for strategies such as *Joint Construction* or *Joint Rewriting*. A recurring tendency in teacher data is that the reading strategies are used more often than the strategies for writing, which is quite interesting as earlier versions of genre pedagogy have a greater focus on writing. It seems as if the R2L Pedagogy Cycle privileges reading as the basis for developing literacy.

A key factor for the success of the R2L PD is adequate support provided to teachers by their schools.

We find examples of both categories among the schools that have participated in the R2LPD over the years. We have also noticed that struggling schools tend to engage in many different development projects, with sometimes conflicting goals. It is therefore important that we continue to strengthen the principals' understanding of organizing and monitoring the R2L PD.

Table 8.2. Effective and ineffective school support for R2L PD

Effective school support	**Ineffective school support**
Principals communicating distinct expectations on the effect of PD. When teachers participate in PD, they are expected to change their teaching strategies	Principals communicating ambiguous and sometimes low expectations for professional development
Stronger framing. New pedagogies on the schedule and all teachers are expected to cooperate with at least one colleague to learn and implement the new pedagogy	Weak framing. Teachers can apply new pedagogies if/when they choose
Senior teachers meet junior teachers regularly to support and monitor teaching according to the new pedagogy	Lack of structured leadership, scaffolding or monitoring of the new pedagogy and its effect
No discussion about lack of time	Teachers communicate lack of time to prepare for and apply new pedagogies

CONCLUSION

Since 2010, Swedish government policy stipulates that school education should be based on a scientific basis and proven experience. R2L fulfills these criteria as the pedagogy is grounded in established theories, and our R2L PD project comprises a scientifically based design with pre- and post-tests.

We have learnt that it takes quite a long time to develop a deep understanding of R2L and that the R2L PD that we have organized is more demanding in comparison with much of the current in-service training in Sweden. The R2L PD is in line with the Timperley et al. (2007) model of professional learning designed to create professional knowledge, as it challenges teachers' underpinning beliefs about the purpose of education, their personal theories of action and their professional identity. The teachers who take R2L pedagogy on board find the R2L PD extremely rewarding as it makes such a difference when it comes to improving students' literacy competence and attainment results, while also enhancing their own notion of professionalism.

A most poignant appreciation of the R2L pedagogy was given by a special education teacher unfamiliar with R2L. After having visited a R2L lesson she gave the following reflective feedback on the pedagogy. According to her, it:

- promotes cross curricular learning and increases content knowledge and understanding e.g., through detailed reading;
- includes cross curricular repetition opportunities which many of the students need;
- provides step by step models of how to read, extract information and express ideas on paper etc.;

- helps students to carry out activities where they follow each step independently, at their level and their speed, e.g., 1. Highlight key words, 2. Write on mini whiteboards etc.;
- promotes inclusive teaching practices which are critical for the self-confidence of all learners, struggling students as well as high achievers; and
- provides students with the foundations they need to become confident communicators and succeed in all academic subjects.

We know that R2L enables teachers to democratize the classroom by affording students equal opportunities to participate in challenging reading and writing activities. Developing student literacy competence is a core task for all teachers; and, as we all know, a high level of literacy competence is a prerequisite for academic success. Having experienced the effects that the R2L pedagogy has on student learning and the empowerment it gives teachers we would like to see R2L being articulated and made part of the curriculum in all teacher training programs. A standard comment from recently trained teachers who participate in the R2L PD is "Why didn't we learn this during our pre-service training?"

NOTE

1 Sweden adopted a nationwide universal voucher program in 1992 as part of a series of reforms designed to give more control over education to towns and schools. Families can choose any school, public or private: Taxpayer money follows the student. This voucher system has led to a growth in mostly for-profit, private schools, also called "free schools".

REFERENCES

Hansson, Å., & Gustafsson, J. (2016). Pedagogisk segregation: Lärarkompetens i den svenska grundskolan ur ett likvärdighetsperspektiv. *Pedagogisk Forskning i Sverige, 21*(1–2) 1401–6788.

Hipkiss, A. M., & Varga, P. A. (2018). Spotlighting pedagogic metalanguage in Reading to Learn – How teachers build legitimate knowledge during tutorial sessions. *Linguistics and Education, 47*, 93–104. https://doi.org/10.1016/j.linged.2018.08.002

Lövstedt, A.-C., & Acevedo, C. (2020). R2L: Sammanfattande projektrapport 2013–2020. https://goteborg.se/wps/wcm/connect/d1a91de6-1862-4242-853f-d7f5772f21e6/R2L-rapport_2013-2020.pdf?MOD=AJPERES

OECD. (2015). *Education at a Glance 2015: OECD Indicators [Elektronisk resurs]*. OECD Publications Centre.

Rose, D. (2016). *Reading to Learn: Accelerating learning and closing the gap (2016 Edition)*. Reading to Learn. http://www.readingtolearn.com.au

Rose, D., & Martin, J. R. (2012). *Learning to write, reading to learn: Genre, knowledge and pedagogy in the Sydney school.* Equinox.
Rose, D., & Martin, J. (2013). *Skriva, läsa, lära.* Hallgren & Fallgren.
SFS Skollag. (2010). Utbildningsdepartementet. https://www.riksdagen.se/sv/dokument-lagar/dokument/svensk-forfattningssamling/skollag-2010800_sfs-2010-800
Skolverket. (2019). Elever och skolenheter i grundskolan läsåret 2018/2019. https://www.skolverket.se/download/18.6bfaca41169863e6a65e7b1/1554323705043/pdf4060.pdf
Timperley, H., Wilson, A., Barrar, H., & Fung, I. (2007). *Teacher professional learning and development: Best evidence synthesis iteration (BES),* New Zealand Ministry of Education.

ABOUT THE AUTHORS

Pernilla Andersson Varga is a teacher of Swedish, Swedish as a second language and English, and holds a PhD in Swedish didactics. She is Senior Lecturer at the Centre for School Development, the city of Gothenburg, where she leads PDPs aiming at strengthening the teaching of literacy. She is also Adjunct Senior Lecturer at the Department of Pedagogical, Curricular and Professional Studies, University of Gothenburg. Her current research concerns issues of equity, genre pedagogy and teachers' metalanguage.

Annette Mitiche is a teacher of science and mathematics. She works as a Development Manager at the Centre for School Development, the city of Gothenburg, where she leads PDPs aiming at strengthening the teaching of literacy. She is currently studying for a PhD at the University of Gothenburg.

Jaana Sandberg has a background in Educational Theatre and Preschool teaching. She is a Development Manager at the Centre for School Development, Gothenburg, where she leads PDPs aiming at strengthening the city schools' teaching for newly arrived pupils and coordination of the R2L Program in Gothenburg.

Susanne Staf is a teacher of Swedish, Swedish as a second language, English and Religion and holds a PhD in Swedish didactics. She works as a Senior Lecturer at the Centre for School Development, the City of Gothenburg, where she leads PDPs aiming at strengthening the teaching of literacy. She is also Adjunct Senior Lecturer at the Department of Pedagogical, Curricular and Professional studies, University of Gothenburg. Her current research includes issues of subject-specific literacy in the social science subjects and the implementation of genre pedagogy.

9

A story of international cooperation: Teacher Learning for European Literacy Education (TeL4ELE)

Claire Acevedo

ABSTRACT

This chapter recounts an ambitious international teacher learning project to develop expertise in Reading to Learn (R2L) pedagogy amongst literacy educators in five European countries, in conjunction with Australia. The project was funded by the European Union from 2011 and 2013. A decade later, many of the chapters in this volume attest to the ongoing impact that this project has had within and beyond Europe (see Lövstedt, Chapter 7; Andersson Varga, et al., Chapter 8; Whittaker, et al., Chapter 10; Gouveia, et al., Chapter 11). The ultimate aim of the project was to improve learning outcomes for students in each country with a focus on educationally disadvantaged students. Groups of key educators from each country were supported to develop expertise in R2L before using it to train classroom teachers in the pedagogy in their national languages. The project evaluation found that teachers responded positively to the new pedagogy and showed improved learning outcomes for all students, with the greatest gains being made by the most disadvantaged learners (Coffin, 2013). This chapter provides insights into the challenges of organizing a large scale, multilayered, multilingual project in different educational cultures, while highlighting the ultimate success achieved by all the participants and the ongoing impact of the learning in Europe.

BACKGROUND TO THE TEL4ELE PROJECT

The catalyst for this international project was the improved literacy outcomes achieved by a pilot Reading to Learn project in Stockholm, led by Ann-Christin Lövstedt and myself, on behalf of the Stockholm Education Administration (Acevedo, 2010, 2014). This project followed an international literacy conference that Ann-Christin had organized in Stockholm in 2007, to learn more about pedagogical methods that would support the academic needs of Sweden's growing linguistically and socially diverse population. The conference brought together key stakeholders in education in Sweden and Denmark. Invited international speakers included key figures in genre pedagogy from Australia, Jim Martin, David Rose and John Polias. Following my relocation to the UK from Australia in 2008, Ann-Christin asked me to work with her on a Swedish pilot project. I had been manager of large teacher professional learning (PL) projects in Australia, including a successful R2L middle years literacy project at the Catholic Education Office in Melbourne with David Rose (Acevedo & Rose, 2007; Culican, 2005, Chapter 3 this volume; Rose & Acevedo, 2006). Following the positive outcomes of the Stockholm R2L pilot, the Education Administration invited me to continue the professional development in Stockholm.

ORGANIZING THE TEL4ELE PROJECT

The idea of seeking European Union support to expand on this success initially came from Ann-Christin. We undertook the EU application (European Commission, 2011) from Stockholm, knowing David and Jim were supportive of the European R2L work and that we already had a firm commitment from our Danish colleagues. Nonetheless, the task of organizing a Europe-wide project with participants from several different countries in multiple languages was an extremely ambitious challenge. It required the development of a network of collaborators in what was, for me, an unfamiliar international environment.

Although, applying for EU funding (as a 'Comenius Multilateral' project) was complex, our objectives of improving literacy and learning outcomes, particularly for disadvantaged learners, via the implementation of an innovative pedagogy, held the promise of findings that would be of significant interest to European educators.

EU funding required a consortium of EU partner countries to jointly develop an application. So we set about contacting possible partners in universities and education organizations around Europe. We focused on organizations that had been working with Systemic Functional Linguistics (SFL) and had an interest in learning more about genre-based pedagogy for reading and writing. The final list of consortium partners for our project application consisted of Sweden, Denmark, Scotland,

Spain and Portugal, with Australia as a 'third country', or non-European participant. Partner organizations included:

- Stockholm Education Administration, Sweden
- National Centre for Reading, Copenhagen, Denmark
- Strathclyde University, Glasgow, Scotland
- Institute of Theoretical and Computational Linguistics, Lisbon, Portugal
- Universidad Autónoma, Madrid, Spain
- University of Sydney, Australia.

All the participating countries had strong reasons to embark on an endeavour to improve literacy as the basis for educational success. However, in spite of our zeal, we were not successful with our first application. We didn't give up, though, but instead took it as a catalyst to develop closer links between the partner organizations. The project leaders from the partner countries collaborated with renewed energy on a second application for the 2011–13 funding period. Ann-Christin and I had already been in meetings with Ruth Mulvad and Klara Korsgaard, from the National Centre for Reading in Copenhagen. So Carlos Gouveia, the project leader in Portugal, hosted a two-day meeting in Lisbon which I attended along with Rachel Whittaker the project leader from Spain. This meeting allowed for in-depth discussion and the development of a new and more dynamic project model that responded flexibly to the learning needs of the experienced educators who would train teachers in R2L across Europe, while also fulfilling the EU criteria. This time we were successful and TeL4ELE got going with the following design and objectives.

THE PROJECT MODEL

The project was to be carried out in two phases, first to train teacher educators (5–7 from each partner country), who would then begin training classroom teachers. In Phase 1 (2011–12), the key educators would learn in the first instance from the participating experts from Australia – Jim Martin and David Rose – during the five, two-day international project meeting workshops, one in each country.

The objectives of Phase 1 (2011–2012) were to:

- build shared knowledge about genre-based literacy pedagogy and the Reading to Learn approach;
- develop national networks of learning partners including teacher education institutions, research organizations, schools, teacher associations and other bodies;
- gather data and produce reports on national curricula, student literacy achievement and key national approaches to literacy education;

- produce learning materials that could be used for teacher training in Phase 2; and
- identify a set of teachers to participate in the school-based implementation in the second phase.

Objectives for Phase 2 (2012–13) were:

- to trial the approach with any necessary adaptations in schools in each national language;
- for each key educator to train at least two classroom practitioners of upper primary and junior to middle secondary students to implement the new pedagogy and support them as they progressively trialed it in the classroom; and
- to collect data for evaluation, namely pre and post intervention reading test scores and assessed writing tasks.

Figure 9.1 uses the imagery of cogs to signify both the reciprocal nature of the project learning in the international meetings as well as the 'mobility' element of the project as the educators travelled to each country over the two-year project period.

The reciprocal learning activities at an international level were mirrored by reciprocal learning events at a national level. The national learning networks of teachers, that were developed and led by the project partners, also met four times during the course of the project for one or two-day meetings. These meetings were jointly facilitated by the national leaders, together with Ann-Christin and myself as the international project leaders from the Stockholm Education Administration. Figure 9.2 illustrates the integrated nature of the international and national layers of learning in the overall project model.

Figure 9.1. Model of international learning

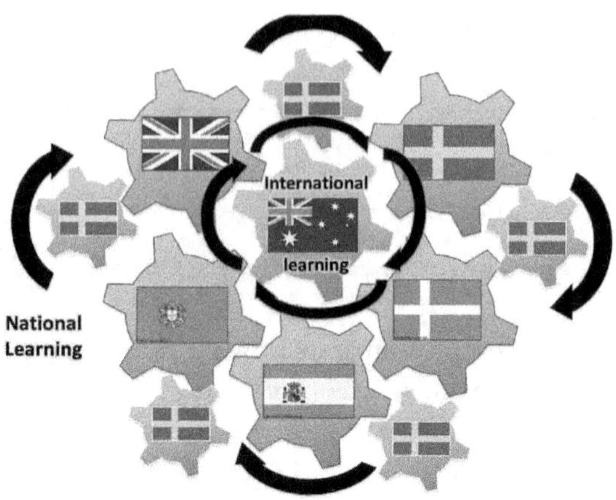

Figure 9.2. National and international learning model

SCAFFOLDING LEARNING: THE TEL4ELE PROJECT MODEL IN ACTION

As we enacted the project model, I came to understand the true impact of the 'mobility' aspect of the project which I had underestimated when making the first unsuccessful application for funding. By travelling to each of the five countries and experiencing the hospitality of each national team as they took pride in organizing social and cultural activities and showcasing their schools, we developed new understandings about the varied educational landscapes. This created tolerance for divergent responses to the pedagogy and built group cohesion as we expanded our notions of how genre-based literacy pedagogy could be implemented flexibly to account for different national contexts.

To respond to the EU aims of fomenting understanding and collaboration between its countries, we established national learning and dissemination networks in each country. This enabled the international project leaders to scaffold the ongoing learning of the educators beyond the international learning meetings while simultaneously drawing on their expertise as knowledgeable leaders in their own fields and national contexts. The dissemination element of the networks operated differently in each country according to local circumstances, but the overall aim was to draw in major stakeholders in literacy education, as well as groups of teachers, some of whom would be trained to implement the R2L pedagogy in their classrooms. This created dynamic literacy learning forums throughout Europe, by enabling the key educators to disseminate their developing expertise in the R2L pedagogy to the wider education community. In Phase 2 of the project, the school-based implementation then provided data for evaluating the efficacy of the pedagogy, while also providing materials for future exploitation.

While the participation of all five partner countries was motivated by the common desire to provide teachers with effective strategies to improve student literacy and learning, each country was also participating in the TeL4ELE project in response to particular local needs. The hope of the consortium partners was that the flexible nature of the SFL-based R2L pedagogy would enable the educators and teachers to apply their learning efficaciously to the diverse needs of their learners in varied contexts to address the shared goal of improving student literacy and learning for all students.

The TeL4ELE project was found by the independent evaluator to be innovative in the way it conceptualized and implemented genre-based literacy pedagogy and in its 'learning through doing' approach to teacher education (Coffin, et al., 2013). A key feature of the project model was the degree of support that teachers received through partnering with teacher educators, which greatly increased the likelihood of the sustainability and success of the pedagogy beyond the life of the project.

This outcome was achieved by enacting the key pedagogic principle of 'scaffolding' for teacher learning which typically underpins student learning in genre-based pedagogy (Bruner, 1986; Vygotsky, 1978). This principle had been used successfully to a develop a multi-site model of teacher learning in previous R2L projects in Australia (Culican, 2005; Rose, 2010) and Sweden (Acevedo, 2010). The TeL4ELE project followed the three-stage model for scaffolding student learning, beginning with teacher modelling, followed by joint practice and finally individual practice. These three stages are schematized in Figure 9.3 (adapted from Wilhelm et al., 2001, p. 91). They are represented in R2L as teaching–learning cycles, of *Preparing*, *Joint*, and *Individual* practice (Rose, Chapter 1 this volume).

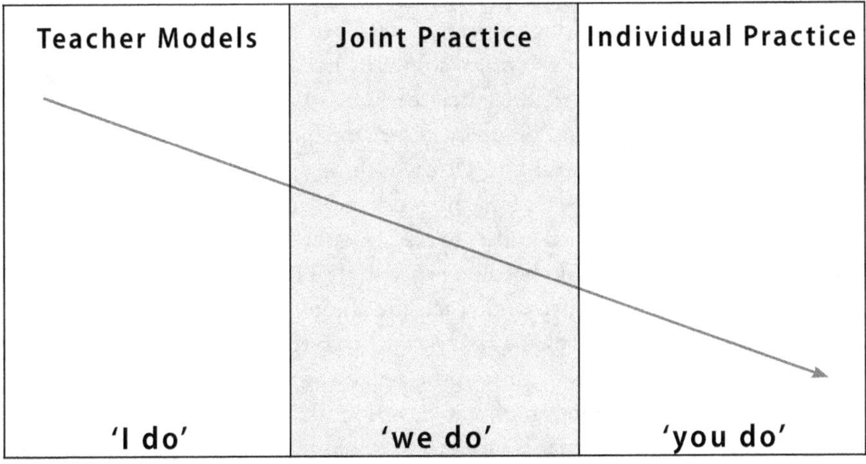

Figure 9.3. Scaffolding student learning

The project model was designed to draw on the pre-existing knowledge and expertise of the key educators from each partner country, using the notion of reciprocal learning. In order to create a strong international team, all the key educators travelled to each of the project countries for two-day learning meetings, firstly in Portugal, followed by Glasgow, Stockholm and Copenhagen. The final project meeting and dissemination conference was held in Spain (keynote lectures can be seen at https://www.telcon2013.com).

LEADING R2L PROFESSIONAL LEARNING IN DIFFERENT EUROPEAN EDUCATIONAL CULTURES

Playing a key role in developing the expertise of 30 educators from five countries, working in six different languages, over a two-year period was, of course, an enormous challenge. So there was a lot to be learnt along the way by all of us. Our aim of developing European experts in R2L pedagogy presented learning challenges for the project leaders as well as the key educators. Along with the R2L experts from Australia, I had to let go of the notion that the TeL4ELE would simply be an iteration of the Australian, English language version of R2L pedagogy in this new diverse context. I had to learn to view the pedagogy from new perspectives and understand how it could be taught and implemented flexibly in response to the different language and cultural contexts we were coming to understand.

Furthermore, we were working with the R2L professional development materials that had been designed for classroom teachers and are based on a 'learning by doing' approach that received a somewhat mixed response from the key educators. While some educators really enjoyed responding to our call for everyone to trial the R2L pedagogy in their own teaching contexts, others, perhaps more comfortable with a lecture style of teaching, were sceptical about the need to have a 'hands on' experience of the pedagogy before training their teachers. So while the international learning meetings led by David and Jim to introduce the fundamentals of the pedagogy, followed the traditional workshop style of teaching with presentations and group work, the learning days at the national network meetings were planned in conjunction with the different national leaders to take account of their differing views about how the key educators should become expert in the R2L pedagogy as well as the range of local issues that impacted on each education environment.

From our experience we were already aware that teacher learning is a nuanced process involving new ideas that may pose a challenge to long-held, or even tacit, beliefs that require the adoption of new classroom skills that may conflict with familiar routines. Our experience is supported by findings from research into teacher professional learning. Timperley et al. (2007) found that new and profound teacher learning based on theories that are not aligned with teachers pre-existing beliefs and understandings needs to be introduced via a careful combination of strategies that enable an enactment of the pedagogy that will provide evidence of its efficacy and a validation of the new theory, thus enabling a 'letting go' of pre-existing, sometimes tacit, theories in a non-threatening manner. This research claims that insufficient attention to either of these elements runs the risk of complete rejection or only partial adoption of the new learning.

In fact, early on in our project one educator left after openly declaring a clash of ideology as the reason. So we were concerned that, unless we could inspire our educators to trial the pedagogy in a classroom setting, we could run the risk that they might reject, or not fully adopt the pedagogy, which could ultimately jeopardize the outcomes of the project. Some authors in this volume (e.g., Andersson Varga et al., Chapter 8; Gouveia et al., Chapter 11; Meehan et al., Chapter 14) also report that some teachers in their R2L initiatives experienced this type of a challenge to their beliefs and understandings, and they describe how they used effective mentoring strategies to support them and work through the ideological and pedagogical struggles to enable them to adopt the R2L approach.

Consequently, providers of R2L teacher learning need to be conscious not only of the difference the new classroom pedagogy might present, but also in the shift in thinking that needs to take place for teachers to consciously change their practice. Hassan and Boccia (Chapter 15, this volume) alert us to the difficulty teachers may have in determining the difference between their current approaches to literacy pedagogy and the R2L approach. Through a close examination of the cognitive approach to reading that underpins their current school curriculum in regional Argentina, the authors carefully compared its features to the text-based pedagogy of R2L. Their analysis shows that without an in-depth examination of the two approaches, surface features, such as the use of modelling, may give the impression that the two approaches are similar.

Such a blurring of boundaries between different approaches can lead teachers to believe they are already implementing a new pedagogy, while they essentially continue with familiar routines in the name of the new pedagogy. In these cases, students are denied the opportunity to take advantage of the benefits of the visible and systematic approach of R2L. Therefore, it is essential that teachers are specifically guided by their R2L professional learning providers to understand the theoretical differences between approaches to literacy learning through the guided enactment of the pedagogy. This type of a theory–practice relationship in R2L teacher learning is developed in cycles of workshops and classroom implementation – or learning by doing.

PARTNERSHIPS BETWEEN KEY EDUCATORS AND TEACHERS

In Phase 2 of TeL4ELE, each of the key educators from each national network worked with two to three classroom teachers, referred to as key teachers (98 key teachers in total). These teachers came from a variety of contexts. Over half were subject specialists in secondary schools, approximately a third were primary school teachers and a third specialized in language and literacy or special needs. In terms of student demographics, about a quarter of the teachers had classes where up to 40% of their students did not speak the national language of the country they were living in and were socio-economically disadvantaged.

Educators drew on the expertise and experience developed in Phase 1 and used the learning materials developed in that time to support the teachers in understanding and implementing the pedagogy. To do this they used a mix of activity-based workshops, seminar discussions and formal lectures as well as modelling the pedagogy and serving as mentors (with 70% of educators spending more than 32 hours on this). Furthermore, a sizeable proportion of the educators (30%) supported the teachers by co-teaching with them in class. They also collaborated on the production of materials throughout the trialling period by helping to identify, analyze and prepare texts (57% of educators worked on between 1 and 5 texts and a further 44% more than 5 texts). Whilst all key educators focused on factual texts, 80% also focused on fiction texts and a further 47% on opinion texts.

The educator–teacher partnership approach of TeL4ELE was an important part of the overall design of the project. The aim was to extend the traditional boundaries of professional development to ensure that the learning was translated into new classroom practices and sustained over time (Acevedo, 2020).

BESPOKE 'SCAFFOLDING' OF LEARNING AT NATIONAL MEETINGS

Following is a series of snapshots that illustrate the variety of approaches to learning that were adopted in each country on the national network learning days to ultimately achieve the development of European educator expertise in R2L pedagogy.

In the case of Sweden, Ann-Christin and I had completed the R2L professional development course with all the key educators in the Swedish team in the pilot project prior to TeL4ELE. The team consisted of experienced teachers who were still classroom practitioners, although some had been newly recruited to take up professional development roles at the Multilingual Institute in Stockholm. Our focus was to provide support for them to enact their new roles as teacher trainers and we decided that these needs could best be met via the continuation of traditional workshop-style learning days. We designed workshops to develop leadership skills and fluency in the pedagogy to ensure that they would feel confident in their new training roles. The development of PD materials in Swedish for teacher training was not a high priority for this group since they were able to use the English materials and had available our lesson plans in Swedish from the pilot study. So we provided workshops where we modelled the teacher learning process, and the future educators worked in groups to plan and rehearse leading possible workshops sessions. We also introduced them to mentoring techniques such as protocols for giving feedback that they could use with their teacher-learners. Details of these processes are described in this volume by Andersson Varga, et al. (Chapter 8) and by Hart (Chapter 5).

In Portugal, the situation was very different. The backgrounds of the educators were varied, so that for some the project would deepen their prior knowledge, while for others it was their first contact with genre pedagogy. Although they were almost all experienced educators, they were not necessarily familiar with the Portuguese school curriculum or teacher professional development. However, due to pre-existing professional relationships, and the leadership of Carlos Gouveia, they worked as a cohesive learning team to gain a solid grasp of the R2L pedagogy. The group was quite self-directed, but articulated their need to learn more about the pedagogy for both literary and disciplinary texts. So in the first year we responded by organizing workshops that modelled the strategies, initially with texts in English and then also in Portuguese. They responded enthusiastically in the classroom simulations and asked probing questions to clarify their understanding of the pedagogy sequence. As it was essential to develop training materials in Portuguese, the group also used time during the learning days to work collaboratively on the analysis of Portuguese texts and the preparation of model lesson plans for their PD materials. In the second year, we were taken to visit the classrooms of some of their R2L teacher-learners to observe their lessons and to provide feedback. As Carlos reports (see Chapter 11 this volume), the TeL4ELE project was the catalyst for ongoing work on a variety of SFL-based genre pedagogy initiatives in Portugal.

The key educators in Spain, apart from the national leader, Rachel Whittaker, were all new to both genre pedagogy and to SFL. The majority were from Faculties of Education and keen to learn more about genre pedagogy as Rachel had a reputation in Spain for her work and publications in the area of SFL (e.g., Whittaker, et al., 2006). The unique feature of the Spanish team was that they were working multilingually. Their teachers worked in Spanish and Basque as L1 or L2, English as a foreign language or as the language of curricula content in bilingual/CLIL[1] classes (schools with two content subjects taught in a foreign language), and French as a foreign language. Translation or summarizing of the R2L PD materials was also imperative for the Spanish team, along with finding suitable sample texts from the national curriculum. So the national learning days in Madrid were structured to meet the diverse needs of this group. We had short plenaries on general topics followed by groups working on different aspects of the project, with Ann-Christin and myself in mentoring roles as we both speak Spanish. One sub-group had been leading the work on translating the R2L materials, which generated learning conversations about defining key terms, concepts and the steps in the pedagogy, which in turn enabled them to develop a more nuanced understanding of both the linguistics and the pedagogy as they determined how meanings could be best conveyed in Spanish. Other groups worked on selecting and analysing texts and developing model lesson plans for the Spanish materials, and we participated similarly in these discussions – often late into the night! During the second year, we provided some workshops in Madrid for the project teachers. An important legacy of the work of this team has been the translation of the R2L reference book, *Learning to write, reading to learn* (Rose & Martin, 2012) into Spanish, *Leer para aprender* (2018).

In Denmark, the key educators were mostly experienced pre-service and in-service educators with backgrounds in SFL and genre writing pedagogy. They were all known to each other, and several of the team had been to Australia specifically to explore the pedagogy. They had also published materials in Danish on the genre writing pedagogy which they used in their education courses. So while they were not so familiar with R2L, their background knowledge and experience meant that they worked as quite independent learners following the international workshops with Jim and David. At our network meetings in Copenhagen, the team members presented the materials they were preparing for their R2L teacher training in Year 2, and we had reciprocal learning discussions around their work. Through the National Centre for Reading, they were very well placed for dissemination and our learning meetings also focused on discussion of the plans they had for making films of their R2L teachers and organizing innovative teacher learning events. In Year 2 of the project, an industrial dispute in Denmark caused a protracted teacher lockout, which meant that their final national learning meeting had to be cancelled and their teachers had a reduced amount of teaching time with their students. However, despite this difficulty, the experience and collaborative working relationships in the team enabled them to solve these issues and achieve the teacher learning aims of the project.

The members of the Scottish team were drawn mainly from tertiary education faculties and, while they routinely worked with pre-service teachers, they also had experience of in-service education. However, they were not familiar with SFL or 'Sydney School' genre pedagogy and some of their team members initially reacted with scepticism to the theories underpinning the approach at the international meetings. This meant that I needed to pay careful attention to their specific learning needs at the national meetings in Scotland if I was to engage them fully in the project. The key advantage for me when working with this group was that there was ample learning material available in English, and no time would need to be taken up with translation. We also already had a reservoir of sample lesson plans in a variety of subject areas that could be used for modelling in the local learning meetings. So I designed workshops that explained the principles of the pedagogy, then modelled the key aspects of the pedagogy using texts from different learning areas and set the educators exercises to prepare texts and lessons. They responded favourably to the exercises as they were able to experience how the planning for R2L classroom pedagogy would benefit their teachers. The discussion of the pedagogical process led me to discover that many of the Scottish educators had been classroom teachers themselves and/or were accustomed to working closely with teachers in schools. So they responded favourably to trialling the R2L pedagogy either with their own tertiary students or by going into classrooms at partner schools to trial the R2L lessons. Consequently, a good deal of the initial scepticism was assuaged through the 'learning by doing' approach of the project.

The achievements from each country were documented and reported on at each international meeting to ensure knowledge exchange and progressive achievement of the project targets. The exchange and dialogue between the international team and national networks enhanced the learning of all involved by encouraging critical reflection on existing practices across the five participating European countries and by facilitating mutual support in exploring, contextualizing and trialling the new genre-based approach to literacy and learning.

EVIDENCE BASED, REFLECTIVE ACTION RESEARCH

This project used a similar approach to data collection that had been used in R2L projects in Australia (e.g. Rose, 2010) and in Sweden (Acevedo, 2010). Data collected on the classroom implementation included evidence of both teacher and student learning. Teacher learning data consisted of some recordings of implementation and reflective teacher responses to a questionnaire designed by the external evaluator of the project. Student learning data included some classroom recordings and student response data, analyses of pre and post intervention writing samples, and pre and post reading comprehension tests.

Teacher learning data

Prior to the project, almost half the project teachers had little or no knowledge of genre pedagogy, and most (80%) had had no prior involvement in professional development programs or university courses relating to the approach. Only three teachers had significant experience in implementing genre pedagogy.

While all involvement in the project was optional and most of it occurred in educators' and teachers' own time, the project evaluation concluded that most teachers developed considerable knowledge and skill with the R2L approach: 85% of the teachers spent at least 10 hours studying and preparing lessons for R2L, with almost half spending more than 20 hours.

In terms of classroom implementation, R2L strategies involve three levels of scaffolding support – reading and writing whole texts, working with short passages in detail, and intensive strategies with one or more sentences (see Chapter 1, this volume). Up to 20% of teachers were able to use all levels of the R2L strategies approximately three times a week, but most were not able to practise this often. While a third of teachers had more than 10 weeks in which to implement the approach almost half the teachers had 5 weeks or less. Factors in this included the one-month teacher lockout in Denmark, and the economic crisis in Spain and Portugal, which led to teacher pay cuts and increased working hours.

Teachers were provided with the R2L resource books, which contain a series of activities to develop their knowledge about pedagogy and language. Most teachers completed the activities in Books 1 to 5, which covered the overall approach, selecting and analyzing texts, *Detailed Reading* and writing, and intensive strategies. On the other hand, fewer teachers were able to complete the activities focused on grammar and discourse. It also emerged through the questionnaire evaluation data that teachers focused more on factual texts than fiction and opinion texts, with approximately a quarter of teachers never preparing or exploring fiction and opinion texts. One likely explanation for this was the subject specialties of many teachers.

Despite teachers' varied starting points and the challenging contexts in which some of them were working, almost all (97%) reported that R2L had had an impact on their approach to working with texts. Almost half of them indicated R2L had a major impact on their understanding of language and learning, including how language operates in different texts and school subjects and on how to approach the teaching of reading and writing. Only 3% felt it had no significant impact.

Student learning data

While the focus of this project was teacher learning, student achievement results were an important part of the efficacy data on the professional development. The teachers conducted pre and post reading tests and 'assessed writing tasks' in order to gauge their students' literacy development as the R2L approach was trialled.

The precise nature of the tests and writing tasks were selected and administered in line with local contexts, opportunities and constraints. However, all teachers provided pre and post test scores from two representative low, medium and high scoring students, using the R2L writing assessment. This assessment uses 14 criteria to measure students' language resources at the levels of genre, register, discourse, grammar and graphic features (see Rose & Martin, 2012, p. 323).

The degree to which students showed an improvement in their reading and/or writing varied across and within national contexts. Nevertheless, across all contexts, pre and post intervention scores on students' reading and writing showed an average overall improvement of 9% in reading and an increase of nearly 15% in writing. As outlined above, this growth was achieved in 5–10 weeks, in three or fewer lessons per week. It was even more remarkable, given the variation in local contexts, opportunities and constraints, alongside differences in teachers' experience and understanding of genre-based pedagogy.

Although all student cohorts showed significant growth, the highest gains were made by students who were educationally disadvantaged through socioeconomic and/or language background, and students who scored low on pre tests. This outcome met the project aim of improving learning outcomes for all students but especially those who are educationally disadvantaged (Coffin, 2013).

READING TO LEARN: AN INNOVATIVE PEDAGOGY IN THE EUROPEAN CONTEXT

The introduction of R2L pedagogy across Europe in the TeL4ELE project proved to make a major contribution in relation to the various concerns raised in the Eurydice report on *Teaching Reading in Europe* (2011). These concerns included:

- improving the knowledge and skills of teachers delivering reading instruction,
- providing teachers with enough support to identify and tackle reading difficulties, and
- ensuring that all subject teachers, not only those teaching the language of instruction have sufficient grounding in the theory and practice of teaching reading.

Reading to Learn focuses on language as a meaning-making resource in all school subjects and therefore the professional development targets all teachers. It draws attention to the fact that language teaching is the responsibility of all teachers, not just language teachers. Furthermore, it shifts the focus of a lack of progress in reading being diagnosed primarily as a student deficit, to an indicator that more powerful pedagogies are needed in mainstream learning contexts to cater for a range of achievement levels in all classrooms. So the R2L genre-based approach to reading proved to be an innovative paradigm shift in classroom pedagogy for all teachers.

DENOUEMENT

Organizing effective teacher learning programs is always a complex undertaking, and bringing together different international contexts can multiply the challenges. Different systems, schools and teachers responded in diverse ways to the R2L pedagogy and to the professional learning according to the opportunities and limitations of their different education systems and curricula. Notwithstanding, the findings of this international project provide a promising picture of the potential of this robust SFL-based pedagogy to transcend international educational boundaries, cultural and linguistic differences, as well as a range of local challenges, to improve learning outcomes for even the most educationally disadvantaged learners.

The legacy of this project is ongoing work with Reading to Learn across Europe, as reported in the chapters in this volume.

NOTE

1 CLIL: Content and Language Integrated Learning is an approach in which a foreign language (frequently English in Spain) is used as a tool in the learning of a non-language subject in which both language and the subject have a joint role.

REFERENCES

Acevedo, C. (2010). *Will the implementation of reading to learn in Stockholm schools accelerate literacy learning for disadvantaged students and close the achievement gap? A report on school-based action research.* Stockholm, Multilingual Research Institute. https://www.researchgate.net/publication/355160739

Acevedo, C. (2014). Reading to learn: Scaffolding democracy in literacy classrooms in Stockholm. In H. Emery, & N. Moore (Eds.). *Teaching, learning and researching reading in EFL* (pp. 298–320). TESOL Arabia Publication.

Acevedo, M. C. (2020). *Bringing language to consciousness: Teacher professional learning in genre-based reading pedagogy.* [Doctoral dissertation, The Open University, U.K.] https://doi.org/10.21954/ou.ro.00011316

Acevedo, C., & Rose, D. (2007). Reading (and writing) to learn in the middle years of schooling. *PEN, 157*, 1–8, NSW, Primary English Teaching Association. https://www.researchgate.net/publication/355182893

Bruner, J. (1986). *Actual minds, possible worlds.* Harvard University Press.

Coffin, C. (2013). *Final report of the independent external evaluator on the TeL4ELE project.* European Union. DOI: 10.13140/RG.2.2.20401.30565

Coffin, C., Acevedo, C., & Lövstedt, A.-C. (2013). *Teacher learning for European literacy education (TeL4ELE) Final Report.* European Union. https://www.researchgate.net/publication/355145686

Culican, S. J. (2005). *Learning to read: Reading to learn: A middle year's literacy intervention research project, Final report 2003–4.* Catholic Education Office Melbourne. DOI:10.13140/RG.2.2.13690.41921

European Commission. (2011). *Lifelong learning programme: Comenius projects,* https://eur-lex.europa.eu/resource.html?uri=cellar:d9ac350d-f880-4b18-a205-80ba147b5afa.0017.03/DOC_2&format=PDF

Eurydice. (2011). *Teaching reading in Europe: Contexts, policies and practices,* Publications Office, European Education and Culture Executive Agency (Eurydice) https://data.europa.eu/doi/10.2797/60196

Rose, D. (2010). Beating educational inequality with an integrated reading pedagogy. In F. Christie & A. Simpson (Eds.), *Literacy and social responsibility: Multiple perspectives.* (pp.101–115). Equinox. https://www.researchgate.net/publication/323549957

Rose, D., & Acevedo, C. (2006). Closing the gap and accelerating learning in the middle years of schooling. *Literacy learning: The middle years,* Australian Literacy Educators' Association, *14*(2), 32–45.

Rose, D., & Martin, J. R. (2012). *Learning to write, reading to learn: Genre, knowledge and pedagogy in the Sydney school.* Equinox Publishing.

Rose, D., & Martin, J. R. (2018). *Leer para aprender: Lectura y escritura en las áreas del currículo* (Ana Bustelo Tortella Trans., R. Whittaker & T. Bordón Revision) Ediciones Pirámide (original work published 2012).

Timperley, H., Wilson, A., Barrar, H., & Fung, I. (2007). *Teacher professional learning and development: Best evidence synthesis iteration (BES),* Wellington, New Zealand Ministry of Education.

Vygotsky, L.S. (1978). *Mind in society: The development of higher psychological processes* (M. Cole, V. Jolm-Steiner, S. Scribner, & E. Souberman, Eds.). Harvard University Press.

Whittaker, R., O'Donnell, M., & McCabe, A., Eds. (2006). *Language and literacy: Functional approaches,* Continuum.

Wilhelm, J. D., Baker, T. N., & Dube, J. (2001). *Strategic reading: Guiding students to lifelong literacy, 6–12.* Boynton/Cook.

ABOUT THE AUTHOR

Claire Acevedo is an Australian educator now based in the United Kingdom where she is an affiliated researcher in Language and Literacies at The Centre for Research in Education and Educational Technology (CREET) at the Open University. She concurrently provides educational services to schools and education sectors across Europe and South America where she leads professional development (in English, Spanish and Swedish). She is experienced in using Systemic Functional Linguistics via 'Sydney School' genre pedagogy to improve reading and writing outcomes for underachieving students in all areas of the school curriculum. She has collaborated with Dr David Rose, University of Sydney, over two decades on the latest research into genre-based reading and she specializes in delivering *Reading to Learn* literacy acceleration professional development to teachers and teacher educators. She is the co-founder and deputy chair of *Reading for Life* (http://reading4life.org) a non-profit association that promotes social justice in society and equity in education all over the world.

10

Working with Reading to Learn at undergraduate level in Spain: A learning journey

Rachel Whittaker, Isabel García-Parejo & Aoife Ahern

ABSTRACT

In this chapter we present three projects which grew out of the European Reading to Learn teacher development programme, Teacher Learning for European Language Education (TeL4ELE) in Spain. These projects have taken the Reading to Learn (R2L) pedagogy to a new context and a new population, that of teachers-in-training. Although Spain has shown improvement in international assessments of reading literacy over recent years (PIRLS and PISA), 20% of primary students, and 16% of secondary still fail to reach the baseline for their age. Despite this problem, there is little focus on literacy over the four years of primary teacher education. Two of our projects aimed to make R2L accessible to inexperienced student-teachers, who were qualifying to teach the different areas of the primary curriculum in Spanish (L1) and in English (L2). The main, long-term innovation project introducing R2L pedagogy to student-teachers aimed to heighten undergraduates' awareness of text genres to improve their teaching and their own competence in writing and included an action research component. This introduction to R2L was integrated into language and literacy subjects, but also led to a second project, taking R2L outside the faculty in a Service-Learning action involving undergraduates working with children at primary schools with high proportions of students from at-risk populations. The third project researched into the impact of the innovation with student-teachers and provides the basis for our reflections on the learning journey of lecturers and student-teachers which close the chapter.

INTRODUCTION: CONTEXT AND CHALLENGES

This chapter presents three interconnected Reading to Learn (R2L) initiatives carried out by the Education Faculty in the Complutense University in Madrid by a small group of lecturers who belong to the research group on multilingualism, literacy and linguistic education, *ForMuLE*, (*Foro de multilingüismo, literacidad y educación*), coordinated by Isabel García-Parejo. The catalyst for the work described in this chapter was the European Comenius Project, TeL4ELE (2011–2013), led by Rachel Whittaker in Spain, which introduced the authors to the Reading to Learn pedagogy (see Acevedo, Chapter 9 this volume). During the TeL4ELE project, a team of Spanish educators developed expertise in R2L and took the pedagogy to the local context and population by designing materials and running courses for 40 in-service teachers, who in turn worked with the approximately 300 pupils in their classes in different languages: Spanish and Basque as first languages, English and French as foreign languages (see Whittaker & García-Parejo, 2018).

Subsequent to TeL4ELE, our team of R2L educators held other short in-service courses and seminars in different parts of the country. As we observed the positive impact of R2L theory and practice on teachers' ability to work with texts and the resulting improvement in literacy outcomes, we were inspired to take the pedagogy to pre-service teacher training. Our bids for teaching innovation projects in the faculty as well as for a research project presented by the *ForMuLE* coordinator were successful, so that, with institutional recognition, since 2013, more than 500 student-teachers have been introduced to the R2L pedagogy in Spanish and English, to prepare them to teach through either or both of these languages (more in García-Parejo & Whittaker, 2017).

In Spain, in the education field, we have a number of challenges to address. One issue is early school leaving, which is a key area of concern for the European Council (2020) and is considerably higher in some regions[1] of Spain than the EU average (Council of Europe, 2020b). Also, while school failure has recently improved, a fifth of male pupils left school in 2020 without obtaining the certificate for completion of obligatory secondary education (Ministerio de Educación y Formación Profesional, 2021).

International studies have highlighted the issue of underachievement in both the primary and secondary years of schooling, which is closely related to groups of pupils abandoning school early. Studies of literacy levels in Spain show a large percentage of low-achievers at mid-primary (PIRLS, Mullis et al., 2017) and mid-secondary (PISA, Organization for Economic Cooperation and Development, 2016). Problems with reading are of course closely related to risk of school failure (Guio-Jaimes & Choi de Mendizábal, 2014) and have consequences for a young person's future access to training and the labour market (Organization for Economic Cooperation and Development, 2013). Literacy educators clearly have a role to play if this situation is to be improved.

The Council of Europe's work on the role of language in education over the past 30 years has great relevance for our initiatives in literacy pedagogy for trainee teachers. This institution considers that one of its most important developments has been 'recognition of the importance of taking into account the language dimension in the teaching and learning of all school subjects in order to ensure access to education for all…' (Council of Europe, 2020a). However, despite knowledge of the role of reading literacy in educational success, and the growing awareness of the genres through which different disciplines create knowledge, this topic is not central to teacher education in Spain. In fact, the curricula designed by the different education faculties in general pay little attention to the linguistic education of future teachers, devoting few, often optional, subjects to the area. In our specific context, in fact, while primary teacher education degrees have recently increased from three to four years in line with European systems, the time devoted to language and language didactics has been reduced by almost half, to a total of 150 hours in a four-year degree.

In this situation, members of *ForMuLE* designed an innovation project[2] to introduce R2L pedagogy into the primary teacher education programme through subjects dealing with language and language pedagogy. The aim was not only to give future teachers competences they would take to the children in their classrooms, but also to improve their own writing and evaluation of some of the genres they would have to teach in the future by enhancing their awareness of text functions, structure and language patterns.

The following sections of the chapter describe how we have gone about taking R2L to Spanish student-teachers, a task which included our on-going learning process as a group. As we went more deeply into the genres of education for our context (in Spanish and in English, both as a foreign language, and to teach content subjects in the growing number of bilingual schools in the country) we also needed to improve our ability to make the pedagogy accessible to teachers-in-training, a population for which it was not originally intended. This meant designing instruments both to help them understand the approach while learning how to plan literacy lessons, and to measure different aspects of our students' uptake of the innovations, information which would allow us to improve our introduction to R2L for them.

Our activities are presented chronologically, first describing the long-term innovation project with which we began our work of initiating student-teachers into R2L, then showing how we evaluated the results in the research project, and finally how we incorporated our experience into an on-going Service-Learning action using R2L. We end the chapter by bringing together the information collected over several years on student-teachers' reactions to the R2L pedagogy and reflecting on our own learning journey with R2L.

TEACHING INNOVATION PROJECT: INTRODUCING R2L TO STUDENT-TEACHERS (2013 TO THE PRESENT)

In 2013, as part of the dissemination strategy for the TeL4ELE project which brought R2L to Spain, the *ForMuLE* group began the innovation project. This initiative was designed to enable us to continue learning about the theory and practice of the pedagogy and to provide structure and visibility to the introduction of R2L to future teachers in the faculty. Funding for the project also enabled us to organize workshops led by Claire Acevedo for the *ForMuLE* group to continue learning about the pedagogy.

A dozen lecturers belonging to the group (some from outside the Madrid region) participated in the project, which took place in two, partly overlapping, phases. One phase focused on our own learning about systemic functional linguistics (Martin & Rose, 2008; Rose & Martin, 2012) and its application to the Spanish educational context; and the other, on introducing R2L to future primary teachers. The subjects with which we worked in the Degree in Primary Education were *Lengua Española* (Spanish Language), *Didáctica de la Lengua* (Teaching Spanish Language), and Teaching EFL Literacy, for students who would be teaching subjects through English (see Ahern et al., 2019; García-Parejo et al., 2017).

In the work with our student-teachers, first we focused on developing knowledge about the genres of schooling. We guided our future teachers to analyze curriculum texts using the genre map (Rose & Martin, 2012). Then we shifted our focus to the pedagogy by modelling the R2L classroom strategies, and finally we guided the students to plan their own R2L lessons (García-Parejo & Ahern, 2019). We showed them how the complete design of a R2L lesson plan entails three basic steps: (i)

Figure 10.1. The group in a workshop with Claire Acevedo (Madrid, December 2016)

Figure 10.2. Analyzing the text

Figure 10.3. Joint rewriting after *Detailed Reading* with student-teachers

careful reading and analysis of the text to scaffold the children's reading, (ii) preparation for writing, and (iii) writing a text of similar characteristics.

To focus their planning for the classroom, we asked the student-teachers to choose a level and subject from the primary curriculum, and then select a text to be studied, both for content and for linguistic reasons. Based on their texts, they had to define the objectives of the whole teaching sequence including these two perspectives and relating them to the curriculum. This preparatory work would guide their decisions in the following steps.

These steps required the student-teachers to think about their future pupils and prepare what they would actually do and say in the classroom. For the initiating R2L classroom strategy, *Preparing for Reading*, our students needed to apply their new knowledge about genres to read their texts carefully, thinking about how they would be able to guide their pupils to understand not just what the text was about, but also what the text was *doing.* This involved identifying the genre and analyzing the stages and phases of their texts so they could prepare their pupils orally to follow with understanding as they read the text to them aloud. Then they focused on a fragment of the text to prepare for the *Detailed Reading* strategy. This required them to select key wordings from the text which would also be used in *Joint Construction* (or *Joint Rewriting*). The students worked together in groups on their plans; and, over the years of the innovation project, they collectively designed more than 80 lesson plans in English and over 50 in Spanish. The lesson plans in Spanish are narrative and factual genres, those in English also include procedural genres (see García-Parejo & Ahern, 2019 for details of this work).

During the hands-on classes, we could see the challenges the student-teachers faced as they went about the selection of texts and the design of their lesson plans. This made us realize that, as they did not have the experience of the in-service teachers for which the pedagogy is designed, they needed more support. To solve this problem, we decided to adapt the original lesson plan pro-forma (Rose, 2018) to our students' incomplete knowledge, making more explicit the different types of preparation required and their role in the actual lesson. Readers can find examples in English and in Spanish on the web of the ForMuLE group www.formule.es, and in the project reports.

In the next section we explain what we learnt about the challenges our student-teachers encountered, revealed in the different types of data we collected and analyzed in the research project.

RESEARCH ON THE IMPACT OF THE INNOVATION PROJECT

In 2016, at the same time as we were introducing different cohorts of student-teachers to R2L in their Spanish and English classes, the *ForMuLE* coordinator was successful in receiving funding for a research project[3]. Its main objective was to evaluate the extent to which the teacher training undertaken in the innovation project had achieved its aims. This included discovering the impact made on our students' ability to design lesson plans, as well as their beliefs about the teaching of written language – here the focus included their evaluation of R2L practices and the innovation project they had participated in (see García-Parejo & Ahern, 2019)[4]. We collected data using different instruments: questionnaires (initial, mid-project, final), focus group discussions and individual and group ethnographic field diaries.

We selected 11 students for the study from the 76 students who were in the third year of the Degree in Primary Education in 2016–17. These students had participated in all the activites and tasks in the Spanish didactics course and gave permission for us to use their work in this research. We used the students' lesson plans for story genres and reports (Rose & Martin, 2012, 2018) given their importance for primary teachers. The sub-corpus we analyzed was, then, a sample from a much wider corpus of lesson plans.

In order to evaluate the students' lesson plans, we designed a template which was validated by two specialists in language teaching. With it we were able to assess the student-teachers' understanding of the genre, and of the field, tenor and mode (Halliday & Matthiessen, 2014) of the text they chose, as well as the way they expressed the objectives of their lessons and put into writing their proposals for applying the different R2L strategies to work with the text in the classroom.

Our analyses of their plans, together with the student-teachers' comments in the field diaries and focus groups, gave us insights into their understandings, and helped us in our own learning. Importantly, we could see how the students appreciated the support the pedagogy provides, enabling them to work in a principled way with all aspects of texts. As a group in the class reported:

> [...] to understand the set of ideas that are transmitted in a text, to understand its composition and structure, whatever the type of text, is a strategy that every primary teacher should be capable of teaching to their students, independently of the area that they teach. The R2L method is a tool that will help us to achieve this goal [5]. (G3–2017G-Assessment)

At the same time, we were able to identify three fundamental areas of difficulty the student-teachers met, challenges which have informed our subsequent work. Firstly, they had trouble identifying and analyzing genres for the primary levels they wanted to work with, as the following comment shows:

> [...] the difficulty of text analysis in narrative texts. It seemed easy at first to divide the texts in its stages and phases, but as I got hands on with the task I began to see the degree of complexity it had. (S-Lst.1-FR)

Secondly, as a result of the previous problem, they found it difficult to formulate clear learning aims for that text, both for content and for language. And, thirdly, it was hard for them to choose the key wordings needed for note-making in preparation for the writing phase (García-Parejo & Ahern, 2019).

We also discovered – and this was important for our purpose of taking R2L to student-teachers – that some students had doubts about the need to work on literacy. They just assumed that, as the children had mastered decoding and were able to write words, nothing more was necessary. This made it clear to us that they needed to experience using R2L in a real-world context to understand the need for the different strategies and the preparation of the lesson plans. An opportunity to fill this gap and to put R2L to work where it was most needed arose when the university called for bids for Service-Learning projects, as we report in the next section.

SERVICE-LEARNING ACTION RESEARCH PROJECTS (2018 TO THE PRESENT)

A stark growth in inequality among schools in the Madrid Region due to policy decisions in response to the evolving demographic and socio-economic trends had been taking place since 2013, while we were offering an introduction to Reading to Learn in language and literacy courses. After six years on the increase in this region, the impact of school segregation, separating children of families with the highest socio-economic status from those of the lowest, was rated the second greatest in the European Union in 2018 (Sanjuán et al., 2019). Seeing the widening gaps in academic achievement caused by this segregation, in early 2019 the *ForMuLE* group members decided to find ways to engage the student-teachers in opportunities to move out of the university lecture halls and try to make an impact in schools using R2L pedagogy in their immediate surroundings.

In the 2018–19 academic year, Aoife Ahern led a pilot initiative with the English as a Foreign Language student-teachers, inspired by successful experiences in Service-Learning projects in numerous other European higher education institutions (Aramburuzabala et al., 2019). This paved the way for a funded project in 2019–20[6] to work with two local primary schools in Madrid with large proportions of pupils from vulnerable socio-economic backgrounds. These two state schools tend to have fewer than the maximum number of pupils per class, as parents in these areas prefer charter schools. This means the state schools receive new pupils whose families arrive in the district throughout the academic year for reasons of displacement or migration. The instability in the student bodies is coupled with a very high turnover of teaching staff. Thus, the learning environment at the two schools is impacted by a range of difficult circumstances and clearly affects pupils' achievement in literacy, as in the rest of the areas of the curriculum.

For the S-L project in the Education Faculty, we had an excellent response to the call for volunteers to participate[7], with 60 second and third-year students, about half working in Spanish and half from the English specialization. Work began with a short, accelerated Reading to Learn seminar made up of four 4-hour sessions, spread over the months of September to November. At that point, none of the students had studied the relevant language teaching courses[8]. Then, in groups of three or four, they chose texts and prepared lesson plans with the help of the lecturers, managing to get them ready just in time for each of their weekly school intervention sessions.

They taught their lessons to pupils in small groups, so that each student worked with 5 or 6 children. Between November 2019 and March 2020, these student-teachers taught a total of 85 lessons, providing support to children in 10 class groups (approximately 200 pupils) between the ages of 5 and 11.

As in previous years, we collected data on the student-teachers' views on the role of literacy instruction in education. This time, though, we could also include the children's attitudes towards literacy learning. The student-teachers' first impressions and observations, after having met the children and obtaining some writing samples to identify their learning needs, highlighted the differences between the literacy abilities of children in the same class. When asked to write, some children were unable to produce anything, so copied something from the blackboard or did a drawing, and others managed a few words or even a paragraph, as the samples in Figure 10.4 from an English Language class show.

Despite the difficulties caused by the difference in ability levels inside the classes, and the student-teachers' very short introduction to the pedagogy, some groups applied the R2L strategies successfully, implementing *Preparing for Reading* and *Detailed Reading* as well as guiding the pupils in *Joint Rewriting* of descriptions or brief texts in genres such as Recounts and Procedures, as they noted in their field diaries:

> We followed the sessions [...] the team created previously: talk about the title, read one or two times, focus in a sentence, learn new vocabulary, then rewrite the sentence changing the vocabulary. (Eng-9)

An important learning moment for our students was when they saw that it was possible to motivate such young pupils to write. According to the initial questionnaire,

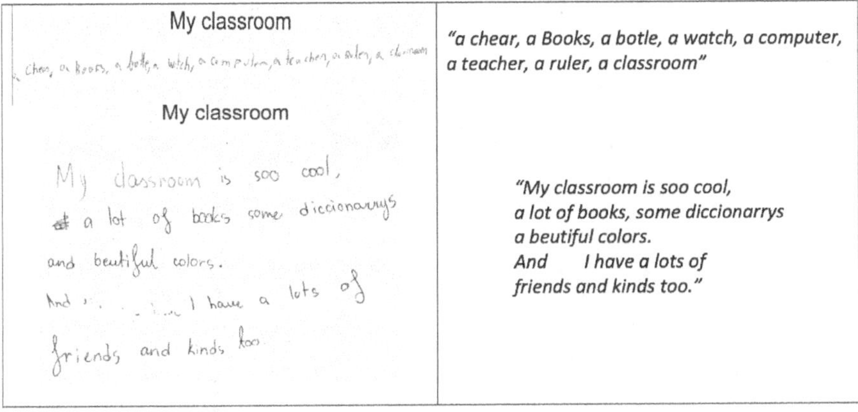

Figure 10.4. Different levels of English in one class

in most cases they had felt that children in primary were apt to show rejection (35%) or indifference (55%) towards writing tasks at school. However, by the time they had completed the first few sessions, their views on children's interest in writing had changed. When they were asked to 'point out any specific aspects of the approach you applied that captured your attention' one group answered:

> The different activities that we did in order for the students to learn how to write. I never thought of that kind of activities. It is fun and entertains the children in a way that other approaches do not. Catching the attention of the children is really important if you want them to learn something. (Eng-8)

Although the project ended abruptly when all the educational institutions in Spain closed down with the Covid-19 pandemic (March 2020), the varied data analyzed show an encouraging set of positive outcomes. One example of the impact on pupils' writing is provided in Figure 10.5, which shows the improvement made by a ten-year-old pupil in writing a description of her classroom in English after one session with the student-teachers.

The student-teachers were amazed that, after one lesson working on a simple text in English in a meaningful way, the child was able to write a series of coherent sentences with varied vocabulary and confident handwriting.

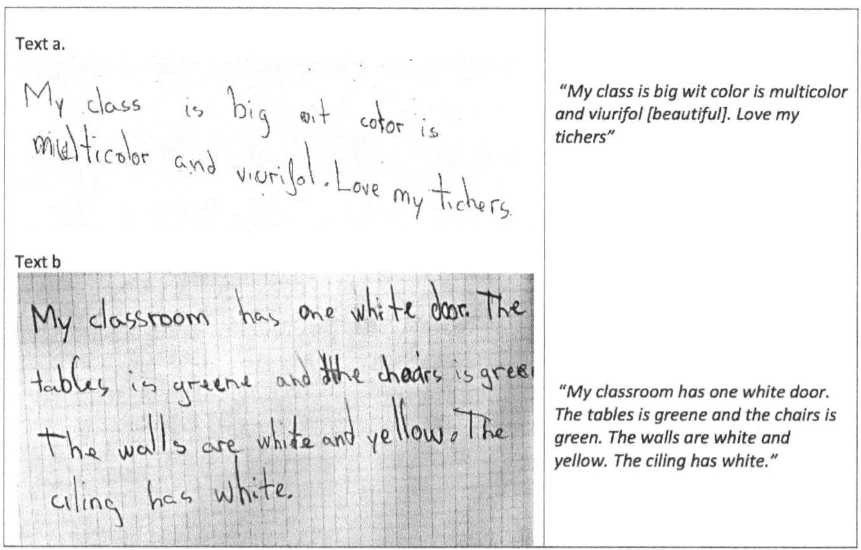

Figure 10.5. Text a: pre-intervention; Text b: rewrite on day 2 of intervention, by 10-year-old pupil (T1-LB-Eng4P)

As they said, they felt that the approach had been effective, and that by to applying it they had made a positive impact on the children's learning. This was corroborated by the children themselves in their questionnaire:

> Lo que más me ha gustado ha sido aprender a hacer frases más cortas, pero con el mismo significado. Lo que menos, es estar tan poco tiempo aprendiendo con vosotros [...] Vais a ser unos profesores fantásticos. [What I liked best was learning to make shorter sentences with the same meaning. What I least liked was to have so little time learning with you ... you're going to be fantastic teachers.] (LB- Sp-Dec-6P2)
>
> Me ha gustado mucho, he aprendido mucho y ha sido muy divertido, paresen profesores completos [I've enjoyed it a lot, I've learnt a lot and it has been great fun, they seem like complete teachers.] (LB-Sp-Dec-6P3)

To close this snapshot of our projects, in the next section we present a general evaluation of the student-teachers' learning about R2L in relation to their future profession.

STUDENT-TEACHERS' EXPERIENCE OF LEARNING R2L

During the years of the innovation project, the student-teachers were asked for their evaluation of the experience with R2L in different ways, as explained above. Among the questions, we asked whether they planned to use R2L when they became teachers, about the the level of challenge they encountered in learning to work with the model, and whether their learning experience had changed the way they thought about teaching writing.

The students' comments on the pedagogy, modelled by the lecturers in the classes, reflect the interest sparked by some of the activities associated with each phase of teaching, above all those related to *Preparing for Reading* and the *Joint Rewriting* of narrative texts:

> I speacially [sic] liked the dynamic that we did in our service learning classes about extracting a sentence from the book, and analysing it in depth. We put this into practice in our sessions and the kids understand the book much better. (Eng-7)
>
> We very much liked the session and especially the joint and individual rewriting. It is what we most like about the method. (G1-Diary27-4)

The group learning to teach in English particularly valued the way this pedagogy allowed them to work on the different linguistic levels such as pronunciation, orthography and grammar in a context that promotes meaningful learning, learning which derives from a text.

They explained that it offers possibilities for addressing not only the curricular area of foreign language teaching, but also for Content and Language Integrated Learning (CLIL). Here, students commented on its applicability, given the diversity of genres that they will face as teachers of 'non-linguistic subjects' in English and in Spanish:

> During the process we have been able to appreciate the usefulness of this preparatory work that should be done on all the texts that are to be used with our future students. We believe that both the work that the teacher must do beforehand and the R2L model can be very beneficial for students. (G1-Diary- 29-4)

With reference to the preparation noted by this group and others, this is where the majority of student-teachers found challenges: choosing suitable texts and establishing linguistic objectives, all of which was new for them. The teachers' work in planning the lesson and applying the model to evaluating pupils' writing was also mentioned, though they considered it less demanding.

Despite the work involved, most of the students said they would certainly use the model in their future teaching, as it was an efficient way to work on literacy:

> Reading to Learn is an approach that provides them with the opportunity to learn step by step, learning through different experiences with the text model and then achieving the main goal which is to write a text using the features studied. (S-Lst.2-FR)

Figure 10.6. Sentence making

> [...] we consider it appropriate for teaching reading and writing in any language and subject. (G1–BLG-Assessment)

> I would choose the Reading to Learn approach, as it tries to solve the fact that some students are not engaged in the language cycle and are left behind. (S-Lst.1-FR)

And as to their views on the teaching of writing, they said yes, somehow, R2L training had changed their approach to teaching writing:

> It is an approach that requires a previous organization from the teacher, which means more work, but is something that if done well, it means that the lesson will develop all right and that students will fulfill the objectives. This previous work to the lesson is because it focuses on the genre of texts, so in this way, children can know that language differs on the purpose you have. And we, as teachers should enable students to read and write in each of them. (S-L st. 4-FR)

And finally, despite the extra work, those who participated in service learning consider this voluntary activity positive and they enjoyed it!

> I have been lucky to have been able to implement this pedagogy (in broad terms) in the service learning project.[...] I can see that works very well. This is a pedagogy I really like. (S-L st.3-FR)

CONCLUSIONS

In this chapter we have told our learning journey, and that of the student-teachers with whom we have been working, as we incorporated R2L into initial teacher-education programmes. Our learning process and research have made it possible for us to explore the characteristics of Spanish school genres, as well as the challenges facing future teachers when they take on the task of teaching reading and writing in one or more languages. We have outlined the insights we have gained from the research we carried out as we were taking R2L to teachers-in-training, and the successes the student-teachers have experienced using the pedagogy. Learning the linguistic and pedagogical model with the help of the instruments we designed gave the students the background they needed to understand how to approach the complexity of reading and writing with the children. Also, we have found that our service-learning project provided the springboard which offered our students the experience they needed in order to understand the real power of R2L. Being able to provide disadvantaged children R2L's scaffolded access to school genres gave meaning to the challenges of the linguistic model and the investment of time in preparation of the pedagogical strategies. We encourage our readers to share such an experience.

NOTES

1 Since the end of dictatorship, and the approval of the 1978 Constitution, Spain has progressively become a virtually federal state, with regional governments administering most areas of public life, including education.
2 The project has been recognized and funded by the Faculty (2014–15, 2016–17, 2018–19). Reports for these projects (Géneros y sociedad I, II y III) can be found at: https://www.ucm.es/buscador?search=garc%C3%ADa+parejo&bci=repositorio
3 Language education and teacher education: exploring the effects of integrating the systemic-functional linguistics-based Reading to Learn approach into the Degree in Primary Education Santander-UCM PR26/16-20348
4 This research also analyzed the effect of knowledge of the functional approach to language on the students' own written texts (García-Parejo & Blanco-Fernández, 2020).
5 Comments written in Spanish have been translated.
6 Reading and Writing in the Languages of Schooling (Leemos y escribimos en las lenguas de la escuela).
7 The TALIS 2018 report shows that 95% of primary teachers in the Madrid Region had chosen the profession motivated by their desire to contribute to society (p. 256).
8 These would begin in the following semester.

REFERENCES

Ahern, A., Whittaker, R., & Blecua, I. (2019). Reading and writing to learn. A principled approach to practice in CLIL/Bilingual classes. *E-Teals*, *9*, 23–40. https://ojs.letras.up.pt/index.php/et/article/view/6103

Aramburuzabala, P., MacIlrath, L. & Opazo, H. (Eds.). (2019). *Embedding service learning in European higher education. Developing a culture of civic engagement in Europe*. Taylor & Francis.

Council of Europe. (2020a). *Languages of schooling*. https://www.coe.int/en/web/language-policy/language-policies

Council of Europe. (2020b). *Tackling today's challenges together: Failure at school*. http://www.coe.int/education.

European Council. (2020). *Europe 2020 strategy*. https://ec.europa.eu/eurostat/statistics-explained/index.php/Europe_2020_indicators_-_education - Continuous_decrease_in_early_school_leaving

García-Parejo, I., & Ahern, A. (2019). La planificación de secuencias didácticas para el desarrollo de competencias discursivas en el marco de un proyecto de innovación docente. In J. V. Salido López, & P. V. Salido López (Eds.), *La competencia lingüística en la comunicación: visiones multidisciplinares y transversalidad* (pp. 87–94). Universidad de Castilla La Mancha.

García-Parejo, I., Ahern, A., & García-Bermejo, M. L. (2017). La 'pedagogía de los géneros discursivos' en Grados de Formación del Profesorado: Presentación de dos proyectos de innovación docente. Monográfica *Lenguaje y Texto*, 69–80.

García-Parejo, I., & Blanco-Fernández, J. (2020). Cambios en la escritura de los estudiantes de un grado de maestro tras su participación en proyectos de innovación docente centrados en la didáctica de los géneros. *E-AESLA 6*, 31–45.

García-Parejo, I., & Whittaker, R. (Eds.). (2017). *Teoría y práctica del modelo Reading to Learn (Leer para aprender) en contextos educativos transnacionales, Sección Monográfica, Lenguaje y Textos, 46*, 1–90. https://polipapers.upv.es/index.php/lyt/issue/view/769/showToc

Guio-Jaimes, J. M., & Choi de Mendizábal, A. (2014). The evolution of school failure risk during the 2000 decade in Spain: Analysis of PISA results with a two-level logistic model. *Estudios sobre Educación, 26*, 33–62.

Halliday, M. A. K., & Matthiessen, C. (2014). *Halliday's introduction to functional grammar* (4th ed.). Routledge.

Martin, J., & Rose, D. (2008). *Genre relations: Mapping culture*. Equinox.

Ministerio de Educación y Formación Profesional. (2021). *Estadísticas de las enseñanzas no universitarias: Resultados del curso 2019–2020. Nota resumen.* https://www.educacionyfp.gob.es/servicios-al-ciudadano/estadisticas/no-universitaria/alumnado/resultados/2019-2020-rd.html

Mullis, I. V. S., Martin, M. O., Foy, P., & Hooper, M. (2017*). PIRLS 2016 International results in reading.* International Association for the Evaluation of Educational Achievement (IEA).

Organization for Economic Cooperation and Development. (2013). *OECD skills outlook 2013: First results from the survey of adult skills.* http://dx.doi.org/10.1787/9789264204256-en

Organization for Economic Cooperation and Development. (2016). *PISA 2015 Results (Volume I): Excellence and equity in education, PISA.*, Paris: OECD Publishing. http://dx.doi.org/10.1787/9789264266490-en

Rose, D. (2018). *Reading to learn: Accelerating learning and closing the gap. Teacher training books and DVDs*. Reading to Learn http://www.readingtolearn.com.au

Rose, D., & Martin, J. R. (2012). *Learning to write, reading to learn: Genre, knowledge and pedagogy in the Sydney school.* Equinox.

Rose, D., & Martin, J. R. (2018). *Leer para aprender: lectura y escritura en las áreas del currículo*. Ana Bustelo Tortella (Transl.). Pirámide. Original work published 2012.

Sanjuán, C., Martínez, L., & Ferrer, A. (2019). *De la segregación socioeconómica a la educación inclusiva.* Save the Children España https://www.savethechildren.es/sites/default/files/imce/docs/mezclate_conmigo-anexo_cm.pdf

TALIS. (2018). *Estudio internacional de la enseñanza y del aprendizaje. Informe español.* Ministerio de Educación y Formación Profesional, Instituto Nacional de Evaluación Educativa, Madrid. https://www.educacionyfp.gob.es/inee/evaluaciones-internacionales/talis/talis-2018.html

Whittaker, R., & García-Parejo, I. (2018). Teacher Learning for European Literacy Education (TeL4ELE): genre-based pedagogy in five European countries. *European Journal of Applied Linguistics 6*(1) 31-57. https://www.degruyter.com/document/doi/10.1515/eujal-2017-0021/html

ABOUT THE AUTHORS

Rachel Whittaker, PhD (English Department, Universidad Autónoma, Madrid), coordinated Spain's team in the project: *Teacher Learning for European Literacy Education* (tel4ele.eu) which brought *Reading to Learn* to a number of European countries (see http://telcon2013.com/, formule.es) and *Lenguaje y Textos* monograph 2017, co-edited with Isabel García Parejo), and supervised the translation of Rose & Martin's *Learning to Write, Reading to Learn* into Spanish as *Leer para aprender: lectura y escritura en las áreas del currículo* (Pirámide 2018). She is active in teacher education and has published a number of articles on *Reading to Learn* pedagogy and on CLIL in Spain.

Isabel García-Parejo, PhD (Spanish Language Pedagogy section of the School of Education, Complutense University, Madrid) has worked as a teacher in Adult Basic Education for eleven years and in teacher education for over twenty-five years. As coordinator of the Forum for Multilingualism research group (formule.es) she participated in the Tel4ele Comenius project and later led teaching innovation projects designed to bring Reading to Learn into L1 teacher education for undergraduates. She has published a number of articles on R2L in Spain and given talks at national and international events (Chile, Columbia, Ecuador, Portugal, USA).

Aoife Ahern, PhD (Foreign Language Pedagogy section of the School of Education, Complutense University, Madrid) has worked in teacher education for over ten years. As a member of the Forum for Multilingualism (formule.es) research group she has participated in teaching innnovation and research focusing on the application of Reading to Learn to foreign language and Content and Language Integrated Learning for pre-service and in-service primary teachers, on which she has given talks and workshops at national and international (Denmark, Ecuador, Finland, Portugal,) events over the past seven years.

11

Learning to use Reading to Learn in Portugal

Carlos A. M. Gouveia, Marta Filipe Alexandre & Fausto Caels

ABSTRACT

This chapter reports on the use of the genre-based literacy pedagogy Reading to learn (R2L) in the cultural, educational and linguistic context of Portugal. R2L was officially introduced during the European Comenius project Teacher Learning for European Literacy Education (TeL4ELE). Following the project, R2L was introduced in pre-service teacher training programmes and in different university courses as part of their literacy development strategies. R2L workshops have been conducted in different parts of the country and there is a growing body of research on the use of R2L in different fields and educational settings (articles, book chapters, theses).

Working closely with teachers and school boards, and creating interdisciplinary teams have proven to be crucial in overcoming initial resistance by professionals who claim to possess prior knowledge of genre principles (language teachers) and by those who fear R2L will compromise content teaching (subject teachers). Lack of materials on genre pedagogy, and the pre-existence of genre-related terminology in the Portuguese curriculum has led to a project to describe and exemplify the genres of the Portuguese curriculum and to promote dialogue between different genre-based approaches in use in Portugal.

INTRODUCTION

This chapter describes how the genre-based literacy pedagogy of the "Sydney School" (hereafter *genre pedagogy*) has been taken up in Portugal following the European Comenius project *Teacher Learning for European Literacy Education* (TeL4ELE), in 2011–2013 (see Acevedo, Chapter 9 in this volume). The chapter places special emphasis on how the third generation of genre pedagogy developed in Australia, *Reading to Learn*, has come to be known and used in schools. We start by providing some background that made the Portuguese participation in the project possible, in terms of researchers, academic and research projects, and the institutions involved in them. We then discuss the TeL4ELE project, focusing on the perspective of the Portuguese team, describing the difficulties faced and the insights gained, and an assessment of the strategies followed to overcome those challenges and continuing working in the aftermath of the project. The final section is entirely devoted to this aftermath, which as a mixture of coordinated group actions and individual entrepreneurship is leading to some very positive results for the future.

BACKGROUND

Systemic Functional Linguistics was introduced at the University of Lisbon, School of Arts and Humanities, in the mid 1980s, by Emília Ribeiro Pedro, who took it also to other universities, particularly to the University of Minho, in formal post-graduate courses taught at the Institute of Arts and Human Sciences/ Instituto de Letras e Ciências Humanas.

SFL in Portugal began the new millennium with the creation of a Masters' Programme in TEFL, at the University of Lisbon. During this course, two dissertations were produced which were clearly framed by SFL: Viegas (2004), on change in Early Modern English, and Tavares (2004), the first dissertation on genre from an SFL perspective to be written in Portugal. These dissertations, together with António Avelar's PhD thesis on register and genre (Avelar, 2008), were supervised by Carlos Gouveia, who was himself engaged with research on genre (Gouveia, 2006a, 2006b). From that moment on, the basis for permanent research work on SFL and genre was set in Lisbon, with regular cooperation between Lisbon and representatives of the Sydney School. Under the auspices of that cooperation, Jim Martin came to the University of Lisbon in February 2006 to teach a first workshop and a series of follow-up workshops in subsequent years, titled *Genre Based Literacy Pedagogy*.

Two other important initiatives were the organization, at the UL, in 2001, of the first DICOEN Conference (International Conference on Discourse, Communication and the Enterprise), convened by Emília Ribeiro Pedro; and, in 2002, of the

14th Euro-International Systemic Functional Linguistics Workshop, convened by Carlos Gouveia. Both events contributed to the development of research in SFL in Portugal, with a strong emphasis on genre. In 2011, the Pre-Congress Institute of ISFC38 (38th International Systemic Functional Congress) was convened by Carlos Gouveia at the University of Lisbon – with workshops by Jim Martin, Susan Hood, Claire Acevedo and Frances Christie. It was via this network of contacts and the intermediation of Jim Martin and David Rose, that Claire Acevedo came to contact Carlos Gouveia with the purpose of submitting a project to the European Commission that would involve the training of teachers on how to use the *Reading to Learn* classroom programme to improve their students' literacy. In Portugal, the project was hosted by ILTEC, a research unit in the national research and development system, congregating researchers from different institutions of tertiary education.

TEL4ELE – TEACHER LEARNING FOR EUROPEAN LITERACY EDUCATION

Overview

ILTEC was a Lisbon-based non-profit organization and research centre associated with the University of Lisbon, the New University of Lisbon and the Foundation for Science and Technology, and became the host institution in Portugal for the European Comenius Project TeL4ELE. The project, conducted from 2011 to 2013, involved teams from five different countries. The Portuguese team was set up with seven members and collaborators from ILTEC's research groups on Discourse and Literacy (Carlos Gouveia, Luís Filipe Barbeiro, Alzira Tavares Santos, António Avelar) and on Language and Linguistic Diversity (Fernanda Botelho, Luísa Solla, Fausto Caels). Due to the characteristics of the project, the group aggregated twenty-two teachers from six different schools in two different regions of Portugal: Lisbon and Leiria.

The first International TeL4ELE Project Meeting was held in 2011 in Lisbon, in which Jim Martin and David Rose ran a workshop involving all the teams in the project and some guests. This meeting was the kick-off for all the remaining work to be done throughout the project, with two distinct moments: a first year devoted to training the team members as literacy experts, and a second year in which these experts trained the teachers in schools, accompanying them with their teaching of the new genre pedagogy, based entirely on *Reading to Learn* (R2L). At this meeting a national literacy profile was drawn which "provided a picture of the literacy environment where the Portuguese team came to create, develop and apply, as part of a teacher training strategy, a new approach to literacy education based on genre and the way the concept feeds knowledge acquisition and the organization of school subjects and disciplines." (Gouveia et al., 2014, p. 3).

The project in Portugal involved the training of seven experts in R2L (year 1), and the subsequent training of 14 teachers, who implemented the pedagogy (year 2). About 250 students from 6 different primary and middle schools participated, with one class being exposed to R2L in all curriculum subjects. During the first year of the project, sample lesson plans were prepared, including both the analysis and annotation of texts as well as the classwork around it. The lesson plans were designed as scaffolding sequences (cycles of tasks) and were based on grammatical and text linguistics concepts from the Sydney School. The lesson plans were presented following a strategy of work that started with the genres the teachers would recognize as such, slowly moving on to genres they were less familiar with, including the genres of school subjects other than school Portuguese (cf. Gouveia et al., 2014, pp. 8–20).

During the second year, preparatory work and teacher training programmes were carried by the national experts. The preparatory tasks combined the translation of the *Reading to Learn* materials and their adaptation to the Portuguese curriculum, the study of the national course books for basic schooling, as well as the elaboration of new materials for the different teaching cycles and the school subjects focused on in each lesson plan. The project was also presented to several schools (potential teacher trainees and school principals), and two websites were created, each one directly related to the regional group of trainers and trainees (Lisbon and Leiria). The teacher training programmes included a 40-hour formal workshop led by the team, plus weekly tutorial work.

Further dissemination of the project was carried out by means of workshops to inform the teaching community, and work with the Ministry of Education, as well as with PROALV (*Programa Aprendizagem ao Longo da Vida* / Lifelong Learning Programme). The collaboration with the Ministry of Education was followed up by a webinar, that was filmed on 5 December, 2013, and made available for the teaching community at the Ministry's webpage (cf. http://webinar.dge.mec.pt/2013/12/05/projeto-tel4ele/).

Stocktaking

The TeL4ELE project was an important milestone in the implementation of R2L in Portugal. Therefore, a brief assessment is justified, identifying some of the achievements and challenges of the project, as well as the perspectives it opened up for future actions.

The project allowed the training of a group of specialists in genre pedagogy. The seven key-members of the Portuguese team started the project with different backgrounds. For some of them, the project allowed the deepening or updating of knowledge; for others it represented the first contact with the genre approach of the Sydney School. The project's emphasis on R2L allowed all key-members to gain an in-depth understanding of the programme's principles and strategies, both in theoretical and in practical terms. However, a need for continued (self) study regarding the language model that supports R2L was also felt by the key-members, who decided to engage further with SFL. They concluded that the planning and execution of the programme's strategies required advanced and holistic textual analysis skills, in terms of genre, register, discourse semantics and lexicogrammar, as these were not fully developed in the project. A comprehensive understanding of the Portuguese educational system was also seen as a need. In order to help teachers with the implementation of R2L, genre experts felt they ought to be familiar with the national curriculum, as well as the reading and writing requirements of different subjects, school years and syllabuses. One of the biggest difficulties of the project, for example, resided in the training of mathematics teachers, as the key-members felt unprepared to deal with the teaching of mathematics and and its subject-specific genres. Through training, study and, in the second year, the interaction with the teachers this difficulty was overcome, but not without some stress and anguish.

The TeL4ELE project featured the participation of a group of highly motivated teachers from different schools, subjects, grades and educational levels. One of the key factors for the success of the training programme was its accreditation by the Scientific-Pedagogical Council for Lifelong Training, SPCLT. In Portugal, continuous or lifelong training is essential for one's career as a basic and secondary education teacher. Engaging in lifelong training courses and scientific events grant teachers credits that will then be acknowledged as boosters for moving on in their career as teachers with the Ministry of Education. Designing the teacher training in the project as an accredited programme with the SPCLT allowed for a formal recognition of the teachers' commitment. In our view, formal accreditation is fundamental when introducing teachers to genre pedagogy, given the duration and the specialized contents of the training programme. The accreditation process of the TeL4ELE teacher training programme had some setbacks, which are explained here, as they show how a genre pedagogy implementation may well depend more on external constraints than on the will and enthusiasm of the people involved. Although the SPCLT accredited the teacher training as a relevant programme, they accredited it as a multidisciplinary training for all the teachers, independently of their subjects. By accrediting it under this modality they failed to recognize its specificity for the expression of content in the subject areas. In doing so, they overlooked the instrumental and cross-cutting role of language in education and didn't recognize the fact that it is through language that the students learn the different subjects. The contribution of genre pedagogy for making curricular content more accessible to students was thus not fully acknowledged by the authorities.

Some teachers expressed initial concerns about the genre approach. Their concerns were different according to the subject they taught: language teachers, for example, had difficulty in recognizing the specificity of the approach assuming that they were already doing in their classes what, in fact, was totally new to them ("I already do this with my students..."); content teachers, in contrast, looked suspiciously at the pedagogy as an overload, something that would reduce their class time for teaching the contents of their subjects ("If I do this I will not have the time to teach them the syllabus contents..."). We retained an important lesson from this initial reaction of our teachers: that a constant and careful dialogue between the genre approach of R2L and teachers' previous knowledge and experience was needed. Slowly, step-by-step, the trainers managed to show the teachers that neither were they already implementing genre pedagogy in their classes nor that implementing it would cause any harm in the teaching of their subjects' contents; on the contrary, the pedagogy was just a different way to teach their subjects' contents with some very important advantages.

For this dialogue to be successful, a spirit of openness was needed by both trainers and trainees. It was in that spirit that some needs and guidelines were identified, like confronting and/or articulating the axioms and assumptions of the Sydney School with the literacy guidelines and demands of the official documents. School Portuguese, for instance, contemplates a wide array of textual categories, (apparently) distinct from the genres of the Sydney School and R2L. The other subjects' curricula and syllabuses, on the other hand, lack accuracy, precision and transparency in their use of verbs and nouns to refer to textual categories and tasks. Doubts concerning teaching materials also surfaced during the training sessions, as texts in textbooks were not necessarily good examples of the genres characterized in R2L, particularly for the identification of social purposes and structures (stages and phases). Whether and to what extent the existence of texts that did not fully show the social purpose and/or the stages of the genre would compromise the implementation of R2L was a central and recurring point of discussion among teachers and teacher trainers.

Teachers involved in the project managed to come to terms with the underpinnings and the strategies of R2L. Those with no prior training and/or experience in teaching literacy took their first steps in the explicit linguistic analyses of texts and in planning reading and writing activities. Despite the 40-hour duration of the training (complemented with tutorials and many hours of autonomous work), the project did not necessarily turn teachers into proficient or enduring users of R2L, with many of them still showing insecurities regarding text analysis, lesson planning, reading and writing strategies dealing with lexicogrammatical patterns (e.g. *Detailed Reading, Joint Construction*) or writing assessment. It became evident, therefore, that the implementation of a genre pedagogy in the Portuguese context would require continuous training, ideally spread over more than one school year. A second major issue concerned the scarcity of training materials in and on Portuguese, taking into account the specificities of the national curriculum and its organization in educational levels and subject areas. Filling this blank was something that was far beyond the goals of the project, thus necessarily extending onwards the translation of fundamental texts by authors of the Sydney School and/or the production of original work in Portuguese.

The different degrees of success in the implementation of the pedagogy by the teachers led us, finally, to ponder the role of the surrounding school environment (see a discussion of this issue in Sweden, in Andersson Varga et. al., Chapter 8 in this volume). The school where the project left more lasting marks had a unique set of variables: i) one of the key-members of the Portuguese team was a staff member, ii) the school management supported the implementation of the project, and iii) the pedagogy was implemented with a single group of students, with all the teachers teaching the group participating in the training. These variables brought teachers a sense of security, as well as the possibility of dialogue and the exchange of experiences. Crucially, it allowed the creation of a multidisciplinary teaching team, in the true sense of the word, in which teachers collaborated in the selection of content, texts and strategies and in the monitoring of the class, no matter the subject. This situation, unusual in the Portuguese education system, where teachers work exclusively with colleagues belonging to the same subject group or department, seems to us a very important condition for the implementation of a programme such as R2L. Teachers of history working with teachers of natural sciences or chemistry and school Portuguese, outside the natural environment of formal meetings to discuss term marks or behavioural problems, was something the teachers had not experienced before. This aspect was highly praised and stressed as an important factor for their professional development and the literacy education of their students.

To round up, TeL4ELE represented the first introduction of R2L in Portugal. The challenges faced within the project led us to understand that a broader and more lasting implementation of the programme would imply interventions on multiple fronts, as described in the next section.

SUBSEQUENT DEVELOPMENTS

This section discusses the work on genre pedagogy carried out in Portugal since the completion of TeL4ELE. It includes initiatives specifically aimed at the dissemination and implementation of R2L, as well as parallel efforts aiming to prepare the ground for a wider and more sustained use of the pedagogy.

Translation of terminology and reference texts

In order to disseminate R2L to Portuguese speakers and to train (future) teachers in Portugal and other Portuguese-speaking countries in the pedagogy, it seemed essential, from the beginning, to have a Portuguese translation of reference texts in the Sydney School. This endeavour started in the TeL4ELE Project, with the translation and adaptation of technical terms related to macro and micro-strategies of R2L and the map of the genres of schooling, including names of genre families, individual genres, social purposes, stages and phases.

Research on genre

It became clear, early on in the TeL4ELE project, that the success of R2L relies heavily on knowledge about genre, which constitutes, in most cases, new territory for teachers in Portugal and other Portuguese speaking countries. The challenge has been to adapt the pedagogy to the Portuguese language, the specificities of the Portuguese education system and the Portuguese teachers' prior knowledge of genre, which is mostly based on a patchwork of different theories not easily accommodated in classroom practices. Hence the initial idea among our trainees that they already do the pedagogy in class. Facing this challenge involved some reflection and some publishing, for two distinct purposes and audiences: scientific and academic, on the one hand, and teacher training courses and programmes support, on the other.

As mentioned in the previous section, there were some previous works on school genres framed by SFL in Portugal, to which one must add Martins (2008) and Gouveia (2006a, 2006b, 2008, 2013a, 2013b, 2013c, 2014). The first major study, however, after TeL4ELE, using the holistic approach of the Sydney School, was carried out by Caels (2016), allowing for the mapping, description and exemplification of the genres used in the subject of natural sciences, as taught in years 5 and 6 of the Portuguese education system. Following a similar approach, a research project on the description of the genres of the subject areas of Portuguese, science and history in both elementary and secondary education was designed. The project was the main endeavour of a newly formed research group, coordinated by Carlos Gouveia and focused on genre and academic discourse, involving researchers with at least two different theoretical perspectives: one of an anglophone origin, basically SFL and R2L, the other, of a francophone origin, involving a composite application of Socio-Discursive Interactionism (Bronckart, 1997) and text linguistics (Adam, 1992).

The research group is named Discurso e Práticas Discursivas Académicas or DPDA (Discourse and Academic Discursive Practices). Outcomes of this project, from a strictly SFL/R2L perspective, include: 1) a database consisting of more than 1000 school texts, transcribed, categorized by grade, subject and genre and segmented in stages and phases, 2) statistical data on the frequency of genres in textbooks,

3) descriptions of genre families and individual genres, concerning their role in the construal of specialized knowledge, their textual structure, and lexicogrammatical patterns.

This ongoing project provides two types of outcomes: scientific texts and texts directed to teaching professionals and practices. The scientific output, directed at peers, helps to build a body of knowledge about the genres in the different subjects and their characteristics (cf. Caels et al., 2020; Caels & Quaresma, 2018a, 2019a, 2019d). The main findings confirm tendencies found in other languages and schooling systems, documented in the literature of the Sydney School. However, the project also enabled the identification of some idiosyncrasies in Portuguese texts.

Texts aimed at teaching professionals, on the other hand, disseminate knowledge on genre, providing in- and pre-service teachers with accurate and accessible descriptions of the literacy demands of different subject areas. To support this aim, a series of free-access resources on the genres of School Portuguese, science and history was designed and put forward, together with a website for the dissemination of genre related knowledge (https://sites.ipleiria.pt/pge/). Resources include:

1 General booklets, one for each subject area, introducing the role of language and literacy in the construction, transmission and evaluation of content-specific knowledge, an annotated map of the genre families and individual genres, statistical data on the representativity of these genres in textbooks, and a brief characterization of each genre (e.g. Caels & Quaresma, 2019b).
2 Specific booklets, focussing on a single genre family or individual genre, providing an in-depth discussion of its social purpose, structure (stages, phases), lexicogrammatical patterns and, whenever relevant, multimodal resources. Text analysis according to genre parameters was also provided, including diagrams on specialized composition and classification taxonomies and activity sequences (e.g. Caels & Quaresma, 2018b, 2018c, 2019c).
3 Support booklets, one for each subject area, containing a variety of sample texts (4–5 for each genre) retrieved from textbooks, and analyzed according to their social purpose, stages, phases and knowledge structure (e.g. Caels & Quaresma, 2017).

Figure 11.1 shows three sample covers, one for each type of booklet (general, specific and support), for the subject area of science.

Apart from this large-scale project, there were also smaller initiatives to map genres in other social contexts or textual resources, as a way to support genre-based classroom interventions. These have taken place mainly as Dissertations and Theses in master's and doctoral programmes in the field of Foreign/Second Language Teaching and Didactics (e.g. Chunyue, 2015; Faquir, 2016; Loureiro, 2016; Morais, 2017).

Figure 11.1. Sample covers of genre resources

In addition to mapping genres in textbooks and other semiotic resources, the need to intervene in two other areas emerged. The first intervention concerned the (critical) analysis of the Portuguese school curriculum regarding the presence, or absence, of genre categories and pedagogical approaches informed by the concept of genre. This analysis has focused mainly on the guiding documents of school Portuguese; it concluded that the documents promote genre-based teaching practices and provide a wide range of textual categories, but these arise from different classification principles with no common criteria (cf. Barbeiro et al., 2020, 2021). The analysis has also taken into account transdisciplinary and integrated perspectives (language and content), both in the syllabuses of school Portuguese and of the other subjects. This type of research is essential. The national educational system already has a set of expectations about what is meant by the notion of genre and which individual genres should be taught. The DPDA group's research has sought, on the one hand, to identify possible omissions in the guiding documents and, on the other, to find points of contact with the approach of the Sydney School (see Hassan & Boccia, Chapter 15 in this volume, for work on this same issue in Argentina). Similar works have been developed in the scope of master's and doctoral research, analyzing guidelines and other official documents for the teaching of Portuguese in other Portuguese speaking countries, such as Mozambique (e.g. Marrengula, 2020) and Cape Verde (e.g. Silva, 2020). A second intervention concerns the dialogue with other genre approaches in use in Portugal. In this context, collaboration with researchers working with the theory of Socio Discursive Interactionism, in particular, which brings together a significant number of researchers in Portugal with several known applications in the field, has proven fruitful and dynamic.

GENRE PEDAGOGY – TEACHER TRAINING, IMPLEMENTATION AND RESEARCH

Despite several attempts, to date it has not been possible to repeat, with other in-service teachers, the teacher training programme implemented within the TeL4ELE project. Overcoming bureaucratic and financial restraints proved difficult. Short-term workshops and training courses have proven more successful in disseminating R2L. In that spirit, several initiatives aimed at both teachers and teacher trainers were held in different parts of the country (Porto, Aveiro, Lisbon, among others). These took place as workshops in conferences and as lectures and workshops in elementary and secondary schools.

Meanwhile, R2L has continued to be used with different levels of application in the different elementary and secondary schools involved in the project. The main application of the pedagogy, however, has been in tertiary education (see further examples of R2L applications in tertiary education in this volume in Millin, Chapter 6; Whittaker, et al., Chapter 10; and Alvarez, et al., Chapter 13). Genre-based teaching started to be formally adopted in some curricular units and courses taught in tertiary education, such as writing courses aimed at international students at the School of Education and Social Sciences, Leiria Polytechnic Institute. It is estimated that, in the last 5 years, around 500 students have been exposed to the programme's strategies in this way. Additionally, genre pedagogy was integrated in post-graduate courses in the MA programme in elementary education, at the School of Education and Social Sciences, Leiria Polytechnic Institute, and in the MA and PhD programmes in Portuguese as a Second/Foreign Language, at the School of Arts and Humanities, University of Lisbon.

As an important development during the years following TeL4ELE, Portugal has seen a major increase in research on genre pedagogy. The use of R2L has been the subject of a growing number of conference papers, journal articles, book chapters, MA dissertations and PhD theses. Regarding subject areas, research has focussed mainly on: Portuguese Language and Literature, Portuguese as a Second/Foreign Language, English as a Foreign language and Scientific Discourse. Strategies of the R2L programme that have received more attention include *Paragraph-by-Paragraph Reading*, *Detailed Reading* and *Joint Rewriting*. See, for example, the research on *Rewriting* by Barbeiro (2015a, 2015b, 2016a, 2016b, 2020), Barbeiro, L. F. & Barbeiro, C. (2016, 2020) and Barbeiro, C. & Barbeiro, L. F. (2019). Other topics include the role of teachers in literacy learning, the use of scaffolding techniques and the use of metalanguage, or genre pedagogy and multimodality (Morais, 2017; Nóbrega, 2018; Nogueira, 2015; Pinheiro, 2017). It is also worth noting that most works defend and/or analyze the use of R2L with more vulnerable audiences, whether students with special educational needs (Barbeiro & Prino, 2016; Fernandes &

Barbeiro, 2016; Pereira, 2015; Prino, 2015), deaf students (Barros, 2015), students of immigrant background (Caels, 2016, in press; Barbeiro, 2017; Mendes, 2014), or students who have Portuguese as a second language in countries like Timor or São Tomé and Príncipe (J. Silva, 2016; J. A. J. Silva, 2017; Cruz, 2017). The latter, in combination with the research on the genres of schooling in Mozambique and Cape Verde mentioned above (Marrengula, 2020; Silva, 2020) account for an important movement of internationalization of genre pedagogy in Portuguese.

CONCLUSION

Research on the use, appropriation and application of SFL-based genre pedagogy has come a long way in Portugal. The purpose of this chapter is to provide an overview of the path trodden so far. Having reached this point, we must stress the potentiality we are facing now. While it has not been possible, thus far, to create a large-scale teacher training project, researchers interested in the use of R2L have developed the manpower and the expertise which allows us to foster applied research individually in different academic contexts. R2L genre knowledge and pedagogy is flowing gently into schools and classroom practices, by insistence, resistance and individual will. The fact that almost all the researchers working with R2L in Portugal, no matter their institution of origin, work together in the same research centre and research group has certainly brought some added value to that flow. Crucially, this collaboration has enabled the creation of a major resource of teaching materials and academic studies to support the continuing development of genre pedagogy in Portugal.

REFERENCES

Adam, J. M. (1992). *Les textes: Types et prototypes*. Edition Nathan.

Avelar, A. (2008). *Géneros e registos do discurso no ensino de línguas: Proposta de aplicação ao ensino de PLE e monitorização em contexto.* [Doctoral dissertation, Universidade de Lisboa].

Barbeiro, C. (2017). *As práticas discursivas nas interações verbais em contexto pedagógico: Contributos da sociolinguística interacional para o estudo do discurso na aula de português.* [Doctoral dissertation, Universidade Aberta].

Barbeiro, C., & Barbeiro, L. (2016). Reescrita conjunta: Entre as propostas dos alunos e a orientação do professor. In J. A. B., Carvalho, M. L. Dionísio, E. Mesquita, J. Cunha, & A. Arqueiro (Eds.), *Atas: V SIELP – Simpósio Internacional de Ensino de Língua Portuguesa // V FIAL – Fórum Ibero-Americano de Literacias* (pp. 65–73). CIEd / Universidade do Minho.

Barbeiro, C., & Barbeiro, L. (2020). Estratégias de interação na reescrita conjunta para o ensino-aprendizagem da escrita. *Indagatio Didactica, 12*(2), 91–108.

Barbeiro, L. (2015a). Rewriting and appropriating language. In l. Gómez Chova, I. Candel Torres, & A. López Martinez (Eds.), *ICERI2015 Proceedings: 8th International conference of education, research and innovation* (pp. 1059–1069). IATED Academy.

Barbeiro, L. (2015b). Reescrita: Domínio e alargamento dos recursos linguísticos. *Exedra (Temático)*, 209–235.

Barbeiro, L. (2016a). The text under construction: The decisions and arguments of writers as the text's first readers in a collaborative writing task. In *INTED2016 Proceedings* (pp. 6191–6201). International Association of Technology, Education and Development (IATED).

Barbeiro, L. (2016b). Paráfrase e reescrita no percurso para a autonomia: Que patamar de proximidade textual? In J. A. B. Carvalho, M.L. Dionísio, E. Mesquita, J. Cunha, & A. Arqueiro (Eds.), *Atas: V SIELP – Simpósio internacional de ensino de língua Portuguesa // V FIAL – Fórum Ibero-Americano de literacias* (pp. 74–83). CIEd / Universidade do Minho.

Barbeiro, L. (2020). Da leitura à reescrita: Propostas e percursos da pedagogia baseada em gêneros. *Educação e Pesquisa, 46*. https://doi.org/10.1590/s1678-4634202046218410

Barbeiro, L., & Barbeiro, C. (2019). O discurso do professor na reescrita conjunta. In F. Caels, L.F. Barbeiro, & J. V. Santos, (Eds.), *Discurso académico – uma área disciplinar* (pp. 69–91). ESECS-Instituto Politécnico de Leiria.

Barbeiro, L. F., Caels, F., & Quaresma, A. (2020). Géneros textuais e interdisciplinaridade nas aprendizagens essenciais. In D. Alves, H. G. Pinto, I. S. Dias, M. O. Abreu, & R. G. Muñoz (Eds.), *Investigação, Práticas e Contextos em Educação – 2020* (pp. 82–90). ESECS-Instituto Politécnico de Leiria.

Barbeiro, L. F., Caels, F., & Quaresma, A. (2021). Aprendizagens essenciais de Português: Mapeamento de géneros textuais e competências associadas. In C. Teixeira et al. (Eds.), *LUSOCONF2019 – II Encontro internacional de língua Portuguesa e relações Lusófonas: livro de atas* (pp. 90–102), Instituto Politécnico de Bragança.

Barbeiro, L., & Prino, C. (2016). Estratégias genológicas: Participação e inclusão de crianças com perturbações da comunicação. In D. Alves, H. G. Pinto, I. S. Dias, M. O. Abreu, & R. G. Muñoz (Eds.), *Atas da IX Conferência internacional investigação, práticas e contextos em educação* (pp. 65-71). ESECS-Instituto Politécnico de Leiria.

Barros, P. L. (2015). *Níveis comuns de referência e pedagogia de género no ensino de português a alunos surdos: Proposta de organização curricular.* [Doctoral dissertation, Universidade Católica Portuguesa].

Bronckart, J. P. (1997). *Activité langagière, textes et discours. Pour un interactionisme socio-discursif.* Delachaux et Niestlé.

Caels, F. (2016). *Os textos de Ciências na disciplina de PLNM: Uma abordagem baseada em Género.* [Doctoral dissertation, Universidade de Lisboa].

Caels, F. (in press). O português como língua veicular de saberes escolares: Pistas para a conceção de materiais didáticos. In C. Castro & A. Madeira (Eds.), *Desenvolvimento de materiais didáticos para Português como língua não materna: Experiências e desafios*. Lidel.

Caels, F., Barbeiro, L. F., & Gouveia, C. A. M. (2020). Géneros escolares segundo a Escola de Sydney: Propósitos, estruturas e realizações textuais. *Indagatio Didactica, 12*(2), 13–32.

Caels, F., & Quaresma, A. (2017). *Exemplos textuais dos géneros de Ciências Naturais.* CELGA-ILTEC.

Caels, F., & Quaresma, A. (2018a). Géneros textuais em manuais de Ciências Naturais. In D. Alves, H. G. Pinto, I. S. Dias, M. O. Abreu, & R. G. Muñoz (Eds.), *Atas da IX Conferência internacional investigação, práticas e contextos em educação* (p. 297). ESECS- Instituto Politécnico de Leiria.

Caels, F., & Quaresma, A. (2018b). *Os géneros em manuais de Ciências Naturais do 2.º e 3.º ciclos do Ensino Básico: Explicação Sequencial.* CELGA-ILTEC.

Caels, F., & Quaresma, A. (2018c). *Os géneros em manuais de Ciências Naturais do 2.º e 3.º ciclos do Ensino Básico: Relatório Composicional.* CELGA-ILTEC.

Caels, F., & Quaresma, A. (2019a). Géneros textuais em manuais de História. In D. Alves, H. G. Pinto, I. S. Dias, M. O. Abreu, & R. G. Muñoz (Eds.), *Atas da IX Conferência internacional investigação, práticas e contextos em educação* (p. 484). ESECS-Instituto Politécnico de Leiria.

Caels, F., & Quaresma, A. (2019b). *Os géneros em manuais de Ciências Naturais do 2.º e 3.º ciclos do Ensino Básico: Mapeamento dos géneros.* CELGA-ILTEC.

Caels, F., & Quaresma, A. (2019c). *Os géneros em manuais de Ciências Naturais do 2.º e 3.º ciclos do Ensino Básico: Géneros procedimentais.* CELGA-ILTEC.

Caels, F., & Quaresma, A. (2019d). Caracterização dos géneros do Ensino Básico e Secundário. In F. Caels, L. F. Barbeiro, & J. V. Santos (Eds.), *Discurso Académico – uma área disciplinar em construção* (pp. 108–133). CELGA-ILTEC / ESECS.

Chunyue, S. (2015). *Seleção comentada e etiquetagem de géneros discursivos para o ensino de aprendentes chineses orientados para os negócios.* [Master's thesis, Universidade de Lisboa].

Cruz, G. (2017). *Produção escrita do português (L2) no 2.º ciclo do ensino secundário em São Tomé e Príncipe.* [Master's thesis, Universidade de Lisboa].

Faquir, O. C. G. (2016). *Didática da escrita em contextos multilingues: o caso de Moçambique – desafios linguísticos, metodológicos e contextuais.* [Doctoral dissertation, Universidade de Lisboa].

Fernandes, T., & Barbeiro, L. (2016). Pedagogia genológica: Intervenção com crianças com necessidades educativas especiais. In D. Alves, H. G. Pinto, I. S. Dias, M. O. Abreu, & R. G. Muñoz (Eds.), *Atas da IX Conferência internacional investigação, práticas e contextos em educação* (pp. 258--264). ESECS-Instituto Politécnico de Leiria.

Gouveia, C. A. M. (2006a). Language, literacy and cultural politics: The debate on the new language curriculum in Portugal. In R. Whittaker, M. O'Donnell, & A. McCabe (Eds.), *Language and literacy: Functional approaches* (pp. 177–188). Continuum.

Gouveia, C. A. M. (2006b). Syllabuses, textbooks and teaching practices: Literacy and language teaching in Portugal. *Veredas, 10* (1 & 2).

Gouveia, C. A. M. (2008). Texto Narrativo. In M. H. M. Mateus, D. Pereira, & G. Fischer (Eds.) *Diversidade linguística na escola Portuguesa* (pp. 113–118). Fundação Calouste Gulbenkian.

Gouveia, C. A. M. (2013a). Writing development in basic school years in Portugal: Report on a pilot project. In *"A scholar for all seasons". Homenagem a João Almeida Flor* (pp. 191–204). Departamento de Estudos Anglísticos/Centro de Estudos Anglísticos da Universidade de Lisboa.

Gouveia, C. A. M. (2013b). A escola como sistema de géneros: conhecimento, aprendizagem e transversalidade. In M. H. M. Mateus, & L. Solla (Eds.), *Ensino do Português como língua não materna: Estratégias, materiais e formação* (pp. 441–461). ILTEC/ Fundação Calouste Gulbenkian.

Gouveia, C. A. M. (2013c). Evolving in confidence: writing across basic schooling. In O. Vian Jr., & C. Caltabiano (Eds.), *Língua(gem) e suas múltiplas faces – Estudos em homenagem a Leila Barbara* (pp. 93–108). Mercado de Letras.

Gouveia, C. A. M. (2014). A compreensão leitora como base instrumental do ensino da produção escrita. In W. R., Silva, J. S.dos Santos, & M. A. Melo (Eds.), *Pesquisas em língua(gem) e demandas do ensino básico* (pp. 203–231). Pontes.

Gouveia, C. A. M., Avelar, A., Barbeiro, L., Botelho, F., Caels, F., Solla, L. & Tavares, A. (2014). *Teacher Learning for European Literacy Education – TeL4ELE – Project outputs from Portugal.* Instituto de Linguística Teórica e Computacional (ILTEC). https://www.researchgate.net/project/Teacher-Learning-for-European-Literacy-Education-TeL4ELE

Loureiro, J. (2016). *Texto e contexto no QECRL e nas propostas dos manuais: explorando as condições de implementação de um ensino de base genológica PLE/PL2.* [Master's thesis, Universidade de Lisboa].

Marrengula, E. (2020). *Do texto ao parágrafo: um contributo para o ensino da escrita no 1º Ciclo do Ensino Secundário em Moçambique.* [Doctoral dissertation, Universidade de Lisboa].

Martins, M. C. (2008). *A contribuição dos significados experienciais para a constituição dos elementos obrigatórios do género narrativa escolar: um estudo de caso.* [Master's thesis, Universidade de Lisboa].

Mendes, M. O. H. (2014). *Abordagem de base genológica no ensino do português como língua não materna.* [Master's thesis, Universidade de Lisboa].

Morais, A. (2017). *Género e multimodalidade na aula de ILE: Compreender e comentar o texto publicitário.* [Doctoral dissertation, Universidade Católica Portuguesa].

Nóbrega, M. S. L. (2018). *Multimodalidade em documento didático: A construção de um vídeo para formação em pedagogia do género.* [Master's thesis, Universidade de Lisboa].

Nogueira, M. F. C. (2015). *Da biblioteca escolar à sala de aula repensando a praxis à luz de uma pedagogia baseada em género.* [Master's thesis, Universidade de Lisboa].

Pereira, T. L. P. F. (2015). *Implementação da pedagogia genológica em alunos com necessidades educativas especiais: Contributos para uma literacia inclusiva.* [Master's thesis, ESECS-Instituto Politécnico de Leiria].

Pinheiro, V. A. G. (2017). *Refletindo sobre a utilização da estratégia Ler para Aprender como meio de redução de erros ortográficos de alunos de 3.º ano de escolaridade.* [Master's thesis, ESECS-Instituto Politécnico de Leiria].

Prino, C. S. (2015). *Abordagem genológica em contexto de jardim-de-infância e crianças com perturbações da comunicação: Alargar o círculo de inclusão.* [Master's thesis, ESECS-Instituto Politécnico de Leiria].

Silva, J. (2016). O *contributo da pedagogia de género para a formação de professores PLE/L2 no contexto Timorense.* [Master's thesis, Universidade de Lisboa].

Silva, J. A. J. (2017). *Contributo de um modelo de base genológica para a formação de professores na Guiné-Bissau.* [Master's thesis, Universidade de Lisboa].

Silva, M. G. V. F. (2020). *Práticas de escrita no Ensino Secundário no contexto de Cabo Verde.* [Doctoral dissertation, Universidade de Lisboa].

Tavares, A. (2004). *Para uma abordagem de género em ILE.* [Master's thesis, Universidade de Lisboa].

Viegas, M. (2004). *Aspectos sistémico-funcionais da mudança linguística em cartas familiares do early modern English.* [Master's thesis, Universidade de Lisboa].

ABOUT THE AUTHORS

Carlos A. M. Gouveia holds a PhD in Applied Linguistics and is an Associate Professor (with professorship) at the Department of English, School of Arts and Humanities, University of Lisbon, Portugal, and a researcher at the Centre for General and Applied linguistic Studies (CELGA-ILTEC), at the University of Coimbra. Presently he is Head of the Graduate Programmeme in Portuguese as a Foreign/Second Language at the University of Lisbon. He has been involved in several research projects and coordinated the Portuguese team of the European Project Teacher Learning for European Literacy Education (2011–2013).

Marta F. Alexandre is assistant professor at the Polytechnic of Leiria and integrated member of CELGA-ILTEC of the University of Coimbra, Portugal. She teaches Linguistic Theories, Discourse Analysis, Portuguese Linguistics and Portuguese as a Second Language. Her activity as a researcher includes: describing academic discourse (focusing the construction and teaching/learning of specialized knowledge in different fields), analyzing social representations (e.g. the representation of food habits in school textbooks), and the description and preservation of popular knowledge (namely folk songs and dances, as well as crafts related to the cycle of the wool).

Fausto Caels is assistant professor at the Polytechnic of Leiria and integrated member of CELGA-ILTEC of the University of Coimbra, Portugal. His research focusses on the description of academic discourse from a genre perspective and the use of genre pedagogy in the areas of Science, History and Portuguese as a Second/Foreign language, both in compulsory and higher education.

12

Bilingual Reading to Learn for ESL Latina immigrant mothers in the United States

Andrés Ramírez & María Gabriela Gutiérrez

ABSTRACT

This chapter describes a bilingual (English-Spanish) extension of the Reading to Learn (R2L) approach (Rose, 2018; Rose & Martin, 2012) with Latina immigrant emerging bilingual adult learners. The adapted R2L methodology was inspired by the language allocation principles of preview–view–review bilingual curricular cycle that systematically uses native and target language in teaching language, through language, and about language (Halliday, 1993). The chapter first rationalizes the pedagogic basis for the adaptation, focusing on the importance of conducting the first stage of the R2L pedagogy cycle, Preparing for Reading, in the native language of the students. It then details how participants were guided through Detailed Reading and Joint Construction which enabled them to produce independent biographical texts in English. Finally, the implications of the bilingual reconceptualization of the R2L methodology are discussed in relation to foreign and second language teaching and learning.

INTRODUCTION

About 40 million people in the United States (immigrant and US born) reported speaking Spanish at home. Spanish speakers have the lowest rates of English proficiency of all US immigrants (Migration Policy Institute, 2018). Faced with this problem, publicly funded adult and workforce programs aim at increasing the levels of English proficiency for adult immigrant populations, so they can be better prepared both for work and for supporting their children's education at home. The federal US government insists on teaching in English only (National Center for Education Statistics, 2003), despite the fact that such practice runs counter to research on best practices for youth and adult immigrants (Lukes, 2011). Adult and workforce programs have no choice but to focus on teaching adult learners in English if they want to receive funds to continue operations.

Support at home for children's academic development is poised to become even more critical as we look at the future in light of modern-day health emergencies and stay at home mandates. Parents Power is one such family literacy program, in which the bilingual Reading to Learn (R2L) approach described in this chapter was applied. Parents Power is an award-winning family literacy program with over a decade of service which has reached over 200 families thus far in the southeast of the USA. Students in the program are emergent to advanced bilingual, or EAB, learners. As with many of these programs in the US, the Parents Power program seeks to: a) teach the parents to read, write, and speak English, b) provide guidance to parents on how to be their child's first and most important teacher, and c) teach parents the professional, communicative and personal skills needed to be involved in nurturing their children for success by encouraging the development of self-confidence.

Andrés Ramirez has been involved with the Parents Power program since 2017, and Maria Gabriela Gutierrez since 2019. The bilingual R2L approach was used in three curricular units during this time, for supporting reading and writing with children at home (Ramirez, 2020, 2022), reading and writing recipes in English, and reading and writing biographies of famous Latinx people. This chapter reports on the curricular unit focused on biographies.

LOST IN TRANSLATION: THE BEGINNINGS

As part of the preparation phase before introducing R2L to the Parents Power program, we visited a classroom for about three weeks. This class consisted of eight Latina mothers with a varied range of proficiency in both English (from entry to intermediate level) and Spanish literacy who came from several different countries (Mexico, Colombia, El Salvador, Venezuela). Some mothers would bring their young children to the class where they were either integrated into some classroom routines or provided with specific children's activities.

The English teacher for the class was monolingual and relied heavily on a Latina assistant as an interpreter for many of the tasks and content in the class in order to accommodate the wide range of English proficiency and Spanish literacy. Despite the official designation of this class as English-only, the reality was that English and Spanish coexisted. Closer observation revealed that the interpreter's main interactions followed the characteristics of the concurrent translation method, in which a teacher and/or an aide constantly alternate between the target language and the students' native language. The translator role in this particular classroom was taken explicitly and more prominently by the Latina volunteer when the main teacher was trying to provide her students with important information about services in the community such as library loans, health education programs, or rights of undocumented immigrants and procedures they should follow if stopped by immigration officers.

Although concurrent translation is one of the most commonly used methods in bilingual classrooms, it is proven to be ineffective (Cuero & Aburumuh, 2008). One documented drawback is that students tend to tune out of the non-dominant language (in this case English) as they overly rely on getting the information in their dominant language. This limits the possibility of high-quality exposure to the target language and negatively affects the motivation of students and teachers. It also becomes extremely taxing for the teacher and boring for students. As content is uttered twice, there is also considerable loss of instructional time which in turn results in "less elaborated language and fewer critical connections to the content" (Cuero & Aburumuh, 2008, p. 170).

READING TO LEARN FOR ADULT EAB STUDENTS

Teaching through R2L in this family literacy context made it possible to think about the adaptations that made sense for this specific emergent bilingual population, in particular when and for what purpose to use Spanish. The key innovation made to the R2L program in teaching adult emergent bilingual students in the Parent Power program was the purposeful use of Spanish in the *Preparing for Reading* lesson component (see other bilingual adaptations of R2L in this volume Lövstedt, Chapter 7 and Kartika-Ningsih, Chapter 17).

Rather than concurrent translation practices, we instead adapted the *Preview–View–Review* pedagogical approach to the R2L strategy of *Preparing for Reading*. Preview–View–Review (PVR) refers to the use of the native language of the students (Spanish) during the Preview and Review portions of the lesson and the use of English during the View portion. It is popular in bilingual education to purposefully and systematically use the native language along with English in learning content. It has the advantages of a) promoting language transfer in an academic setting, b) making content comprehensible, and c) building and/or activating background knowledge. *Preparing for Reading* in R2L supports learners to follow a text with comprehension, by providing a step-by-step oral summary of how the text unfolds, in terms the learners can all understand. This support was enhanced in the bilingual approach here, by providing this step-by-step summary in the students' first language.

THE POWER OF READING TO LEARN

This section demonstrates how through purposeful guidance informed by genre theory (Martin, 1999, 2009) and the pedagogical principles of R2L (Rose, 2018; Rose & Martin, 2012), immigrant mothers in the Parent Power program were able to independently produce highly appropriate texts in the expected genre. Their accomplishments are exemplified in the following section which provides details on the curricular unit with emphasis on the students' growth in language control.

CANTINFLAS AS A MODEL: A BIOGRAPHICAL TEXT TO ENHANCE LATINX CONTRIBUTIONS TO USA

During the fall of 2019, we conducted an R2L unit with the help of two student teacher interns. The genre focus was on biographical texts. The goal was to write about a famous Latinx character of the students' choosing. They were to identify such a character, conduct research on their life, write a biographical recount, and prepare to present their work in front of the class. This genre focus was based on a task set by the Latina volunteer, who was now the main teacher of the class. The unit started with students writing autobiographical sketches with the hope that these would serve as models for biography writing. The text below is representative of the kind of text students wrote about themselves.

> I am Adriana Resendiz. I am 26 years old. I have one girl. She is 8 years old. I like to listent to music all day. My favorite colors are black and withe. I like drack chocolate. I like puppies. I was born in Mexico. My favorite food is tacos. I want a house. I want to visit Francia.

Clearly, such personal accounts would do little to scaffold the kind of sequencing in time and organization in life stages required of the biographical recount the mothers were asked to produce at the end of curricular unit. Instead, we chose to model the R2L sequence with an adapted biographical recount of the famous Mexican comedian, Cantinflas (Table 12.1). This model was constructed with the genre stages and phases of a canonical biographical recount (Rose, 2018, Book 2). The stages

Table 12.1. Cantinflas: model of a biographical recount

Orientation	Mario Fortino Alfonso Moreno Reyes (12 August 1911–20 April 1993) professionally known as Cantinflas is considered by many as the most successful Mexican humorist of all time. His humor, with Mexican linguistic features of intonation, vocabulary, and syntax, is beloved in all the Spanish-speaking countries of Latin America and Spain. His popularity gave rise to expressions such as cantinflear, cantinflada, and cantinflesco, among others.
Life Stages early life	Mario Moreno grew up in the tough neighborhood of Tepito. He was one of eight children born to Pedro Moreno Esquivel, a mail carrier, and María de la Soledad Reyes Guízar, a housewife. He married Valentina Ivanova Zubareff, a Russian who adopted Cantinflas' son born of another woman. He made it through difficult situations with his quick wit and intelligence that he would later apply in his films.
fame	He became popular with his portrayal of Cantinflas, an impoverished peasant of poor origin, who wears his trousers held up with a rope, a rugged coat and a battered hat. This Cantinflas character soon turned him into an iconic figure not only in Mexico, but also in other parts of Latin America. In 1956, his stellar appearance as Cantinflas in his American film debut *Around the World in 80 Days* earned him a Golden Globe for best actor in a musical or comedy. Moreno was referred to as the "Charlie Chaplin of Mexico," but Charlie Chaplin himself once commented that Cantinflas was the best comedian alive.
retirement	Following his retirement, Moreno devoted his life to helping others through charity and humanitarian organizations, especially those dedicated to helping children. His contributions to the Roman Catholic Church and orphanages made him a folk hero in Mexico.
death	Cantinflas died of lung cancer on 20 April 1993 in Mexico City because he was a lifelong smoker. Thousands of people appeared on a rainy day for his funeral. He was honored by many heads of state and the United States Senate, which held a moment of silence for him.

and phases are labelled here, but the model was initially presented to the students without these components.

PREPARING FOR READING

In *Preparing for Reading*, we first gave an overview of the whole text in Spanish. Then for each paragraph, we first prepared in Spanish, and read the paragraph in English. It is easy to understate the importance of the *Preparing for Reading* within the R2L pedagogy cycle. Careful preparation of the whole text and each paragraph provides solid ground for all students, but it is *essential* for emergent bilingual students in order to lower their semiotic load and anxiety. They will not only understand what is happening at each step as the text is read and discussed but will be ready and motivated to listen more attentively and begin adventuring to produce much more of the target language. In this specific case, the possible difficulties arising from the fact that the biographical text is in the non-dominant language

(English) is minimized by the familiarity and cultural affinity with the Cantinflas character who all the mothers knew. Crucially, preparing the text in Spanish in the way shown above helps ease the language shift transition as the whole text is summarized in Spanish and then each specific paragraph is read in English.

The value of *Preparing for Reading* is greatly amplified for EAB students as cross-linguistic connections may become key meaning potential for bilinguals. Previewing genre phases is especially important for bilingual learners in two ways. First, its schematic structure may trigger their experience with texts of the same genre in another language. Second, students' bilingualism is an asset, as linguistic and content knowledge encoded in the first language is recognized and is called upon explicitly as a resource for English learning. Foregrounding field and genre in this way has broad implications for EAB students in other ways. As is widely documented in the US (Short & Fitzsimmons, 2007), new learners of the language are doing "double the work", learning new content as well as new language. By introducing knowledge in *Preparing for Reading*, EAB students can focus on language development.

An excerpt from the lesson plan for *Preparing for Reading* is shown below. This curricular guide was written for pre-service teachers visiting from La Salle University in Bogotá, Colombia, who were observing the class, including author Gutierrez.

Lesson plan for *Preparing for Reading*

1. **Prepare what you will say to introduce the text as a whole. This is done in Spanish**
   This is a text that tells us about the life of one of the most important comedians of all times in Mexico. Mario Moreno, most commonly known as Cantinflas. The text first tells us about who he was, when and where he was born, and some peculiarities of his humor. The text then tells us a bit about his life and his family, how and why he became famous, and the later stages of his life.
2. **Prepare each paragraph by providing a description of what will be read in each paragraph. Paragraph 1 (in Spanish)**
   The first paragraph tells us about Cantinflas real name, when he was born, when he died, and how important and famous he was. Then, it tells us about his humor, and when he was popular. Finally, it tells us about some words that people created based on the Cantinflas character and personality.
3. **Then read the first paragraph in English**
   Mario Fortino Alfonso Moreno Reyes (12 August 1911–20 April 1993) professionally known as Cantinflas is considered by many as the most successful Mexican humorist of all time. His humor, with Mexican linguistic features of intonation, vocabulary, and syntax, is beloved in all the Spanish-speaking countries of Latin America and Spain. His popularity gave rise to expressions such as cantinflear, cantinflada, and cantinflesco, among others.

DETAILED READING

Following *Preparing for Reading*, the sequence in the lesson turned to *Detailed Reading*. In *Detailed Reading*, each sentence was read in detail. We first reviewed the paragraph, then ensured that all students could identify the sentence under focus. The sentence was then prepared in Spanish and read in English. Table 12.2 is a reconstructed interaction from this moment in the lesson.

Following the sentence preparation, students were guided to identify each piece of information, using simple focus questions, such as *What is Cantinflas' real name? When was he born? When did he die? How else was Mario Moreno called? What was his occupation? How do we know he was good?* After identifying each meaning, the class was directed to highlight the wording. Some meanings were also elaborated, such as synonyms for the word *humorist*. The *Detailed Reading* process was repeated with every sentence in the text and students ended up with the original text highlighted as shown in Figure 12.1.

Table 12.2. Teacher-led *Detailed Reading* interaction

Teacher	*OK. Vamos a empezar con el primer párrafo. Recuerden que este párrafo nos revela el verdadero nombre de Cantinflas, donde y cuando nació y murió, y que hacía. Además nos da información acerca de las características de su humor y las palabras que incluso creó él mismo y que se volvieron populares.* OK. Let's begin with the first paragraph. Remember that this paragraph reveals the true name of Cantinflas, what he did, and where and when he was born and died. Besides, it gives us information about his humor and some unique characteristics and how he even created words himself that then became popular.	Review paragraph
	Pueden identificar la primera oración? Pongan su dedo en esta oración. Empieza con la palabra Mario y termina con el punto después de la palabra "time". *La tienen?* Can you identify this first sentence? Put your finger on the first sentence. It begins with the word *Mario* and finishes with the period after the word *time*. Do you have it?	Focus sentence
Students	*Si.* [pointing to the sentence] Yes.	Identify sentence
Teacher	*Esta oración es parte de la orientación. Esta oración nos dice el verdadero nombre de Cantinflas, cuando murió, cuando nació y en donde.* This first sentence is part of the orientation. In this sentence, it tells us the real name of Cantinflas, what he did and where, and the dates of his birth and death. *Mario Fortino Alfonso Moreno Reyes (12 August 1911–20 April 1993) professionally known as Cantinflas is considered by many as the most successful Mexican humorist of all time.*	Prepare sentence

CANTINFLAS

Mario Fortino Alfonso Moreno Reyes (12 August 1911 - 20 April 1993) professionally known as Cantinflas is considered by many as the most successful Mexican humorist of all time. His humor, with Mexican linguistic features of intonation, vocabulary, and syntax, is beloved in all the Spanish-speaking countries of Latin America and Spain. He was so popular that created expressions such as cantinflear, cantinfiada, and cantinflesco, among others.

Mario Moreno grew up in the tough neighbourhood of Tepito. He was one of eight children born to Pedro Moreno Esquivel, a mail carrier, and Maria de la Soledad Reyes Guizar, a housewife. He married Valentina Ivanova Zubareff, a Russian who adopted Cantinflas son born of another woman. He made it through difficult situations with his quick wit and intelligence that he would later apply in his films.

He became popular with his portrayal of Cantinflas, an impoverished peasant of poor origin, who wears his trousers held up with a rope, a rugged coat and a battered hat. This Cantinflas character soon turned him into an iconic figure not only in Mexico, but also in other parts of Latin America. In 1956, his stellar appearance as Cantinflas in his American film Debut "*Around the World in 80 Days*" earned him a Golden Globe for best actor in a musical or comedy. Moreno was referred to as the "Charlie Chaplin of Mexico," but Charlie Chaplin himself once commented that Cantinflas was the best comedian alive.

Following his retirement, Moreno devoted his life to helping others through charity and humanitarian organizations, especially those dedicated to helping children. His contributions to the Roman Catholic Church and orphanages made him a folk hero in Mexico. Cantinflas died of lung cancer on 20 April 1993 in Mexico City because he was a lifelong smoker. Thousands of people appeared on a rainy day for his funeral. He was honored by many heads of state and the United States Senate, which held a moment of silence for him.

Figure 12.1. Highlighted text after *Detailed Reading*

At the teacher's discretion, sentence preparations can begin to occur in English depending on how comfortable students feel. The questions themselves can also be in English as long as they are simple, and students are answering without difficulty. A good indication is the success of students responding accurately. This type of constant positive reinforcement and continued success motivates further learning of all students, but it is critical for students who are being instructed in a language other than their own.

Although preparation with this level of detail requires dedication and time, the advantages far outweigh this drawback. Effective preparation eliminates the time-consuming and counterproductive practice of asking a lot of unprepared open questions, especially when the topic, the genre, and even the language are new to students. Asking unprepared questions is time-consuming because students may give answers that are not appropriate, are unrelated to the topic, or simply do not advance the purpose of the lesson. This is counterproductive because the students engage in a guessing game that ends up creating differences between students in terms of whose answers get affirmed, not taken or dismissed more often. This kind of guess-what-is-in-my-head interactions can be taxing for all students, but they are certainly a source of higher anxiety and doubt for new learners of a language who may not be willing to participate as much. As Rose (2018) puts it: "The purpose of asking questions is not simply to engage students, but as steppingstones in building knowledge. The elaboration is the goal of the question, so we need to get the right answers in order to elaborate, and all our students must be ready for each elaboration." (Rose, 2018, Book 1, p. 49).

NOTEMAKING

Following *Detailed Reading* of the whole text, the highlighted words then became the basis for the *Notemaking* activity, in which students took turns to dictate from the text and scribe on the board. Figure 12.2 shows one of the students, accompanied by her baby, serving as a scribe. Each separate bulleted list item in the picture depicts different handwriting. This provides evidence of the collaborative and dynamic nature of this activity as students took turns as scribes when coming to the board.

An excerpt from a student's notebook is shown in Figure 12.3. Each of the bullet points corresponds to the highlighted words belonging to a separate sentence in the text.

Figure 12.2. *Notemaking*

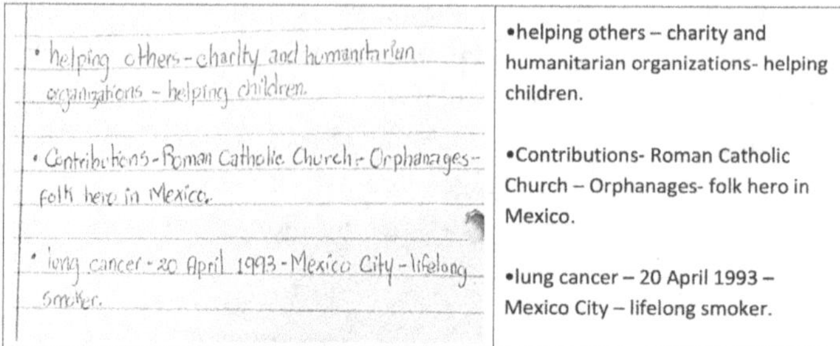

• helping others - charity and humanitarian organizations - helping children.	•helping others – charity and humanitarian organizations- helping children.
• Contributions - Roman Catholic Church - Orphanages - folk hero in Mexico.	•Contributions- Roman Catholic Church – Orphanages- folk hero in Mexico.
• lung cancer - 20 April 1993 - Mexico City - lifelong smoker.	•lung cancer – 20 April 1993 – Mexico City – lifelong smoker.

Figure 12.3. Student's notebook

Through dictating and scribing, students engage collaboratively and simultaneously in negotiating appropriate language formatting in a skills-integrated way by pronouncing, reading, writing, and listening to the highlighted words. This active, intermodal process promotes both language skill integration and group accountability through friendly correction of pronunciation, spelling, and punctuation in the context of a text that by this time is well known by students.

JOINT CONSTRUCTION

Once notes had been written for the whole text, the information was grouped by labelling the genre stages and phases. A new text was then jointly constructed from the notes with the guidance of the teacher. The new text was constructed sentence by sentence using the same genre stages and phases, but with sentence patterns that differed from the model. Again, students took turns to scribe the text on the board, as the class contributed ideas, guided by the teacher. Figure 12.4 shows the same student with her baby scribing the new text on the board.

Figure 12.4. Scribing during *Joint Construction*

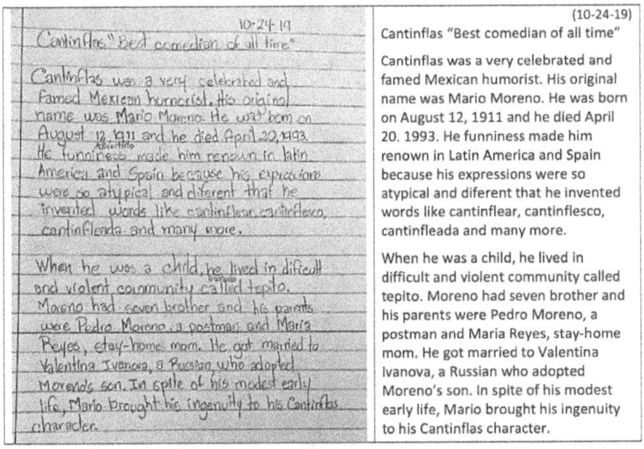

(10-24-19)
Cantinflas "Best comedian of all time"

Cantinflas was a very celebrated and famed Mexican humorist. His original name was Mario Moreno. He was born on August 12, 1911 and he died April 20. 1993. He funniness made him renown in Latin America and Spain because his expressions were so atypical and diferent that he invented words like cantinflear, cantinflesco, cantinfleada and many more.

When he was a child, he lived in difficult and violent community called tepito. Moreno had seven brother and his parents were Pedro Moreno, a postman and Maria Reyes, stay-home mom. He got married to Valentina Ivanova, a Russian who adopted Moreno's son. In spite of his modest early life, Mario brought his ingenuity to his Cantinflas character.

Figure 12.5. *Joint Construction* of Cantinflas biography

An excerpt from the jointly constructed text, copied into students' notebooks, is shown in Figure 12.5. The field and structuring of the new text is parallel with the model, but the mode is less highly written, sentence patterns are different, and the information is re-organized.

INDEPENDENT RESEARCH AND WRITING

Following these joint activities of *Detailed Reading*, *Notemaking* and *Joint Construction*, students were tasked with reading new texts and writing their own biographical recounts of Latinx personalities influential in United States affairs, such as Sonia Sotomayor, Jorge Ramos, Cesar Conde, Rafael Reif, Cesar Chavez and others. Figure 12.6 shows independent student writing which was the product of their own research. The excerpt from the biographical recount included the familiar stages of Orientation and Life Stages as well as the phase "fame" already encountered in the Cantinflas text. However, it also included whole new phases on activism, and awards.

The data collected provides strong evidence that while the students gathered a lot of information about their chosen characters, they did so purposefully and were able to categorize it to put it to good use in the task. As they gathered information, they were able to categorize and better organize such information through the main stages of biographical recounts. Even though the task was in English, they did not shy away from researching and using information in Spanish. The purposeful use of this linguistic capital by the mothers suggests that they saw their first language as an asset to their English learning just as it had been emphasized through the R2L bilingual pedagogy sequence.

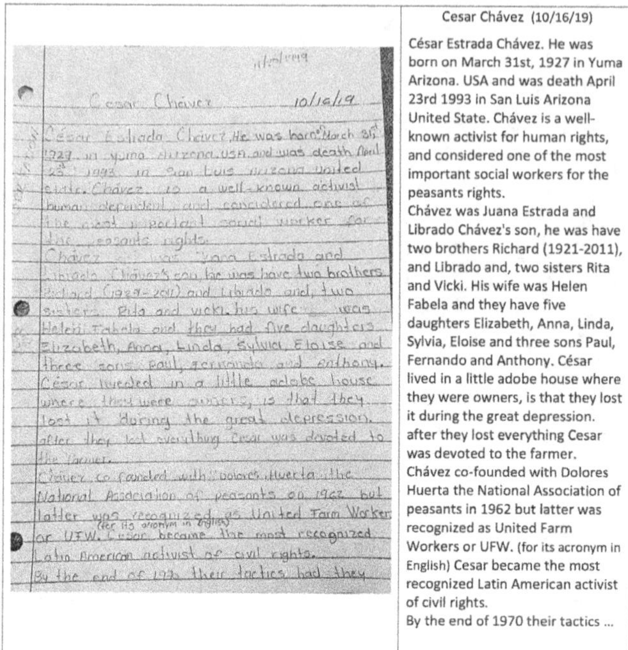

Cesar Chávez (10/16/19)

César Estrada Chávez. He was born on March 31st, 1927 in Yuma Arizona. USA and was death April 23rd 1993 in San Luis Arizona United State. Chávez is a well-known activist for human rights, and considered one of the most important social workers for the peasants rights.
Chávez was Juana Estrada and Librado Chávez's son, he was have two brothers Richard (1921-2011), and Librado and, two sisters Rita and Vicki. His wife was Helen Fabela and they have five daughters Elizabeth, Anna, Linda, Sylvia, Eloise and three sons Paul, Fernando and Anthony. César lived in a little adobe house where they were owners, is that they lost it during the great depression. after they lost everything Cesar was devoted to the farmer.
Chávez co-founded with Dolores Huerta the National Association of peasants in 1962 but latter was recognized as United Farm Workers or UFW. (for its acronym in English) Cesar became the most recognized Latin American activist of civil rights.
By the end of 1970 their tactics ...

Figure 12.6. *Independent Construction* – biography of Cesar Chávez

IMPLICATIONS

Several implications can be drawn from the work presented here, for second/foreign language teaching in general and for the R2L approach in particular. Three implications discussed below are the treatment of errors, the integration of content and language, and, more extensively, the issue of the role and use of the native language in teaching and learning, related to bottom-up and top-down approaches.

Treatment of errors

Language teaching approaches tend to reinforce learning by modeling correct language usage once students make mistakes. This reactive way of treating mistakes is contrary to R2L. As demonstrated in this chapter, all tasks in R2L circle around reading and writing. In this approach, patterns of texts, or how meanings work in text, are sequentially, redundantly, and systematically, prepared, studied and deconstructed through the activities of *Preparing for Reading, Detailed Reading, Note Making*, and *Joint Construction*. As a result, mistakes are the least of the worries in R2L since they tend to be surface errors that do not affect meaning making.

By foregrounding the higher-level features that make up texts – Bernstein's (2000) "recognition rules" – learners are better equipped with tools to create texts in context (Bernstein's "realization rules") and develop the potential for expanding their repertoire from the known to the new (Bernstein's "analogic potential"). When mistakes do occur, they do not have a significant effect on meaning because they are usually concerned with lower-level features such as grammar and graphic features such as spelling, punctuation, and presentation. As the teacher continually reads and models, both higher and lower-level features become meaningfully redundant for students. During *Detailed Reading*, students are carefully guided through prepared questions that are easy to answer as they are text dependent and not based on guesses or opinions. If students do not respond successfully, it is the teacher who must adjust the questions to students. During *Notemaking* and *Joint Construction*, words are pronounced and spelt for the scribe in a non-threatening collaborative task without assessment purposes. Hence for EAB learners, low level mistakes such as pronunciation are largely avoided.

As second/foreign language methodologies have traditionally paid close attention to grammar, the idea of grammar being a low-level feature may cause surprise to some. However, the pedagogic focus for grammar in R2L is not on systems of grammar in a developmental plan, syllabus or plan of study, but on the meaningful use of words and structures in contexts. For example, instead of starting with grammar exercises, such as transforming isolated sentences from simple present into simple past, curricular units in R2L start from modeling a text such as the Cantinflas biographical recount. The genre and register of the text naturally trigger systems of wordings, such as verbs in past in the Life Stages of the biographical recount (*grew up*, *was*, *married*, *adopted*, *made*). These can be pointed out during *Detailed Reading* and modelled during *Joint Construction*. Such instances provide multiple opportunities for students to develop their progressive contextual understanding of grammar features.

Integration of content and language

Integration of content and language has long been a topic of debates and teaching frameworks in second and foreign language teaching (Snow et al., 1989). However, as Halliday (1993) reminds us, all human learning is a process of making meaning – a semiotic process, simultaneously learning language, learning through language, and learning about language. The students in this study learnt language (new vocabulary and grammar), learnt through language (lives of famous Latinx) and learnt about language (how to structure a biography in English).

In learning how to mean, learners must process the complexity of language simultaneously at the levels of context, text, sentence, and words, regardless of whether it is in a first or second/foreign language. The R2L lessons presented here offered explicit pedagogic sequences that led students to tackle this complexity at the level of text, using the stages and phases in the model to produce their own coherent writing. They also learnt to arrange sentences in meaningful grammatical chunks with appropriate words that built the topic, and to choose appropriate words and master their pronunciation and spelling.

The conceptual framework proposed here through R2L offers language and content teachers a systematic approach to the identification and instruction of language aims within content teaching. We believe that the implications of integrating language and content teaching must be guided by a linguistic theory of "text-in-context" that is mainly concerned with how people make meaning in language such as SFL and an integrative, text-centered, top-down approach such as R2L if content-based instruction is to be implemented effectively.

Bottom-up/top-down approaches to language learning and the use of the native language

Widely used approaches in second/foreign language treat language as a ladder, with small chunks of language such as phonemes and morphemes at the bottom, followed by words, sentences, paragraphs and finally a text at the top. These approaches emphasize developing language from the bottom up, in an ascending path toward the top of the ladder. Scores of materials in foreign/second language learning follow structural principles in their design. An example is practising grammatical structures of the verb *to be* before practising the present continuous tense which uses *to be* as an auxiliary. Another popular bottom-up method is Total Physical Response (TPR), which begins with simple commands that are then combined with new vocabulary. The entry point of these methods is to first master the smallest components of language such as phonemes or simple grammatical structures or simple commands and then move up to words, sentences and finally to texts.

In contrast, R2L prioritizes function and not structure as its main entry point. The preferred path starts in a top-down fashion as it proceeds from discussing the field and purpose of whole texts, down to deconstructing patterns in sentences, to words, down to phonemes and letters to then move upwards again through patterns of words, sentences and ultimately text. Other popular second/foreign language methods such as the natural approach or the language experience approach with constructivist principles anchored in romantic progressivism also favor learning in a top-down fashion that focuses on meaning first, but explicit teaching is not important, as parts, they say, come naturally later (Ovando et al., 2006). Unlike R2L, there is no systematic building up of language resources as it is assumed learning through input is enough to produce appropriate output.

Bottom-up approaches leave little room for meaningfully tapping into the first language as a resource to advance the second. As languages differ most at lower ranks (phonemes, morphemes, words), native language knowledge is not as useful for bottom-up language teaching. Although EAB learners know how to express themselves in their native language, it is unlikely they are conscious of how that native language works, let alone how it can be used to advance the second. Thus, intelligent and accomplished adults are positioned in a deficit-based perspective as "not knowers," with higher probability of experiencing vulnerability, lack of knowledge, and insecurity when approaching second/foreign language learning. These feelings become an additional unnecessary heavy burden on foreign/second language learner's shoulders as they trudge up the ladder of language learning.

In contrast, top-down methodologies such as R2L not only welcome but are enhanced by the knowledge encoded in the first language of the students. Indeed, adult learners are not only positioned as expert users of texts, but this expertise is harnessed through purposeful lesson strategies that tap naturally into the knowledge encoded in their first language. Considering R2L's starting point is with texts, emergent bilinguals are positioned on linguistic high ground and openly called to meaningfully use their common sense and experience narrating, arguing, or recounting in their native language to speed up second/foreign language acquisition. As the result of R2L strategies, the students in this study were able to transfer general knowledge associated with genre and register encoded in Spanish (recognition rules) to the same genre and register in English (realization rules). Linguistically speaking, this transfer makes sense as languages are much more similar at higher levels of genre and register. Under this approach, even adults without high levels of academic literacy are positioned in an assets-based perspective that not only promotes further and deeper learning but makes them and their native linguistic capital valued, accepted, and key when approaching second/foreign language learning. This explains how students were able to produce appropriate texts in English after just a few class sessions. It is also consistent with results on the effectiveness of R2L reported around the world in Sweden (Acevedo & Lövstedt, 2014), Spain (Whittaker, 2014), Portugal (Gouveia, 2014), and Australia (Carusi-Lees, Chapter 4 and Culican, Chapter 3 this volume, Rose & Martin, 2012).

The work described in this chapter suggests a principled course of action for considering the addition of bilingual instantiation to the Reading to Learn approach when teaching EAB learners. Although the core of the suggested changes regarding the inclusion of the native language of the students in instruction were directed at the *Preparing for Reading* cycle, bilingual instantiation may be appropriate at different R2L stages, such as *Notemaking* and *Joint Construction* (Kartika-Ningsih & Rose, 2021). In classrooms where multiple native languages are represented, alternative means of conducting the *Preparing for Reading* strategies in the native language of the students can be considered. Such alternatives include help from school personnel or community volunteers to accompany the student or students, co-teaching with a bilingual teacher, adapting the *Preparing for Reading* lesson plan to distribute to appropriate students in advance, and engaging the native speaker parents at home.

CONCLUSION

The talented students in the program described here were elevated to the high linguistic ground that understanding meaning and purpose in texts provides. They were purposefully, resolutely, and gently escorted down through each level of language to reach the smallest components of the focus text and discrete language skills. Invigorated by the conviction of contextualized knowledge, they then began their journey up the language levels once again as they collaboratively reconstructed words and sentences from their notes to form a new text that paraphrased the original. This purposeful two-way linguistic journey prepared them to remain anchored in high linguistic ground, keenly aware not only of what the new task demanded but of all the newly discovered tools, to independently create new texts.

With the growing number of international migrants, there is a great possibility of increasing numbers of immigrants who speak a language other than that of the host countries. The culture, talents, experience, and valuable knowledge encoded in their first languages is a valuable resource for learning the target language, acculturating, and being able to contribute to the host country. We offer the bilingual R2L design described here as our humble tribute to Halliday's view of linguistics as an ideologically committed form of social action. We hope teachers around the world find meaningful insights in its proposal that they can themselves apply in their own contexts.

REFERENCES

Acevedo, C., & Lövstedt, A.-C. (2014). *Teacher Learning for European Literacy Education: Project outputs from Sweden*. Stockholm Education Administration, European Union. https://www.researchgate.net/publication/355160985

Bernstein, B. (2000). *Pedagogy, symbolic control and identity: Theory, research, critique*. Taylor and Francis.

Cuero, K., & Aburumuh, H. (2008). Concurrent translation method. In J. M. González (Ed.), *Encyclopedia of bilingual education*, (pp. 169–171). SAGE Publications, Inc. DOI: 10.4135/9781412963985.n71

Gouveia, C. (2014). *Portugal Project Outputs, Teacher Learning for European Literacy Education*. Lisbon: Instituto de Linguística Teórica e Computacional (ILTEC), The Hague: European Union

Halliday, M. A. K. (1993). Towards a language-based theory of learning. *Linguistics and Education*, *5(2)*, 93–116.

Kartika-Ningsih, H., & Rose, D. (2021). Intermodality and multilingual re-instantiation: Joint construction in bilingual genre pedagogy. *Ikala, Special issue on Appliable Linguistics in Language Education: SFL in Practice*. 26(1), 185–205. https://doi.org/10.17533/udea.ikala.v26n01a07

Lukes, M. (2011). 'I understand English but I can't write it': The power of native language instruction for adult English learners. *International multilingual research journal*, *5*(1), 19–38. DOI:10.1080/19313152.2011.539488

Martin, J. R. (1999). Mentoring semogenesis: 'genre-based' literacy pedagogy. In F. Christie (Ed.), *Pedagogy and the shaping of consciousness: linguistic and social processes*, (pp.123–155). Cassell (Open Linguistics Series).

Martin, J. R. (2009). Genre and language learning: A social semiotic perspective. *Linguistics and Education*, *20*, 10–21.

Migration Policy Institute. (2018). Frequently Requested Statistics on Immigrants and Immigration in the United States. Retrieved, March, 8, 2020. https://www.migrationpolicy.org/article/frequently-requested-statistics-immigrants-and-immigration-united-states#Demographic,%20Educational,%20and%20Linguistic%20Characteristics

National Center for Education Statistics. (2003). National assessment of adult literacy. Washington, DC: Author. Retrieved May 8, 2022. https://nces.ed.gov/naal/

Ovando, C., Combs, M., & Collier, V. (2006). *Bilingual and ESL classrooms: Teaching in multicultural contexts.* McGraw Hill.

Ramirez, A. (2020). The case for culturally and linguistically relevant pedagogy: Bilingual Reading to Learn for Spanish-speaking immigrant mothers. *System*, *95*, 102379.

Ramírez, A. (2022). Emergent Bilingual Latina/o/x Parents Read in English to Their Young Emergent Bilingual Children at Home. In D. Caldwell, J. Martin, & J. Knox (Eds.), *Appliable Linguistics and Social Semiotics: Developing Theory From Practice*, (pp. 437–456). London: Bloomsbury.

Rose, D. (2018). *Reading to Learn: Accelerating learning and closing the gap. Teacher training books and DVDs.* Reading to Learn, http://www.readingtolearn.com.au

Rose, D., & Martin, J. R. (2012). *Learning to write, Reading to learn: Genre, knowledge and pedagogy in the Sydney school.* Equinox.

Short, D., & Fitzsimmons, S. (2007). *Double the work: Challenges and solutions to acquiring language and academic literacy for adolescent English language learners – A report to Carnegie Corporation of New York.* Alliance for Excellent Education.

Snow, M., Met, M., & Genesee, F. (1989). A conceptual framework for the integration of language and content in second/foreign language instruction. *TESOL Quarterly*, *23*(2) 201–217.

Whittaker, R. (2014). *Teacher Learning for European Literacy Education. Spain project outputs*. European Union. https://www.researchgate.net/publication/355161518_Teacher_Learning_for_European_Literacy_Education_Tel4ELE_Project_Outputs_from_Spain

ABOUT THE AUTHORS

Andrés Ramírez is Associate Professor in the Department of Curriculum and Instruction at Florida Atlantic University. He teaches courses in TESOL education, curriculum theory, systemic functional linguistics (SFL) and critical discourse analysis. His research explores culturally and linguistically responsive pedagogies that promote the literacy and language development of Emergent to Advanced Bilingual students (EABs) with special emphasis on Latina/o/x EABs populations. He furthers his interests in this area through the use of the genre-based Reading to Learn pedagogy.

María Gabriela Gutiérrez is a graduate in Languages – Spanish, English and French – from La Salle University, Bogota, Colombia. As part of her internship in pedagogy at Florida Atlantic University, USA, she became a Reading to Learn teacher apprentice under the supervision of Andrés Ramírez in the *Parent Power* program. As she develops her expertise in the R2L methodology she plans to use it as the cornerstone of her future professional practice in Colombia and beyond.

13

Introducing Reading to Learn into higher education teaching in the Colombian Caribbean

Sergio Álvarez Uribe, Norma Barletta, Teresa Benítez & Nayibe Rosado-Mendinueta

ABSTRACT

This chapter describes how Reading to Learn (R2L) is being used by the Spanish faculty at the Universidad del Norte (UN) in Barranquilla, Colombia, in a comprehensive, campus wide approach to student and teacher literacy education, the Communicative Competence (ECO) program. The development of the ECO program in response to the growing student need for support with academic literacy is explained using examples from the genre-based teaching program. The chapter also focuses on how the program operates to recruit, educate and provide ongoing support to faculty members from a range of disciplines as they learn to incorporate literacy teaching strategies from R2L in their discipline areas. Examples of the results of this process for both staff and students are provided and followed by a discussion of the successes and challenges of the initiative. This program of support for both student and teacher learning has been ground-breaking for UN and is offered here as inspiration for other tertiary educators as well as those working in a range of other contexts.

THE BACKGROUND FOR A LEARNING COMMUNITY

Education is a human right and it is fundamental to development. Goal four of the 2030 Agenda for Sustainable Development Goals to transform the world intends to ensure inclusive and equitable quality education and promote lifelong learning opportunities for all. In Colombia, quality education is indeed a key challenge. The results of the students that took the PISA test in 2018 were lower than the average of students from other participating countries. Only 44 per cent of the students who enter first grade finish high school, and from those who enter a higher education institution only about fifty per cent obtain a degree (Ministerio de Educación Nacional, 2018). The Colombian Caribbean region, which comprises 21 per cent of the population of the country and several of the departments with the lowest achievement levels in the national standardized examination (SABER11), has traditionally lacked political leadership, especially one that would focus on the compelling need to develop education for all its citizens (Meisel, 2018).

In this context, the Universidad del Norte, a non-profit private university in Barranquilla, founded in 1966 under the initiative of a group of local businesspeople, intends to meet the social, economic, political, environmental and cultural needs of the Caribbean region and the country. With about fifteen thousand students enrolled in undergraduate, postgraduate and continuous education programs, today it is one of the most important and prestigious universities in Colombia with several national and international accreditations.

Every semester, Universidad del Norte receives a considerable number of students, many of whom are not prepared to face the demands posed by the learning tasks they have to tackle in tertiary education. These demands derive to a great extent from the characteristics of the written language students need to master to have access to the knowledge and social practices of the disciplines they have chosen to study. Also, the unpreparedness has to do with the insufficient attention paid to the development of academic literacy in the primary and secondary school years (Carlino, 2003; Fernández & Carlino, 2010; González et al., 2016), when students are expected to gradually move away from the oral registers and get familiar with the written form characteristic of advanced literacy (Christie, 2002; Colombi, 2002). The resulting deficiency often threatens students' success in their pursuit of a university degree and a professional career.

This situation became evident at the turn of the 21st century when, in trying to comply with the competence approach to education the country had embraced, a group of researchers at Uninorte carried out the first diagnosis of the reading competence of first semester students (Colectivo Comunicación, 2002). The results were quite worrisome, but they clearly showed for the first time the enormous challenge ahead. This chapter will share the success story of how the Universidad del Norte has faced this challenge, and how the Spanish department's teaching of academic literacy, slowly but steadily, introduced, adopted, and adapted an SFL genre theory and a genre-based, literacy pedagogy – Reading to Learn (Rose & Martin, 2012/2018) – into higher education teaching.

With the sponsorship of the academic provost office, the university launched the Communicative Efficacy program (ECO from its initials in Spanish). Its main purpose was to provide students with systematic support to develop academic literacy so that they become successful learners while studying at the university, but also to help them develop effective communication skills for their lives as professionals, citizens and leaders in our society.

Two main actions were undertaken from the very start of the program in the year 2006. First, two communicative competence courses were included in the basic education component as a requirement for first-year students of all academic programs. In addition, all the students were asked to take a reading diagnostic test before the first day of class and an exit exam after finishing the second communicative competence course, as a way to measure the contribution of the program to reading development at that point.

Second, a teacher development program was offered for content-area faculty so that they would intentionally and systematically help students cope with their reading and writing challenges, contributing to the students' literacy development. This program was based on the ideas of textlinguistics (van Dijk, 1980) and the communicative approach, although the pedagogic guidelines were not entirely clear.

For several years, the results of the reading examination, based on the PISA reading test, did not demonstrate a solid and sustained advance in the students' reading competence. Furthermore, there was no clarity regarding how involved the content-area faculty were, and in what ways they were contributing to the students' literacy development. It became evident that the communicative competence (ECO) courses alone were not sufficient for the students' academic literacy improvement and that the faculty of the different disciplines needed better guidance if they were to teach reading and writing in their courses.

Almost a decade later, thanks to the connection with educational linguists that attended the congresses of the Latin American Association of Systemic Functional Linguistics (ALSFAL), the ideas of genre-based pedagogy (GBP) reached our institution. Ingrid Westhoff, Cecilia Colombi and Gillian Moss were the first to offer courses and workshops at Uninorte on Systemic Functional Linguistics (SFL) and its applications in the teaching of reading and writing at university level. As a result, the faculty in the Spanish Department became a learning community and it now follows a unified language-based teaching and learning perspective.

Clearer objectives were then developed to ensure that, following the first-year program, students should continue their literacy development by taking two discipline-based ECO-courses – that is, courses from faculty members who have received R2L training and were committed to teaching the language of their disciplines explicitly.

FINDING ALLIES

There has been a slow but steady process of engaging faculty willing to teach the language of their disciplines explicitly. Some members of the faculty think this is an additional (and unnecessary) burden to their already difficult job; others think literacy teaching is something appropriate for secondary school; still others feel they have no time for that because their syllabus is already packed with important concepts and skills. So a number of strategies have been put in place to find the allies needed to implement the program successfully.

First of all, the Office of Academic Projects addressed all the heads of departments and program coordinators to explain the ECO program and to select two courses per major in which reading and writing could be systematically addressed. The selection process was not immediate and has taken place in different ways. At one point, the heads of the departments made a call for teacher-volunteers among the faculty. Fortunately, before being invited to participate in the ECO teacher education program, some faculty were convinced of the need to do something about their students' literacy skills and they enthusiastically endorsed the initiative and appreciated every workshop and the accompanying individual mentoring to support classroom implementation.

Additionally, all faculty hired by the university receive introductory pedagogic training that includes a glimpse at a reading lesson within a content class. It is a workshop led by the Spanish department which a number of the newly-employed teachers find very useful. The result has been that they spontaneously sign up for their courses to become ECO-courses, which is a commitment to incorporate the explicit teaching of literacy in their disciplines. These workshops are also periodically offered to experienced faculty of different departments to motivate them to join the program.

The Spanish department has also used the Center for Teaching Excellence at Uninorte (CEDU) to publicize the ECO program as a possibility for course transformation, as a pedagogic laboratory and as a learning community for teachers to plan, implement and evaluate pedagogic strategies focusing specifically on the teaching of reading and writing in their disciplines. Finally, teachers that have turned their courses into ECO-courses have spread their successful experience by word of mouth, and this has attracted other allies to the program.

Finding allies has been a challenging process. In some programs where students traditionally have lower literacy skills from the start, more faculty have signed up to become ECO-teachers, while within some other programs there are still no such teachers. Time is always an issue. The university counts participation in the ECO program as one possible goal among the four goals each teacher must fulfil in their annual assessment. But, despite the value given to that pedagogic commitment, in some cases, the tension between a teacher's professional growth and other responsibilities becomes evident. At the moment of writing this chapter, there are 43 ECO-courses and 40 ECO-teachers in 20 out of the 27 academic programs open today.

TRAINING IN R2L FOR A LONG-TERM COMMITMENT

Participating in the ECO program, transforming a course into an ECO-course, and becoming an ECO-teacher demand a long-term pedagogic commitment: 1) attending a series of workshops about genre-based pedagogy and R2L methodology; 2) designing, implementing and evaluating one pedagogic sequence for reading a disciplinary text and one for writing a particular genre with the assistance of a language specialist; and 3) continuing teaching the same course every semester (or several times). After the first implementation, the support by the language specialist decreases but never stops, especially when the ECO-teacher decides to prepare a new pedagogic sequence.

The workshops determine the faculty commitment. They are taught during summertime by a specialist in the R2L program, Claire Acevedo. Here is an example of a typical sequence of presentations and workshops for the content-area faculty:

- The impact of genre-based pedagogy on learning
- The pedagogic principles
- Reading to Learn in action
- Joint writing pedagogic sequence
- Assessing writing in the R2L pedagogy

The first session familiarizes the attendees with the origins of genre-based pedagogy and the R2L experience, the rationale for developing the program, and some of the results obtained so far. It puts special emphasis on the key role of language in all learning processes and how reading and writing skills are usually presumed in the content classroom, even though students have had quite different reading and/or writing experience in primary school and secondary education.

In the second session the R2L specialist synthesizes the main theoretical tenets underlying the pedagogy. Three topics are usually covered: 1) Bernstein's (2000, 2003) ideas about pedagogic discourse and how it can contribute to democratizing knowledge; 2) The sociocultural notion of scaffolding within the zone of proximal development towards increasing development of students' autonomy. It is from this principle that the pedagogy unfolds. It progresses from a teacher who explicitly explains and models the reading and writing processes (I do, you watch) to a joint practice in which teacher and students work together (I do, you help; and you do, I help) to a stage where students can work independently (you do, I watch) (Wilhelm, et al., 2001); 3) Genre theory and the notions of genre, stages and phases. There is always an opportunity for teachers to practice analyzing short texts to identify genre, stages and phases.

The third workshop offers practical experience for teachers to prepare a reading lesson. The workshop leader explains the pedagogic sequence in the R2L pedagogy (Rose, 2018) and provides a model of how the teacher should analyze and prepare a text that is going to be read in class. The lesson planning process includes three elements: 1) Selecting a suitable text according to the curriculum, the field under discussion, the purpose of the lesson, the degree of technicality and abstraction that students need to get familiar with, and the genre the text belongs to, including its suitability as a reference model for subsequent writing; 2) Identifying the stages and phases of the complete text; 3) Planning how to prepare students for reading the text, or a complex and important text fragment. Planning *Preparing for Reading* has two components: a) preparing background information to facilitate general understanding of the text, selecting relevant pictures and key technical terms to be explained; and b) preparing guidance regarding how the text unfolds, its genre, its purpose, stages and phases – that is, writing a script explaining, before actual *Paragraph-by-Paragraph Reading*, what the text is doing (describing, explaining, evaluating, etc.). In other words, the participating faculty get experience in walking the students through the text, so that the students get a general picture of its structure and meanings before actually facing it in detail. Workshop participants apply this planning process to real texts in their disciplines.

The fourth workshop deals with the teaching of reading for writing. This includes *Detailed Reading* of texts, identifying key information, *Notemaking*, and using notes for writing new texts. The workshop leader models the identification of key words for notemaking and the formulation of the type of questions and comments that the instructors should make with their students during detailed reading. This is the scaffolding cycle (Prepare–Task–Elaborate) to guide students in the identification of key words (Prepare), to involve students cognitively (Task), and to provide additional explanation or discussion about the meaning of the text (Elaborate) (see Rose, Chapter 1 in this volume). Finally, the participants are invited to identify any linguistic resources that are useful for understanding and for writing a new text of the same genre. This workshop also addresses the difference between writing a text of the same genre as the reading text, and writing a text of a different genre. In the latter case, a text of the target genre is deconstructed with the aim of clarifying the structure of the target genre.

The last workshop offers a general view of reading and writing assessment practices, based on the explicitness of each genre purpose, stages and options for phases.

Guided reading and writing practice of academic texts provides deeper understanding of the topics studied and raises awareness of the linguistic features that construct successful texts of a given genre. This knowledge about academic language usually takes years to develop and might not even happen if students were to deal with the text independently.

THE ONE-YEAR JOURNEY TO AN ECO-COURSE

Once content-area teachers are enrolled in the ECO program, they embark on a one-year teacher development journey where they receive one-to-one support from a language specialist (mediator) to transform their courses into an ECO-course. During this period, participant teachers are guided in the design, implementation and evaluation of a pedagogic sequence for reading and/or writing a particular genre. This process starts with an interview to identify: teachers' beliefs about reading/writing teaching and learning; their pedagogic practices for teaching and evaluating these competencies; the types of texts they use in their subjects, the characteristics of those texts, and the purposes they pursue with them; and the greatest difficulties their students encounter when managing those texts and their strategies to help them overcome these difficulties. During the interview, the characteristics of the ECO program are explained to the participating teachers and the genre(s) to be taught during the implementation are negotiated.

Then, teachers are instructed in how to analyze the schematic structure and the most relevant characteristics of a genre through a joint analysis of a sample text. This analysis is recorded in a format (see Table 13.1) to aid teachers in deciding which parts they will focus on for instruction during the implementation of the R2L cycle, according to the objectives they aim to achieve with the text.

Table 13.1. Analysis of text characteristics

ANALYSIS OF TEXT CHARACTERISTICS	
Text title	
Genre	
Social purpose	
Topic	
Purpose or main idea of each stage/section	
HyperThemes	
Comments of detailed analysis	

After the analysis, teachers receive support in planning genre-based reading and writing lessons. Lessons focused on reading for learning purposes follow the steps of the TLC adapted by Universidad del Norte (Moss et al., 2016): *Contextualization, identification of text structure and purpose, detailed reading, (re) representation of text's ideas, critical reaction to text, and self-evaluation of comprehension* (see the lesson planning form in Table 13.2)

Lessons focused on reading for writing purposes follow most of the steps of the R2L teaching cycle, as suggested by Acevedo and Rose (2007): *Preparing for Reading, Detailed Reading, Preparing for Writing, Joint Construction, Independent Construction* (see the lesson planning for writing form in Table 13.3).

Table 13.2. Reading lesson plan proforma

UNIVERSIDAD DEL NORTE INSTITUTIONAL PROGRAM COMMUNICATIVE EFFICACY ECO TEACHER-DEVELOPMENT PROGRAM READING PEDAGOGICAL SEQUENCE			
TEACHER: **CLASS:** **TEXT:**			
READING OBJECTIVES (Must be aligned with the objectives of the subject)			
CLASS STEPS			
STEPS	**OBJECTIVES**	**TEACHER'S & STUDENTS' ACTIONS**	**MATERIALS**
Contextualization			
Text structure and purpose of the text			
Detailed Reading			
(Re) representation of text ideas			
Reaction to text ideas			

Table 13.3. Reading for writing lesson plan proforma

UNIVERSIDAD DEL NORTE
INSTITUTIONAL PROGRAM COMMUNICATIVE EFFICACY
ECO TEACHER-DEVELOPMENT PROGRAM
WRITING PEDAGOGY SEQUENCE

TEACHER:

CLASS:

TEXT/GENRE:

WRITING OBJECTIVES (Must be aligned with the objectives of the subject)

DESCRIPTION OF THE WRITING TASK:

TEXT SCHEMATIC STRUCTURE:

IMPORTANT REMARKS:

The text must exhibit adequate use of:

- Coherence and cohesion resources
- Grammar, spelling, and punctuation
- Academic register
- APA norms in text citations, reference list, and overall text format.

CLASS STEPS

STAGES	OBJECTIVES	TEACHERS & STUDENTS' ACTIONS	MATERIALS
Preparation for reading (contextualization and text structure and purpose)			
Detailed reading (Text deconstruction)			
Joint construction			
Independent construction			

In this planning stage of the teacher development program, the team jointly plans a lesson and negotiates the activities and instructional materials that will be applied in each stage of the lesson. Special emphasis is placed on the types of questions that teachers will ask during detailed reading and the information they will provide as elaborations to scaffold students' comprehension of the text's content and linguistic characteristics.

Table 13. 4. Procedure text rubric

Criteria	Description	Performance levels			
		Excellent	Good	Acceptable	Needs improvement
Purpose	The purpose of the text is clear. It corresponds to the procedure report genre				
Schematic structure	The stages and phases of the text are appropriate to a procedure report (title, introduction, materials, procedure, results and observations, conclusion, and bibliography).				
Information	The information provided at each stage is sufficient and relevant to the topic.				
	Documentation from reliable academic sources is evidenced.				
Cohesion and coherence	Each part of the text develops the proposed theme and contributes to the achievement of the communicative purpose. The overall meaning of the text is clearly identified.				
	Appropriate use of cohesive elements (textual markers, reference, reiteration, etc.) is evidenced to link all parts of the text logically and effectively.				
Grammar and spelling	Exemplary use of grammatical and spelling rules is evident.				
Punctuation	There are no significant errors in punctuation that affect the clarity of the text.				
Lexis and register	The language used evidences awareness of the audience and context.				
References	Applied APA standards correctly in citations and references				

Assessment plays a crucial role in the support provided to participant teachers during this stage. Lesson planning also includes negotiation of the activities and instruments that will be used to evaluate students' achievement of the proposed objectives. Here, teachers receive support on how to design activities to evaluate students' reading comprehension, for example DARTS or graphic representations, and rubrics to evaluate writing, based on Reading to Learn material (Rose, 2018) (see Table 13.4).

Once lessons, activities, materials, and evaluation instruments are designed, content-area teachers implement their pedagogic sequence in the classroom. This implementation is recorded for further observation and analysis with the mediator. The analysis includes a guided reflection about the strengths and weaknesses observed during the lesson, and an action plan for further implementations. An example of the reflection questionnaire is provided in Table 13.5.

Table 13.5. Post-implementation reflection questionnaire

POST-IMPLEMENTATION REFLECTION QUESTIONNAIRE
Teacher's name: Subject: Program: Semester: Class implementation date: Below you will find a series of questions that will guide you as you watch the video of the implemented class. Feel free to add information that you consider pertinent and that is not covered in the questionnaire. These questions will guide the conversation with your ECO facilitator about the implemented class.
• What was/were the objective(s) of this class? • To what extent was the class implemented as planned? What was done as planned and what was not? • If there was a variation, what was it? What was the reason for the variation? • How do you think the students perceived your class? Did they like it? Did they seem interested? Did you perceive any rejection? • Do you feel that the methodology implemented in the class helped the students to produce their text? Was it evident that they needed this mediation? • Which parts of the class went well? How do you know? • What parts didn't go so well? How do you know? • What would you do differently if you were to teach this same class with another group? • Were there any objectives that you did not achieve? Why were they not achieved? • How did you perceive your class? Did you feel satisfied with what you did? Why?

After one year of work in the teacher development program, participating subject-area teachers who accomplish all the objectives are credited as ECO-teachers and their subjects as ECO-courses.

TEACHERS' REFLECTIONS AND EMOTIONS

Evaluation for improvement and decision making have been built-in to each iteration of the ECO program through data collection techniques such as classroom observation, focus groups and surveys. Some highlights from the data collected from focus groups and observations in 2020 providing an overview of participant reactions follow. In general terms, teachers shared insights in relation to reading and writing, the benefits for their students, the supporting role of the language specialist and their own professional growth during the accompaniment process.

One conclusion from teachers' reflections about the applicability of R2L informed practices is students' improved reading comprehension. For example, one teacher recalls that his new practices had moved from explaining the meaning of content in readings to co-constructing understanding in interactions with the students. He adds that:

> Now, it is faster, and they understand the ideas better, as we do this together and focus on the structure of the genre and the features of the text, especially those that make it difficult.

During a lesson, we observed how a teacher identified the genre and purpose of the text he was about to read with his students. In this particular case, he was interested in unveiling the implicit meanings in a specific news story so that his class of future engineers could engage in a process of critical reading.

> Our text can be classified as a piece of news. Notice that the main function of news stories is not to inform something, but to retell something. Therefore, then, we do not expect it to strictly stick to the truth, but to tell us something and it may try to make an impression on readers. (...) Reports have a different purpose. They adhere to the truth, they are exhaustive and meticulous. (...) So, you are going to read captivating elements rather than elements of the super proved truth. (...) The idea is that this makes a good impression so that the reader says: How interesting! I want to read more.

Here is how the same teacher modelled the deconstruction of a text and the process of underlining key words in order to unveil the key ideas:

> Let's deconstruct the text. Let's take the news story, take out a pencil or pen and let's begin to underline things that make us understand the text better. First, let's see the title: *The bike that allows you to charge your cell phone*. Here is the bicycle, a key word, and we have its picture. We perceive it's a static bike [...]
>
> In the subtitle we find the first special clues. It says: "After 60 minutes pedalling". It is important to underline this part (he underlines it) because 60 minutes pedalling has the time factor. And it also has the effort or power depending on the power that a person can pedal, and that time will gather a certain amount of energy. (...) It says it will provide energy for "about 60 light bulbs". Let's note it down (he underlined it) and we can immediately think of how much each light bulb needs. This is not specified yet. (And continues reading) "It makes your TV set stay on for five more hours" so here we have a TV set (he underlines it) and we have "five more hours" and we underline...

As another teacher described the gains his students made from his implementation of R2L, he highlighted their enhanced control of learning tasks as a result of experiencing reading as a shared social activity. It seems R2L not only allowed the students to understand the discipline-related readings, but also to develop competencies that teachers highlight as complementary and of great importance for the teaching-learning process such as the "strengthening of critical/analytical thinking" and the "appropriation of strategies pertinent to the reading purposes". These enable learners to transfer what they have learnt to solve other tasks in different contexts.

Concerning the writing process in R2L, teachers recognize that using R2L strategies has enabled students to structure their written texts according to disciplinary expectations. One teacher explained that students are learning "how to structure the content and do it well; that it does not have to be long but well written and understandable, so the truth is that this activity has been enriching for my subject."

In a writing-oriented class, we observed a teacher's deconstruction of a sample article by walking students through structure, social purpose, and the most important linguistic and graphic features of the text. She then asked students to search for information about a topic of their interest for writing an article, and to take notes to construct the different parts of the text. Following is an example of how the teacher guides a student during *preparing for writing* by focusing on how to narrow the topic for writing a journal article and how to organize the information in the different stages of the text.

Q:	*Let's see, Mayra, what do you want to write about?*	**Teacher clarifies the topic**
M:	*I want to write about Russian constructivism, but as today, in modernity, and how it has influenced design in some fields nowadays.*	
T:	*Russian constructivism was an artistic movement, so what you want to write about is how that movement is reflected in design today, something like that?*	Teacher recasts the student's answer to narrow down the topic
M:	*Yes, teacher, how that movement has influenced many artists today and how they use it in a more modern and contemporary way.*	
T:	*O.k. I think that's cool. Keep in mind that this is initially a description; then, with Russian constructivism you can initially highlight some categories that situate this phenomenon in time and space and some concepts that allow us to understand what Russian constructivism is. Afterwards, what you are commenting, Mayra, you can leave it for the last part of analysis or evaluation. Let's see how the influence of Russian constructivism can be seen in modern design, or in some authors. It seems to me that it is very good.*	Teacher affirms student's answer, elaborates on shifting purposes for different stages: Introduction to contextualize the topic: description/definition and the body of the text to evaluate and interpret with examples
	You can take the same into account for the topic "architecture of Germany" and also "Hirohiko Araki". They will have to have first a description and then you can have that other part that can be something more evaluative, an interpretation, or an analysis.	The teacher reminds student about general organization of these texts

Teachers also conclude that using R2L has had an impact on students' academic performance. Teachers relate such change to students' awareness of texts resulting from the modeling and teaching around text now taking place in class. They see that this has enabled students to appropriate the content they read and use it to produce clearly written texts in the expected genres to demonstrate their disciplinary learning. They recognize that students are taking an active role in this process. These reflections reinforce the importance and usefulness of R2L in supporting students learning to read and write in the disciplines.

Evidence of teachers' appropriation of R2L was found in the way they use the strategies with the content of their disciplines, and through their self-evaluations of their learning process. When commenting on her participation in the program, one teacher said that it "allowed me, not only to develop skills to use R2L, but also helped me to grow as a teacher." Having experts to guide and accompany them in the planning, creation, implementation and evaluation of the process has been fundamental for ECO teachers to learn and grow and embrace the program. This individual mentoring support has contributed to the teachers personal and professional growth. The teachers valued the feedback received in their teaching and the support in their learning experience as novice R2L practitioners. This scaffolding of their learning supported them to use and appropriate the R2L pedagogic strategies. This confirms the importance of carefully considering how to help them to critically evaluate their teaching as well as mediate their emerging R2L practices.

Institutionally, results are also positive. The students' scores in the Colombian national standardized test (Saber Pro) that include reading competences have been improving consistently. Since 2016, students placed in higher levels of achievement (3 and 4) have increased 11%. These results suggest that the ECO program is yielding fruits. Such indications are pivotal to sustain institutional efforts and secure resources geared towards students' development of ECO across the curriculum.

FINAL COMMENTS

Reading to Learn has provided the Universidad del Norte with a strong and useful theoretical and methodological foundation to organize and implement a reading and writing program. It has supplied proven pedagogic sequences that carefully scaffold students in their academic literacy development (see also Millin, Chapter 6 this volume for findings from a tertiary setting in South Africa). Just as the R2L program scaffolds learners before they are able to perform independently, the ECO teacher development program emulates this process, by offering continued scaffolding for faculty willing to teach reading and writing from a language-based learning perspective. It has provided these teachers with a common language to talk about texts and a toolbox to teach literacy.

We have travelled a long distance from where we started on this journey. Along the way we have changed and improved our program, the courses, the teaching and learning processes for both students and staff. However, we still face many challenges. As we close this narrative, we highlight some of the factors that have contributed to the success of the experience as well as various challenges that need to be overcome to spread this program to other areas of the university experience.

Staff participation and satisfaction with the possibilities that R2L has opened up for them, in terms of professional development, are very high. The broadening of pedagogic possibilities to enrich their disciplinary teaching has been recognized as a result of this experience. The teachers' feelings of achievement and gain are really inspiring and indicative of our success story.

However, an institution-wide campaign is needed to position the program at the forefront of all our students, teachers and administrators' minds. Such a campaign would help construct a unified institutional discourse around Reading to Learn, increase academic staff participation in the program, align the efforts of diverse agents, secure resources for the continuation of the program and create shared understanding and visions about the benefits that this program brings to its different stakeholders, particularly to the students.

Finally, continuous efforts are required to better understand faculty needs and characteristics. As adult learners, in-service professionals, coming from various walks of life (both disciplinary and pedagogic), the ever-growing numbers of faculty from different content areas pose an ever-changing challenge in deciding on the nature of the mediation and scaffolding strategies that best suit their needs. This is an area of constant learning and adaptation for the ECO program.

REFERENCES

Acevedo, C., & Rose, D. (2007). Learning to Read, Reading to Learn – A Middle Years Literacy Intervention Project: Success for all Learners in the Middle Years of Schooling (5–9). *The International Journal of Learning: Annual Review 13*(11), 73–84. doi:10.18848/1447-9494/CGP/v13i11/45095

Bernstein, B. (2000). *Pedagogy, symbolic control and identity: Theory, research, critique* (rev. ed.). Rowman & Littlefield Publishers.

Bernstein, B. (2003). *Class, code and control. Vol. 5. The structuring of pedagogic discourse.* Routledge.

Carlino, P. (2003). Alfabetización académica: Un cambio necesario, algunas alternativas posibles. *Educere, 6*(20), 409–420.

Christie, F. (2002). The development of abstraction in adolescence in subject English. In M. Schleppegrell & M. C. Colombi (Eds.), *Developing advanced literacy in first and second languages: Meaning with powe*r (pp. 45–66). Lawrence Erlbaum.

Colectivo Comunicación. (2002). *Comprensión y competencias lectoras en estudiantes universitarios. Resultados de una investigación*. Ediciones Uninorte.

Colombi, C. (2002). Academic language development in Latino student writing in Spanish. In M. Schleppegrell & M. C. Colombi (Eds.), *Developing advanced literacy in first and second languages: Meaning with power* (pp. 67–86). Lawrence Erlbaum.

Fernández, G., & Carlino, P. (2010). ¿En qué se diferencian las prácticas de lectura y escritura de la universidad y las de la escuela secundaria. *Lectura y Vida, 31*, 6–19.

González, Y., Jiménez, J., & Rosas, J. (2016). Prácticas lectoras de estudiantes universitarios con fines de escritura académica. *Revista Electrónica Actualidades Investigativas en Educación, 16*(1), 1–19.

Meisel, A. (2018). *El liderazgo y el futuro del Caribe colombiano*. Editorial Universidad del Norte.

Ministerio de Educación Nacional. (2018). *Referentes de calidad. Una propuesta para la evolución del Sistema de Aseguramiento de la Calidad.* Imprenta Nacional de Colombia.

Moss, G., Benítez, T., & Mizuno, J. (Eds.). (2016). *Textos que se leen y escriben en la universidad: una mirada desde los géneros discursivos*. Universidad del Norte.

Rose, D. (2018). *Reading to learn: Accelerating learning and closing the gap. Teacher training books and DVDs.* Reading to Learn http://www.readingtolearn.com.au.
Rose, D., & Martin, J. R. (2012). *Learning to write, reading to learn: Genre, knowledge and pedagogy in the Sydney school.* Equinox.
Rose, D., & Martin. J. R. (2018). *Leer para aprender. Lectura y escritura en las áreas del currículo* (Ana Bustelo Tortela Trans.). Pirámide (original work published 2012).
Van Dijk, T. (1980). *Texto y contexto.* Cátedra.
Wilhelm, J. D., Baker, T. N., & Dube, J. (2001). *Strategic reading: Guiding students to lifelong literacy, 6–12.* Boynton/Cook.

ABOUT THE AUTHORS

Sergio Álvarez Uribe is a full-time teacher-researcher at Universidad del Norte in Barranquilla, Colombia. His research interests include academic language development and assessment; knowledge about language for teacher development; argumentative studies; cohesion analysis; extracurricular and co-curricular language development; creative and art-based research methods; and instructional design informed by genre-based pedagogy.

Norma Barletta is an associate professor at Universidad del Norte in Barranquilla, Colombia. She teaches at the Spanish, Foreign Language and Education departments. Her research interests center around L1 and L2 language and literacy teaching and learning as well as language use in social contexts. She is particularly interested in discourse analysis, issues of ideology and identity, and applications of genre-based pedagogy.

Teresa Benítez is a full-time teacher-researcher at Universidad del Norte in Barranquilla, Colombia. She belongs to the Language and Education research group. Her research interests include Language (L1 and L2) teaching and learning; applications of genre-based literacy pedagogy in educational contexts; teacher development; curriculum development and instructional materials design.

Nayibe Rosado-Mendinueta is a language teacher and a teacher educator at Universidad del Norte in Colombia. Her research interests reside in the intersection of students' and teachers' learning and how languages affect the construction of reality in contexts such as classrooms and in other institutions that surround us.

14

Reading to Learn in an Argentine context: Implementing the pedagogy in primary schools

Patricia V. Meehan, Angélica Gaido,
Liliana Anglada & María Belén Oliva

ABSTRACT

This contribution reports on the implementation of Reading to Learn (R2L) in primary schools in a Spanish-speaking, Latin American context, in Córdoba, Argentina. The focus of the first stage in this pilot project was to train in-service teachers in charge of teaching the disciplinary areas of the social and natural sciences in the application of the pedagogy. This process involved acquainting them with the most central notions about the theory of language underlying R2L. This chapter begins by describing a shift of attention from language-learning at the university level to learning the language of specific disciplines at the primary school level, and the need to explore the earlier stages of schooling in terms of prevalent teaching practices, school curricula and educational policies. The chapter also provides an account of teachers' background assumptions and practices and an overview of a teacher-training plan based on the genres often featured in school textbooks to teach the disciplines. The final section covers aspects concerning the implementation of that plan.

THE CÓRDOBA CASE: HOW IT ALL STARTED

As teacher-researchers involved in the implementation of the R2L programme in primary schools in Córdoba during 2018 and 2019[1], we had previously worked extensively with undergraduate students as part of our teaching positions within the university system. After a number of years of working with students in the translator and teacher-training programmes at the Faculty of Languages, National University of Córdoba, it became quite clear that the students had difficulty with the comprehension of task rubrics and with the organization of ideas in their written texts. We were involved in the teaching of grammar to students of English as a foreign language and realized that our students experienced two major difficulties when doing homework assignments and when answering exam questions. On the one hand, some students failed to understand the tasks that they were required to perform and, on the other, those students who were able to comply with the task often had difficulties in organizing the ideas logically in their writing so as to produce cohesive and coherent texts. Initially, we attributed the difficulties in understanding the task and in performing the writing activity to a lack of mastery in the target language, i.e. English. We therefore tried to help our students to improve their skills in the target language by having them write more frequently and work on remedial activities.

With the passing of time, the repetition of situations like those described above generated explorations into other possible causes for those difficulties (Gaido, 2015). We entertained the idea that the problems surfacing at the university level were more serious than those resulting from linguistic interference (Carlino, 2005; Moyano, 2010; Natale, 2012; Navarro, 2014) and that their origin could be traced back to gaps in the students' earlier schooling. The fact that the students were not able to produce texts in compliance with instructional verbs in the rubrics such as "describe", "classify", "define", "explain" or "discuss", verbs which are quite transparent if we compare English and Spanish, indicated that the problem had started earlier and was not solely related to the language being learned. The students' lack of text organizational skills manifested itself in a failure to establish appropriate connections between ideas, and difficulties in signaling stages in their writing indicated that they had not been prepared to assemble texts in their native language at earlier stages of schooling. Ultimately, the difficulties seemed to point to a lack of genre awareness.

These reflections justified our looking into other levels of formal education as more appropriate areas to begin working – that is, areas or stages of development where learners could be given effective tools to prevent the kinds of difficulties that we had detected among university students. In this way, we would be tackling and resolving those difficulties early on. In other words, we thought it would be more advantageous and a good investment to shift the focus of attention from higher to lower levels of education; perhaps primary school students who had already learned how to read and write needed to be trained in the application of specific reading and writing strategies based on a functional model of language like those being applied at the university level, most of them drawn from the R2L pedagogy (Rose, 2016; Rose & Martin, 2012, 2018). This training would facilitate primary school learners' work with disciplinary texts, safeguard them from falling behind and guarantee their inclusion and permanence in the educational system.

EXPLORING THE TERRITORY

Before we could offer educational institutions what we thought would be an effective pedagogical approach to the development of literacy skills in the earlier stages of formal schooling, it made sense to look into the policies and practices prevalent in primary education. Furthermore, if many of the difficulties at the university level could be attributed to the limited or ineffective preparation provided by high schools and primary schools, we had to understand what was happening at those earlier stages of schooling. In order to develop an understanding of that educational context, we began by studying a number of documents that are meant to guide institutional actions and teachers' practices. We wanted to determine the place given to reading and writing and the pedagogical recommendations concerning the teaching of these two skills in national and state documents[2].

The official documents reveal that reading and writing skills are centre-stage in the first three years of primary school education and even though they continue to play an important role in the last three years, there are no clear specifications as to how teachers can make new disciplinary knowledge available to their students via an emphasis on reading and writing skills. There seems to be a preoccupation with how the development of these skills should run across the curriculum, i.e., across all areas of knowledge, but little is explicitly stated concerning the role played by language as the mediator or carrier of content. As far as the notion of genre is concerned, there are suggestions as to what types of texts the students should read, and some genres are mentioned in passing. These genres, however, are not described as key elements in the organization and the teaching of classes. In the guidelines and recommendations laid down in these documents, it is assumed that teachers will know what strategies to use and how to put them into practice to guide the students in the discovery of the relationships between a number of dimensions: field knowledge, the purposes and structure of texts, and the language used to put that field knowledge into specific genres (Gobierno de Córdoba, 2011; Ministerio de Educación, 2004, 2011).

The limited guidelines on how to handle texts, content knowledge, and linguistic resources available in the ministerial documents prompted us to find possible ways to reach out to in-service teachers. We hoped that in-service teachers would be willing to learn about and then try out the R2L pedagogy in their classrooms. However, we were hesitant as to where to begin and how to approach them. After considering a number of possibilities, we decided that the most direct way to do so was to target the Ministry of Education in Córdoba. In May 2017, we wrote a proposal to be submitted to the ministerial authorities. After getting the endorsement of the Dean of the Faculty of Languages, we presented the document to them and obtained an appointment. We wanted the authorities to consider the implementation of the R2L programme in the teacher-training colleges' curricula as well as to encourage school principals to pilot the methodology in their schools. The meeting was partially successful in that the ministerial authorities showed an interest in our project, but the concrete results that we were hoping for did not come to fruition.

In spite of this setback, we did not give up and, in August that same year, Claire Acevedo visited Córdoba to have a personal interview with Prof. Delia Provinciali, Secretary of the Ministry of Education, and a board of educational advisers. Claire did not discuss the pedagogy but went straight into modelling the classroom pedagogy with the participants in the meeting. This resulted in two of the advisers to the Secretary of Education attending the R2L training workshop that we offered after the 12th ALSFAL Conference in Córdoba in November 2017. Around 30 in-service teachers of state and private schools attended the workshop (Figure 14.1). Some of them became interested in further learning about the R2L pedagogy and they were invited together with a few other teachers who had not attended that workshop to be part of three other workshops the following year. These

Figure 14.1. Teacher training workshop

workshops aimed not only at informing teachers about the R2L programme but also at gaining a commitment from school principals and recruiting teachers who had become interested in the pedagogy. By the end of those training sessions, three schools and some of their teachers were ready to commit themselves to implementing the pedagogy.

In what follows we address two main aspects of the implementation of the plan. First, we cover the challenges encountered when making teachers aware of the network of genres proposed by the Sydney School and the theory of language on which it is based; i.e., we describe what we did initially and the adjustments that we had to make. Second, we present the steps that we took in order to scaffold the R2L programme in the three schools that became involved in the project and also describe some instances of its implementation and in-service guidance.

INVESTIGATING GENRES AND CHALLENGING PREVIOUS ASSUMPTIONS

When we started planning the teacher-training workshops, what we first pondered over was how much theory to include. Approaches to new paradigms and perspectives are never simple; and thus, to avoid discouragement, for the initial training sessions we aimed at selecting key aspects of the theory that would be functional for understanding the pedagogy and putting it to work. The challenge at this stage then was to equip teachers with the basics for perceiving the written texts used in the class as linguistic vehicles encoding the discipline specific content and for selecting and analyzing those texts.

Central to this aim was the introduction of the network of genre families in the school curriculum and the underlying conceptualizations about genres and their social purposes (Rose & Martin, 2012). Teachers found the new proposal rather overwhelming because of the delicacy in the description of genres, which they constantly compared against the small set of text types that they were acquainted with – expository, argumentative, narrative, instructional. These labels (together with their underlying concepts and rather unclear defining criteria) seemed to be firmly rooted in the teachers' minds. To find a way around, we thought of delving into the teachers' previous knowledge of text types to compare the theoretical bases and scope of their background assumptions against the genre network that we were proposing. This comparison would allow us to make adjustments to the original genre map and offer a more accessible one.

Given that the teachers undertaking the training worked in the areas of natural and social sciences, the texts used to reorient the work with genres were only the ones with which content was taught and learnt in these disciplines, generally known in the school context as "expository" texts. This reduction of the whole network to the family of informing genres was aimed at making the textual universe more manageable. To get a more accurate idea of the metalanguage used to refer to these texts and the teachers' implicit conceptualizations, we designed a brief survey which we later administered to teachers in the schools involved. The instrument included two texts from textbooks used in local primary schools, one of them describing an entity (a report) and the other explaining a phenomenon (an explanation). Respondents were asked to label them and then justify the reasons for the selected "name".

As we could see, the teachers had little idea about labelling a text according to its purpose. The labels they used were "expository", "descriptive" and "informative" for the first text, and "expository", "explanatory", "informative" and "narrative" for the second text. As regards the justifications, in both cases the reasons tended to overlap, the most recurrent ones being that the purpose of the texts was to describe, inform, explain and that they made use of comparisons and exemplifications, and specific vocabulary. These responses revealed rather diverse and diffuse defining criteria, namely purpose (explain, inform, describe), discourse strategies (exemplification, comparison) and type of lexis (specific vocabulary). This variety of labels and criteria was also observed in the primary school language textbooks that we examined to analyze how the texts that inform are taught and understood.

It was clear that both the teachers and the researchers needed explicit shared criteria for the texts about natural and social sciences used in our local primary school context. We therefore carried out a mapping of the genres of the core textbooks. The recurrent genres found were in line with those prototypically used in these knowledge areas (Martin & Rose, 2008; Rose & Martin, 2012), namely reports, explanations, procedures and two types of chronicles (historical accounts and historical recounts). These findings guided the design of the genre map for these disciplines.

With the data gathered during our field research, we planned an approach to genres aimed at meeting the demands of the teachers in our local context. We designed a reduced, adapted version of the map of informing genres, including reports, explanations, and the two types of chronicles found in the school textbooks. As they did not pose a challenge, procedures were not included so as to reduce the network as much as possible. This was accompanied by a brief explanation and guiding questions oriented to the identification of systemic oppositions. The chart[3], which is presented as Table 14.1, was meant to function as a guide for teachers' text identification and analysis when preparing lessons. The guidelines accompanying the chart were as follows:

HOW TO IDENTIFY THE GENRES OF INFORMING TEXTS

The texts that you use to teach various disciplines, which you generally know as expository, informative or explanatory texts, can be grouped together in the family of **informing genres**, as their overall purpose is to give information about the natural or the social world. In the school context, these texts make use of exemplifications, elaborations, comparisons and other discourse strategies to make the content more accessible to students. However, it is important to notice that the texts belonging to the informing family may **do different things** considering the **type of phenomenon** they inform readers about and the more specific purpose they aim at. These aspects will determine **forms of organization** of the content that make one genre different from the other. That is, the functional components or **stages** that contribute to the structuring of knowledge in the text will vary from genre to genre. Table 14.1 shows the informing genres you use in your disciplines.

When we find an informative text, we can identify the genre it belongs to by asking a series of questions based on the criteria established at the top of Table 14.1 (the type of phenomenon discussed in the text and the specific purpose). These questions allow us to narrow down the universe of possible informative genres as we rule out other possibilities.

Table 14.1. Informing genres (adapted from Rose & Martin, 2012, p.130)

GENERAL purpose	**Type of phenomenon**	**SPECIFIC purpose**	**Stages* (show how content is structured in the text)**	**Label**
TO INFORM	Entity(ies)	Classifying and describing 1 type of entity	Classification^Description (of **different aspects** of the entity)	Descriptive report
		Classifying and describing different types of entities	Classification^ Description: **types**	Classifying report
		Describing parts of a whole	Classification^ Description: **parts**	Compositional report
	Activity/ process (cause/effect)	Explaining a sequence	Phenomenon^ Explanation: **step 1, step 2...**	Sequential explanation
		Multiple causes – one result	Phenomenon (outcome) ^Explanation **(factor 1, 2...)**	Factorial explanation
		One cause – multiple results	Phenomenon (cause) ^Explanation (**consequence 1, 2...**)	Consequential explanation
		Results of contingent cause	Phenomenon^Explanation (condition 1, 2...)	Conditional explanation
	Facts/events	Stages in history — Recounting: temporal	Background^Stages: 1, 2...	Historical recount
		Stages in history — Explaining: causal	Background^Stages: 1, 2...	Historical account

*Examples, comparisons, elaborations, etc. are likely to be found in any of these genres.

For example, if we identify a text that describes an entity, such as a plant, a social group, etc., we can rule out texts that are organized around an activity or a fact/event. On the other hand, on the basis of this identification we can ask further questions, questions that inquire about the specific purpose of the text, to see whether what is involved is the description of only one entity, of different entities or of parts of a whole. Once we finish asking the questions, we can look at the expected stages (and phases) of each genre, which show how the content of the text is typically structured. In other words, the stages represent how knowledge is organized in the text[4].

SCAFFOLDING THE TEACHERS: THE PREPARATION PHASE

After finishing the cycle of workshops on genres and the general guidelines on R2L, there came the moment to prepare the teachers to actually apply the pedagogy in the classroom. Our team of researchers split into three smaller groups and each group took care of a particular school. We held on-site personal meetings with the teachers participating in the pilot project and started out by asking the teachers to read and revise the pedagogy (Rose & Martin, 2018). We then exchanged views and explained aspects that were not altogether clear. As a second step, we provided the teachers with sample lesson plans based on texts drawn from the natural and social sciences textbooks published in Argentina. The main objective was to imbue them with the essence of the pedagogy by illustrating it through texts that were culturally familiar to them.

Once the teachers seemed to have grasped the methodology, they were asked to prepare a lesson plan based on material that they were planning to use soon. This step took some time, for it required providing important feedback and revision. At this stage, we could see that they had not completely understood the purpose of the R2L model, which is to teach meaning rather than just to check reading comprehension. As a matter of fact, the main problem was that most of the questions the teachers prepared to use in the *Detailed Reading* stage followed the old tradition of merely checking understanding of content, rather than focusing on the language used to express that content. For example, there was a group of third grade teachers (with students aged 8–9) who had to prepare their lesson plan based on a text entitled *Los problemas ambientales* ("Environmental Problems") (Kotliar et al., 2012). The opening paragraph read:

> Tanto en el campo como en la ciudad existen **problemas ambientales.** Estos problemas son ocasionados por **actividades y comportamientos humanos**, que **perjudican** el ambiente... [There exist **environmental**

> **problems** both in the countryside and in cities. These problems are the result of **human behaviour** and **activities** that **damage** the environment. (our translation)]

The teachers successfully identified the lexical items (in bold type) crucial for the understanding of the text and which students would later need to recover and use in the *Joint Construction* stage. However, the phrasing of the questions did not seem to be effective. One of the teachers' questions was "In the title, what words indicate what the text is about?" Even though some of the 8-year-olds, the most gifted ones, would most likely have answered "Environmental Problems", this would not ensure understanding but mere repetition of the two words they could see. In turn, we suggested splitting the question into two in order to focus on the meaning of each lexical item at a time:

a) "Who can see in the title a word that means something that is an inconvenience?" (Expected answer: **Problem**),
b) "Who can see in the title a word that means "related to the natural world?" Expected answer: **environmental**).

Another question these teachers suggested was: "Read the second line and answer: Why are these activities and human behaviour bad for the environment?" (the expected answer was ***damage***). Again, the question was clearly aimed at checking the understanding of "content", rather than teaching meaning. The improved version we recommended was: "Who can see in the second sentence a word that means **to harm**?" The teachers were not really convinced about our suggestions for the "improved" questions and, when asked why, they said they found the answers to the questions too obvious.

All this work gave rise to enriching interaction between ourselves, in our roles as trainers, and the teachers as trainees. These discussions revealed that deeply rooted methodologies are difficult to change (this issue is also discussed in Andersson Varga, et al., Chapter 8 this volume). Once the preparation phase was apparently complete, there came the moment to actually try out the pedagogy with the students in the classroom.

SCAFFOLDING THE TEACHERS: THE IMPLEMENTATION PHASE

We formed teams made up of senior and junior researchers to attend the classes. Once in the different schools, we devoted a few minutes to explaining why we were there, so that the children would not feel too anxious during the class.

During the classroom implementation stage, we experienced some breakthrough moments with the teachers. One of the third-grade teachers who during the preparation phase had found the answers to the questions in the *Detailed Reading* stage too obvious, soon changed her mind. To her surprise, all her students – high and low achievers – enthusiastically cried out the correct answers to the questions asked during *Detailed Reading*. She also did an excellent job when elaborating on particular difficult concepts. After this rich and active exchange on the meanings of key words, the teacher was finally able to value the ultimate aim of R2L. At the end of the class, she approached the researchers and said: "But then it's language that we have to teach!"

Another teacher stated that she began to realize the power and effectiveness of the pedagogy when she noticed that the students started to experience success. She carefully followed all the steps suggested in the pedagogy; but she realized that, at first, she felt rather hesitant and unsure of what she was doing. Little by little she gained confidence and enthusiasm as her students, especially the weak ones, shyly started to participate and feel, probably for the first time, proud of themselves whenever they provided a correct answer. Later on, she wrote an email to the team to thank us for the opportunity and said: "Suddenly, the students were participating not only more actively but in a more orderly way; they understood the text and *I* understood the real scope of the pedagogy!"

Another aspect that was enriching and crucial for the students' active participation and understanding of key lexical items was the culminating *elaboration* move in the R2L interaction pattern during the *Detailed Reading* and the *Joint Construction* stages (Figure 14.2).

In order to elaborate on complex language, the teachers unpacked nominalizations, worked on the derivation of words and referred to topics previously studied.

Figure 14.2. Joint construction of a primary school text

Table 14.2. Unpacking nominalizations

	sp		phase
1	T	*Who can identify in the first sentence a proper noun that has been capitalized?*	focus wording
	St	*Association for the Conservation and Study of Nature.*	identify wording
2	T	*What is an association? What word does "association" come from?*	focus derivation
	St	*From to associate*	propose derivation
	T	*Good!*	affirm
		A synonym would be to unite, to join, to get together.	elaborate definition
3	T	*Now...who gets together in associations?*	focus figure
	St	*People!*	propose entity
	T	*We understand, then, that people associate, join, or get together for the conservation and study of nature.*	elaborate figure
4	T	*Ok, let's look at the nouns "conservation and study". What words do they derive or come from?*	focus derivation
	St	*To conserve and to study.*	propose derivation
	T	*Excellent!!*	affirm
	T	*A synonym of conserve can be look after.*	elaborate definition
		So, we can say that "Association for the Conservation and Study of Nature" refers to a group of people that get together to study topics related to nature because we need to look after nature".	elaborate sequence

For example, one of the fifth-grade teachers needed to help her students understand a noun group which involved a series of nominalizations: "**Asociación** para la **conservación** y **estudio** de la naturaleza" [**Association** for the **conservation** and **study** of nature (nominalizations in bold type) (our translation)].

Table 14.2 contains an excerpt of the classroom discourse showing how this fifth-grade teacher unpacked the nominalizations with the purpose of elaborating on complex concepts (our translation). This took four learning cycles to accomplish. In the first cycle the teacher guides students to identify the nominal group as "capitalized". In the second, she asks them to derive the activity "associate" from the first noun and elaborates with a commonsense synonym. In the third, she guides them to identify the "people" involved in this activity and elaborates the whole figure realized by the nominalization: "people associate, join, or get together". In the fourth, she again asks them to derive activities from "conservation and study". She then elaborates – first by defining "conserve", then with a commonsense paraphrase of the whole sequence realized by the nominalization.

When this teacher was interviewed on her experience with R2L, she said: "I have realized the importance of spotting complex language when I'm planning the class at home. I can anticipate my students' problems in advance, and this allows me to elaborate on the complicated stuff more effectively. Now I see that my students can genuinely learn new content".

REFLECTIONS ON THE IMPACT OF R2L IN CÓRDOBA

After the classroom interventions using R2L, we can conclude that our project had numerous achievements. One of the most salient ones was that the teachers involved in the pilot programme felt grateful for having at long last been able to tackle the difficulties their students faced in class. They also referred to the positive impact the approach had on low-achieving students who would normally not dare participate, simply because they do not understand what the texts mean. These students showed a renewed enthusiasm for the lesson as they were able to give valid answers, which were praised by their teacher in front of the class. Such explicit approval generated self-confidence with an obvious positive effect on the children's performance.

The preparation of the activities involved in the *Detailed Reading* stage led the teachers to a more careful reflection on language, i.e., lexical and grammatical elements that can be problematic for comprehension, and therefore that need to be reflected upon through interaction. The teachers placed themselves in their students' position when deciding what to ask and how to design the questions that would trigger understanding of the key ideas of the text or paragraph. They explained that this new approach enabled them to anticipate more clearly the problems related to the information packed in complex language than when they used their previous methodologies.

As a general rule, most teachers insisted that apparently the students responded more promptly because there was no tension in the air. The students felt comfortable in a relaxed class. This did not mean a boring class; on the contrary, being stress-free, the class atmosphere favored the students' active partipation.

Along with these achievements, we encountered some obstacles on the way. The main problem for us was the integration of the notion of genre by most of the teachers in their actual classes. Although we explicitly worked with their previous assumptions about text types and adapted the genre network to make it more manageable, most teachers found it hard to identify the genre and the schematic organization of the text that their students would be reading. And when dealing with genres in class, some of the teachers addressed the purpose of the text and some other elements connected to text structure but not at an initial stage or before plunging into reading. We hypothesize that these limitations may have to do with the complexity of learning a new taxonomy of texts, which presupposes understanding that those texts are the linguistic realization of discipline related activities concerning the natural and social world. This change of paradigm is likely to involve recurrent instances of practice and reflection, for which time is an essential element.

We should also acknowledge that the first interventions with R2L are time-consuming in both preparation and implementation. As teachers in our context are overloaded with work and content to teach, they are likely to experience difficulty in enacting the pedagogy with enough frequency to develop fluency. Thus, we suggest the implementation of the pedagogy with short extracts from each text until the teachers grasp the dynamics of the learning cycle. This might foster shorter interventions but a more frequent application of the methodology.

Another aspect that deserves attention is the institutional support given to the implementation of the pedagogy. In this sense, we noticed a direct relation between the progress of R2L in those schools where the authorities supported it and the opposite in those where the teachers were eager to participate but the authorities were not supportive enough (see also Andersson Varga et al., Chapter 8 for more on this same topic).

After the classes we observed we concluded that deeply rooted methodologies are very difficult to change and that providing teachers with theory and examples, no matter how clear they might be, is not always enough. It is only through the actual and frequent classroom application that the benefits of the R2L can be seen and valued (see more in Acevedo, Chapter 9 in this volume).

A GOAL WITHOUT A PLAN IS JUST A WISH

We are well aware of the fact that the implementation of Reading to Learn in Córdoba is still at an initial stage and that our results cannot be generalized. However, they are very encouraging since they have had wide acceptance and have been seen as positive and innovative within the school communities where we have applied the pedagogy. Teachers, who at first distrusted its benefits, ended up welcoming a methodology that contributed to the students' achievement. This is what Rose (2005) refers to as "democratizing the classroom".

We still have in sight our original goal from 2017, which was to have the education authorities contemplate the implementation of the R2L programme in the teacher-training colleges in Córdoba. Our project, which started as an on-site training of a small group of teachers, has taken one step forward. We have designed an on-line course to supplement our on-site training. This on-line course was piloted in 2022 with a group of experienced teachers, who provided us with valuable feedback for the definitive course, which we plan to launch for wider audiences across the province. The ultimate beneficiary – as ambitious as it may sound – is, and has always been, the whole educational system in Córdoba. We are convinced that if our projects enable the implementation of R2L pedagogy in the classrooms, students at primary schools will improve their reading and writing skills. This will in turn result in a better performance of secondary school students, who will hopefully have greater access to higher education and ultimately to better jobs, and a more critical participation in society. Facilitating access to knowledge and learning for all students alike is the best way to democratize education and Reading to Learn fast tracks the process.

NOTES

1 This article reports on some of the work done as part of a four-year research project entitled *Lectoescritura y reflexión lingüística: bases esenciales para la adquisición de conocimientos disciplinares en la escuela primaria* (in English, Reading-writing and linguistic awareness: Foundations for the acquisition of disciplinary knowledge in primary schools). This project, which was carried out between 2018–2022, was supported by *Secretaría de Ciencia y Tecnología, Universidad Nacional de Córdoba.*

2 These guidelines and recommendations are featured in the documents known as *Núcleos de Aprendizajes Prioritarios (NAP)* and *Diseño Curricular (DC)* for the Province of Córdoba 2011–2020.

3 This is the translated version of the original, in Spanish.

4 The questions designed to guide the identification of genres of the informing family are presented in the Appendix.

APPENDIX

Questions to identify the genres of the informing family

What **type of phenomenon** does the text inform about?

a. Does the text describe an **entity**?
   If it does: Is it about **one** entity?
   Is it about **different types** of entities?
   Does it describe **parts** of a whole?

b. Does it expose the causes and effects of **an activity or process**?
   If so: Does it explain a sequence of events?
   Does it explain various causes and one outcome?
   Does it explain one cause and various consequences?
   Does it explain the effects of **contingent** causes?

c. Is it about historical **facts or events**?
   If it is: Does it organize the events in time?
   Does it present causes and effects of the facts or events?

REFERENCES

Carlino, P. (2005). *Escribir, leer y aprender en la universidad. Una introducción a la alfabetización académica.* Fondo de Cultura Económica.

Gaido, A. (2015). *Text production in undergraduate education: Functional and cognitive complexities.* [Master's Thesis, Universidad Nacional de Córdoba]. https://rdu.unc.edu.ar/handle/11086/4530

Gobierno de Córdoba. Ministerio de Educación y Cultura. Dirección de Planificación y Estrategias Educativas. (2011). *Diseño Curricular de la Educación Primaria 2011–2020.* https://www.igualdadycalidadcba.gov.ar/SIPEC-CBA/publicaciones/EducacionPrimaria/DCJ_Primario-23-02-2018.pdf

Kotliar, D., Magallanes, J., Fernández de Reboursin, B., & Salussoglia, E. (2012). *Mica y sus amigos 3.* Santillana.

Martin, J. R., & Rose, D. (2008). *Genre relations: Mapping culture.* Equinox Publishing.

Ministerio de Educación, Ciencia y Tecnología de la Nación. Consejo Federal de Cultura y Educación. (2004). *Núcleos de aprendizajes prioritarios. 1er. Ciclo EGB/Nivel Primario.* http://www.bnm.me.gov.ar/giga1/documentos/EL000977.pdf

Ministerio de Educación, Ciencia y Tecnología de la Nación. Consejo Federal de Cultura y Educación. (2011). (3ra ed.). *Núcleos de aprendizajes prioritarios. 2° ciclo. Educación primaria. 4°, 5°, 6° años.* http://repositorio.educacion.gov.ar:8080/dspace/bitstream/handle/123456789/109594/NAPsegundociclo2011.pdf?sequence=1

Moyano, E. (2010). Escritura académica a lo largo de la carrera: un programa institucional. *Signos, 43*(74), 465- 488. http://dx.doi.org/10.4067/S0718-09342010000500004

Natale, L. (Ed.). (2012). *En carrera: Escritura y lectura de textos académicos y profesionales.* Universidad Nacional de General Sarmiento.

Navarro, F. (Ed.). (2014). *Manual de escritura para carreras de humanidades.* Editorial de la Facultad de Filosofía y Letras, UBA.

Rose, D. (2005). Democratising the classroom: A literacy pedagogy for the new generation, *Journal of Education, 37,* 131–167.

Rose, D. (2016). *Reading to Learn: Accelerating learning and closing the gap (2016 Edition).* Reading to Learn. http://www.readingtolearn.com.au

Rose, D., & Martin, J. R. (2012). *Learning to write, reading to learn: Genre, knowledge and pedagogy of the Sydney school.* Equinox Publishing.

Rose, D., & Martin, J. R., (2018). *Leer para aprender. Lectura y escritura en las áreas del currículo* (R. Whittaker & T. Bordón, Trans.). Ediciones Pirámide (original work published 2012)

ABOUT THE AUTHORS

Patricia V. Meehan is a teacher of English from the Facultad de Lenguas, Universidad Nacional de Córdoba. She holds an MA in English Applied Linguistics. She taught ESL/EFL at bilingual schools for 20 years and has been a senior Examiner for English B (IBO) since 2004. She's a permanent Full Professor in the Chair of Contrastive Grammar at Facultad de Lenguas, Universidad Nacional de Córdoba and has been in the area of International Affairs at Universidad Nacional de Córdoba since 2016. Her current research includes systemic functional linguistics and genre pedagogy.

Angélica Gaido is a teacher of English and holds an MA degree in English and Applied Linguistics from Facultad de Lenguas, Universidad Nacional de Córdoba, Argentina. She has taught EFL undergraduate and graduate courses on grammar and linguistics. Her current research focuses on the relationship between knowledge about language, reading and writing skills development and content learning. Her areas of interest revolve around language literacy, genre pedagogy, and functional aspects of grammar and language.

Liliana Anglada graduated as a translator and teacher of English from the Facultad de Lenguas, Universidad Nacional de Córdoba. She holds an MA in Applied Linguistics (Ohio University) and a PhD in English (Texas Tech University). She has taught EFL/ESL undergraduate and graduate courses on language, grammar and linguistics and acted as director of the doctoral programme at Facultad de Lenguas from 2016 to 2022. Her research interests include systemic functional linguistics, EFL writing instruction and genre pedagogy.

María Belén Oliva is a teacher of English, graduated from the Facultad de Lenguas, Universidad Nacional de Córdoba. She has been the vicedean of this institution since 2021 and was also vicedean from 2014 to 2017. She holds an MA in English Applied Linguistics (Facultad de Lenguas). She has taught EFL/ESL undergraduate and graduate courses on language, traditional grammar and systemic functional grammar. She has done research into discourse analysis, traditional grammar and systemic functional linguistics.

15

Reading to Learn and cognitive approaches to reading in the EFL context: Engaging in dialogue

Samiah Hassan & Cristina Boccia

ABSTRACT

This chapter is based on the findings of a study conducted in Mendoza, Argentina, that compared an L1 cognitive reading program – Plan de Lectura y Escritura Mendoza (PLEM) – widely used in our local, public primary school setting with Reading to Learn (R2L).

The key element of our local program is a cognitive instructional model (IM) that follows Fisher et al. (2009) and centrally consists of a cycle designed to develop learners' reading comprehension skills as they receive intensive training in cognitive and discourse strategies. We studied this model and compared its key features and theoretical underpinnings with the R2L model (Martin & Rose, 2005; Rose, 2006; Rose & Martin, 2012, 2014) with a view to establishing a common ground between both models. Finding how R2L can complement and enhance the IM is important to optimize pre- and in-service work with L1 teachers and, more specifically, EFL teachers – a group that already receives instruction in a functional, contextual model (strongly SFL-based), very compatible with R2L. The study teases out the similarities and differences between IM and R2L and identifies the ways in which R2L can strengthen the local model. In doing so, we take a first important step towards delineating a carefully scaffolded reading teaching and learning cycle both for young local teachers who need a substantial amount of guidance and for our learners for whom reading comprehension is a major challenge. Taking as our starting point the instructional model, as currently used in official L1 teacher training offered to school directors and teachers in Mendoza, is a strategic move aimed at identifying what the model has in common with R2L and, critically, at enhancing the power of the model that is officially used.

ORIENTATION TO THE STUDY

This is an exploratory study of the reading program that is being extensively followed in our local, public L1 and, prospectively, EFL studies, with a view to establishing ways in which it can engage in conversation with, and be further specified by, R2L. The result of this study will be used to develop teaching and learning material for pre-service students at the EFL Teacher Training college at the Universidad Nacional de Cuyo (UNCuyo) and for in-service teachers as part of the EFL literacy program on *Teaching Genres in the EFL Classroom*.

In an attempt to strengthen the impact of PLEM (*Plan de Lectura y Escritura Mendoza*), we have focused on reading comprehension as a key literacy challenge that students struggle with at all levels in public, state-funded education. We have strategically taken the instructional model (IM) that is central to the program as our starting point with a view to highlighting the common ground that can be established with R2L and then we move on to suggest how R2L can further specify and enhance IM/PLEM[1].

We studied national and provincial official curriculum guidelines for primary and secondary schooling for Language (L1) and EFL, had interviews with key educational instructors and attended training on PLEM. We studied the few documents uploaded to the regional School Board website (Dirección General de Escuelas – Mendoza https://www.mendoza.edu.ar/) and the instructional model as described in *In a reading state of mind: Brain research, teacher modeling, and comprehension instruction* by Fisher et al. (2009) and its accompanying audio-visuals. The specialists in charge indicated to us that this was the main source of the local program. A wider perspective on the model has been attained from Pearson and Gallagher (1983), Fisher and Frey (2013, 2014), McVee et al. (2019), and Webb et al. (2019).

We studied the reading program and its theoretical underpinnings focusing on the role they assign to reading instruction in the curriculum, their main target population, the key pedagogical assumptions, the role of the teacher, and the role of metalanguage. Within these areas we established the common ground with R2L and identified the differences between both programs. Finally, we defined the space for elaboration and specification of the IM/PLEM.

We positioned ourselves as knowers of the R2L pedagogy,[2] with extensive experience with contextual, functional frameworks, particularly with the Sydney School genre teaching and learning cycle (Martin & Rothery, 1991; Rose & Martin, 2012). We have studied the numerous, sound results obtained from the application of R2L in different contexts around the world, many of which are included in other chapters in this volume.

The local scope of this study is taken as a starting point to tease out and foreground the ways in which an approach to reading informed by cognitive linguistic studies on reading can enter into productive conversation with the functional and contextual R2L framework. We take up Halliday's invitation to explore the ways in which his functional systemic theory of language and its applications in education, more specifically the R2L framework, can enter into useful dialogue with other theories and applications. This seems to us a mandatory first step to facilitate conversations with specialists in charge of curricular planning and of the design and implementation of pre- and in-service training in our local context.

The chapter reports on results related to the ways in which both models can be combined, ways in which they seem incompatible, and ways in which we could move beyond the differences. We will review

- the local context in which the pedagogy has been implemented up to March 2020;
- the key features of IM/PLEM;
- the similarities and the differences with the R2L framework;
- the ways in which R2L can specify and expand the framework and enhance local pre- and in-service training.

ORIENTATION TO THE LOCAL CONTEXT

We will briefly describe the local context in which the study was conducted. The regional School Board in Mendoza designed a program to foster reading and writing in local schools as an institutional priority to reduce social inequalities related to literacy. This program was, at least partly, a response to two international and regional assessment tests for academic progress (PISA, APRENDER) which revealed insufficient levels in reading competence. In 2018, students in Argentina ranked 63 in a group of 79 countries evaluated in the PISA tests for reading. Even when these results are better than those obtained in 2012, they place the country below the median in Latin America. APRENDER 2018, conducted in year 6 of primary state and private, urban and rural schools, revealed that 54.4% of the students surveyed had a satisfactory and basic level of understanding of what they read. If results are compared based on students' socio-economic level, the results clearly show that the lower the level, the lower the percentage of advanced level readers. As the graph in Figure 15.1 shows, 61.4% of learners from lower socio-economic levels have satisfactory

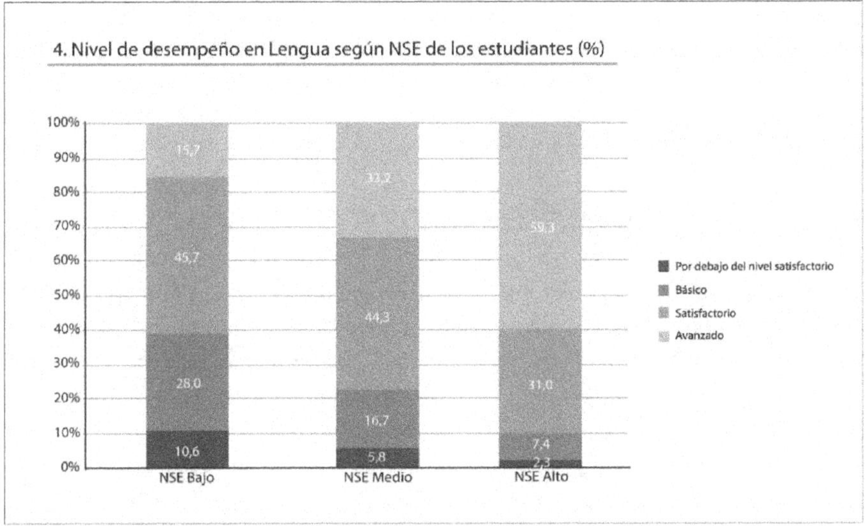

Figure 15.1. APRENDER (2018) – L1 level based on learners' socio-economic level

or advanced reading performance, while nearly 90.3% of learners in the higher socio-economic sector have this same level combined and only 9.7% have basic or below basic performance.

Partly in response to these results, the local School Board designed PLEM. The program included an instructional model, unified guidelines for the selection of texts for all schools, at all levels, and open access to a selection of texts – ranging from international, regional, classical and modern children's tales, legends and myths, poems and songs to longer narratives, plays and non-fiction texts.

The reading expectations proposed for primary, secondary and higher education are: decoding (K, years 1 to 3); comprehension (years 4 to 7); interpretation (years 8 to 10); constructive reading (as they complete secondary schooling with disciplinary orientations); intertextual reading (higher education).

In 2019, a new phase was implemented for primary and some secondary schools in an effort to develop fluency in reading, understood as the basic decoding of letters and words. The program – *Puentes de Lectura* (Reading Bridges) – featured daily 20-minute reading aloud periods to improve basic decoding, renewed efforts to develop comprehension strategies and reading clubs for teachers and learners. The return to the very basic practices of decoding for fluency is a clear indication of how challenging reading literacy is in primary schooling.

The success of PLEM depends on key participants in the program: education and school authorities, in charge of designing the implementation of the program (including the availability of libraries, teacher professional training, and family participation); teachers, who are expected to seek and participate in professional development, foster students' interest and self-confidence and lead them through reading to access cultural wealth; students, who are expected to become "experienced" readers; and families, who are invited to accompany, encourage, comment on, and value the reading experience.

THE IM/PLEM READING PROGRAM

IM/PLEM proposes a cycle of instructional modelling aimed at developing learners' reading comprehension skills through intensive training in the cognitive and discourse strategies that teachers model to them. These strategies relate to solving the meaning of words, understanding text structures and becoming aware of language features as applied in the course of shared reading with students.

The cycle, as described in Fisher et al. (2009); and Fisher and Frey (2013), unfolds along four components as shown in Table 15.1.

A crucial feature of the model is that, as the cycle unfolds, the teacher gradually shifts the responsibility of the cognitive load to the learner through increasingly self-regulated activities (especially from ii to iii). The comprehension strategies explicitly

Table 15.1. Components of the IM (Fisher et al., 2009; Fisher & Frey, 2013)

i) focus lesson	The teacher prepares for reading by "establishing purpose, modeling or demonstrating skills and concepts, and conducting teacher think-alouds" (Fisher & Frey, 2013, p.2). Teachers prime their students for the reading and language learning purpose of the lesson.
ii) guided instruction	Teacher and students read together; the teacher shares his/her impressions of the text and the strategies s/he applies as s/he reads and sorts out difficulties. Main strategies include: predicting, clarifying, summarizing, visualizing, comparing, monitoring, determining importance, connecting (text to self; text to text; text to world), making inferences via activating background and prior knowledge, inductive and deductive reasoning (e.g., establishing hierarchies of subject matter), using "robust questions, prompts and cues to scaffold when necessary as students put new knowledge into play" (Fisher & Frey, 2013, p. 2). Learning is expected to occur as students "get an opportunity to try it for themselves" and see if they understand (Fisher & Frey, 2013, p. 4). Graphic organizers (to represent macro and superstructure) are used and note taking is conducted.
iii) productive group work	Students work together applying strategies practiced with the teacher in ii); teachers "take a step back", transferring part of the cognitive load to students. Collaborative, "interdependent" work is conducted: looking for information, problem solving, reasoning on the text.
iv) independent work	Students build fluency as they read, review concepts, consolidate and apply skills, extend or deepen knowledge and think metacognitively about the different behaviors they have engaged in.

modelled for students to imitate and internalize are those that are demanded by the text, according to the teacher's judgment.

The critical purpose of the cycle is to repeatedly apply strategies (i.e., predicting, clarifying, summarizing, visualizing, comparing, monitoring, determining importance, connecting) that the teacher models once and again for students to mimic, use and internalize so that they become reading comprehension skills that can be applied independently to other texts. These skills become "imposed on biological structures" (Fisher et al., 2009, p. 15) that are then called upon for the complex reading process.[3]

Local IM/PLEM instructors explained that the strong cognitive orientation of the cycle is accompanied by teaching and learning discourse strategies that draw upon Van Dijk's (1980) model of critical discourse analysis.[4]

COMPLICATION I – R2L AND IM/PLEM COMPARED

In an attempt to establish a common ground between both models and tease out the differences between them, we will briefly review aspects of both programs in terms of their main target population, the role of reading instruction in the curriculum, their key pedagogical underpinnings, the role of the teacher, and the role of meta-language. As we do this in Table 15.2, we will presume familiarity with R2L, (Rose & Martin, 2012) mentioning its key features without necessarily explaining them. In the table, similarities are written across both columns and differences are shown in individual columns.

Based on the features of both methodologies, IM/PLEM and R2L can be placed in the topological representation of pedagogies proposed by Martin and Rose (2005) and Rose and Martin (2012), after Bernstein (1990). In so doing, a wider, more panoramic perspective on the model can be gained in terms of R2L itself and other models (Figure 15.2).

IM/PLEM shares features with progressive pedagogies that prioritize internal cognitive activity and the internalization of strategies via repeated action, as is the case with the pedagogies in the upper left quadrant. Yet, interestingly, IM/PLEM stresses features such as the social dimension of learning in interaction, the explicit naming and repetition of cognitive strategies, the importance of scaffolding towards autonomy; and it assigns an active role to the teacher as instructor. These features can be said to pull the model closer to the bottom right quadrant, where R2L is situated.

The common ground that seems to surface between both pedagogies is a first, encouraging step with a view to working out areas of cooperation between IM/PLEM and R2L in a context in which cognitive models are increasingly drawn upon in pre- and in-service training, particularly in L1 and increasingly in L2. A partial resolution of our challenge so far.

Table 15.2. R2L and IM/PLEM compared

Aspect	R2L	IM/PLEM
Main target population	Target learners mostly come from oral language traditions at home with little or insufficient reading practice with their parents.	
Role of reading instruction in the curriculum	Reading and writing are integrated across the curriculum and embedded in subject areas in primary and secondary schooling. A central, initial role is assigned to reading for literacy development, starting with orality and progressing towards written texts. Writing is conceived as a mode to apply, consolidate and assess knowledge – of content, genre, language – initially acquired via reading.	
Their pedagogies	R2L is a literacy program designed to teach students at all levels of instruction to read and write curriculum texts. It lays out delicately specified and principled phases of teacher–learner interactions that first provide maximum support in terms of semiotic load then gradually move towards increasing student autonomy.	IM/PLEM is a reading comprehension model that scaffolds students' interaction with a text in terms of the cognitive skills involved in reading. Guided, explicit instruction on the strategies used by good readers is sequenced so strategies are internalized as skills learners will subsequently deploy themselves.
	R2L's key theoretical underpinning is SFL; Bernstein's sociology of learning and Vygostky's socio-interactive view on learning.	IM/PLEM draws heavily on cognitive psychology and findings from neurology; it introduces the social dimension of learning following Vygotsky and Piaget's internal organization of knowledge as schema building.
	Both pedagogies aim at gradually developing students' reading comprehension by guiding them through a carefully scaffolded process of socially developed learning. This resonates with Joan Rothery's notion of "guidance through interaction in the context of shared experience" (as explained in Rose and Martin, 2012 p. 58), a principle which, in turn, is associated with new-Vygotskyan notions of scaffolding. Both approaches propose strong pedagogical support towards increasing autonomy. IM/PLEM proposes strong scaffolding with the teacher holding all the cognitive responsibility as initial decoding and comprehension strategies are applied; cognitive responsibility is gradually transferred to students.	

(*continued*)

Table 15.2. (*continued*)

Aspect	R2L	IM/PLEM
Their pedagogies (*continued*)	R2L, in turn, describes this transfer as a *semiotic* one: the teacher is initially responsible for managing the semiotic load (+ ID [instructional discourse]; + RD [regulatory discourse]); load is gradually transmitted to learners with varying degrees of strength with respect to ID or RD.	
	As the IM/PLEM unfolds in stages, mimicry and repetition become key pedagogical practices that foster the consolidation of learning at all levels, context, discourse-semantics, lexico-grammar and expression. "Watch me as I do it" is a key practice.	
	We assume familiarity with the carefully principled learning activities in R2L at the scale of text, paragraph, sentence, word groups and words arranged to provide strong initial semiotic support towards students' increasing autonomy.	
Role of teacher	As both models propose a visible and interventionist pedagogy, a strong role is assigned to the teacher who explicitly intervenes in the teaching and learning process. IM/PLEM describes teachers as actively transmitting the mental reading strategies applied as reading is prepared for or conducted.	
Role of meta-language	Both models promote learning *about* aspects associated with reading: the cognitive processes implicated (IM/PLEM) and the key features of language and of the texts being read (R2L). The primary object of teaching and learning dictates the relevant meta-language. Even when these objects can differ, importance is assigned to explicit discussion.	

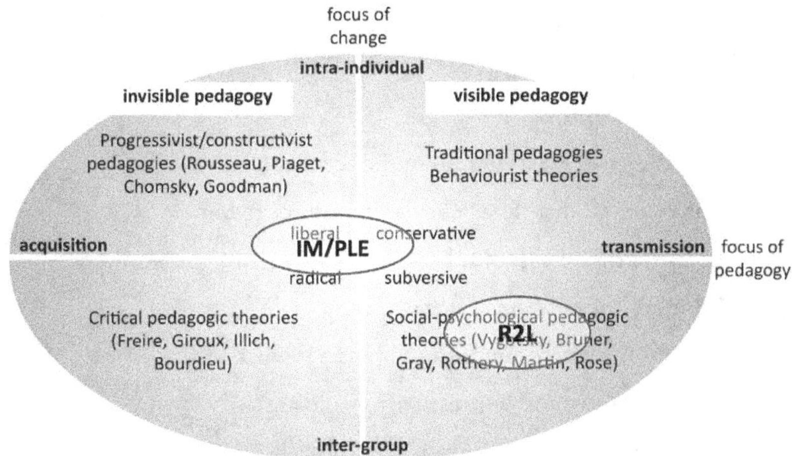

Figure 15.2. Types of pedagogy (Rose & Martin, 2012, p. 318)

COMPLICATION II – THE DIFFERENCES

We will now revisit some of the aspects of the encouraging panorama summarized above. As we fine-tuned our analysis, a few difficulties emerged regarding the key object of the teaching and learning practice, the nature of the scaffolding the models design, and the level of difficulty of the texts used. As we briefly discuss these differences, we suggest preliminary ways to resolve them.

The object of the teaching and learning practice

The key focus of IM/PLEM is the teaching and learning of reading comprehension, a goal that is pursued most clearly through the teachers' repeated description of their thinking through direct modelling or think-alouds as they deal with the text. So, the key object of the instruction is the behaviors that, when imitated and repeated, should become internalized as reading skills that students will develop. As we know, R2L also engages students in active work with the text. The critical focus is the KAL (knowledge about language), and about texts that students will acquire and apply to their future efforts to read. This is done mainly through a top-to-bottom perspective: the generic and situational features of the text are described, and the discourse-semantic and lexico-grammatical resources implicated are taken up throughout the phases of the model. Teachers can interactively guide students as the reading occurs and the areas of discussion are, in fact, the features of the text and of the language used. It is the text, the author or narrator that says, expresses, repeats, includes, compares, etc.

Based on the sample work by instructors and all the material on IM/PLEM we have been able to access, we observed that teachers model their thinking using utterances such as:

> The title **gives me a clue** about the content ...
>
> **But I can tell** that the poem was important to him
>
> **I predict** that she'll come back ...
>
> **I think I know** what this means ...
>
> **I'm chunking** some important phrases in my mind ...
>
> **I don't understand because** why would anybody ...
>
> **I'm inferring** the meaning of ...
>
> **I'm beginning to understand** ...

The following is an excerpt of a teacher's comments after reading a passage aloud:

> Now I have even more questions. I wonder how spiders eat if they don't have mouth parts. I can't really visualize that, so I think I'll look for more information to answer my question. I do remember something very interesting. I didn't know that spiders are found all over the world. I think that the most interesting spider is the one that lives underwater in silken domes. Now that is something I need to know more about. (Fisher & Frey, 2014, p. 12)

As modelling takes place and teachers verbalize what their mental processing is, the information that is projected is about the text itself: inferences based on background information, predictions, and vocabulary. The text is, in fact, talked about, as the object of the teachers' mental activity. IM/PLEM stresses the cognitive strategies at stake that, in turn, reveal the features of the text.

Interestingly, this is what teachers "model", yet, as we observed in the sample videos, as the students work interactively with each other, they naturally shift to discussing what happens in the text itself (and not really what "their thinking" is), as in:

> It's really important for him to have the poem there.

Or, imitating the teacher's use of mental processes they'll go as far as saying:

> **I think** ...
>
> **I'm predicting** they will show us the poem ...
>
> **To me,** the poem is ...

Students' efforts to "reveal their inner voice" seem at times forced and rather artificial to them. Modelling the mental processing involved in understanding a text seems to have a two-fold, not always clearly defined purpose: voicing the way the text is approached *and* voicing what is understood about the text.

Interestingly, as well, mental processes are the focus of the anticipation and recapitulation phases during instruction, as in the following example:

> We are going to talk about **thinking aloud**; **ways to think aloud** in order **to understand** what we read. I'm going to model **it** for you, to show you what **it** looks like **to think out loud**, to have your **inner voice**. And then you try **it** out yourselves. (Video 6, Fisher et al., 2009, our emphasis)

In this example, clearly, the purpose of the instruction is the mental processing itself.

Even when we hope the reader can establish the differences between the examples we just reviewed and R2L classroom interactions, we will include and comment on an exchange during the detailed reading of the story of *Fantastic Mr. Fox*, from Rose and Martin (2012, p. 158):

Teacher	Prepare sentence	***The next sentence tells us*** *he's almost right out of his hole. Watch and I'll read it. "He was almost right out in the open now."*
	Prepare	***At the start it says*** *how far out he was.*
	Focus	*[student name] Can you see how far out he was?*
Student	Identify	*Almost right out*
Teacher	Affirm	*Exactly.*
	Direct	***Let's highlight*** *almost right out.*
	Focus	*So if he's almost right out, what part of him might still be in the hole?*
Student	Propose	*His tail*
Teacher	Affirm	*That's exactly right.*
	Elaborate	*All the rest of him is probably outside, and just his long bushy tail is still inside.*
Teacher	Focus	*[student name]* ***Can you see the words that mean*** *outside? Almost right out...?*
Student	Identify	*In the open.*
Teacher	Affirm	*Excellent.*
	Elaborate	***The open means*** *outdoors where there's nowhere to hide.*
Teacher	Focus	***So how would*** *he feel about being out in the open?*
Student	Propose	*Scared. Worried...*
Teacher	Affirm	*Absolutely.*
	Elaborate	***That's why*** *he's creeping out so slowly.*

During the exchange above (bold added) the teacher prepares students to read a sentence and to observe the patterns in which qualities are described, and guides them to locate information in the sentences and to highlight it, to find synonyms and to learn the meaning of words. Only after the concrete, literal sentences and words are identified and explained does the teacher move on, ask for predictions (based on information in the text) and establish logical relations – all aspects of the *text itself*.

In our view, the clarity of the focus of the interaction – the concrete, visible or traceable features of language and the text itself towards inference and interpretation

– is a definite advantage of the logic that scaffolds the interaction (see also Ramírez & Gutiérrez, Chapter 12; Meehan et al., Chapter 14; and Kartika-Ningsih, Chapter 17 in this volume).

The IM/PLEM has a less focused purpose: both learning about the strategies that will lead students to become skilled readers (the *how*) and, in a somewhat subsidiary manner, developing knowledge about a text, how it works and the language that is implicated (the *what*). Exactly where and how this happens as the modelling occurs is not clear from the material we have had access to. Even when teachers do model their thinking about the text (an aspect that seems to be at the core of a cognitive model), students also need to be guided to work with the text itself and its features – identifying, underlining, highlighting and talking about it. This constitutes a first space for an R2L contribution to IM/PLEM. The focus of the methodology can be, in fact, dual – both the KAL and texts and the mental processing strategies – yet this focus needs to be explicitly embedded in a principled manner into the design of the interactions.

Sharpening the focus of the teaching and learning practice would be, in itself, an important step forward. Additionally, firmly grounding the practice in an understanding of the concrete features of the text seems essential before moving on to other strategies as proposed by IM/PLEM, such as predicting, visualizing and comparing. Fine-tuning the teaching and learning practice and consolidating the KAL and texts following R2L's detailed, principled framework which is, in turn, substantiated by a comprehensive theory of language and texts as is SFL, would be most certainly a significant step forward in the effectiveness of the instruction imparted in our schools.

The nature of the scaffolding that is built

The examples we just discussed also show another important difference between both reading programs: how the cycle is designed in terms of detailed scaffolding both for teachers and students. We will now compare the core interactive work between teacher and learner.

The components of the cycle proposed by IM/PLEM were reviewed in Table 15.2. We will now focus on the guided instruction phase in which the teacher establishes the purpose of the lesson and shows the students how to enact the behaviors of competent readers. A variety of possible strategies are used by the teacher as she guides students from initial decoding towards comprehensive understanding. No two texts are dealt with in the same way, the model argues, and teachers are to choose and model strategies according to what the instantiated text demands. With no further guidance or sequencing, too many decisions seem to fall on the teacher. This is, we believe, a potential ground for confusion: teachers are expected to model their thinking as they approach the particular features of each text, without a stable approach that can be replicated with other texts and that can, in turn, become the approach that students gradually take up themselves with increasing autonomy. The teachers' comments on the text on spiders we included above illustrates a typical teacher intervention during guided instruction. The approach has no principled internal structuring, an ad-hoc rendering of mental processes chosen for this particular text.

We will now briefly consider the nuclear structuring of the cycle proposed by R2L that unfolds in phases: prepare, focus, identify, affirm and elaborate (Figure 15.3). It models a very regulated and principled interaction. Each phase is very carefully contextualized in the previous one as work proceeds from text to phase, sentence, phrases, words and parts of words.

These five elements flesh out exactly what occurs as teachers and students interact with a new text; it "formally describes the micro-interactions" that take place (Martin & Rose, 2005, p. 259). As students are prepared to focus on meanings and wordings, they are guided at the micro-level, where most of the initial difficulties are found. Only once the concrete wordings are specifically associated with the meanings expressed, is elaboration conducted. As elaboration proceeds, focusing on contextual, discourse-semantic, lexico-grammatical or expression features of the text, students are encouraged to work beyond their current level of capabilities.

Elaboration is the space that requires teachers to be well trained so that they can explicitly help students understand what is important about a particular, instantiated text. This is, we believe, the space that poses a major challenge for training: teachers need to become familiar with notions of text and language that will inform their approach to texts. This is where the SFL model of language and text that underpins R2L can be called upon. Elaboration can extend students' knowledge of lexis, structures and discourse patterns and encourage them to visualize and infer connections across the text and to interpret the context and its impact on the text.

All this work towards developing students' KAL and about texts is conducted only after the details of the texts have been worked out in the very principled *prepare–focus–identify–affirm* sequence.

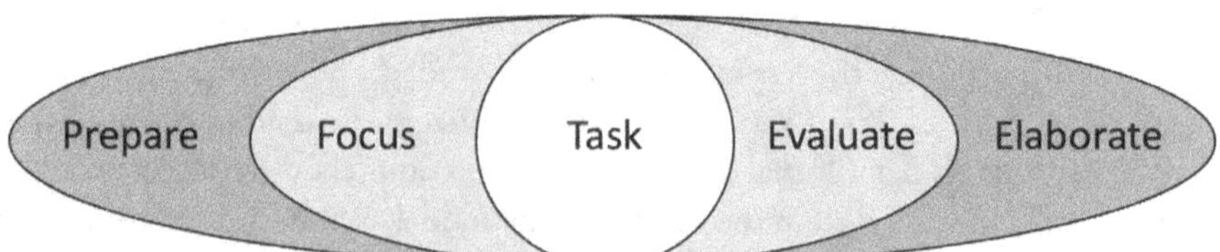

Figure 15.3. Five general elements of a learning activity (Rose & Martin, 2012, p. 11)

We can only very briefly mention some additional features of the design of R2L:

- principled progression from stronger to weaker waves of classification and framing;
- sequencing of phases that neatly build on each other as the interactions unfold;
- a systematic, predictable pattern of preparation, imitation, repetition and application;
- careful cueing from meaning to wording, especially when metaphor is involved;
- alternation between common-sense and more specialized expression depending on who holds the semiotic pressure in the interaction;
- careful shunting between specialized or technical wordings and their unpacked alternatives, back to incongruent equivalents and so on;
- multimodal variations as the work with texts unfolds.[5]

A detailed analysis of the design of the interactions involved in both models brings out the critical difference between *explicit* teaching that both models propose and the idea of *explicit and principled* teaching that is illustrated by the R2L learning activity just reviewed. Only when instruction is explicit and when it follows a principled, predictable logic can it really contribute to meaningful and "visible" reading literacy development.

Level of difficulty of the texts

The recommended level of difficulty of the texts that students are expected to read is another area in which both frameworks differ. IM/PLEM strongly advocates the use of texts that are not challenging for students and cautions that too much work with a single text (due, for example, to the number of new words or complex structures) simply will not work (Fisher et al., 2009, p. 26; p. 67). Reading, it is argued, should be motivating, interesting and comprehensible to students.

R2L, as we know, favors the use of texts that are somewhat beyond students' individual capabilities. Careful scaffolding, involving the notion of "guidance through interaction in the context of shared experience" (Rose & Martin, 2012, p. 58) is designed to enable all students, of varying abilities, to read and understand texts that are beyond their current capacity. This is a way to ensure that students, whatever their socio-economic background, can access texts that further their literacy development.

In our view, the best way to deal with this difference is by showing concrete results that can be achieved when we are given the opportunity to work with teachers, familiarize them with R2L, use texts that are beyond students' individual capabilities and evaluate results. Reconsideration of the texts that can be used with students can follow.

Only a brief, final comment follows on a further difference between both models that cannot be overlooked, yet will not be discussed in detail in this chapter. IM/PLEM draws upon findings from neurolinguistics that insist on a phonic, letter-phoneme correspondence approach for the first steps in the reading process. R2L, proposes a whole-word approach to reading. Rose and Martin (2012) insist that if students "know the words orally, they can easily be guided to recognize them visually" (p. 231). The discussion of these two clearly contrasting positions is beyond the scope of this chapter. Actually, it is an issue that needs to be sorted out only for the early stages of children's learning, when basic decoding takes place. As neuroscience advances and we come to better understand what exactly the case is, more discussion by the experts will surely ensue.

The key points that need to be foregrounded for concrete steps to be taken towards articulating both models are, we believe, those concerning the key objects of the teaching and learning practice and the nature of the scaffolding teachers construct during the reading practice. As we have tried to establish, even when IM/PLEM strongly supports explicit modelling and imitation as the crucial behavior in teaching and learning practice, the exact object of teaching is not in sharp focus and, very importantly as well, the interaction teachers and students need to engage in does not follow a principled cycle in which each step is clearly nested and grounded in the previous one. Failure to set up a practice that is both explicit and principled will stand in the way of designing a visible curriculum, for both teachers and students. This critical difference between the models pushes them apart in terms of their pedagogic conceptions. On these grounds, in contrast to what we proposed in Figure 15.2 (p. 251), we have relocated IM/PLEM towards the upper, left quadrant, as shown in Figure 15.4.

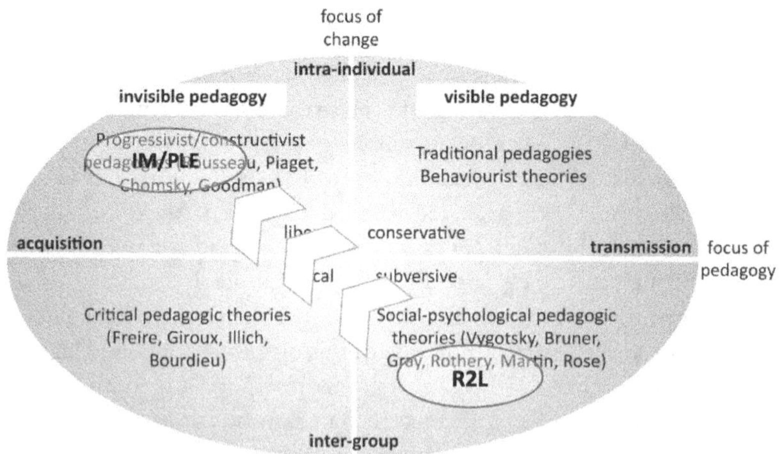

Figure 15.4. Types of pedagogy (Rose & Martin, 2012, p. 318)

As we hope the review of the IM/PLEM has shown, the model actually resonates with pedagogies of both the intra- and inter-group types. It strongly argues for the use of teaching and learning strategies that are explicitly modelled by teachers and imitated by students in the context of socially shared experience, with a view to having an impact on students' cognitive behavior, as acquired skills. What decisively leads us to reconsider the pedagogy as a clear cut social-psychological performative pedagogy is, as we have argued above, the blurred focus of the modelling that is conducted (alternatively the thinking of expert readers and aspects of language and of the text) and the lack of a principled and systematic approach to the text that will provide teachers and students with a strong scaffolding that does not wholly depend on the teachers' ad-hoc, subjective appreciation of the particular instantiated text. Our analysis has foregrounded the critical difference between explicit teaching and explicit teaching that is based on principled, systematic and predictable criteria. The distinction between one and the other is enormous; only the latter will take us firmly towards a visibly shared curriculum.

Identifying these difficulties, far from constituting a barrier for the articulation of both models, allows for a sharp visualization of the exact area we need to work on. In terms of our applied research narrative, we have spotted exactly what the conflict we are faced with is; what our obstacles are.

FINAL COMMENTS – CODA

The analysis and comparison of both instructional models, IM/PLEM and R2L, in terms of the model of language and text that underpins them, the pedagogy and the mental or educational sociology they draw upon have foregrounded not only key similarities and differences but also significant features of each model that have come sharply into focus. We can more clearly spot the potential areas of articulation that will make it possible to take concrete steps for R2L to enhance IM/PLEM by further specifying critical stages, especially the core micro-cycle within detailed reading. This possibility is particularly important in terms of:

- teacher training: teachers themselves, need strong scaffolding to be able to conduct a practice that progressively becomes a fixed, predictable design they can hold on to.

Additionally, once the basic decoding of the text has been conducted, R2L allows for space for teachers to elaborate on the features of the instantiated text. The SFL model of language and text that underpins the R2L framework can be used to train teachers – whose KAL and text is often weak or incomplete – and to strengthen their understanding of how language does what it does in a text. KAL and text is more likely to become a visible aspect of the curriculum.

- the scaffolding of students' path towards autonomy: students are repeatedly exposed to ways of systematically approaching a text and language from initial decoding to interpretation as part of a visible curriculum of literacy practices.

Interestingly, the invitations made at the end of the books in which the models are described (Fisher et al., 2009; Rose & Martin, 2012) sharply foreground the differences between both approaches.

Fisher et al. (2009, p. 122) quote Vygotsky (1997) as he observed: "Through others, we become ourselves." Modelling is argued to be at the root of "how we continue to grow as learners".

Rose and Martin (2012, p. 332) quote Bernstein as he proposes the "three interrelated rights" we have as human beings to individual enhancement, inclusion and participation.

The latter is a goal that will take our learners much farther as they become public, integrated and participatory individuals. This goal takes more than talking about strategies and mental processes. Critically, it takes talking about the empowering semiotic phenomena we want our students to learn to decipher and comprehend and make their own.

NOTES

1 We will refer to the instructional model and the general program as IM/PLEM, for short.
2 We have carefully studied the R2L model and have ample experience with the teaching and learning pedagogical cycle. We have not actually used the R2L cycle itself in teacher training as yet.
3 We do not have space to include the historical, psychological and neural perspectives supporting the IM and we are interested in moving on to the comparative analysis of both models.
4 For an accessible presentation of Van Dijk's framework, see *The Routledge Handbook of Critical Discourse Studies,* Flowerdew & Richardson (Eds.) 2018.
5 We do not have space to review these features, which are all taken up in Rose and Martin (2012), and in Rose, Chapter 1 in this volume.

REFERENCES

APRENDER. (2018). Test Results. http://www.argentina.gob.ar/sites/default/files/informe_mendoza_primaria_2018_0.pdf

Bernstein, B. (1990). *Class, Codes and Control. IV. The Structuring of Pedagogic Discourse.* London: Routledge.

Bernstein, B. (1996). *Pedagogy, symbolic control and identity: Theory, research, critique*. Taylor & Francis.

Fisher, D., & Frey, N. (2013). *Engaging the adolescent learner: Gradual release of responsibility instructional framework*. International Reading Association.

Fisher, D., & Frey, N. (2014). *Better learning through structured teaching. A framework for the gradual release of responsibility*. ASCD.

Fisher, D., Frey, N., & Lapp, D. (2009). *In a reading state of mind. Brain research, teacher modeling, and comprehension instruction*. International Reading Association.

Flowerdew, J., & Richardson, J. (2018). *The Routledge handbook of critical discourse studies*. Routledge.

Martin, J. R., & Rose, D. (2005). Designing literacy pedagogy: Scaffolding asymmetries. In R. Hasan, C.M.I.M. Matthiessen & J. Webster (Eds.), *Continuing discourse on language* (pp. 251–280). Equinox.

Martin, J. R., & Rothery, J. (1991). *Literacy for a lifetime: Teachers' notes*. Film Australia.

Mendoza Reading Programme. http://bases.mendoza.edu.ar/aplicaciones/legales/gestion/documentos/5dcb8f_1822--.pdf

McVee, M., Ortlieb, E., Sharples, J., & Pearson, D. (2019). *The gradual release of responsibility in literacy research and practice*. Emerald Publishing.

Pearson, P. D. & Gallagher, M. C. (1983). The instruction of reading comprehension. *Contemporary Educational Psychology*, *8*(3), 317–344.

PISA Programme for International Student Assessment. (2020). http://www.oecd.org/pisa/pisaenespaol.htm

Rose, D. (2006). Reading Genre: A new wave of analysis. *Linguistics and the human sciences*, *2*(3), 185–204.

Rose, D., & Martin, J. R. (2012). *Learning to write, Reading to learn: Genre, knowledge and pedagogy in the Sydney School*. Equinox.

Rose, D., & Martin, J. R. (2014). Intervening in contexts of schooling. In John Flowerdew (Ed.), *Discourse in context: Contemporary applied linguistics*, *3*, (pp. 273–300). Bloomsbury Academic.

Van Dijk, T. (1980). *Estructuras y funciones del discurso. Una introducción interdisciplinaria a la lingüística del texto y a los estudios del discurso*. México: Siglo XXI Editores

Vygotsky, L. S. (1997). *The history of the development of higher mental functions*. (M.J. Hall, Trans.). New York: Plenum.

Webb, S., Massey, D., Goggans, M. & Flajole, K. (2019). Thirty-five years of the gradual release of responsibility: Scaffolding towards complex and responsive teaching. *The Reading Teacher*, *75*(1), (75–83). https://doi.org/10.1002/trtr.1799

ABOUT THE AUTHORS

Samiah Hassan is full-time professor in the undergraduate EFL teacher training and translation course of studies at Facultad de Filosofía y Letras, Universidad Nacional de Cuyo, Mendoza, Argentina where she teaches General English. She holds an M.A. in Applied Linguistics. She is also academic coordinator of immersion programs of Spanish as a foreign language. Her teaching and research interests are mainly in the area of teaching and learning genres in EFL contexts. She is co-director of a research project that analyses how genres are taught in various educational contexts.

Cristina Boccia is full professor at the EFL teacher training and translations studies at the Facultad de Filosofía y Letras, Universidad Nacional de Cuyo. She teaches General English, Linguistics and Genre studies. She holds an M.A. in Applied Linguistics and is working towards her PhD. Her teaching and research interests are Appraisal especially in academic and scientific discourses; teaching and learning of genres; materials and professional development, all in the EFL context.

16

Maths process modelling: A Reading to Learn curriculum genre

Ingrid Westhoff & Raimundo Olfos

ABSTRACT

This chapter reports on how Reading to Learn (R2L) can be used to respond to the need for more effective pedagogical approaches to address the challenge of underachievement in mathematics in Chile. It describes the positive results achieved by the specifically designed R2L approach for maths teaching in a pilot study in Sweden (Lövstedt & Rose, 2015). It then discusses how this provides a model for improved maths instruction in the Chilean context. The underlying principles and the steps in each stage of the R2L approach (Rose, 2019) are explained. The chapter then shows how the maths strategies can be enacted, with examples of lesson plans and classroom interactions in problem solving in primary school mathematics education.

INTRODUCTION

Latin America's education systems were facing many challenges well before the onset of the COVID-19 pandemic. Unfortunately, the damaging effects of this global health crisis have deepened and further amplified educational challenges, especially for the most vulnerable students (Berlanga et al., 2020). Reports of underachievement in literacy and mathematics from national and international assessments for the school population in Chile exemplify the challenges facing Latin America as a whole. PISA 2018 Maths results show that approximately 51.9% of Chilean students have not achieved the basic competencies as they scored below level two on a six-level scale of development (Agencia de Calidad de la Educación, 2019b; OECD, 2019). TIMMS shows that Chile's student performance is below average for Mathematics and Science in grades 4 and 8 (Agencia de Calidad de la Educación, 2019a). Results from the Chilean Education Quality Measurement System (SIMCE) reveal that 76% of the school population in fourth grade have an insufficient or emerging level and the Education Quality Agency (2018a, b) reports stagnation in recent years in the areas of mathematics and reading. Confidence in Mathematics is also an issue: a study performed by Pisa 2012 shows that 59% of OECD students worry that maths lessons will be difficult for them, thus undermining academic achievement (OECD, 2015). This problem of apprehension was confirmed by findings that 52% of children in the 4th year of primary school in Chile report fear Maths evaluations (Agencia de Calidad de la Educación, 2018b). This is worrying evidence that needs to be urgently addressed, considering the fundamental role maths plays in the understanding of subject content such as Physics (Doran, 2018), History, Music and even Art (MINEDUC, 2012). Furthermore, it is evident that these issues may have a lifelong impact, as the Program for International Assessment of Adult Competencies (PIAAC) revealed that 62% of Chilean adults are unable to solve basic mathematical operations (OECD, 2016).

Results from a project conducted by Felmer et al. (2015) show that teachers present limitations in the use of heuristics and offer few opportunities for their students to develop as problem solvers. This may be associated to reduced opportunities to practice problem solving during their teacher training course. A range of factors related to the classroom teaching and learning of mathematics contribute to the lack of achievement reported. Aravena and Caamaño (2007) state that poor development of mathematical competence is a result of students not recognizing what they are learning, or understanding the purpose of the learning and its relevance to other disciplines. On the other hand, Abello-Cruz and Montaño-Calcines (2013) argue that the problem is caused by students' lack of ability to interpret what they read, and the basic barriers it creates. From a pedagogic perspective, the national curriculum promotes a constructivist model, but as practicing teachers are not trained in its implementation, they revert to using the same traditional teaching methods that were used when they were at school. Teacher workload is a factor that is likely to limit teacher development. For example, a teacher with 44 hours a week can work at three year levels, distributed in 38 teaching hours, 4 planning hours and 2 administrative hours. A further factor highlighted in studies reported in Pino-Fan et al., (2018) is that there is an imbalance between disciplinary and pedagogical knowledge in teacher education. Primary school teachers acknowledge having a lot of pedagogic knowledge, but little disciplinary knowledge. On the other hand, secondary school teachers report having disciplinary knowledge, but little knowledge of pedagogy. Furthermore, the Sociedad de Matemática de Chile (2010) states that teacher training is currently one of the key causes of the "poor" performance of students and that the problem is carried over to higher education, thus producing an "illiteracy of reasoning" in the Chilean population.

Faced with these monumental concerns and persistent underperformance, there is a need to find effective pedagogic approaches to teach maths, especially to disadvantaged students. Fortunately, teachers have freedom to make pedagogical decisions regarding theories, methods and models to use in their teaching. By the same token, such freedom requires teachers to have a broad disciplinary and pedagogical knowledge that allows them to choose the most effective methodology for all their students including the most vulnerable ones.

Given this context, this article presents a didactic sequence to teach addition of fractions with the same and different denominators in 5th grade. It is based on the Australian Reading to Learn program (Rose & Martin, 2012, 2018), inspired by an experience in primary schools in Stockholm (Lövstedt and Rose, 2015) and in the teacher discourse described in Rose (2014, 2018, 2021).

READING TO LEARN FOR TEACHER DEVELOPMENT IN STOCKHOLM

In 2010, the Multilingual Research Institute in Stockholm carried out a three-month study on the application of Reading to Learn (R2L) strategies in the teaching of maths with teachers in 11 elementary schools, some with 90% of students whose mother tongue was not Swedish. Twenty teachers and 500 students from 1st to 6th grade of various socioeconomic levels took part in the program (Lövstedt & Rose, 2015). Teachers attended workshops that included genre-based pedagogy (Martin & Rose, 2007, 2008), Reading to Learn strategies, reflection on teachers' pedagogic theories and lesson plan construction. Data-collection consisted of pre- and post-test results, class videos, photographic and written evidence. Overall performance improved significantly. The lowest performing students made the most outstanding progress, with an increase of almost 23% in achievement (Figure 16.1). The other groups also showed improvement, although not as marked. This suggests that the strategies had an overall positive effect, but they mainly demonstrated their potential with low-achieving students.

Teachers reported being pleasantly surprised by the results and by the positive dynamics generated in the classroom. The strategies made them reflect on the importance of language in the teaching of mathematics. They improved their teaching skills by gaining new teaching tools and they developed a greater understanding of their mathematical objects[1]. The students became more involved in the learning process, achieved greater concentration and showed more interest in the subject. Conceptual understanding improved, especially for those whose mother tongue was not Swedish (Acevedo, 2010). The experience also increased their self-esteem and self-confidence (Lövstedt & Rose, 2015).

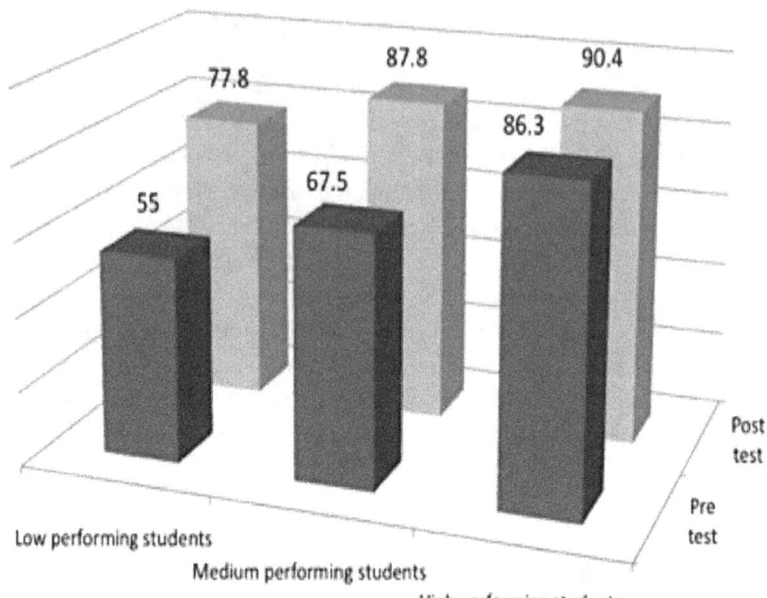

Figure 16.1. Comparison of pre and post test results (%) (Lövstedt & Rose, 2015, p. 11)

Figure 16.2 shows a representation of the procedure used by a 2nd grade student to add two-digit numbers using a number line with the written procedure below. The multimodal nature of maths is manifested in its semiotic resources linked and highlighted to contribute to learning (O'Halloran, 2005, 2010).

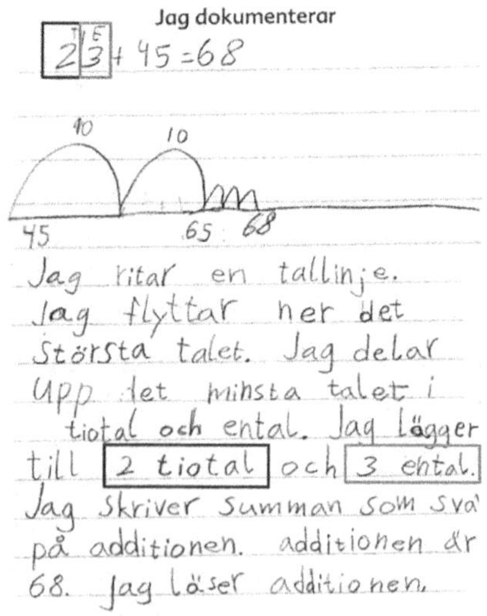

Figure 16.2. Representation and procedure for addition. (Lövstedt & Rose, 2015, p.14).

English translation:

> I draw a number line. I write down the largest number. I divide the smallest number into tens and ones. I add [2 tens] and [3 ones]. I write the sum as the solution to the addition. The addition is 68. I read the addition. (Lövstedt & Rose, 2015, p.14)

SYSTEMIC FUNCTIONAL LINGUISTICS, READING TO LEARN AND MATHEMATICS

Systemic Functional Linguistics (SFL) developed by Halliday (1978) and Halliday & Matthiessen (2014) has provided the theoretical basis for studies of discursive genres and the teaching of different disciplines among many other applications. Unlike other linguistic theories, SFL has, since its inception, sought to be an applied theory "designed to have the potential to be applied to solve problems that arise in communities around the world, involving both reflection and action" (Matthiessen, 2012, p. 436).

R2L is underpinned by "Sydney School" genre pedagogy, which has the aim of making the discourses of schooling available to all learners in order to reduce the gap between high and low achieving students. It is a visible pedagogy, designed to enable students to successfully meet the school's academic requirements. Genre theory, derived from SFL, is a language-based theory of learning (Halliday, 1993). It is based on the premise that effective teaching involves providing the learner with explicit knowledge about the language of the school subject genres. Sydney School researchers defined genre as a "staged goal-orientated social process" (Rose & Martin, 2012, p.1). Christie (2002) described two types of key genres involved in education: knowledge genres, the knowledge to be learned, and curriculum genres, as classroom practice. Knowledge genres are those through which disciplinary knowledge is transmitted and learning is shown. In the case of mathematics, the most common knowledge genres and their functions are: Definitions: defining technical concepts; Explanations: explaining mathematical principles; and Problem solving: solving problems using various procedures. In this chapter, the curricular genre in focus is the *Maths process modelling* (MPM) genre, which has the purpose of recording the steps of a maths process in written form (Rose, 2021). The pedagogical activity of the MPM comprises 1) lesson stages and lesson phases/steps; 2) the learning cycle; and 3) illustrations of specific classroom discourse.

CURRICULUM GENRE: MATHS PROCESS MODELLING

Teacher Demonstration, *Guided Practice*, and *Joint Construction* are the three contextual stages of the maths process modelling (MPM). What the teacher does at each stage is illustrated in Table 16.1 (NESA & Rose, 2018; Rose, 2019). It should

Table 16.1. Stages of Mathematical Process Modelling

Stage 1	**Teacher demonstration** In the first stage, the teacher demonstrates the mathematical process with a worked example that has been carefully planned beforehand. The teacher explicitly describes each step of the process as it is modelled. The first step is to read the problem, which may be written on the board or appear in a text. After reading, the students are asked to identify key information in the problem/question. The teacher writes this information sequentially on the board. The teacher then demonstrates how to use the information to solve the problem.
Stage 2	**Guided practice 1** In this stage, a second problem is selected and written on the board. The teacher asks students to say each step of the process to solve the problem. Because the teacher has explicitly modelled each step previously, students' responses approximate what has already been modelled. Although responses may not be exact, it is important to acknowledge the response and adjust it as necessary. In this way, students' understanding is affirmed. **Guided practice 2** Another worked example is practised with another problem and more students are asked to say each step of the process and write it on the board. It is important to try to include as many students as possible in this stage, including those who may be reluctant to respond. After modelling the steps twice[2], most students will be able to provide an appropriate answer and the teacher can continue to affirm students' understanding. It is this experience of success that engages students in their learning and can be used to engage all students in learning mathematics.
Stage 3	**Joint construction** Finally, the whole procedure is scribed as a sequence of steps. Students take turns to write each step on the board. The class tells the scribe what to write with the teacher's guidance. This activity is known as *Joint Construction* because the class is jointly constructing a text with the guidance of the teacher. The text in this case is a procedure for completing a mathematical process. Students should keep a copy of the procedure so that they can refer to it if they wish when they are solving problems. This process helps all students to achieve; less able students are provided with an opportunity to understand and remember the steps needed to undertake a mathematical process, while more able students have the opportunity to better explain how they solve problems.

(Rose, *Reading to Learn, Book 9, Planning for success in Maths*, 2019; NESA & Rose, 2018)

be noted that the teacher carefully plans the teaching activity before the lesson. She chooses the words she will use in each step and the type of questions she will ask. She starts the lesson by introducing and preparing the topic, frontloading the content and providing strong context to the learning. In the primary grades, such an introduction may involve a real-life situation, role play or narrative. In secondary maths, it may involve activating prior knowledge, and/or establishing "how the topic fits in" (Rose, 2019). After this introduction, the teacher applies the 3 stages before students can move on to individual problem solving, homework or formative or summative assessments.

SOCIAL CONTEXT OF LANGUAGE

The actual modelling of maths process occurs in a social context called register, i.e., field, tenor and mode (see Rose, Chapter 1 this volume). These three dimensions are: the pedagogical activities that happen in the classroom; the pedagogical relationships that are built between teacher and learner; and the modalities through which meanings are presented.

Pedagogical activities are structured in three hierarchical segments: lesson stages, activities and micro-activities. The lesson is structured according to the stages of the MPM already described: *Teacher Demonstration (TD), Guided Practice*[n] *(GP)* and *Joint Construction (JC).* The activities are made explicit in the lesson plan which consists of different steps/phases according to content or skill. Finally, micro activities consist of learning cycles of a specific micro activity. Table 16.2 illustrates the organization of the pedagogical activity for the topic of addition of fractions with same and different denominators.

Table 16.2. Organization of the pedagogical activity (adapted from Rose, 2021, p. 264)

Steps	What the teacher says
1	Read the task
2	Write important information
3	Model the expression for leftover pizza
4	Determine if the denominators are equivalent
5	If they are not equivalent, amplify or simplify any of the fractions so that they have common denominators
6	Make denominators equivalent
7	Add the numerator and keep the denominator
	In the case of subtraction of fractions of different denominators, the only difference is that the numerators are subtracted instead of added. The procedure does not change
8	Verify if the fraction is irreducible
9	Answer the question

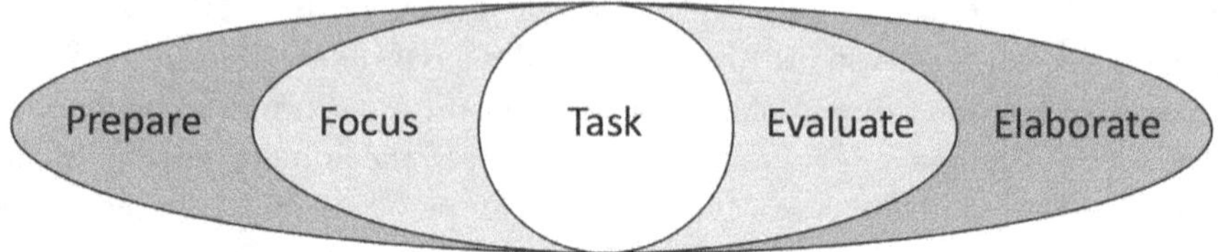

Figure 16.3. Nuclear and marginal phases of the R2L learning cycle (Rose & Martin, 2012, p. 11)

All these segments use the R2L learning cycle (LC) to do the lesson, as in Figure 16.3. This cycle consists of five nuclear and marginal structural phases. Every pedagogical activity always focuses on a learning task, i.e. the teacher explicitly prepares for the task to be achieved, explicitly guides the visual focus of attention to the task, the students perform it and the teacher evaluates it, finally, the teacher alone or with the students elaborates/extends the knowledge.

Pedagogical relationships include the roles that the teacher and the students take independently or jointly in the interaction and the pedagogical acts that are carried out. The roles that the teacher can play are: presenting knowledge, evaluating students, and leading an activity. During the interaction, the teacher can activate students' attention by asking them to remember, inviting reasoning or involving everyone in the task.

Pedagogical modalities are the sources of knowledge or meaning, the modes that teacher and student have to access them and to record meanings. Knowledge can be found in the environment, in written format or orally. The meanings present in the environment can be shown, for example, by pointing with a gesture towards the information written on the blackboard. Students access it by looking at the blackboard. The written mode comprises text, symbols (equation), images, diagrams, or audio visuals. Finally, the oral source comes from the knowledge of the teacher, student, or previous classes. Meanings can be recorded by writing texts, notes, or symbols such as equations or expressions. They can also be drawn on diagrams, in pictures.

The analysis of the pedagogical discourse done by Rose (2014, 2021) and Kartika-Ningsih and Rose (2018) has shed light on how teaching and learning happens, how teachers promote or discourage successful learner identities. This analysis is very useful for the teachers because it allows them to observe and reflect on the way language is used and on their teaching practice, and to become aware of their successes and mistakes in order to modify when necessary. All this was taken into account when planning part of the didactic sequence.

CENTRAL SKILLS FOR THE DEVELOPMENT OF MATHEMATICAL THINKING

The Chilean maths curriculum (MINEDUC, 2012) proposes the Concrete–pictorial–symbolic learning model (COPISI), based on the Singapore maths method, Concrete–Pictorial–Abstract[3]. It seeks to develop mathematical thinking through four interrelated skills: representing, modelling, problem solving, and arguing and communicating. The use of concrete, pictorial and symbolic representations entails being able to move between different semiotic modes along a continuum from concrete and everyday to abstract maths representations. Learners need to be able to model so they can capture the complex patterns of reality, and to express them in a simplified and abstract version using mathematical symbols. Students should be able to solve routine and non-routine problems and to apply what has been learned creatively in complex situations, with more than one solution, with several steps and involving different maths areas. Finally, students are expected to explain and communicate maths reasonings. In summary, these four skills should contribute to the development of logical, abstract and complex thinking.

It is worth highlighting the radical importance of problem solving in maths and other subjects. This requires the mastery of previously acquired maths concepts, operations and relationships and their integration with new knowledge. It also requires students to explain the processes instead of memorizing them. At the same time, the role of memory in the activation of prior knowledge is essential, since the ability to remember what has been learned is the basis for building new knowledge. Memory and comprehension are interconnected requirements for developing mathematical thinking.

FRACTIONS AND THEIR REPRESENTATIONS

Authors such as Behr et al. (1983) have highlighted the importance of the different modes of representation of fractions and the difficulties involved in the transition between them, thus enriching Bruner's works on concrete, pictorial and symbolic representations (Valdemoros, 1997). These authors stress the significance of representing fractions in a figurative, numerical and written way. This is congruent with the Chilean COPISI method when considering how the student transitions from concrete things to pictorial and finally symbolic modes of representation (see Figure 16.4).

Clear and engaging visuals add to a solid understanding of concepts. The curriculum points out the importance of these representations, stating that students construct the meaning of maths objects better when they link their representations

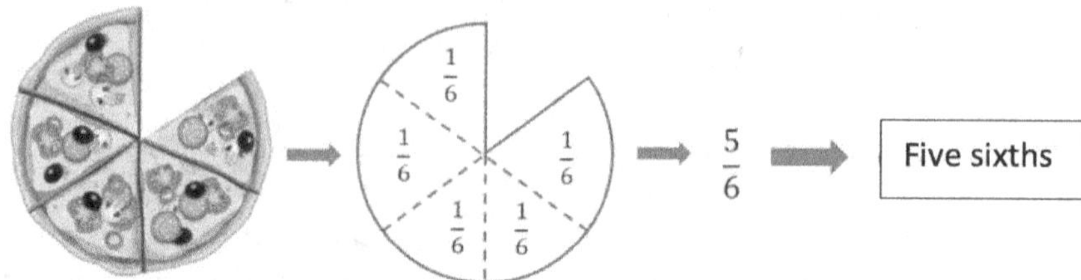

Figure 16.4. Representations of the fraction 5/6

from the concrete to those that require a higher level of abstraction. This constant exchange between different modes of representation promotes a deeper understanding of the mathematical object under study (Macías, 2014). Now, having established the complexity of the discipline, we turn our attention to the didactic sequence.

LESSON PLAN FOR R2L MATHS PROCESS MODELLING

Reading to Learn highlights two important steps to be considered when planning. These are: discussion of prior knowledge, a prerequisite for new learning, since without it, it is impossible to carry out any teaching task successfully, let alone reach all students; and a pre-test and post-test to show students' progress. The following is the suggested sequence:

- Carry out a pre-test
- Review prior knowledge
- Apply the lesson plan for R2L maths process modelling
- Carry out a post-test

Table 16.3 shows a typical plan for teaching maths according to the Chilean curriculum: contents, objectives, skills and attitudes. The contribution of Reading to Learn can be seen in the pedagogic activities embodied in the math process modelling genre and its corresponding stages: *Teacher Demonstration – Guided Practice" – Joint Construction* and the nine Phases/steps of the pedagogical activity.

Generally, planning in Chilean schools is by units, approximately 4 per year, and planning is not done for each topic, as this is in the course book (Vidal, 2010). The lesson is structured in three steps: Beginning: previous content; Development: knowledge, skills and exercise; End: evaluation and metacognition. During the Beginning, the teacher asks questions for students to recall prior knowledge and contextualizes through an activity so they can discover how to perform the task or solve a problem. Due to the great disparity of mathematical knowledge among students in the same grade, this can go on for much longer than the allotted time and end up derailing the whole pedagogical plan by generating a disruptive or distracting

Table 16.3. A typical plan for teaching maths according to the Chilean curriculum

Unit	Fractions, decimal numbers and algebra
Content	Addition and subtraction of proper fractions with different denominator
Learning objectives (LO)	LO9. Solve additions and subtractions with proper fractions with denominators less than or equal to 12, pictorially and symbolically; amplifying or simplifying OA13. Solve routine and non-routine problems, applying additions and subtractions of proper fractions or decimals to the thousandth
Prior knowledge	Addition and subtraction of fractions of equal denominator; amplification and simplification of fractions; equivalent fractions
Key concepts	Proper fraction, amplification, addition, fractions, denominator
Lesson stages	Math process modelling: 1. Teacher demonstration 2. Guided practice^n 3. Joint construction
Phases of the teaching activity	9 steps
Maths skills	Representing, modelling, arguing and communicating, and problem solving
Attitudes	Manifest an orderly and methodical working style, express and listen to ideas in a respectful way, approach the search for solutions to problems in a creative and flexible way
Materials	Prior knowledge guide: definition of key concepts; maths and attitudinal skills poster; pre-test, post-test
Allotted time	9 teaching hours for both Learning Objectives

environment. In fact, according to the experience of Latin American colleagues and the contributors to this article, this step is time-consuming and takes time away from practice, automation of procedures, problem solving and reflection on what has been learned, therefore it has to be carefully prepared so students can focus on the topic.

The R2L lesson plan begins with a detailed planning of the mathematical object and the steps to demonstrate it. It is organized according to stages, phases and functional cycles: *Teacher Demonstration, Guided Practice*^{n} and *Joint Construction.* Depending on the level, the teacher meaningfully contextualizes or relates the topic to previous content; demonstrates the steps to solve the task; practices variations of the task according to students' needs, using the skills demonstrated by the teacher; finally, the teacher and students jointly write about the procedure, while developing communication and argumentation. Introducing the maths content in this way guarantees that all students, and not just the most advanced, will be ready to successfully engage with problem solving. We believe that the teacher who does not have a functional, object-based mathematical plan and a well-defined and structured methodology runs the risk of blurring the lesson goal, and thus only the most advanced students manage to keep up with the pace of the class and learn.

The R2L lesson plan explicitly articulates the content with the core skills of the curriculum while providing a powerful scaffold for evidencing the achievement of the skills, thus linking the different pedagogical modes of numeracy, graphics and natural language. In this way, natural language is revalued as a fundamental tool for doing maths.

Reading to Learn provides explicit directions for teachers at every stage of the maths process modelling. This explicit planning is illustrated in detail in Table 16.4 where students are asked to add fractions with different denominators. In column 1, the teacher uses 9 steps to demonstrate the solution to the task. Column 2 involves some questions with which the teacher will engage the students' participation. Column 3 shows the teacher's elaborations to the answers as notes or diagrams.

Stage 1: Teacher demonstration

The task is to use proper fractions to determine how many slices of pizza are left over. Figure 16.5 shows the number of slices that were left over from two pizzas.

The teacher demonstrates the use of key maths skills specified in the curriculum. For example, representing something pictorially, a pizza into symbolic language, a fraction. Modelling how students have to translate an expression from everyday language 'sum' into mathematical language '+'. The lesson plan explicitly illustrates the use of the important skills of modelling or representing. If students do not develop these skills, they are not able to work mathematically with anything in the real world.

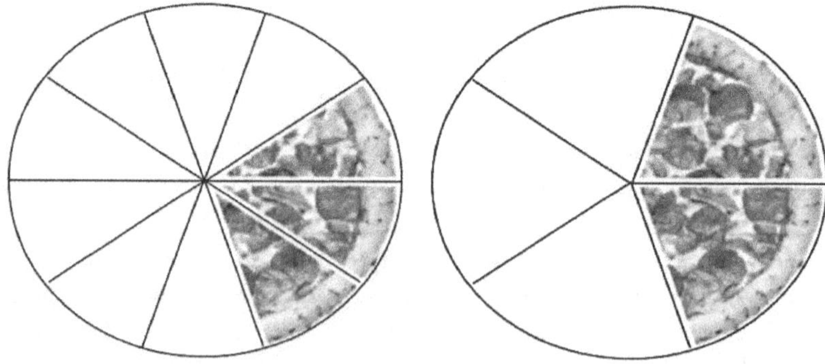

Figure 16.5. Pictorial representation of leftover pizza slices

roblem: How much pizza was left over?

ble 16.4. Lesson plan for R2L maths process modelling

Steps (what the teacher says)	**Questions** (from the teacher to the class)	**Example** (teacher writes or draws on the board)
Read the question	What does it say?	The following slices were left over from two pizzas (image as per Figure 16.5)
		How much pizza was left over in total?
Write down the important information in the question	What is the first important information?	There were slices left over from two pizzas
	How do I represent the leftovers in a fraction?	There were 3/10 of the first pizza and 2/5 of the second pizza
	What is the next important information?	We need to know how much was left over in total
Model the expression for the total leftover pizza	What operation do I use to find out the total number of slices there are?	Addition.
	What mathematical expression models the leftover pie?	$\frac{3}{10}+\frac{2}{5}$
Determine whether the denominators are equal	What are the denominators of the fractions?	Point to the blackboard 10 and 5
	Are they equal?	No
	What do I do then?	Equal the denominators
If they are not equal, amplify (multiply) or simplify (divide) any of the fractions to equal denominators	How can I make the denominators equal?	Amplifying or simplifying any of the fractions
	Can I simplify 3/10 to a fraction whose denominator is 5?	No
	Can I amplify 2/5 to a fraction whose denominator is 10?	Yes $\frac{2.2}{5.2}=\frac{4}{10}$
	What number do I use to amplify 2/5?	
Equal denominators	To which fraction is 2/5 equivalent?	$\frac{3}{10}+\frac{2}{5}=\frac{3}{10}+\frac{4}{10}$
Add the numerators and keep the denominator	Are the denominators the same?	Yes
In the case of subtraction of fractions of different denominators, the only difference is that the numerators are subtracted instead of added. The rest of the procedure does not change	How do you add fractions of equal denominators?	$=\frac{3+4}{10}=\frac{7}{10}$
Check if the fraction is irreducible	Can I simplify this fraction?	No
Answer the problem	What did we want to find out?	Total leftover pizza
	What is the answer?	In total there was 7/10 of pizza left over

Step 2: Guided practice[n]

Following the *Teacher Demonstration (TD)*, the lesson continues with *Guided Practice (GP)*. Here the nuclear and marginal phases of the learning cycle (see Figure 16.3) illustrate how the learning takes place. The exchanges in Table 16.5 (opposite) have been written to illustrate how the pedagogy can be enacted in the classroom.

Figure 16.6 shows the number of slices of cake that were left over from two cakes at a birthday party.

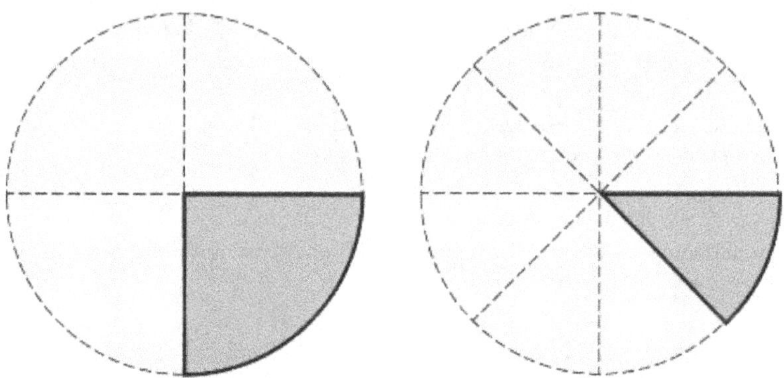

Figure 16.6. Pictorial representation of leftover slices of cake

As can be seen from the example of interaction, *Guided Practice[n]* provides scaffolding through repetition of the process steps, keeping the same words used in the *Teacher Demonstration*. The teacher mainly guides by directing attention with focus questions, the students put into practice the ability to argue and communicate. They also take on the role of the teacher by writing the maths workings on the board, as they know what to do. This is labelled as elaborating here. In this stage, the teacher takes a secondary role and is only concerned with affirming the accomplishment of the task. Practising different situations helps to automate the procedure. In the case of students with difficulties, the *GP[n]* is repeated, giving them more and more autonomy (Table 16.5).

Problem: How much cake was left over?

Table 16.5. Guided practice[n]

		Illustrative classroom exchanges for *Guided Practice*	**phase**
1	T	*What is the next step?*	focus
		[raise your hand]	
		S1	
	S1	*Write down the important information*	propose
	T	*Exactly*	affirm
		Write it down on the board	elaborate
	S1	*[goes to the board and writes]*	
2	T	*Who can tell me what the first important piece of information is?*	focus
		[raises hand]	
	S2	*There were leftover pieces of 2 cakes*	propose
		Very good	affirm
	T	*Who can tell me what is the second important piece of information?*	focus
		[raises hand]	
	S3	*We need to find out the total amount of cake that was left over*	propose
		Perfect	affirm
3	T	*How do we represent the leftover pieces as fractions?*	focus
	S4	*The first one would be 1/4*	propose
	T	*Good*	affirm
	T	*Why is it 1/4?*	focus
	S4	*Because the cake is divided into 4 and only 1 of 4 is left over*	propose
	T	*Excellent*	affirm
		Go ahead and write the fraction	elaborate
	S2	*[goes to the blackboard and writes 1/4]*	
	T	*Good*	affirm
	T	*In the case of the second cake, who can tell me what fraction represents the leftovers?*	focus
	S5	*There was 1/8 left over*	propose
	T	*Why is it 1/8?*	focus
	S5	*Because the second cake is divided into 8 portions and only one of them was left over*	propose
	T	*Excellent*	affirm
		Go ahead and write the fraction	elaborate
	S5	*[goes to the board and writes 1/8]*	
	T	*Ok*	affirm
4	T	*Which operation allows me to determine the total amount of cake left over?*	focus
	S6	*Addition*	propose
	T	*Perfect*	affirm
	T	*Which mathematical expression models the total leftover cake?*	focus
	S7	*1/4 plus 1/8*	propose
	T	*Excellent*	affirm
		Go to the blackboard and write it down	elaborate
	S7	*[Writes: Leftover cake = 1/4+1/8]*	

Stage 3: Joint construction of the steps of the procedure

In this third and final stage, teacher and students collaborate to jointly construct the procedure on the board and argumentation and communication are reinforced. Due to space constraints and to avoid repetition, the joint construction of the procedure is written below.

> *I read the statement and identify the important information. I model the mathematical expression to solve the problem. I determine if the denominators are equal. If they are not, I amplify or simplify some of the fractions. I make denominators the same. I solve the addition or subtraction of fractions of different denominators. I check if the resulting fraction is irreducible. I solve the problem.*

Problem solving

Once students are familiar with the process, they can advance to solve non-routine problems, a process which is structured in five generic steps, as shown in Table 16.6.

In sum, organizing the pedagogical activity as a "staged, goal-oriented social process", i.e. as an MPM provides an order, a clear structure on the organization of the whole class. The detailed planning that the teacher does before the lesson makes her aware of the complexity of the mathematical object, of the procedure necessary for the learner to perform the task and of the scaffolding potential of the learning cycle. The learning cycle is, metaphorically, a versatile toolbox that allows actions to be taken and pedagogical relationships to be built. Depending on the different stages of the pedagogical activity, some tools are chosen rather than others. For example, in *TD* the teacher explicitly prepares by giving or recalling prior knowledge about the task in order to reduce cognitive load and thus anxiety; directs the learner's visual attention to identify the object of study or the step needed to perform the task; provides feedback on the task performed and creates a positive attitude towards learning and a feeling of achievement. Finally, once the environment is prepared, the teacher elaborates, illustrates the use of maths skills, teaches; or it is the

Table 16.6. Problem solving steps (Rose, 2019)

1	Read the problem and the question.
2	Identify the facts that help solve the question by writing them down numerically.
3	Determine the missing piece of information or the solution to the problem.
4	Choose the operation/operations and skills I need to solve the problem.
5	Determine the result. Answer the question.

learner who elaborates when she is sure of her knowledge. In short, pedagogical relationships and the different phases of the learning cycle in which exchanges are negotiated build successful identities, encourage autonomy and collaborative work by involving the whole class in the resolution of the task through joint construction.

CONCLUSION

In this chapter, we have analysed the difficult situation of the learning of maths in Chile and presented an adaptation of the Stockholm R2L maths project, the *Maths Process Modelling* curriculum genre (MPM), as a way to provide teachers with viable and explicit pedagogic alternatives for teaching maths so that key disciplinary knowledge is provided to all students, including those placed at risk by socioeconomic factors, and without watering down rigorous disciplinary content in the process. Teaching maths requires teachers to have access to the multiple pedagogical modalities of maths language, such as symbols, images and diagrams. The new pedagogy described here gives teachers a principled way to approach the complex semiotic processes at stake in the pedagogical activity and to plan successful lessons with greater knowledge and confidence.

It is also important to highlight that traditional education methods overemphasize teaching, while constructivist education overemphasizes learning and discovery. The R2L didactic sequence generates a dialogue between deductive and inductive methodologies complementing both and balancing their use, both to teach and to allow the discovery of new knowledge in contexts of vulnerability. It does not assume an ideal learner, but a real one. This consideration is very necessary for disadvantaged student populations which have not yet achieved basic competencies such as reading and writing. It is suggested that these sequences be made compatible with lesson studies (Isoda & Olfos, 2010), to assess the potential for greater impact on effective and meaningful learning of the math process modelling curriculum genre.

The interdisciplinary work with maths and language allows the participant math teachers to become fully aware of the crucial role language plays in teaching. From the SFL perspective, concepts or skills are realized through language, they do not exist outside the language used to refer to them (Halliday, 1978). Therefore, learning the language of a discipline implies learning the discipline itself; in fact, language and learning cannot be separated (Schleppegrell, 2007). This way of looking at language allows the teacher to see that maths skills are not obscure processes that occur in the mind, but linguistic processes that can take a linguistic, pictorial or mathematical/symbolic form and therefore they can be taught explicitly and more effectively. It is the university's responsibility to make sure that future teachers know the characteristics of disciplinary discourses, like the language of maths, biology, history, philosophy, physics, etc. The discipline responsible for this is educational linguistics. It is essential that it be present in the university curricula of education degrees.

This chapter is an invitation to explore R2L and to apply its strategies in action research projects in other international contexts. As educators and researchers, we need to stop describing the reality we already know, or blaming society for having students who do not know how to read or do maths. We no longer want to hear students saying "I am bad at maths", "I never knew what it was for", or reaching year 12 saying "I never understood maths". We need to act. It is time for politicians, researchers, practitioners and parents to empower themselves and provide students with the tools they need to succeed in their schools and in their lives.

NOTES

1 Mathematical objects are anything you can "do mathematics on". More formally, an object has a definition, obeys certain properties, and can be the target of certain operations e.g., numbers, functions, triangles, matrices, groups and more complicated things such as vector spaces and infinite series are all examples of mathematical objects.

2 *Guided practice* may be repeated as many times as necessary according to needs of the group, this is indicated as *Guided practice*^{n}

3 The Singapore maths method is focused on mastery, which is achieved through intentional sequencing of concepts. Some of the key features of the approach include the CPA (Concrete, Pictorial, Abstract) progression, number bonds, bar modelling, and mental math.

REFERENCES

Abello-Cruz, A. M., & Montaño-Calcines, J. R. (2013). Leer y comprender para aprender Matemática. *VARONA*, *57*.

Acevedo, C. (2010). *Will the implementation of Reading to Learn in Stockholm schools accelerate literacy learning for disadvantaged students and close the achievement gap?* Multilingual Research Institute, Stockholm Education Administration.

Agencia de Calidad de la Educación. (2018a). Informe nacional resultados SIMCE 2017. *Revista de Educación, Mineduc.* http://www.revistadeeducacion.cl/resultados-simce-2017-pocos-avances-y-grandes-desafios-en-educacion-media/

Agencia de Calidad de la Educación. (2018b). *Informe nacional de la calidad de la educación 2018.* Ministerio de Educación, Chile.

Agencia de Calidad de la Educación. (2019a). *TIMSS 2019 Estudio internacional de tendencias en matemática y ciencias.* Ministerio de Educación, Chile.

Agencia de Calidad de la Educación. (2019b). *Informe de resultados PISA 2018 competencia lectora, matemática y científica en estudiantes de quince años en Chile.* Ministerio de Educación, Chile.

Aravena, M., & Caamaño, C. (2007). Modelización matemática con estudiantes de secundaria de la comuna de Talca, Chile. *Estudios pedagógicos, 33*(2), 7–25.

Berlanga, C., Morduchowicz, A., Scasso, M., & Vera, A. (2020). *Reabrir las escuelas en América Latina y el Caribe: Claves, desafíos y dilemas para planificar el retorno seguro a las clases presenciales.* División de Educación, BID.

Behr, M., Lesh, R., Post, T., & Silver, E. (1983). Rational number concepts. In R. Lesh and M. Landau (Eds.), *Acquisition of mathematics concepts and processes* (pp. 91–125). Academic Press.

Christie, F. (2002). *Classroom discourse analysis.* Continuum.

Doran, Y. (2018). *The Discourse of physics: Building knowledge through language, mathematics and image*. Routledge.

Felmer, P., Perdomo-Díaz, J., Cisternas, T., Cea, F., Randolph, V., & Medel, L. (2015). *La resolución de problemas en la matemática escolar y en la formación inicial docente*. Estudios de Política Educativa, 1(1), 64–105.

Halliday, M. A. K. (1978). *Language as social semiotic: The social interpretation of language and meaning.* Edward Arnold.

Halliday, M. A. K. (1993). Towards a language-based theory of learning. *Linguistics and education* 5, 93–116.

Halliday, M. A. K., & Matthiessen, C. M. I. M. (2014). *An Introduction to functional grammar.* Routledge. (4th ed. 1985)

Isoda, M., & Olfos, R. (2010*). El enfoque de resolución de problemas en la enseñanza de la matemática a partir del Estudio de Clases.* Ediciones Universitarias de Valparaíso, P. Universidad Católica de Valparaíso.

Kartika-Ningsih, H., & Rose, D. (2018). Language shift: analysing language use in multilingual classroom interactions. *Functional linguistics,* 5(9) https://doi.org/10.1186/s40554-018-0061-0

Lövstedt, A.-C., & Rose, D. (2015). Reading to Learn Maths: A teacher professional development project in Stockholm. Multilingual Research Institute, Stockholm. https://www.researchgate.net/publication/354521625_Reading_to_Learn_Maths_A_teacher_professional_development_project_in_Stockholm

Macías, J. (2014). Los registros semióticos en matemáticas como elemento personalizado en el aprendizaje. *Revista de investigación educativa conect@2, 4*(9), 27–57.

Martin, J. R., & Rose, D. (2007). *Working with discourse: Meaning beyond the clause.* Continuum (1st edition 2003).

Martin, J. R., & Rose, D. (2008). *Genre relations: Mapping culture*. Equinox.

Matthiessen, C. M. I. M. (2012). Systemic-Functional linguistics as appliable linguistics: social accountability and critical approaches. *D.E.L.T.A., 28*, 435–471.

MINEDUC. (2012). *Bases curriculares primero a sexto básico*. Unidad de Curriculum y Evaluación. Ministerio de Educación de Chile.

NESA & Rose, D. (2018). *Planning for success in secondary maths*. NSW Education & Standards Authority. https://educationstandards.nsw.edu.au/wps/portal/nesa/k-10/learning-areas/mathematics/planning-for-success-in-secondary-mathematics

OECD. (2015). "Does math make you anxious?". *PISA in Focus,* No. 48, OECD Publishing. https://doi.org/10.1787/5js6b2579tnx-en.

OECD. (2016). *Skills Matter: Further results from the survey of adult skills.* OECD Skills Studies, OECD Publishing.

OECD. (2019). *PISA 2018 results (Volume I): What students know and can do.* PISA, OECD Publishing.

O'Halloran, K. L. (2005). *Mathematical discourse: Language, symbolism and visual images.* Continuum.

O'Halloran, K. L. (2010). The semantic hyperspace: Accumulating mathematical knowledge across semiotic resources and modalities. In F. Christie & K. Maton (Eds.), *Disciplinarity: functional linguistic and sociological perspectives,* (pp. 217–236). Continuum.

Pino-Fan, L. R., Guzmán, I., Larraín, M., Vargas, C. (2018). La formación inicial de profesores en Chile: 'voces' de la comunidad chilena de investigación en educación matemática. *UNICIENCIA, 32*(1), pp. 68–88.

Rose, D. (2014). Analysing pedagogic discourse: an approach from genre and register. *Functional linguistics, 1*(11). https://doi.org/10.1186/s40554-014-0011-4

Rose, D. (2018). Pedagogic Register Analysis: mapping choices in teaching and learning. *Functional linguistics, 5*(3). Springer Open Access, http://rdcu.be/HD9G

Rose, D. (2019). Reading to learn: Accelerating learning and closing the gap. Teacher training books 1–9 and DVDs. Sydney: Reading to Learn http://www.readingtolearn.com.au

Rose, D. (2021). Doing maths: (de)constructing procedures for maths proceses. In K. Maton, J. R. Martin and Y. Doran (Eds.), *Teaching science: Knowledge, language, pedagogy.* Routledge.

Rose, D., & Martin, J. R. (2012). *Learning to write, Reading to learn: Genre, knowledge and pedagogy in the Sydney School.* Equinox.

Rose, D. & J. R. Martin (2018). *Leer para aprender. Lectura y escritura en las áreas del currículo.* Pirámide (original published in 2012).

Schleppegrell, M. J. (2007). The linguistic challenges of mathematics teaching and learning: A research review, *Reading & writing quarterly, 23*(2), 139–159.

Sociedad de Matemática de Chile. (2010). *Culpan a formación de docentes por mal desempeño estudiantil en Matemática. La Tercera.* https://www.latercera.com/noticia/culpan-a-formacion-de-docentes-por-mal-desempeno-estudiantil-en-matematica/

Valdemoros, M. E. (1997). Recursos intuitivos que favorecen la adición de fracciones: estudio de caso. *Educación matemática, 09*(03), 5–17.

Vidal, C. (2010). El libro de texto de matemáticas en Chile en el último siglo 1910–2010. *Facultad de Educación,* Universidad Alberto Hurtado, 1–21. https://repositorio.uahurtado.cl

ABOUT THE AUTHORS

Ingrid Westhoff completed a Master of Education degree at the University of Sydney where she specialized in the use of Systemic Functional Linguistics and Genre pedagogy; she has a Diploma in Philosophy from Universidad de los Andes. She has worked as a lecturer in English for Specific Purposes, Systemic-Functional

Linguistics and Didactics of Reading and Writing (UCSConcepción, UAndes UNABello). She is a director of the foundation Educar para Crecer, preparing volunteer tutors in RtL for disadvantaged families and promoting action research among teachers in reading and writing. She has worked for many years in Chile with the Reading to Learn teacher development program.

Raimundo Olfos is a lecturer at the Pontificia Universidad Católica de Valparaíso with an interest in Reading to Learn pedagogy. He holds a Master's degree in mathematical education from the University of Santiago de Chile and completed his PhD at the University of Wales and post doctorate at King's College, London. He is Chair of the Teacher Trainer Strand in the Doctoral Program of the Didactics of Mathematics, President of the Sociedad Chilena de Educación Matemática and Director of the Asociación Chilena de Investigadores en Educación. He is also an Associated researcher at the Centro de Investigación Avanzada en Educación (UChile, PUCV, UdeC).

ACKNOWLEDGEMENTS

Many thanks for the comments and ideas provided by many Chilean teachers. Specially to maths teachers Angel Salvo, PUCV and Juan Pablo Gonzalez (PhD candidate).

17

Application of Reading to Learn methodology in EFL classrooms: A bilingual approach

Harni Kartika-Ningsih

ABSTRACT

This chapter describes an intervention program which applied R2L for teaching English and science at two public schools with similar multilingual environments yet different socio-economic backgrounds in Bandung, West Java, Indonesia. It involved Year 8 students (aged 14–15) who were mostly speakers of both Sundanese and Indonesian.

A bilingual R2L intervention program was designed to address three persistent challenges. First, there was a wide gap in students' competence in written English with only a few students achieving the expected writing outcomes. Secondly, the current teaching practices seemed to overemphasize knowledge about language, neglecting the field or disciplinary subject knowledge. Lastly, interactions involving code-switching between L1 and L2 is discouraged despite the fact that Indonesia is a multilingual nation where Bahasa Indonesia is the national language and the medium of instruction at school (L1) and English is taught as a compulsory foreign language subject (L2). In addition, even when code-switching is used, the practice is more pragmatic and spontaneous than systematic for pedagogic purposes.

The R2L methodology was adopted and extended to suit this multilingual environment. The extension involves the use of L1 and L2 reading texts and a systematic pattern of interactions from L1 to L2 throughout the teaching programs. The result from the students' pre and post writing outcomes indicates impressive progress in the students' written language development, particularly with regard to text organization, use of scientific terminology and grammatical elements.

THE CONTEXT

Social justice in language education is an ongoing issue in Indonesia and this was the impetus for developing the Reading to Learn bilingual program (hereafter bilingual R2L) in response to the needs of English as foreign language classrooms in Indonesia. As a multilingual nation with around 300 languages, language policies are designed to maintain national unity, preserve local culture and identity, and enable people to take part in global affairs. In everyday life, a regional language is often used for convenience along with the national language, Bahasa Indonesia. Bahasa Indonesia is the predominant language of education. English is a foreign language that plays a significant role in Indonesian education since it is the language used in global affairs and the specialized discourses of disciplines such as science, history and economics. Given Indonesia's position in the global marketplace, fluency in English for all school students has become a necessity (Musthafa & Hamied, 2014). Studying in universities requires competence in English since the university entrance exams and teaching materials include articles and even textbooks in English. Thus, the teaching of English as a foreign language (EFL) has become as important as the teaching of Bahasa Indonesia. Changes in the national EFL curriculum tend to follow current global trends in the development of linguistic and educational theories.

Bilingual R2L in Indonesia was developed in 2014, a decade after the adoption of the Sydney School genre pedagogy in the national EFL curriculum. The systemic functional linguistics (SFL) genre-based approach, known locally as the SFL GBA (hereafter GBA) was introduced in 2004. GBA offered a principled way of thinking about English language and literacy that could inform the teaching of English as a foreign language in Indonesia. It marked a shift in pedagogy from teaching traditional grammar and the 'communicative approach'. This was timely since the Reform Era[1] in the early 21st century was a huge turning point in the history of the country, affecting all areas of life, including its educational system. Since that time, education in Indonesian has encouraged and even demanded the active participation of its citizens in many walks of life in national, and especially international arenas. As a result, English literacy has gained a more significant position in the educational system (Emilia, 2011) and GBA has played a significant role in the EFL curriculum (Kartika-Ningsih & Gunawan, 2019). This could be observed in the prescribed school textbooks for subject English which outlined the social purpose and the generic structures of recount, procedure, narrative and argument genres, among others.

Despite its profound impact, research on GBA was far from comprehensive in terms of addressing multilingual issues in Indonesian EFL classrooms. In the Indonesian context, multilingualism has different patterns of language use compared to contexts such as the US where there is co-existing multilingualism as different languages are spoken mainly within particular language communities (see Ramírez, Chapter 12 this volume). In Indonesia, as in other multilingual communities, different languages are freely exchanged and often become part of the repertoire in the spoken discourse of different language users as in South Africa (see Hart, Chapter 5 and Millin, Chapter 6 this volume). Code-switching is common, as well as responding using a different language. The current strategy to address multilingualism where L1 translation is used for teaching and regulating classroom behaviours is not sufficient. This context created an opportunity to develop an innovative bilingual R2L program by extending the pedagogy to meet the specific needs of EFL classrooms in Indonesia.

FROM GBA TO BILINGUAL R2L

In the late 1990s, the SFL GBA was introduced into the curriculum in Indonesia by a group of scholars who had studied in the Department of Linguistics at the University of Sydney (Agustien, 2006; Wachidah, 2001). A major push in developing genre pedagogy in Indonesia, through teacher training and conferences, was led by Professor Emi Emilia (2011), who had studied in Australia with Frances Christie. In 2006, a national conference on English was held in Bandung, West Java, organized by the English Students' Association and the English Education Department of Universitas Pendidikan Indonesia. I was a member of the committee team for the Association working on the seminar program and I assisted in preparing for Professor Christie's plenary talk on GBA. Professor Christie's visit was timely because her talk provided a much-needed explanation about the new pedagogy for English teachers in Indonesia. That was also the time that the name SFL GBA was adopted in Indonesia and the theory used to inform the kind of knowledge genres used in schools was explicitly stated. It was through Professor Christie's talk that I learnt about the pedagogy and knowledge genres for the first time.

This event was the catalyst for a series of teacher training sessions, organized by universities and the local and national government in West Java, to assist teachers in implementing the new genre-based curriculum. In 2008, Emilia invited Dr. David Rose to provide a training program in Reading to Learn for the postgraduate students at the Universitas Pendidikan Indonesia in Bandung. Following the training, the implementation of R2L in a vocational school in Bandung, West Java, was reported on by Widianingsih in her Master's thesis in 2010, subsequently published as a journal article (Widianingsih, 2012). This created an early interest in R2L and, in 2011, the university invited Professor Jim Martin to train a group of EFL schoolteachers and to give a talk to a group of postgraduate students. At this time, I was working as Emilia's research assistant and was introduced to Professor Martin and assisted him during his training program and talk. The GBA Teaching/Learning Cycle was the focus of his training and the new knowledge about pedagogy was significant for teachers. This experience led me to Sydney to pursue a PhD with Professor Martin at the University of Sydney.

In the first semester of my doctoral studies, Professor Martin brought up R2L in a supervision meeting and recommended that I should study David Rose's work. He gave me as a gift a copy of *Learning to Write, Reading to Learn* (Rose & Martin, 2012). This was my proper introduction to R2L and became a faithful companion throughout my PhD years and beyond. The outline of the book provided a framework to guide me in carrying out my research. During this time, I constantly had questions related to EFL teaching challenges and the status quo of the GBA in Indonesia. How did the EFL curriculum evolve and influence teaching and learning practices? What kind of adaptation had we made to genre pedagogy in Indonesia? What were the challenges of GBA practices after years of implementation? I had previously developed good networks of English teachers and postgraduate students through the good fortune of working as Emilia's research assistant in Indonesia. The scholarly exchange and discussion the networks provided were influential, and the teachers later assisted me in conducting my doctoral research in their schools. However, at this stage, I was still far from possessing sufficient knowledge about language and pedagogy to understand the relationship between these two kinds of knowledge in genre pedagogy.

In 2012, I was trained for the first time in R2L. Following Professor Martin's advice, I attended an R2L workshop run by Claire Acevedo, as part of the International Systemic Functional Congress held in Sydney. When Professor Martin took sabbatical leave, Dr. David Rose took over my PhD supervision and we began to focus intensively on the Indonesian bilingual R2L project. Dr. Rose invited me to attend his training workshops for teachers at a Sydney high school, which gave me the opportunity to learn and practise R2L pedagogy with a group of practising teachers. At that time, Dr. Rose gave a me a task to think about typical Indonesian classrooms and how R2L could be recontextualized for them. I felt he had taken me under his R2L wing. Through a series of meetings, he guided me to develop an R2L program for EFL in Indonesia. We had lengthy discussions about the multilingual context, pedagogy, and SFL in language education.

During this training period, I was able to identify two key elements of R2L that would guide me in extending the pedagogy to address the issues faced in teaching English in multilingual classrooms. Firstly, the goal of R2L to 'close the gap' resonated with my struggle to distribute knowledge equally among students in the classroom. Inequality in achievement was most apparent in the students' writing results. While some students in each class made progress in writing, the majority still struggled. Figures 17.1 and 17.2 illustrate writing results typically found across classrooms in Grade 8 (14–15 years old), in Indonesian high schools. Students were asked to write a description about their favourite animals, such as cats and rabbits.

These texts indicate common challenges faced by many Indonesian students when writing in EFL. They are very short texts showing significant problems with English grammar and punctuation. Typical teacher feedback for such texts would include revising grammatical errors, punctuation or spelling, and suggestions to 'write more'. However, the same mistakes were often repeated, so that students such as these faced the risk of falling behind and not being able to develop their L2 language skills. As a result, the gap in writing results widens over time.

The second aspect of R2L that particularly inspired my bilingual classroom work was the design of learning exchanges to support all students to participate successfully. This was an eye-opener as it was closely linked to the multilingual nature of classroom talk in Indonesia. Interaction in multilingual classrooms has been a topic of heated debate between proponents of L2 only, or allowing L1 with L2 (e.g., Garcia & Li, 2014; Lin, 2013). However most Indonesian teachers would use L1 pragmatically to assist students in learning L2 and to control classroom behaviours.

The cat
I have a Pet it is a cat. The colour OF my
cat is white. Every morning, I always Feed
the cat wit Fish. Habits that my cat always
want to be loved. I am there Fore verry happy
cats.

Figure 17.1. Pre-program student writing sample No. 1. The cat

Rabbit
Rabbits are tame animals, it's like to eat carrots, it's can
Jumped up and down. it's are cute animals, it's are intelligent
animals, it's have long ears, it's fur is very soft. it's meat is
very tasty. it's a herbivore. it's color is white. grey and brown.
it has a small body

Figure 17.2 Pre-program student writing sample No. 2. Rabbit

The design of learning exchanges in R2L served as an ideal platform to systematically plan for the use of L1 and L2.

The two elements of R2L discussed above were key early considerations in the bilingual R2L design. Since genre pedagogy is interventionist in nature, the next step was to design an intervention program right in the heart of the multilingual classroom setting. The aim was to pilot the bilingual R2L project which deliberately used and systematized L1 and L2 through R2L (Kartika-Ningsih, 2020). The project was carried out for two months and took place in two schools in Bandung, where the teachers and the students spoke three languages and had previously used genre pedagogy.

INNOVATIONS IN THE R2L BILINGUAL PROGRAM

Innovating on R2L for multilingual Indonesian classrooms involved several considerations about subject English and the dynamics of language learning. One key issue was that EFL teaching in Indonesia put an emphasis on grammatical knowledge in a traditional sense, alongside teaching a variety of text types in the GBA curriculum, almost to the exclusion of content or field knowledge (Kartika-Ningsih & Gunawan, 2019). So one consideration was to focus on knowledge about language that was related to subject disciplines. Another was to actualize deliberate and systematic L1 involvement in the bilingual program design. My goal was to structure the use of L1 *and* L2 to make teachers conscious about the choice of which language to use in order to scaffold their students in learning L2. Thus, the R2L bilingual program was designed to include three main components. First, it integrated the teaching of subject English and biology, a choice suitable for the curriculum at the time of the research. Second, it included the explicit use of reading texts in both L1 and L2. Third, it systematized teaching in both L1 and L2.

EFL AND BIOLOGY

The need to integrate EFL and biology in the Indonesian curriculum responded to the issue of international standardized schools and the trend of Content and Language Integrated Learning (CLIL) at the time of the study. The R2L bilingual program involved 'embedded literacy practice', placing literacy learning in the specific subject domain (Rose & Martin, 2012). In line with this perspective, the program was contextualized into lessons which integrated units in English and biology – science taught in English.

A starting point was to select units of study in the Indonesian science curriculum which could be taught in English. In the 2013 English curriculum, subject English required the teaching of different text types. The Year 8 English curriculum prescribed 'texts in interpersonal, transactional and functional discourse in the forms of description' (Ministry of Education and Culture of Indonesia, 2013). Such texts include the description genre, that describes a specific person, place, object or thing, such as the text, 'The cat' (Figure 17.1), and the report genre, that classifies and describes general phenomena, such as the text, 'Rabbit' (Figure 17.2).

In the biological science curriculum, students are apprenticed into four skills: to observe, inquire, collect and process information and to communicate. When students learn to classify living things, they are apprenticed 1) to identify the characteristics of living and non-living creatures; 2) to understand the procedures of classifying living and non-living creatures based on the characteristics being observed; 3) to collect data and classify things, plants, and animals in the surrounding area; and 4) to present the results of data analysis from the observation in the form of spoken or written texts. These skills align with the functions of descriptive reports. The program was thus designed to focus on learning to write the descriptive report genre as part of a biodiversity unit in the biology curriculum, focusing in particular on an endangered bird species from Indonesia.

BILINGUAL READING TEXTS

As texts are the basis of teaching in R2L, the task of text selection for the bilingual program involved 1) choosing high-stakes reading texts for the program – two in Indonesian and one in English, and 2) sequencing the texts to be used in each language in each stage of the R2L pedagogy cycle. Three R2L criteria were used to guide the text selection (Rose, 2020, Book 2) based on genre and register comparative criteria in L1 and L2. First, in terms of the *field*, the texts provided key information in the curriculum unit to be taught. Second, the texts provided good models of the target *genre* for writing science reports. Third, in terms of *mode*, the texts were at an appropriate level for the stage of schooling, although they were above the independent reading level of many of the students. The sequence of the texts moved from L1 to L2, and from more familiar to less familiar topics. In addition to this, the texts were selected on the comparability of the topics, consisting of a written text presented as a list of information, including names, description, habitat, behaviour, voice, and range of distribution, and an image of the bird species.

The two L1 (Bahasa Indonesia) reading texts were about endangered birds from Indonesia and the third reading text was in L2 (English) about an endangered bird from Australia. Those texts were written for biologists and bird watchers. The

Indonesian texts were sourced from a website for Indonesian national bird conservation, so these were high stakes reading material for the students, even though they are written in Bahasa Indonesia. The first reading text was about *Nisaetus bartelsi,* or the Javan Hawk-eagle, an eagle species that inhabits the island of Java. It is a very popular bird in Indonesia since it is the symbol on the national coat-of-arms, the Garuda bird. Its popularity would provide the students with the necessary prior knowledge, assisting them in shifting their 'common sense' perspective of the Garuda bird to the 'uncommon sense' or a scientific perspective of the Garuda as bird species.

The second reading text was about *Ninox ios,* or the Cinnabar Hawk-owl, an owl species that inhabits Sulawesi. It is a less familiar species than *Nisaetus bartelsi,* and most of the students had never heard of it. This text had less information in terms of the species' identification, as there was less data recorded about the species. However, as the students would first learn about the Garuda from a scientific perspective, they would be prepared to then learn about a different bird which they had not known before.

The third reading text was in English taken from an encyclopaedia about extinct and endangered birds of Australia (Taylor, 2012). The text was about the Purple-crowned Fairy-wren, selected to represent an endangered bird outside of Indonesia. No student had heard about this bird species, as Australian birds were relatively unknown to them. This text was targeted at English speaking bird watchers and biologists, so it was particularly challenging for the Indonesian speaking students. It consisted of a written text with detailed information about the species, the history of the discovery of the bird, names, taxonomy, description, voice, habitat, and others, and an image. Extracts from this text were chosen that were comparable to the Indonesian texts, including names, description, voice and habitat.

The differences in the three reading texts showed the students that not all reports contain the same amount or types of information. The information provided depends on several factors, such as the research undertaken to observe particular species, and selection of information to be included in the report. As this reflected the work of scientists in writing reports in biology, analysing the reading texts was part of apprenticing students into the work of bird biologists.

BILINGUAL LEARNING EXCHANGE

Each reading text was used in one iteration of the R2L teaching cycle, giving three iterations before the final writing task. Stages of the cycle included *Preparing for Reading, Detailed Reading, Joint Construction* and *Independent Construction.* Throughout the stages, other modalities such as use of images (see Figure 17.3)

Figure 17.3. Intermodal and multilingual classroom teaching

and intermodal activities (see Kartika-Ningsih & Rose, 2021), and two languages, were used to different degrees. Learning exchanges were designed to systematize L1 and L2 use.

L1 and L2 were used to a different degree throughout the implementation of the three iterations. In the first and second iterations, using L1 reading texts, L1 was prioritized in Prepare and Focus phases of exchanges. Exchange 1 illustrates the use of L1 to identify important lexical items in the text about Nisaetus bartelsi, in the first iteration (see Kartika-Ningsih, 2019a). English glosses are given in italics below the Indonesian.

Exchange 1. Use of L1

sp	exchange	phase
T	Nah sekarang kita (...) mengenai nama-nama Nisaetus bartelsi karena dia punya banyak nama. *Now we (...) about the names of Nisaetus bartelsi, because it has a lot of names.*	Prepare
	Ini ada satu nama yang disebutnya nama Latin. *There's this one name which is mentioned as the Latin name.*	
	Apa nama Latinnya? *What's the Latin name?*	Focus
Ss	*Nisaetus bartelsi.*	Identify
T	OK, good. Nisaetus bartelsi.	Affirm

In Exchange 1, the students' task is to identify the Latin name in the reading text. The teacher uses L1 to prepare and focus the task. As the students identify Nisaetus bartelsi successfully, she affirms in L2. This was the first instance of L2, used for a positive evaluation.

By the third iteration, the students had grown familiar with the patterns of exchange and with identifying key information in the text. This time, the L2 reading text was used and L2 was used more for preparing and focusing tasks, as well as for evaluations. On the other hand, L1 was still often used for directing students. In Exchange 2, the teacher prepares by naming the sentence to focus on in L2, and then directing attention in L1 (see Kartika-Ningsih, 2019a). She then focuses the task in L2. After a student identifies the correct wording, the teacher elaborates by defining the meaning of 'malurus' in L1.

Exchange 2. Use of L2

speaker	exchange	phase
T	Now I want you to focus on the first sentence. Yang ini ya. *This one.* [reads sentence aloud]	Prepare
	I want you to find the genus of this species.	Focus
S	Aku tahu! Malurus! *I know! Malurus!*	Identify
T	OK, good! Very good! Malurus!	Affirm
	Malurus artinya bulu ekor yang halus. *So Malurus means 'soft tail feathers'*	Elaborate

In summary, L1 was more often used for preparing and focusing tasks in the first iteration. But by the third iteration, L2 was used in almost all exchanges aimed at identify the wordings. This pattern led to the development of a language shift, or the meaning-making process realized in two (or more) languages. This involved 'translating', or bringing equivalent meanings from L1 to L2, and 'code-switching/mixing', or using two or more languages in the spoken discourse (Kartika-Ningsih, 2019a; Kartika-Ningsih & Rose, 2018). The key idea of the 'language shift' system is that it pushes forward our understanding of the meaningful choices of L1 and L2 use in multilingual classrooms. Potentially, it can further be used as a platform to choose which language is to be used in order to assist students in learning L2.

THE DEVELOPMENT OF WRITING

The goal of the lesson sequence was for the students to independently write a report about an endangered bird species from Indonesia. Following the three R2L iterations outlined above, students researched data from the internet, particularly from a website dedicated to bird conservation in Indonesia (www.burung.org). In general, writing results indicated significant progress as post-intervention texts were longer and successfully achieved the purpose of writing reports about a bird in L2. This progress was evidenced in work across all grades. In particular, the post-intervention texts indicated the development of control of the genre and the field in their use of technical terms, grammar and presentation (spelling, graphic features, and use of images), which had all been part of the teaching program. In terms of text stages and phases, most of the texts followed the generic structure of reports, including Classification and Description stages. Phases in the Description stage all included an appearance phase followed by various other phases such as habitat or voice.

The text in Figure 17.4 is a post-intervention text that was independently researched and written by the author of the pre-intervention text 'The cat' in Figure 17.1. It is a report on the Indonesian passerine, *Monarcha boanensis*, a bird endemic to South Maluku. The Classification stage covers the scientific name, taxonomic rank, and Indonesian name. The Description stage is realized through appearance and habitat phases. In addition to this, the student writer also used colours to indicate different stages of the report and added a photo and an image of the bird.

Table 17.1 outlines the generic structure of the text *Monarcha boanensis* by student No. 1 in Figure 17.4. The student has clearly distinguished stages and phases with distinct paragraphs and text colouring. In the original, the title is dark blue, the first paragraph is green, the second paragraph red, and the last paragraph orange. The drawing of the bird is black and white, similar to the original printed photo in the top right corner. The writing displays strong control over the technical field and the mode, and technical lexis is used appropriately. In the Classification stage, the terms *Monarcha boanensis*, *genus* and *species* are used to classify the bird, and the scientific rule of binomial nomenclature appears, with the genus capitalized and the species written in lower case. In the Description stage, the appearance phase describes the parts of the bird, beginning with its size, then the different colours of the feathers on the 'upper parts' and 'under parts'. In the habitat phase, the terms endemic and local distribution are used appropriately. Unlike the pre-intervention text in Figure 17.1, there are now no significant grammatical errors, no spelling errors, and the presentation is excellent, including handwriting, page design and illustrations.

Figure 17.4. Post-program text *Monarcha boanensis* by student No. 1

Table 17.1. Stages and phases of *Monarcha boanensis* (Figure 17.4) by student No 1

Stages	phases	clauses
Classification		The scientific name of the Black-chinned Monarch is Monarcha boanensis. Monarcha is the genus, boanensis is the species. The Black-chinned monarch is called Kehicap biak in Indonesian.
Description	appearance	Monarcha boanensis is 16 centimetres long. Its upperparts, head side, and chin are black. Its under parts and cheek are white.
	habitat	The bird is endemic in Boano, South Maluku. Its local distribution is at foot of a hill about 150 metres.

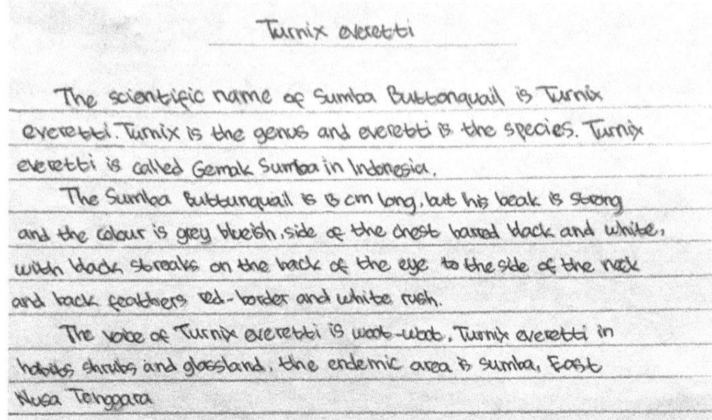

Turnix everetti

The scientific name of Sumba Buttonquail is Turnix everetti. Turnix is the genus and everetti is the species. Turnix everetti is called Gemak Sumba in Indonesia.

The Sumba Buttunquail is 13 cm long, but his beak is strong and the colour is grey blueish, side of the chest barred black and white, with black streaks on the back of the eye to the side of the neck and back feathers red-border and white rush.

The voice of Turnix everetti is woot-woot, Turnix everetti in habits shrubs and glassland, the endemic area is sumba, East Nusa Tenggara

Figure 17.5. Post-program text *Turnix everetti* by student No. 2

Figure 17.5 shows another post-program text written by the author of the pre-text 'Rabbit' in Figure 17.2. The text is a report that classifies and describes the *Sumba Buttonquail*, a local species from East Nusa Tenggara, *Turnix everetti.*

Table 17.2 outlines the generic structure of the text. The Classification stage includes the scientific name, the taxonomic rank and the Indonesian name. The Description stage has three phases, appearance, voice and habitat. It includes terms which refer to parts of the species (e.g. *beak, side of chest*), and distinctive qualities (*beak – strong, grey blueish*) and the habitat where the species can be found (endemic – Sumba, East Nusa Tenggara). This text also displays effective control over the technical field and the mode and technical lexis is used appropriately. However, this student still has some grammatical problems, such as the overly long sentence in the appearance phase, with an inappropriate 'but'. Although there are no spelling errors, handwriting is legible, and paragraphing appropriate, the presentation is not at the standard of *Monarcha boanensis* (Figure 17.4 and Table 17.1). Still, since this text was written by one of the struggling learners of the bottom class, the progress demonstrated promising written language development.

These two examples from the students' post-texts demonstrate progress in using the scientific terms in bird biology expected in the report genre. Moreover, the use of bird biology terms was found across all post-texts. The use of these terms in the post-intervention texts shows progress in two ways. First it indicates a shift from everyday ways of describing things, illustrated in the pre-program texts 'The Cat' (Figure 17.1) and 'Rabbit' (Figure 17.2), to effective use of more uncommonsense meanings, using technical terms typically found in scientific writing. Secondly, it demonstrates control over L2 knowledge of bird biology. Using terms in L1 presents its own challenge; thus, having the ability to control the writing of a factual report and to use terms in L2 is an indication of significant progress.

Table 17.2. Stages and phases of *Turnix everetti* (Figure 17.5) by student No.2

Stages	**phases**	**clauses**
Classification		The scientific name of Sumba Buttonquail is Turnix everetti. Turnix is the genus, and everetti is the species. Turnix everetti is called Gemak Sumba in Indonesia.
Description	appearance	The Sumba Buttonquail is 13 cm long, but his beak is strong and the colour is grey blueish, side of the chest barred black and white, with black streaks on the back of the eye to the side of the neck and back feathers red-border and white rush.
	voice habitat	The voice of Turnix everetti is woot-woot. Turnix everetti inhabits shrubs and glassland the endemic area is Sumba, East Nusa Tenggara.

ENVOI

Reading to Learn is the latest generation of genre pedagogy with success reported across the world (Rose & Martin, 2012), including its application involving bilingual classrooms in different multilingual contexts such as South Africa, the US and Sweden (e.g. Hart, Millian, Ramirez and Lövstedt in this volume). For Indonesian EFL classrooms, the R2L bilingual program has proven a significant advance. It is innovative in addressing the challenge of multilingual classrooms, using both L1 and L2 systematically for L2 teaching. This intervention showed that the R2L methodology can be fine-tuned and recontextualized for different linguistic environments while simultaneously fulfilling the demands of the curriculum. The principles of selecting and analyzing texts, for example, can be applied in different languages, allowing the linguistic understanding of the text to be used for the teaching activities. The design of learning exchanges has proven useful for deploying L1 and L2 systematically in instruction, which is a major step for bilingual education.

The development of the bilingual R2L program for my doctoral research has opened up further interesting projects dealing with multilingual issues. In 2015, I had the chance to develop an academic reading and writing program for ESL postgraduates at the Learning Centre at Sydney University, with Jing Hao and Helen Drury. This program received much positive feedback from the participating students. In 2018, in my hometown of Bandung, I developed a trilingual project for teaching Sundanese cooking discourse using English and Indonesian for student teachers (Kartika-Ningsih, 2019b). In 2020, I was involved with a team to develop R2L specifically for teaching IELTS writing (Damayanti, et al., 2020).

I have learnt valuable lessons and gained invaluable experience from working on an innovative R2L bilingual program. All of this would not have been possible without the generosity of the mentors and colleagues who have helped me to develop the R2L methodology in my national context. More broadly, I believe that bilingual R2L has a promising future for multilingual language education. After all, using students' multilingualism to advantage, rather than viewing it as a hindrance, is an effective way to provide democratic access to language education.

NOTE

1 Since the resignation of President Suharto on 21 May 1998, Indonesia has been on the Post-Suharto era. This period of transition is known as the Reform Era (*Era Reformasi*).

REFERENCES

Agustien, H. (2006, February). *Genre-based approach and the 2004 English curriculum.* [Plenary lecture]. UPI National Seminar, Bandung.

Damayanti, I. L., Kartika-Ningsih, H., & Dharma, N. S. (2020, November). *Reading to Learn program for teaching IELTS writing tasks.* [Paper presentation]. The Thirteenth Conference on Applied Linguistics (CONAPLIN 13), Bandung, West Java, Indonesia.

Emilia, E. (2011). *Pendekatan Genre-based dalam Pengajaran Bahasa Inggris: Petunjuk untuk Guru.* Rizqi Press.

Garcia, O., & Li, W. (2014). *Translanguaging: Language, bilingualism and education.* Palgrave Macmillan.

Kartika-Ningsih, H. (2019a). Implementing the Reading to Learn bilingual program in Indonesia. In K. Rajandran & S. Abdul Manan (Eds.), *Discourses of Southeast Asia* (pp. 145–163). Springer. https://link.springer.com/chapter/10.1007/978-981-13-9883-4_8

Kartika-Ningsih, H. (2019b). Pengajaran bahasa daerah melalui rancangan metapedagogi multibahasa berbasis genre in Memajukan peran bahasa dalam kancah kontemporer Indonesia: Penguatan strategi dan diplomasi di berbagai bidang. Seminar Internasional Kebahasaan held by Pusat Pengembangan Strategi Diplomasi Kebahasaan, Kementerian Pendidikan dan Kebudayaan (the Ministry of Education and Culture). http://badanbahasa.kemdikbud.go.id/lamanbahasa/content/prosiding-seminar-internasional-kebahasaan-tahun-2019

Kartika-Ningsih, H. (2020). Language shift: bilingual exchange structure in classroom interactions. In J. R. Martin, Y. J. Doran & Giacomo Figueredo (Eds.), *Systemic functional language description: Making meaning matter* (pp. 307–330). Routledge.

Kartika-Ningsih, H., & Gunawan, W. (2019). Recontextualisation of genre-based pedagogy: The case of Indonesian EFL classrooms. *Indonesian journal of applied linguistics*, *9*(2), 335–347. https://ejournal.upi.edu/index.php/IJAL/article/view/20231

Kartika-Ningsih, H., & Rose, D. (2018). Language shift: analysing language use in multilingual classroom interactions. *Functional Linguistics*, *5*(1), 1–22. https://doi.org/10.1186/s40554-018-0061-0

Kartika-Ningsih, H., & Rose, D. (2021). Intermodality and multilingual re-instantiation: Joint construction in bilingual genre pedagogy. *Ikala, Special issue on appliable linguistics in language education: SFL in practice*, *26*(1), 185–205. https://doi.org/10.17533/udea.ikala.v26n01a07

Lin, A. (2013). Classroom code-switching: three decades of research. *Applied linguistics review*, *4*(1), 195–218. http://hdl.handle.net/10722/184270.

Ministry of Education and Culture of Indonesia/Kementerian Pendidikan dan Kebudayaan. (2013). *Kerangka Dasar dan Struktur Kurikulum 2013.*

Musthafa, B., & Hamied, F. (2014). Teaching English as a foreign language in Indonesian schools in the Reform Era: What do teachers have to say? *The new English teachers*, *8* (2). http://www.assumptionjournal.au.edu/index.php/newEnglishTeacher/issue/view/35

Rose, D. (2020). *Reading to Learn: Accelerating learning and closing the gap (2020 Edition).* Reading to Learn. http://www.readingtolearn.com.au

Rose, D., & Martin, J. (2012). *Learning to write, reading to learn: Genre, knowledge and pedagogy in the Sydney school.* Equinox Publishing.

Taylor, S. (2012). *John Gould's extinct and endangered birds of Australia.* National Library of Australia.

Wachidah, S. (2001). *EFL learning autonomy and output planning: A case in a Javanese-dominated general high school (sekolah menengah umum) in Indonesia.* [Doctoral dissertation, University of Sydney].

Widianingsih, S. (2012). Scaffolding interaction cycle in Reading to Learn program. *Semantik STKIP Siliwangi*, *1*(1). http://e-journal.stkipsiliwangi.ac.id/index.php/semantik/article/view/99

ABOUT THE AUTHOR

Harni Kartika-Ningsih, is Assistant Professor in the Linguistics Department, Universitas Indonesia. She received her doctoral degree from the Linguistics Department, Sydney University and did her postdoctoral fellowship in the Department of Curriculum and Instruction, at the Chinese University of Hong Kong. Her research interests include genre pedagogy, multilingualism, bilingual education, and pedagogic discourse. She can be reached through her email harni.kartika@ui.ac.id.

Index

Note: Page numbers followed by 'f', 't' and 'n' refer to information in tables, figures and notes respectively

www.ingramcontent.com/pod-product-compliance
Lightning Source LLC
LaVergne TN
LVHW010443080826
844660LV00026B/1206

* 9 7 8 1 8 0 0 5 0 3 2 4 3 *